Teacher's Manual

**TEN BASIC STEPS
TOWARD CHRISTIAN MATURITY**

and

**HANDBOOK
FOR CHRISTIAN MATURITY**

TEACHER'S MANUAL

for the

Ten Basic Steps Toward Christian Maturity

(Individual Booklets)

and the

Handbook for Christian Maturity

(Compilation of 11 Booklets)

BILL BRIGHT

CAMPUS CRUSADE FOR CHRIST

Arrowhead Springs, San Bernardino, California 92414

1982

TEACHER'S MANUAL
for TEN BASIC STEPS TOWARD CHRISTIAN MATURITY booklets
and for A HANDBOOK FOR CHRISTIAN MATURITY
by Bill Bright

Revised Edition, 1982. Second printing, 1983.

A Campus Crusade for Christ Book
Published by
HERE'S LIFE PUBLISHERS
P. O. Box 1576
San Bernardino, CA 92402

ISBN 0-918856-97-8
Library of Congress Catalog Card No. 81-67819
Product No. 35-111-4

FOR MORE INFORMATION, WRITE:
L.I.F.E. — P. O. Box A399, Sydney South 2000, Australia
Campus Crusade for Christ of Canada — Box 368, Abbottsford, B. C., V25 4N9, Canada
Campus Crusade for Christ — 103 Friar Street, Reading RGI IEP, Berkshire, England
Campus Crusade for Christ — 28 Westmoreland St., Dublin 2, Ireland
Lay Institute for Evangelism — P. O. Box 8786, Auckland 3, New Zealand
Life Ministry — P. O. Box / Bus 91015, Auckland Park 2006, Republic of So. Africa
Campus Crusade for Christ, Int'l. — Arrowhead Springs, San Bernardino, CA 92414, U.S.A.

FOREWORD

The greatest spiritual awakening of all time is taking place today. More people are hearing the gospel; more people are receiving Christ; more people are committed to helping fulfill the Great Commission than at any other time since the church was born almost 2,000 years ago.

Here in the United States, one-third of all adults identify themselves as born-again, evangelical Christians, according to the Gallup Poll. Every Sunday more than 85 million people are in church and 125 million people listen to Christian radio and television programs regularly according to the National Religious Broadcasters.

But we have a problem — a very serious problem. These encouraging, unprecedented statistics are not reflected in the life of our nation. Our Lord has commanded us to be the salt of the earth and the light of the world. But there is little evidence of the influence of Christianity in the media, in education, in government or in other major areas of influence. What has gone wrong?

As a part of our ministry, we take hundreds of thousands of surveys — working with pastors, other Christian leaders and students. The statistics compiled as a result of these surveys are cause for great concern, as we discover that more than 50% of the members of the churches in America are not sure of salvation (in some churches that figure might be 5%, in others 95%, depending on the denomination and the leadership of the church). Ninety-five percent of the members do not understand the ministry of the Holy Spirit, and 98% are not regularly sharing their faith in Christ.

It was for the purpose of helping to meet this critical need that the *Ten Basic Steps Toward Christian Maturity* were written. An immature, surrendered Christian can be used by the Lord in limited ways. But as the Christian grows in maturity his effectiveness also grows. To be an influence for Christ in his community or in the world, he must learn how to grow spiritually. His knowledge of how to introduce men and women to the Savior must increase and he must be able to help other believers reach a higher level of maturity in Christ. An in-depth study of God's Word is a major factor in accomplishing these things.

This Bible study series was especially designed and written to help Christians gain that necessary growth. As a result, individuals and groups alike have been stimulated to explore the riches of God's Word and find spiritual nourishment.

Written originally with the college student in mind, this material has become equally effective with high schoolers and with adults. Now being used by churches, home Bible study groups, military and prison chaplains and Christian groups across America, it has been translated into a number of other languages and is being taught in many other countries as well.

When the need for a single volume became evident, one which could be used more easily by one person for private Bible study and personal spiritual growth, the *Ten Basic Steps* booklets were revised and compiled into the *Handbook for Christian Maturity*. While still intended mainly for group use, it is now designed so that an individual Christian can benefit greatly from it.

However, if you would like to lead others in the studies, this *Teacher's Manual* will facilitate effective use of the *Handbook* or the booklets in a group situtation. The manual is so prepared that even inexperienced teachers can lead and teach the Bible studies successfully. You will find complete instructions on pages 15-22.

Feelings of hopelessness and inadequacy are sensed often in the face of the desperate needs evident in the world today. An internalizing of the material presented here will help to dispel these feelings and will challenge the concerned Christian to seek new heights in communicating his faith.

Nearly every major doctrine of Christianity has been carefully considered and clearly presented. Any person seeking spiritual truth will be generously rewarded as he or she reads and studies these pages. Christians will be strengthened as they allow the teachings to change their lives.

Our prayer is that these books will bless and enrich your life, and that you will be further encouraged to grow to full maturity in Jesus Christ. We trust also that the effectiveness of your personal witness for Him will be greatly enhanced.

— Bill Bright

TEACHER'S MANUAL

TEN BASIC STEPS TOWARD CHRISTIAN MATURITY
HANDBOOK FOR CHRISTIAN MATURITY

CONTENTS

A WORD TO THE TEACHER

Would you like to know how to teach the Bible? *You can!*

This *Teacher's Manual* for the *Ten Basic Steps Toward Christian Maturity*
(11 individual booklets) and the *Handbook for Christian Maturity* (a compilation of
those booklets) has been designed and written to enable even a new Christian to
lead and teach Bible study groups.

The *Ten Basic Steps Toward Christian Maturity* and the *Handbook for Christian
Maturity*, together with this *Teacher's Manual*, are products of necessity.

As the ministry of Campus Crusade for Christ expanded rapidly to scores of
campuses across America, thousands of students committed their lives to Christ —
as many as four or five hundred on a single campus. Individual follow-up of all
new converts soon became an impossibility. Who was to help them grow in
their new-found faith?

A Bible study series designed for new Christians was desperately needed, a
study which would stimulate individuals and groups alike to explore the depths and
the riches of God's Word. Though several excellent studies were available, there
was nothing which we felt met the particular need of these college students.

In 1955, several members of our staff were assigned to assist me in the preparation of materials which we hoped would stimulate both Christian growth and
evangelism in a new believer. The contribution by campus staff members was
especially significant because of their constant contact with students, introducing
them to Christ and meeting regularly with them to assist them in their
Christian growth. Thus, the *Ten Basic Steps Toward Christian Maturity* — a study in
"follow-up evangelism" — was the fruit of our combined labor.

The unusual popularity of this Bible study series soon posed an additional
problem — a teacher's manual was needed. No longer could one staff member
teach all of the many Bible study groups organized on a single campus. Also, many
other groups were now requesting use of these materials. As the Campus Crusade
for Christ ministry expanded to new campuses and many additional workers joined
our staff, I found it necessary to be away from my ministry on the campus at
UCLA where the work was first launched. My wife, Vonette, was recruited to
substitute. In order properly to supervise the many Bible studies on the campus, she
found it necessary to appoint a leader for each Bible study group. Each week
Vonette prepared lesson plans and met with all the leaders to teach them the
material they would teach their individual Bible study groups.

This was the beginning of the *Teacher's Manual* for the *Ten Basic Steps*. Since that
modest beginning, many other members of the staff have contributed generously to
the present volume which you hold in your hands. On occasion, for example, I
have found myself involved in research and writing sessions which involved several
of our staff, all seminary graduates, several with advanced degrees, one with his
doctorate in theology. More important, all of them are actively engaged in
"winning men, building men and sending men" for Christ.

Although thousands of hours have been invested in writing these materials, we
are still confident they can be improved. You can be of great assistance by advising

us of any suggestions which you may have, or of corrections in reference or in content which should be made.

This *Teacher's Manual,* the *Handbook for Christian Maturity* and the *Ten Basic Steps Toward Christian Maturity* all have been prepared with the prayer that they will encourage multiplied thousands of students and adults around the world to become true disciples of the Lord Jesus Christ.

INTRODUCTION

I.   *The Purpose of the Ten Basic Steps*

Young people today, and adults as well, study a little of nearly everything, but all too often give minimal or no time to a study of the Bible. Yet the Bible undoubtedly has had a more profound effect on history than any other book has had. It played a major role in the founding and molding of western culture — the daily life of every American would be vastly different if the Bible had never been written. No person can be considered well-educated without at least a general knowledge of the Bible.

The *Ten Basic Steps* are designed to give you an efficient means for systematic study of the Bible and of the Christian faith it teaches. The result of this study should be two-fold in your life.

First, the study should communicate knowledge. Without a knowledge of at least some biblical teaching no person can become a Christian, and no Christian can live the Christian life. A great many people reject Christianity and a great many Christians live miserable, defeated, frustrated lives for no reason except that of sheer ignorance. The psalmist said, "The unfolding of Thy words gives light" (Psalm 119:130), and Jesus taught that the truth would make us free (John 8:32).

Second, this study should communicate power to your life. Hebrews 4:12 says, "The Word of God is living and active, and sharper than any two-edged sword, and piercing as far as the division of soul and spirit, of both joints and marrow, and able to judge the thoughts and intentions of the heart."

The Bible differs from all other books in that it is a living book, and through it the life and power of God are communicated to the life of an individual. Men and women by the thousands, including Augustine, Luther, Wesley and many others have changed history because God used the Bible to change them.

Even as your group begins to study the *Ten Basic Steps,* in the *Handbook* or in the individual booklets, a change should come over the members. They should begin displaying more consistent Christian living, more love, more devotion to Christ, more patience and more desire to spread the Christian message. At the same time a decrease in pride, jealousy, gossip, harsh words, etc., should be evident. Also, some should receive Christ as Savior.

In this study, several things will be emphasized:

(1) *The distinctiveness of Christianity.* No religion makes provision for the breach between God and man which Christianity calls sin, but Christianity does deal with it — not by what man can do for God, as taught in all religions, but through what God has done for man in sending His Son, Jesus Christ, to die on the cross.

(2) *The distinctive claims of Christ.* Many people feel that Christ was only a good moral teacher, but this study will make clear that He claimed to be no less than deity, and is either the true God or a liar and impostor.

(3) *The abundant life which God has for every Christian through the power of the Holy Spirit.* The lives of many people have been utterly transformed through an understanding of the abundant life God has for them and of the doctrine of the filling of the Holy Spirit (see Step Three, "The Christian and the Holy Spirit").

II. *The Value of the Ten Basic Steps*

A. The *Ten Basic Steps Toward Christian Maturity* are designed specifically to help each Christian in the following ways:

1. To give him a general knowledge of the Bible.
2. To provide him with a systematic plan of study.
3. To acquaint him with the major doctrines of the Christian faith.
4. To help him with problems he is facing.
5. To motivate him to be active in sharing the gospel, developing a fruitful ministry and in leading others to experience the same spiritual growth.

B. This study is good for the new Christian because it:

1. Aids his spiritual growth.
2. Increases his familiarity with the Bible.
3. Teaches him the basic doctrines of his Christian faith.
4. Helps him find scriptural solutions for the problems of his life.
5. Inspires and equips him to begin to share the gospel.

C. This study is good for the older Christian because it:

1. Gives him tools he can use to help another person find Christ or to help a weak Christian grow in his faith.
2. Helps him establish a systematic devotional and study plan.

D. This study is good for the non-Christian because it:

1. Helps him to understand the Bible.
2. Presents the claims and person of Christ.
3. Clearly shows him how to become a Christian, gives him an opportunity to receive Christ and teaches him how to live the Christian life.

A faithful study of the *Ten Basic Steps Toward Christian Maturity* and of the other material in this *Teacher's Manual* will prepare you for a more comprehensive ministry, giving you a thorough understanding of the biblical principles upon which your faith is based. It will focus and strengthen your own purpose and will assist you in your continual appropriation of the power of the Holy Spirit for a more joyous, triumphant Christian life.

INSTRUCTIONS FOR TEACHING THE
TEN BASIC STEPS TOWARD CHRISTIAN MATURITY

This course of study is designed to give your students a broad survey of Christianity. They will meet its central figure, Jesus Christ, and will study its authoritative literature, the Holy Bible. They will learn of the nature, privileges and responsibilities of the Christian way of life, and will discover the secret of the power of the Holy Spirit to transform men and give them a continually abundant life.

I.   How to Organize a Bible Study Class

Organizing a class to study the *Ten Basic Steps* should be done only after prayer for God's leading and blessing. Classes may vary in size from just one person to several. Generally, you will approach others with whom some previous contact has been made, though announcement may be made concerning the Bible class to others at your job, or your dormitory, or neighborhood, as the case may be. Often those to whom you have witnessed but who have not yet received Christ will be interested.

New Christians and others who need follow-up are also likely prospects. Choose the ones you think would be best to start with, pray about each one individually and then see each one personally. After you have made the contacts, you may choose a definite meeting place and time.

If the study is in your room at school or your living room at home, be sure it is neat, attractive in appearance and well-ventilated. Choose a place where you will be free from interruptions. If several days lapse between the contact and the first Bible study, remind those involved. Make an announcement, speak to them personally, phone them or send them each a card.

If you have had no experience teaching one of these classes, and feel unsure of yourself, you might ask an experienced teacher to take the first one or two classes, and observe the methods used.

In selling people on the idea of a Bible study, it is important to avoid pressuring them. At the same time, however, you must avoid a negative or apologetic attitude. The best way to promote interest and enthusiasm is to be interested and enthusiastic about it yourself. Here are some suggested approaches to a prospective student:

"John, when we've talked before, you've expressed an interest in knowing more about Christianity and the Bible. I wish you'd take a look at this book for a minute (show him the Introductory Step, "The Uniqueness of Jesus," or the complete *Handbook*). This really has been a tremendous help to me in learning more about the Bible in a short time. (Show him Lesson 1.) I think this could be a real help to both of us, John, if we could study it together."

Or, "John, we're starting a class of several who are eager to study the Bible, and we feel that if we did it together we would all benefit. Why don't you join us?"

With patience and prayer, you will be led to those whom God would have in your class.

15

II. Role of the Teacher

The purpose of the teacher is not to be an "answer checker," but to supplement the student's own study. *You should not monopolize the time,* but should be prepared to answer the student's questions and to bring out the deeper things from the Word of God which the students may have missed. Stimulate their thinking and motivate them to dig deeper for more knowledge than is required.

As the teacher, you should be able to show the student how to apply the new knowledge which he has acquired to his life, for real learning does not take place until there is a change in one's thinking, attitudes or actions. The Master Teacher is our Lord Jesus Christ. He knows the needs of every pupil. Allow Him first to be your teacher; then, yielding to Him, let Him teach your students through you.

III. How to Lead a Group Bible Study

These lessons are prepared in such a way that they can be used with groups of Christians, non-Christians or mixed groups. For those who have had very little background in the study of the Bible, few ways of getting into the Scriptures are as effective as the group method. In a group the new student is encouraged immediately to participate, to say something himself. This sharpens his desire to learn, for he realizes that he is not only receiving but also is giving to others.

This opportunity for individual expression *is important for building leaders.* Each group should have as one of its chief goals the producing of leaders for other groups. A note of caution: if one person dominates the discussion and does not allow others to participate, the leadership-training goal is frustrated.

A. Basic Principles of Group Bible Study
  1. The multiple purpose of Bible study should be:
     a. for students to learn of Christ;
     b. to encourage Christians in holy living;
     c. to provide an opportunity for evangelistic outreach.
  2. The emphasis of all Bible studies should be evangelistic, to introduce non-Christians to Christ.
  3. The activity should be the study of the Scriptures, not a general discussion. The whole point is to learn the contents of the Bible and to increase in the knowledge of Christ.
  4. The discussion should follow the definite outline of study as set forth by the lesson plan.
  5. Certain groups, although following the same curriculum as others, may be geared to specific needs. For instance, there could be a special group for working people, another for new Christians, a different group for more advanced students, etc.

6. Ideally, no group should be more than ten people. It may be less. If more than ten, intimacy is lost. It is best to sit in a circle.

7. For larger groups, such as a church Bible study, two sessions are suggested; the first led by the pastor for 20 minutes or so to introduce and provide background for the study; the second session led by several trained discussion leaders of smaller groups.

B. The Group Leader

1. You, as the group leader, are not a lecturer, but a discussion leader. You should not dominate the discussion, but should lead it, draw it out. You should be well prepared to suggest ideas, give background material and ask questions to keep the conversation rolling when it lags. If another member is saying something productive and to the point, you should not be anxious to insert your own thoughts, but should guide, clarify and summarize. You should see to it that the discussion stays centered on the definite chosen passages of Scripture.

2. The group leader should never leave the group once it has started. If materials have to be secured or extra chairs are needed, you should appoint someone else to get them.

3. When several groups are meeting in the same room, care should be taken not to place them so close together that they disturb each other. You should sit facing the other groups so that as much as possible your people are not distracted by things happening outside your own circle.

4. You should know everyone in your group by name and refer to them often by their names. You should see to it that new people are introduced before the discussion begins.

5. You will want to contact all visitors during the week after their visits and invite them back.

C. How to Keep the Discussion Moving (too fast = shallow; too slow = tedious)

1. Ask the group to read the passage to be discussed, each person taking a verse.

2. Invite one member to summarize the passage in his own words before any questions are asked about it.

3. When going over the study questions, ask specific people to answer them. This will keep each person on his toes. However, care should be taken to avoid embarrassing anyone. When you ask a question of a group member, be sure he answers it aptly. If he stumbles, help him along and make him think he did answer it, at least in part. Compliment him on his response. A person should not be allowed to feel that he has failed. This is especially true of new members of your study group.

4. Restate the question in different words, from another point of view.

5. If possible, have several parallel passages worked out for each study Scripture and for each question. If everyone looks blank when you ask the question and no one has anything to say, suggest that one of them look up the parallel passage which you give him.

   a. Have him read the passage.

   b. Ask, "What similarity do you see between this passage and the one we have been studying?"

   c. Ask, "What light does this new passage throw upon the original question?"

6. After one person has made a point, ask others if they agree. Have them state their reasons. Often a great deal can be learned by disagreeing over a passage. At the end of the discussion have someone summarize the points that have been made. It is sometimes better for the leader to do this.

7. Apply the passage personally. Ask, "What significance does this have for us today?" "What does this mean to you?" "How does (or will) it affect your life?"

8. There probably will be some who do extra studying of the lessons. Have them briefly share their results. Be sure to commend them for their effort.

9. Use questions that stimulate discussion, such as:

   a. What do you think this passage means?

   b. What can we learn from this passage about God, Christ, ourselves, our responsibility, our relationships to others, etc.?

10. Ask, "What don't you understand about this passage?" Be sure that all unusual words are clearly defined. Have a different translation read. (It will be your responsibility as leader to have that translation on hand.)

11. Keep the discussion relevant and personal.

12. Keep the discussion non-argumentative.

13. Use brainstorming and buzz groups for variety and stimulation in your discussion group.

D. Characteristics of Good Questions

1. Questions should be brief and simple. The pupil should be able to grasp the meaning quickly.

2. Questions should be clear, with only one possible interpretation as to what is meant. This demands great care in the choice of words and phrasing of sentences.

3. Questions should provoke thought, which will test judgment, not merely memory.

4. Questions should never suggest answers.

5. Questions should not offer the student a choice between two possible answers contained in the question, because such questions do not

compel the student to think but rather to guess.

6. Questions should not be stated in the words of the text, pamphlet or notes being used. This results in verbatim repetition of content rather than encouraging thoughtful assimilation of ideas. [This does not apply to the questions in the lessons of the *Handbook* or the *Ten Basic Steps*. Many of those questions require specific answers and should be considered just as they are.]

7. Questions should be adapted to the knowledge and experience of the pupils with special attention being given to both the quickest and the slowest members of the class and with an opportunity for answering given to each.

8. Questions should prepare the person for further study, starting a train of associated ideas.

9. Questions should be logical and interrelated.

10. Questions should fulfill an essential purpose and not be asked merely for the sake of asking.

11. Questions should be asked in a conversational, spontaneous way, as if personally addressed to each member of the group before one is selected to answer.

E. Techniques of Questioning

1. Questions should be asked in an informal way, implying that the student is able to answer.

2. Questions should be distributed so that all have as equal an opportunity to learn as possible. This should not involve a purely mechanical distribution; e.g., alphabetically, seating order, etc.

3. Strike a balance between letting volunteers answer and stimulating shy people to respond.

4. A person should be allowed sufficient time to answer. Do not be impatient. A rapid placing of questions with insufficient time to answer will distract rather than develop the thinking skill.

5. The answer should not be suggested by word, hint or inflection of the voice, or in any other way.

6. Plan your questions so as to lead the class through the material in an organized way.

7. Usually, neither answers nor questions should be repeated since this tends to make people inattentive. However, if for any reason the question is not understood, it will need to be asked again.

8. When a person says he is not able to answer a question you should assume this is true. Don't prod.

9. The question should apply to both the material and the immediate situation.

10. Care should be taken not to ask too many questions, especially in a deliberate way.

11. Sometimes you should not respond or agree with the answer but move ahead to clarify information in the lesson.

(Much of the above material has been edited from suggestions received from Mrs. Frank Renwick, a well-known Bible teacher.)

IV. Lesson Plans

NOTE: In order to be able to teach this series of studies most effectively, you should make yourself familiar with the "Instructions for Individual Study of the *Handbook for Christian Maturity,*" which begin on page 13 of the *Handbook.* Written especially for use by the individual student, these instructions include:

> Summary of the Steps
> Organization of the *Handbook* studies
> Memorization
> How to Study the Lessons.

Ten Basic Steps Toward Christian Maturity may be taught in either of two different ways:

1. according to the Summary Lesson Plan, which is a brief overview, completing one entire Step at each session;

2. with a more detailed study completing one lesson at each session.

A separate lesson plan is included for each of these two procedures. Subject matter for these Lesson Plans is found in the corresponding lessons in the *Ten Basic Steps Toward Christian Maturity* booklets and in the *Handbook for Christian Maturity.*

Teacher's Objective: This is your aim — what you will want to accomplish as you teach each lesson. Keep in mind informational, motivational and life application or action-response goals, and prepare your lesson so as to meet these goals.

Teacher's Enrichment: This supplementary material has been prepared especially for your personal benefit. If you have time to share this material with your students when you teach, you all will be blessed. If not, the lesson still will be complete without it. In any case, your own understanding and appreciation of the truths of God's Word will be richer.

Class Time: Work through each lesson first yourself, of course, answering the questions and making your own observations. When you've internalized the information, and applied the truths to your life, you will be much better prepared to assist your students to benefit from the lessons.

Suggested Opening Prayer: These prayers have been written simply as patterns for you to follow. You may use them or not, as you feel led. The intent of each is to focus on the truth being studied at the time and on the implementation of that truth into the student's life.

> NOTE: Student material in *Handbook for Christian Maturity* and *Ten Basic Steps Toward Christian Maturity* booklets (1983 revision) is reproduced and "boxed" here for your convenience. Suggested answers appear in appropriate blanks. Page numbers mentioned refer to the *Handbook,* and that material may be found in the corresponding Step and Lesson in the individual booklets.

Introduction: The reprinted students' objectives will help you establish and reach the desired informational, motivational and action goals for each lesson.

It is important that you continually encourage your students to memorize the indicated verses and to review them regularly in order to retain what they have learned. Challenge the students to be faithful to this spiritual exercise and give them frequent opportunities in class to demonstrate that memorization.

The suggested Bible reading should be done on the student's own time rather than in class, ahead of time if possible, in preparation for the group study. We want to be sensitive to the possible spiritual immaturity of new Christians, so you will not find Bible reading instructions in the Introductory Step. It is believed the students will be more attuned to the benefits of regular Bible reading by the time they reach Step One, and will be anxious to begin.

Discussion Starter: Your opening question and the resulting discussion should stimulate thinking but not necessarily supply answers, as this will be accomplished during the Bible study. Guide the discussion and keep it going by interjecting further questions. For example, if someone replied to the opening question with, "I would show him what the Bible says," you could ask the individual to name specific verses. Do not correct wrong answers at this time, but use them to stimulate group thinking further by asking if other class members have different opinions.

Lesson Development: Opening paragraphs which precede the Bible study in many of the lessons may be handled in any one of several ways. For variety and interest, you will want to use different methods as you teach the lessons. Some suggestions are:

1. You may read the material aloud while students follow along.

2. Everyone may read it silently.

3. You may ask a different student to read each paragraph (when there are several) or each sentence (if only one paragraph). This will give you an opportunity to evaluate each student's reading ability without putting him or her under too much pressure.

4. When you have determined which students are capable of reading aloud without being embarrassed about their ability, you may ask one of them to read while others follow along.

As you come to the questions from the students' books, discuss each of them, encouraging the students to provide answers either from the Scriptures or from their own thinking, whichever is appropriate. Share the answers suggested in this manual *only if necessary.*

Information and questions included in the development of the lesson (in addition to the "boxed" material) are supplied to enhance and deepen the students' appreciation of the subject. You, as the teacher, will probably not be able to utilize all of this material, so you should prayerfully consider what is most vital for your particular class.

Conclusion and Application: This is the time to move from the informational aspect of the lesson to motivation and action. It is now that you lead your students to personal decisions. Many of the Life Application questions should be answered by the students privately, silently, without public discussion. Your role is to guide their thinking, and then guide them through the prayer time. You should plan frequent opportunities for the group members to make definite commitments to the Lord.

Suggested Closing Prayer: These prayers are prepared for the purpose of aiding you in leading the students to a point of commitment to the Lord. An effective procedure is to read aloud the prayer for the lesson you have just studied, or write it on a blackboard, or have it duplicated and hand out a copy to each student, so everyone will be familiar with its contents. Discuss it as necessary, then either you or one of the students may lead the group in the prayer, giving the students a time of direct communication with God on the matter. Again, information, motivation and commitment to action should be kept in mind as significant goals.

Additional Background Material: May be used for further development of the lesson if time permits, but is not necessary to a proper understanding of the truth presented.

Summary Lesson Plan: Located at the end of the material for each Step, this plan may be used in either of two ways:

1. as a *review* of the entire Step (Even though there is a recap lesson, teaching this summary lesson in addition to the recap will prove beneficial in reinforcing what has been learned.);

2. as a means of *teaching* the entire Step in *one session.* If you elect to use this method of teaching the *Ten Steps,* you should take the time to study all the material included for each Step. You may feel it wise to use different questions from those listed. You are encouraged to get to know your own group, and use the material that is most appropriate to meet the needs of your particular students.

We pray that God will supernaturally open your mind and heart as you begin studying the truths presented here, and that your learning and your teaching will result in experiences of blessed spiritual growth and fruitful life and ministry.

INTRODUCTORY STEP
The Uniqueness of Jesus

SPECIAL NOTE TO THE TEACHER: It is best if the students have been able to read the article, "The Uniqueness of Jesus Christ," beginning on page 27 of the *Handbook for Christian Maturity,* before the first Bible study session is held.

However, if this is not possible, try to make arrangements for them to read it before the next session and go ahead and teach this lesson. Of course, you should read it carefully yourself and make it your own. Also, you will want to be prepared to refer to the section, "Your Opportunity" (beginning on page 41), at the time indicated in the development of Lesson 1.

LESSON ONE

WHO IS JESUS CHRIST?

Teacher's Objective: To present Jesus Christ as the Son of God, to acquaint the students with His claims, and to enable them to recognize Him for who He is.

Teacher's Enrichment: (May be shared with students if time permits.)

Jesus Christ, conceived of the Holy Spirit (Matthew 1:18), came into the world through the means of human birth—of the virgin Mary (Luke 1:26-35; 2:7). Throughout His life upon earth as a man, Jesus Christ withstood all temptation to sin (Matthew 4; Hebrews 4:15) and lived His life here completely without sin (2 Corinthians 5:21 — "Him who knew no sin . . ."). While He was upon the earth, Jesus performed many miracles, including healing the sick, restoring sight to the blind and raising the dead (Matthew 8:1-16; 9:27-33; Luke 8:41-56).

At the close of His short, earthly ministry, Jesus willingly submitted Himself to the shame and pain of death by crucifixion in order to die for the sins of the world, ". . . that we might become the righteousness of God in Him" (2 Corinthians 5:21). Dead and buried for three days, He arose (Matthew 28; 1 Corinthians 15:4-20), and appeared to many other people as well as to His disciples.

After forty days (Acts 1:3) Jesus ascended into heaven, where He is today at the Father's right hand (Romans 8:34), our great eternal High Priest, interceding for us before the Father (Hebrews 5 and 7, particularly 7:25—"Hence, also, He is able to save forever those who draw near to God through Him, since He always lives to make intercession for them").

CLASS TIME

Suggested Opening Prayer

Dear Father, as we begin our studies in this series, we ask that You will open our hearts and minds to the truths You have for us. Help us understand them and appropriate them to our lives. We thank You for the opportunities we are looking forward to and for each person who is interested enough in his or her Christian growth to attend the Bible study. Now help us with this particular lesson as we are introduced to Jesus Christ and as we determine for ourselves who He really is.

(Teacher: In this opening session, even though everyone may know you, introduce yourself again, welcome everyone to the study, and be sure all the students have met each other.)

(Introduction: Be sure students understand objective memory work.)

Introduction
OBJECTIVE: To personally recognize Jesus Christ as the Son of God.
TO MEMORIZE: John 14:6.

Discussion Starter

(Ask for brief responses to this question:) Who is Jesus Christ?

Lesson Development

(Have the class share these paragraphs in any of the ways suggested on page 21 of the Instructions for Teaching.)

Some additional fulfilled prophecies:

The exact amount paid for His betrayal and several related details: Zechariah 11:12; Matthew 27:9-10.

He would be scourged and spit upon: Isaiah 50:6; Matthew 26:67.

He would be given gall and vinegar: Psalm 69:21; Matthew 27:34, 48.

It has been said that if one could know what would occur five minutes in the future, he would need but two weeks to rule the world. The Bible miraculously foretells hundreds of events. Minute details are recorded. In many cases, prophecies preceded their fulfillment by hundreds, sometimes thousands of years. Some prophecies related to cities and countries, such as Tyre, Jericho, Samaria, Jerusalem, Palestine, Moab and Babylon. Other prophecies related to specific individuals.

Jesus Christ is the subject of more than 300 Old Testament prophecies. His birth nearly 2,000 years ago and events of His life had been foretold by many individual prophets over a period of 1,500 years. History confirms that even the smallest detail came about just as predicted. It confirms beyond a doubt that Jesus is the true Messiah, the Son of God and Savior of the world.

The following are some amazing predictions concerning Jesus Christ, together with the record of their fulfillment:

His birth: Isaiah 7:14; Matthew 1:18, 22, 23.
His birthplace: Micah 5:2; Luke 2:4, 6, 7.
His childhood in Egypt: Hosea 11:1; Matthew 2:14, 15.
The purpose for His death: Isaiah 53:4-6; 2 Corinthians 5:21; 1 Peter 2:24.
His betrayal: Zechariah 11:12, 13; 13:6; Matthew 26:14-16; 27:3-10.
His crucifixion: Psalm 22; Matthew 27.
His resurrection: Psalm 16:9, 10; Acts 2:31.

He will come again in glory to judge the nations: Psalm 50:3-5; Ezekiel 21:27; Zechariah 14:1-7; Luke 1:31-33; Philippians 2:10-11; all to be fulfilled.

Bible Study

A. *Jesus' claims concerning who He is:*

State in your words the claims Christ made concerning Himself in the following verses:

1. John 10:30   *He claimed to be the Son of God.*

What did those who heard what Jesus said understand Him to mean?   *That He was God.*

Jesus Christ is eternally existing (John 8:56-58). In order to free men from condemnation for their sin, He took upon Himself the form of man, becoming totally human, yet totally divine (Philippians 2:6-7).

1. His *humanity* is illustrated by His birth of a human mother, His natural human growth and development (Luke 2:40), His physical emotions, His need for sleep, His hunger and His thirst.

2. His *deity* is pointed out by the name "Immanuel" (God with us) (Matthew 1:23), by His witness to Himself (John 5:17-19; 10:30-33) and by the witness of the writing apostles.

> 2. John 14:7 *He referred to God as "My Father."*
> _____
>
> 3. Matthew 28:18 _____
> *He claimed deity by claiming authority.*
>
> 4. John 14:8, 9 _____
> *He claimed His mission was to the Father.*
>
> 5. John 14:6 _____
> *He claimed to be the only way to God.*

Peter later states in Acts 4:12, "There is salvation in no one else; for there is no other name under heaven that has been given among men, by which we must be saved."

To prove His claims, Jesus preached sermons which have never been equalled (Matthew 5-7) and performed miracles, such as feeding 5,000 people with five loaves of bread, walking on water, controlling the wind and forces of nature, healing the desperately sick, giving life to a man who had been dead four days and finally rising from the dead Himself.

> B. What others said about who He was:
>
> 1. His followers:
>
> Peter (Matthew 16:16) _____
> *"Christ, the Son of the living God."*
>
> How did Christ respond to what Peter said (v. 17)? ___
> *He commended Peter; said God had revealed it to him.*
> Martha (John 11:27) *"The Christ, the Son of God, which should come into the world."*
>
> Thomas (John 20:28) *"My Lord and my God."*
>
> How does Christ's response to what Thomas said (v. 27) apply to you? _____

Some other conclusions about who Jesus was (note that at the time these statements were made, none of these men were disciples — they were independent observers):

John the Baptist: "Behold the Lamb of God" (John 1:29-36).

Philip: "Him of whom Moses in the law and also the prophets wrote, Jesus of Nazareth" (John 1:45).

Nathaniel: "the Son of God, the King of Israel" (John 1:49).

The Centurion: "Son of God" (Matthew 27:54).

> 2. His enemies:
>
> John 10:33 *He was guilty of blasphemy, saying He was God.*

Testimony of Leader

(Your testimony as discussion leader — allow about two minutes — will prove effective at this point. In presenting your testimony, try to touch upon your examination of the evidence regarding Christ and your personal testing of His claims by inviting Him into your life *and* by making Him your Lord and Master.

If you cannot in complete honesty say you have made Christ your Lord and Master, it is best that you not testify at all.)

JESUS CLAIMED TO BE GOD.

Two Alternatives

His claims were FALSE.

His claims were TRUE.

Two Alternatives

He is Lord.

He knew His claims were FALSE.	He did not know His claims were FALSE.

Two Alternatives

You can ACCEPT.	You can REJECT.

He made a deliberate misrepresentation.

He was sincerely deluded.

He was a LIAR.

He was a LUNATIC.

C. *Importance of the truth about His identity*

According to the above passages, Jesus claimed actually to be God. He made the kinds of claims that only a person who presumed he was God would make and He was termed God by both friends and enemies without ever attempting to deny it. He even commended His followers for thinking thus.

1. Suppose Jesus Christ were not God. If He knew He was not God and that none of those claims were true, what could we conclude about Him? _____

2. Suppose Jesus were sincerely wrong. Suppose He sincerely believed all these fantastic claims, even though they were not true. What could we conclude about Him? _____

3. Does either of the above answers make sense to you? ___ Why or why not? _____

4. Who do *you* believe Jesus is and on what do you base that belief? _____

It is interesting to consider Jesus' claim to be God, to be the author of a new way of life. Interestingly enough, wherever this message has gone, new life, new hope and purpose for living have resulted. If His claims were false, a lie has accomplished more good than the truth ever has.

Conclusion and Application

The Bible tells us "God so loved the world, that He gave His only begotten Son, that whoever believes in Him should not perish, but have eternal life" (John 3:16). In other words, the great chasm between God and man cannot be bridged by man's effort but only by God's effort through His Son, Jesus Christ. Religion and philosophy have been defined as man's attempt to find God. Christianity has been defined as God's only means of reaching man.

Life Application

1. Why is it important that you personally recognize Jesus Christ for who He really is? _____

Our lives are filled with many activities— such as studies, finances, athletics, social life, business and home life—with no real purpose or meaning.

Jesus wants to come into your life and give you that needed meaning and purpose. He wants to forgive your sins and bridge the chasm between you and God. He does not want to come into your life simply as a guest, but He wants to be in control. Regarding the Lordship of Christ, Romans 10:9 says, "If you confess with your mouth Jesus as Lord, and believe in your heart that God raised Him from the dead, you shall be saved."

> 2. Have you invited Jesus Christ into your life? (See "Your Opportunity," page 41.) _____
>
> 3. What changes do you expect to experience in your life as a result of your trusting Christ? _____

Suggested Closing Prayer

(Give an opportunity for those present to silently invite Christ into their lives if they have not previously done so. Then, you close in audible prayer:) Thank you, Father, that we can trust the Word of Christ, and thank You for answering the prayers of those present.

ADDITIONAL BACKGROUND MATERIAL

Some parallel Scriptures referring to Jesus' claims:

He claimed power to forgive sins — Matthew 9:6.

He allowed Himself to be worshipped as God — Matthew 14:33; John 20:25-28.

Other things He said: He should have the same reverence as God — John 5:23; He would raise all humans from the grave and judge them — John 5:27-29; He would give everlasting life to all who trust in Him — John 6:47; He was eternal — John 8:58; He would return to earth — John 14:1-3.

•   •   •

The story is told of a devout member of a Hindu sect who was confronted with the claims of Christ. To him all life was sacred — cow, insect, cobra. Yet he could not grasp the Christian concept that God actually visited this planet in the flesh, in the person of Jesus Christ. One day as he walked through the fields wrestling in his mind with this concept, he saw thousands of ants around an ant hill in the path of a plowing farmer. Gripped with concern you and I would feel for hundreds of people trapped in a burning building, he wanted to warn them of their impending destruction. But how? He could shout to them, but they would not hear. He could write in the sand, but they would be unable to read. How then could he communicate with them? Then, the realization came. If he were an ant, he could warn them before it was too late. Now, he understood the Christian concept. God became a man — Jesus Christ — in order to communicate His love and forgiveness to us.

LESSON TWO

THE EARTHLY LIFE OF JESUS CHRIST

Teacher's Objective: To present Jesus Christ as the greatest person who has ever lived and to lead students to the conclusion that His moral character, teachings and influence upon history demonstrate that He is God.

Teacher's Enrichment: (May be shared with class if time permits.)

THE INCOMPARABLE CHRIST

"More than nineteen hundred years ago there was a Man born contrary to the laws of life.

"This Man lived in poverty and was reared in obscurity. He did not travel extensively. Only once did He cross the boundary of the country in which He lived; that was during His exile in childhood. He possessed neither wealth nor influence. His relatives were inconspicuous and had neither training nor formal education.

"In infancy He startled a king; in childhood He puzzled doctors; in manhood He ruled the course of nature, walked upon the billows as if pavements, and hushed the sea to sleep. He healed the multitudes without medicine and made no charge for His service.

"He never wrote a book, yet all the libraries of the country could not hold the books that have written about Him. He never wrote a song, and yet He has furnished the theme for more songs than all the songwriters combined. He never founded a college, but all the schools put together cannot boast of having as many students. He never marshaled an army, nor drafted a soldier, nor fired a gun; and yet no leader ever had more volunteers who have, under His orders, made more rebels stack arms and surrender without a shot fired. He never practiced medicine, and yet He has healed more broken hearts than all the doctors far and near.

"Every seventh day the wheels of commerce cease their turning and multitudes wend their way to worshipping assemblies to pay homage and respect to Him. The names of the past proud statesmen of Greece and Rome have come and gone. The names of the past scientists, philosophers, and theologians have come and gone, but the name of this Man abounds more and more.

"Though time has spread nineteen hundred years between the people of this generation and the scene of His crucifixion, yet He still lives. Herod could not destroy Him and the grave could not hold Him. He stands forth upon the highest pinnacle of heavenly glory, proclaimed of God, acknowledged by angels, adored by saints, and feared by devils, as the living, personal Christ, our Lord and Savior."

— Author Unknown

CLASS TIME

Suggested Opening Prayer

Our Father, we commit this lesson into Your hands today and we ask that You will reveal to our hearts how Christ's moral character, His teaching and His influence upon history prove conclusively that He is indeed God the Son.

(Introduction: Be sure students understand objective memory work.)

> **Introduction**
>
> OBJECTIVE: To see that Christ's earthly life confirmed His deity.
> TO MEMORIZE: John 1:12.

Discussion Starter

(Ask for possible responses to this statement and discuss:) "Yes, Jesus was a great leader, but there have been many other good teachers as well. I don't see why the teachings of Jesus are necessarily any more important than those of other great men."

Lesson Development

(Discuss answers to questions in students' books.)

> **Bible Study**
>
> **HEAVEN**
> GOD BECAME MAN
>
> A. *The entrance of Jesus Christ into the world*
>
>   1. On the basis of His statement in John 17:5, where was Jesus Christ before He came into the world? ____
>   *With the Father.*
>
>   2. Read Matthew 1:18-23. In your own words summarize the circumstances which surrounded Jesus' birth. ____
>   *Students should answer in their own words.*
>   _____
>   _____
>   _____
>
> The New Testament passes over the next 30 years of Jesus' life almost in silence. Apparently the gospel writers were more anxious to portray what kind of a man Jesus was than to give us a chronological biography.
>
> B. *The character of Jesus Christ:*
>
>   1. What do you learn about Jesus' character from the following:
>
>   Mark 1:40-42 ___ *Compassionate: "moved with compassion."*
>
>   Luke 23:33, 34 ___ *Forgiving: "Father, forgive them."*
>
>   John 2:13-17 ___ *Zealous*
>
>   John 13:1-5 ___ *Humble.*

2. "The character of Jesus has not only been the highest pattern of virtue, but the strongest incentive to its practice, and has exerted so deep an influence that it may be truly said that the simple record of three short years of active life has done more to regenerate and to soften mankind than all the disquisitions of philosophers and than all the exhortations of moralists."

W. E. H. Lecky,
History of European Morals

C. *Jesus Christ as a teacher:*

1. What was some of the *content* of Christ's teaching about:

   a. The new birth in John 3:1-8? *It is absolutely necessary in order to see the kingdom of God.*

In His conference with the religious leader Nicodemus, Jesus clearly explains that just as one enters the world as a physical being through physical birth, one can become a spiritual being (child of God, John 1:12) only through a spiritual birth.

b. His claims about Himself?

John 10:11 *"Good Shepherd...lays down His lif*
for the sheep.
John 13:13, 14 *Teacher and the Lord.*
John 15:1, 5 *"The vine, you are the branches.*
Matthew 5:17 *Came not to abolish but to ful-
fill.*

Jesus refers in Matthew 5:17 to prophecy and the Old Testament. He read from Isaiah 61, the great prophecy of the Messiah, and laid the scroll down with the statement, "This day has this Scripture been fulfilled."

John 11:25, 26 *"The resurrection and the life."*
Which of these claims do you feel is most important and why? _____

c. His demands of those who would follow Him?
Mark 8:38 *Not to be ashamed of Him.*
Matthew 9:9 *Immediate obedience.*
Matthew 11:29 *"Take my yoke...learn of Me."*
Luke 9:23 *"Deny himself...take up his cross."*
Matthew 19:28 *To follow Him.*
Which of these demands do you find it easiest to follow? _____

_____

How do you think Jesus wants you to deal with the difficult ones? _____

Jesus' demands are not simply for ethical obedience; they are for utter self-committal to Himself. They represent the "totalitarian" claim of Jesus.

"Everyone who shall confess me before men, him will I also confess before my Father who is in Heaven" (Matthew 1:32; Luke 12:8; Mark 8:38).

"He that receiveth you, receiveth me; and he that receiveth me receiveth Him that sent me" (Matthew 10:40; Luke 10:16; Mark 9:37). Here is one who knows His cause to be the cause of God.

"He that loveth father or mother more than Me, is not worthy of Me; and he that loveth son or daughter more than Me is not worthy of Me; and he that doth not take up his cross and follow Me, is not worthy of Me" (Matthew 10:37; Luke 14:26; Mark 8:34).

"Believe on the Lord Jesus Christ, and thou shalt be saved" (Acts 16:31). His demand for faith in Himself is as insistent as Paul's words to the Philippian jailer.

2. Read carefully Matthew 7:7-12 from the Sermon on the Mount. In what verse do you find the following teaching methods illustrated?

Effective repetition of ideas — Verses 7 & 8.

Relevant illustrations — 9 and 10

Practical application — 11

Clear summarization — 12

3. What was even more important than Christ's effective teaching methods (Matthew 7:29)? His authority. Where did He get this authority (John 13:49, 50)? From His Father--"Just as the Father has told Me."

The Impact of Jesus Christ on History: The British scholar W. H. Griffith Thomas said, "In the case of all the other great names of the world's history . . . experience has been that the particular man is first a power, then only a name, and last of all a mere memory. Of Jesus Christ the exact opposite is true. He died on a cross of shame, His name gradually became more and more powerful, and He is the greatest influence in the world today . . . .

"The present social status of men, women, and children is so familiar to us that we sometimes fail to realize what it was before Christ came. In the Roman world the father had absolute right over his children to sell, to enslave, to kill them. It is Christianity that has made these atrocities impossible. Woman was the living chattel of her husband, as she is still in some parts of the world. It is through Christianity that she has obtained a new status, and now in Christian countries 'Home' receives its true and full meaning. The slavery of the Roman Empire was . . . absolute . . .often exercised with cruelty and ferocity. But Christianity proclaimed the universality and brotherhood of all men in Christ, and thereby struck at the root of slavery, and wherever the Gospel of Christ has had its way, slavery has been compelled to disappear."

Caleb Cushing, statesman and former Attorney General of the United States, suggests, "The Christian religion levels upward, elevating all men to the same high standard of sanctity, faith and spiritual promise on earth as in heaven. Just so is it, that, wherever Christianity is taught, it inevitably dignifies and exalts the female character."

Conclusion and Application

Throughout the pages of history, Jesus Christ transformed lives. Today He is continuing to provide spiritual reality — fellowship with God — to those who receive Him as Savior and Lord.

> **Life Application**
>
> Give at least three reasons you feel you can trust Jesus' teachings:
>
> _____
>
> _____

Suggested Closing Prayer

(Leader: If there are those present who need to invite Jesus Christ into their lives, this would be a good time to guide them in this step. Preface the closing prayer time with:) We have seen how Jesus' character, His teachings and His influence upon history prove that He is the Son of God. If you have never asked Him to come into your life, to take the throne of your heart, do it now. In Revelation 3:20, Jesus Himself is speaking. He says, "Behold, I stand at the door (of your heart and life) and knock; if anyone hears my voice and opens the door (inviting Him to enter), I will come in." Ask Him to come in — to save you from sin, to empower you to live the kind of life He wants you to live, to enrich your life with His presence, power, peace, and pardon. Ask Him to guide you continually, as we take a few minutes for silent prayer.

(Then after an appropriate amount of silent time, you close in audible prayer:) We thank You, Father, for what we have learned today and for always listening to our prayers and we thank You for the answers we receive now.

(After praying, add:) He will answer our prayer. 1 John 5:14-15 tells us that if we ask anything according to His will, He hears and answers. Verses 11 and 12 tell us that when Christ comes into our lives, we then have eternal life, our sin is forgiven and we now have access to God in prayer. We become children of God (John 1:12). With Christ in our lives, we have peace with God. Jesus Christ within provides power to live and experience the "abundant life" of which he spoke (John 10:10b). He can now direct us in lives of purpose and fulfillment.

LESSON THREE

THE DEATH OF JESUS CHRIST

Teacher's Objective: To demonstrate to the students the significance of Christ's death and the importance of receiving Him as Savior and Lord, and to give them another opportunity to invite Him into their lives.

Teacher's Enrichment: (May be shared with class if time permits.)

The 22nd Psalm was written hundreds of years before Jesus went to the cross, yet it contains amazingly detailed prophecy of what was to happen there. Christ desired that no one miss the point that this was a prophecy of the cross; therefore at the end of the three hours of darkness at the crucifixion, when God had turned His back upon His Son, Christ cried out in the Hebrew language the first verse of this Psalm: "My God, My God, why hast Thou forsaken Me?" (See Matthew 27:45-49; Mark 15:33-37.)

This searching question of Christ has mystified many. Some have even gone so far as to suggest that this is Christ's final admission that His life and claims had been a hoax. Such a suggestion demonstrates either a lack of scholarship in failure to investigate the facts or an intentional distortion of the Scripture to keep from personally facing the claims of Christ.

Christ points us to three things by quoting this particular verse:

1. *He was forsaken of the Father* on the cross. Christ had enjoyed fellowship with the Father from eternity past. He had lived a life as man that was well pleasing to the Father. He had no sins of His own to die for, yet on the cross He took upon Himself the sin of the world. As a result He was cut off from fellowship with God the Father. His cry is an admission of this agony of soul.

2. *The explanation of His cry,* as found in verse three of the Psalm, "Yet, thou art holy, O thou who art enthroned upon the praises of Israel." In other words, God in His holiness cannot have fellowship with sin, thus He had to turn His back upon His beloved Son. Because God is holy, Christ, bearing our sins, was forsaken on the cross.

3. *This prophecy of His death.* He wanted us to realize that His death on the cross was not just a tragic event in history, but that it was the climactic event in God's dealing with sin. It was an event completely foreknown of God and planned according to His purpose (1 Peter 1:18, 19).

As one reads the first part of Psalm 22, he becomes aware of some exact details that were fulfilled on the cross:

Verse 1: The words of Christ, "Why hast Thou forsaken Me?"— Matthew 27:46.

7: Christ was scorned and derided by the mob — Matthew 27:39.

8: Words of scoffers, "Let God deliver Him" — Matthew 27:43.

16: Christ's hands and feet were pierced — Matthew 27:35.

18: Soldiers cast lots and divided His garments — Matthew 27:35; Mark 15:24; Luke 23:34; John 19:24.

There could be no more fitting way for Christ to point to the awful price He paid in dying for our sins, as well as to give clear testimony of His faith in God's purpose, than for Him to cry, "My God, My God, why hast Thou forsaken Me?"

CLASS TIME

Suggested Opening Prayer

Dear Father, we thank You for meeting with us today and we ask that You will help us understand the meaning and significance of the death of our Savior as we study Your Word.

(Introduction: Be sure students understand objective memory work.)

Introduction

OBJECTIVE: To understand the meaning of Christ's death on the cross; and the importance of receiving Christ as Savior and Lord.

TO MEMORIZE: Romans 5:8.

Discussion Starter

(Ask the group:) Have you ever heard this: "I believe that Jesus was a martyr — public opinion turned against Him, and He died for His cause. I don't understand how this has anything to do with me personally in my search for purpose and meaning in life"? What do you think would be a good response? (Ask for several ideas.)

Lesson Development

(Have the class share this material in any of the ways suggested in the Instructions for Teaching on page 21.

Then move on to a discussion of the questions and their answers.)

NOTE: The Bible teaches that death means separation, not cessation of existence. *Physical death* is separation of the soul (the immaterial or spiritual part of man) from the body (the material part of man) with the resulting decomposition of the body. *Spiritual death* is the separation of man from God. Both physical and spiritual death are the results of sin.

Actually, man was created to have fellowship with God, but because of his stubborn self-will, he chose to go his own independent way, and the fellowship was broken. Remember the floor lamp? (See page 32). Pull the plug from the socket and the light goes out. This is what the Bible says has happened to man.

The results of this separation are not only gross sins like murder, immorality, stealing, etc., but also worry, irritability, lack of purpose in life, frustration, desire to escape reality and fear of death. These and many other conditions are evidence that man is cut off from God, the only One who can give him the power to live an abundant life.

Bible Study

A. *The need for the death of Jesus Christ:*

1. Read carefully Romans 3:10-12 and 3:23.

   How many times does the writer use terms like "all," "none," or their equivalents? _Eight times._

   Why do you think he repeats these terms so much? _____

   _____

   What does this tell you about moral, respectable people?

   _____

Read Romans 1:13-20. Notice especially verse 20: ". . . His eternal power and divine nature, have been clearly seen, being understood through what has been made, so that they are without excuse." Why can God rightfully punish anyone who glorified Him not as God?

Read Romans 1:22-32. What mental, physical and social problems have resulted from man's choice to go his own independent way?

> **2. What is the result of sin (Romans 6:23)?** _Spiritual and physical death._
>
> **B. The result of the death of Christ:**
>
> **1. Read 2 Corinthians 5:21 carefully.**
>   How good does it say Christ was? _He "Knew no sin."_
>   But what happened to Him when He died? _He became sin on our behalf._
>   What was the result for you? _We can become the righteousness of God in Him._
>
> **2. How did Christ feel about such a death (Hebrews 12:2)?** _He submitted voluntarily. knew it would bring joy, endured the cross, despised the shame._
> **3. What did Christ teach concerning His death (Mark 8:31,32)?** _He would suffer, be rejected, killed, and rise again._
> **4. Why did He die for us (1 Peter 3:18)?** _"That He might bring us to God."_

The apostle Paul emphasizes many times in his writings the fact that Jesus Christ is the one mediator between God and man, by the blood of His cross (Colossians 1:20; 1 Corinthians 2:2), removing the sin barrier between God and man.

Peter shows that Jesus is the one way to God (Acts 4:12; 1 Peter 1:2, 18-19; 2:21, 24; 3:18). See also Ephesians 2:16, 18 ("through Him we have access to the Father") and 1 Timothy 2:5 ("one mediator . . . Christ Jesus").

> **C. Significance of the death of Christ:**
>
> **1. What is the only thing we can do to make sure that the death of Christ applies to us so we can be saved (Acts 16:31)?**_____
> **2. Why can't we work for salvation (Ephesians 2:8, 9)?** _It is by grace, not works, so no one can boast._

(For an in-depth study of the true significance of the death of Christ, including an examination of the terms reconciliation, propitiation, redemption, sacrifice, atonement and justification, see the Additional Background Material at the end of this lesson. This information may be used in class or omitted, according to time available.)

> **Life Application**
>
> 1. Read John 3:18 carefully.
>
>   What two kinds of people are described here? _____
>   *Believers and non-Believers.*
>
>   What is the only reason that one kind is condemned?
>   *Because he does not believe in the Son of*
>   *God*
>
> ▷ According to what the Bible says here, are you condemned
>   or uncondemned? _____
>
> ▷ 2. According to 1 John 5:11, 12, do you have eternal life?
>   _____
>
>   (Do not confuse 1 John, the Epistle, near the end of the
>   New Testament, with the Gospel of John.)
>
> 3. According to that same passage, how can you know?
>   _____
>   _____
>
> 4. Have you made the decision to accept Christ's death on
>   the cross for you, and have you accepted Him into your
>   life as Savior and Lord? _____

(Students should not answer these two questions aloud.)

Conclusion and Application

Apart from Jesus Christ, it is impossible for man to know God. By His death on the cross, Christ became your substitute, taking upon Himself the penalty for your sin. This can become effective for you right now, if you receive Him as your personal Savior. Ask Him to forgive your sin, come into your life, and guide you to live for Him. If you already know Christ as personal Savior, pause now to ask His guidance in sharing these truths with those who do not know Him.

Suggested Closing Prayer

(Observe a time of silent prayer to give opportunity for those who either wish to receive Christ as Savior, or pray for guidance. Then you close in audible prayer:) Thank You, God, for the promise that Christ is in our lives and He will never leave us.

ADDITIONAL BACKGROUND MATERIAL

TRUE SIGNIFICANCE OF THE DEATH OF CHRIST

Some of the most important and yet least understood questions of the Christian faith are: "Why did Christ have to die in my place?" "What is the significance of Christ's physical death to me?" "Why couldn't God redeem man without Christ's physical death in his place?"

The answers to these questions make up the very heart of the gospel. They must be understood before a person can really experience personally the great liberating power of Christ's death.

God has chosen to reveal these answers in certain *words* which carry concepts of the truths. Words which explain the meaning of Christ's death are:

1. Reconciliation   4. Sacrifice
2. Propitiation   5. Atonement
3. Redemption   6. Justification

RECONCILIATION. *Definition:* To change a person from enmity to friendship. The theological meaning applies only to man, who is said to be born at enmity with God. This enmity is caused by the guilt feeling man has for the barrier of sin he has erected between himself and God. Reconciliation is that aspect of Christ's death on the cross which removed the barrier of man's sin and its consequences and thus took away the guilt.

Reconciliation is *sufficient* for ALL MEN, but only *effective* for those who accept it personally by faith.

Scriptures: 2 Corinthians 5:14-21; Romans 5:6-11; Colossians 1:20-22.

PROPITIATION. *Definition:* Satisfaction. Deals with the character of God.

God will not compromise His attributes of righteousness and justice which were outraged by man's deliberate violation of God's will. But God's love motivated Him to provide a way whereby He could bring man back into fellowship with Himself *without compromising* His absolute righteousness and justice. God's holy character demanded that man's sin be paid for. Man, who is born a sinner, could not do this because he had no righteousness (Isaiah 64:6). Therefore, God Himself came into the world in the person of Jesus Christ, who was born without sin and never committed an act of sin. Possessing the righteousness of God, He qualified to bear all of the wrath of God which was due the human race. In so doing He *satisfied* the demands of God's holy character and set God's love free to pour out upon the human race in what the Bible calls GRACE. This is propitiation.

Scriptures: Romans 3:21-27; 1 John 4:10; 2:2.

REDEMPTION. *Definition:* There are three Greek words which are translated "redeem": 1. to buy; 2. to buy out (remove from sale); 3. to ransom in order to set free.

Every person is born into the slave market of sin, so to speak (John 8:34). In the slave market, however, there is no means of self-liberation or rescue (Ephesians 2:8-9). Only by the price of death can one be freed from that market (Romans 6:23). There is no slave who can redeem himself or any other slave. Only a free man, one without sin, is able to purchase any slave.

Christ the Redeemer. There is only *one* free (sinless) man who has ever lived, Jesus Christ (Hebrews 4:15; 2 Corinthians 5:21). The Bible liberally attests to the fact that man has at no time obeyed the commands of God. Because of this fact, God provided the plan of redemption and Himself became the Redeemer of mankind in the person of His Son.

By paying the ransom price of His shed blood, Jesus Christ purchased man out of sin and set him free to become a son of God (Galatians 3:13; 1 Timothy 2:5-6; 1 Peter 1:18-19; Galatians 4:4-5). Christ has made this provision of redemption on the cross, but in order for a person to be released from the slave market of sin, he must accept that provision. This he does by receiving God's Son (Ephesians 1:5).

Scriptures: John 8:32-36; Colossians 1:14; Romans 3:24; Ephesians 1:7; Hebrews 9:12.

Prophecies concerning the Redeemer, or Messiah, are numerous and unmistakably clear in many cases. God Himself became the "kinsman redeemer" in the person of His Son, Jesus Christ.

Seed of the woman — Genesis 3:15.

Seed of David — 2 Samuel 7:12-16; Jeremiah 23:5.

Virgin birth — Isaiah 7:14.

Divinity:

His name to be Immanuel or "God with us" — Isaiah 7:14.

His name also to be Wonderful Counselor, Mighty God, Eternal Father, Prince of Peace — Isaiah 9:6.

Priestly office:

A priest after the order of Melchizedek — Psalm 110:4.

A priest upon His throne — Zechariah 6:12-13.

Eternal kingship — Isaiah 9:7; Daniel 7:14.

Prophetic office — Deuteronomy 18:15.

SACRIFICE. *Definition:* The act of offering something to a deity in propitiation or homage; especially, the ritual slaughter of an animal or person for this purpose. Also, that which is so offered.

The sacrifices in the Old Testament pointed forward to the sacrifice of Jesus Christ on the cross. They served as perfect symbols, completely fulfilled in His death.

Sacrifices were divinely instituted for the instruction of the people of Israel. They were object lessons, teaching the sinful condition of the people and showing them that God had provided a way by which they could be reconciled to Him. The principle of substitution was illustrated as early as the time of Abel (Genesis 4:4). Sacrifices were intended to point to the coming one, who would fulfill all sacrifices so that ". . . there no longer remains a sacrifice for sins . . ." (Hebrews 10:26).

Scriptures: Isaiah 53:7; Luke 23:9.

ATONEMENT. *Definition:* The reconciliation of God and man brought about by the life and death of Jesus Christ.

The Old Testament Day of Atonement, which occurred once each year, was of major significance to the Israelites. It required spiritual preparation on the part of the people who were to "afflict their souls." The day, and the events which transpired, prefigured that day when Christ, our High Priest, entered heaven itself to intercede for us before God.

It was necessary that the priest first be atoned for, before he could be a representative of the people before God. As "without shedding of blood there is no forgiveness," the high priest was instructed to use blood in the ceremony of making atonement for himself and for the congregation.

The ground of appeal for atonement or forgiveness is not the goodness or any merit of the individual but the nature of God Himself. The means through which atonement is granted is through the grace and mercy of God.

Scriptures: Exodus 30;10; Leviticus 16:11, 15; Numbers 14:15-20; Isaiah 48:9-11; Hebrews 9:22.

JUSTIFICATION. *Definition:* To free man of the guilt and penalty attached to grievous sin.

Being Himself *just,* God cannot be expected to justify any but those who have kept His law — yet there are none who have been able to do that. Keep in mind that to be "justified" means to be acquitted of guilt, resulting in the elimination of condemnation. The result is restoration to fellowship with God and eternal life.

Man cannot in any sense earn acquittal, or favor in the sight of God, but can approach Him only through Christ, in faith and repentance for sin. Even this would not be possible, except through the great plan of redemption which God instituted. Salvation is the gift of God and not of works, lest any man should boast.

Scriptures: John 3; Romans 6:23; Ephesians 2:9.

LESSON FOUR

THE RESURRECTION OF JESUS CHRIST

Teacher's Objective: To present historical, factual evidence regarding Christ's resurrection, to consider the importance of this event to us as individuals and to lead students to build their Christian experience upon this basis.

Teacher's Enrichment: (May be shared with class if time permits.)

Appearances of Jesus Christ
Between His Resurrection and His Ascension

1. To certain women as they returned from the sepulchre, after having seen the angel who told them He had risen — Matthew 28:1-10.

2. To Mary Magdalene at the sepulchre, probably upon her second visit to it that morning — John 20:11-18; Mark 16:9-11.

3. To the apostle Peter, before the evening of the day of the resurrection, but under circumstances of which we have no details — Luke 24:34; 1 Corinthians 15:5.

4. To the two disciples, Cleopas and another, on the way to Emmaus on Sunday afternoon — Mark 16:12, 13; Luke 24:13-35.

5. To the ten apostles (Thomas being absent) together with others whose names are not given, assembled together on Sunday evening at their evening meal — Mark 16:14-18; Luke 24:36-40; John 20:19-23; 1 Corinthians 15:5.

6. One week later, to all the eleven apostles, probably in the same place as the preceding appearance — John 20:26-28.

7. To several of the disciples at the Sea of Galilee, while they were fishing (the exact time is undesignated) — John 21:1-23.

8. To the apostles and over five hundred others at once on an appointed mountain in Galilee — Matthew 28:16-20; 1 Corinthians 15:6.

9. To James, under circumstances of which we have no details — 1 Corinthians 15:7.

10. To the apostles at Jerusalem, immediately before the ascension from the Mount of Olives (forty days after the resurrection) — Mark 16:19; Luke 24:50-52; Acts 1:3-8.

CLASS TIME

Suggested Opening Prayer

Our Father, we thank You for meeting with us again today and we wait with expectant hearts for the insight You will give us regarding the resurrection of our Savior, Jesus Christ. We pray that the historical, factual truth of this event will become real to us and that our Christian experience will be built upon this firm basis.

(Introduction: Be sure
students understand
objective
memory work.)

Discussion Starter

(Ask the class:) Each spring, Easter comes around, reminding us of the
resurrection of Jesus Christ three days after His death. How do we know Jesus
actually did rise from the dead? How many items of evidence can we think of?

Lesson Development

(Have the class share this
material in any of the ways
suggested on page 19 of the
Instructions for Teaching.)

Jesus' crucifixion had apparently disbanded and demoralized
His followers. That little band was now terror-stricken and
scattered. His enemies were celebrating their victory. But three
days after His crucifixion a miracle occurred: Jesus rose from the
dead.

Within a few weeks His once cowardly followers were fearlessly proclaiming His resurrection, a fact that changed the
entire course of history. Followers of Jesus Christ were not those
who followed the ethical code of a dead founder, but rather
those who had vital contact with a living Lord. Jesus Christ lives
today, and anxiously waits to work in the lives of those who will
trust Him.

THE REAL DIFFERENCE

"The great difference between present-day Christianity
and that of which to us we read in these letters is that to us it is
primarily a performance, to them it was a real experience.
We are likely to reduce the Christian religion to a code, or
at best a rule of heart and life. To these men it is quite
plainly the invasion of their lives by a new quality of life
altogether. They do not hesitate to describe this as Christ
'living in' them.

"Mere moral reformation will hardly explain the transformation and the exuberant vitality of these men's lives —
even if we could prove a motive for such reformation, and
certainly the world around offered little encouragement to
the early Christians! We are practically driven to accept
their own explanation, which is that their little human lives
had, through Christ, been linked up with the very life of
God.

"Many Christians today talk about the difficulties of our
times' as though we should have to wait for better ones
before the Christian religion can take root. It is heartening
to remember that this faith took root and flourished
amazingly in conditions that would have killed anything
less vital in a matter of weeks.

"These early Christians were on fire with the conviction
that they had become, through Christ, literally sons of God;
they were pioneers of a new humanity, founders of a new
kingdom. They still speak to us across the centuries.
Perhaps if we believed what they believed, we might
achieve what they achieved."

J. B. Phillips, Foreword to *Letters to Young Churches*

(Proceed to a discussion
of the questions and
the answers.)

Bible Study

A. *Four proofs that Jesus actually rose from the dead*

1. *First Proof: The resurrection was foretold by Jesus Christ,
   the Son of God.*

What had Jesus told His disciples in Luke 18:31-33?
He would be killed and rise again the third day.

If Jesus had clearly stated He would rise from the dead, and then had failed to do so, what would this say about Him? _____

2. Second Proof: The resurrection of Christ is the only reasonable explanation for the empty tomb.

What did Jesus' friends do to make certain His body would not be taken (Mark 15:46)? *Rolled a stone against the entrance to the tomb.*

What did Jesus's enemies do to make sure His body would not be taken (Matthew 27:62-66)? *Made the grave secure with guards and seal on the stone.*

But on Sunday morning the tomb was *EMPTY!*

Regarding the empty tomb, see Mark 16:1-8, especially verse 6 — "He has risen; He is not here."

NOTE: If Jesus had not been killed, but only weakened and wounded by crucifixion, the stone and the soldiers would have prevented His escape from the tomb. If Jesus' friends had tried to steal His body, the stone and the soldiers would likewise have prevented them. Jesus' enemies would never have taken the body since absence of His body from the tomb would only serve to encourage belief in His resurrection. **Only His resurrection can account for the empty tomb!**

3. Third Proof: The resurrection is the only reasonable explanation for the appearance of Jesus Christ to His disciples.

List all the individuals or groups who actually saw the risen Christ, according to what the apostle Paul wrote in 1 Corinthians 15:4-8: *Cephas, the twelve, 500 brethren, James, all the apostles, Paul.*

If Christ did not rise from the dead, what should we then conclude about all these witnesses (1 Corinthians 15:15)? *They would be false witnesses.*

Does the above answer make sense to you? _____
Why or why not? _____

What else would be true, if Christ did not rise from the dead (1 Corinthians 15:17)? *Your faith is worthless; you are still in your sins.*

When Christ appeared to His followers, what things did He do to prove it was not an hallucination (Luke 24:36-43)? *Asked them to touch Him and see, and ate a piece of broiled fish.*

"Twelve of the twenty-three verses, or over half of the first sermon (of the divinely established church), deals with the Resurrection of Jesus Christ . . . If that doctrine were removed there would be no doctrine left. For the Resurrection is propounded as being: (1) the explanation of Jesus' death; (2) prophetically anticipated as the Messianic experience; (3) apostolically witnessed; (4) the cause of the outpouring of the Spirit, and thus accounting for religious phenomena inexplicable; and (5) certifying the Messianic and Kingly position of Jesus of Nazareth.

> **4. Fourth Proof:** *The resurrection is the only reasonable explanation for the beginning of the Christian church.*
>
> Within a few weeks after Jesus' resurrection, Peter preached at Pentecost, and the Christian church began.
>
> What was the main subject of his sermon (Acts 2:14-36)? *The resurrection of Christ.*

"Thus the whole series of arguments and conclusions depends for stability upon the Resurrection" (W. J. Sparrow-Simpson, *The Resurrection and Modern Thought*, London 1911, p. 230).

"The Christian church rests on the resurrection of its Founder. Without this fact the church could never have been born, or if born, it would soon have died a natural death. The miracle of the resurrection and the existence of Christianity are so closely connected that they must stand or fall together" (Philip Schaff, *History of the Christian Church*, Vol. I, p. 172).

> If Jesus' body were still in the tomb, how do you think his audience would have responded to this sermon?
>
> But how did they respond (Acts 2:37, 38, 41, 42)? *They repented, were baptized, added to the church, and continued in their Christian lives.*

Dr. H. D. A. Major, Principal of Ripon Hall at Oxford, editor of the *Modern Churchman,* made this statement: "The Christian church . . . was founded on faith in the Messiahship of Jesus. A crucified messiah was no messiah at all. He was one rejected by Judaism and accursed of God. It was the Resurrection of Jesus . . . which proclaimed Him to be the Son of God with power" (*Mission and Message of Jesus*, New York, 1938, p. 213).

> **B.** *The results of the resurrection*
>
> 1. What does the resurrection tell us about:
>   a. Jesus Christ (Romans 1:4)? *He "was declared the Son of God with Power."*

> b. The power God can now exercise in our lives (Ephesians 1:19, 20)? *It is of "surpassing greatness... in accordance with the working of the strength of His might."*
> c. What will eventually happen to our bodies (Philippians 3:21)? *(They will be transformed "into conformity with the body of His glory"--made like His.*
> 2. If we can believe the miracle of the resurrection, why do you think it would be logical to believe in all the other miracles Jesus performed?

Conclusion and Application

"We have evidence that a very few weeks after the event Jesus Christ's followers, who had scattered in dismay, were reunited at Jerusalem . . . bound together in a religious society through a common conviction . . . They were fully persuaded that He was alive, and that he had been seen by individuals and by groups of his followers. They were eagerly expecting that He would quite shortly return as the Messiah of their race . . . The strength and the sincerity of their conviction were tested by persecution and proved by their steadfastness. The religious quality of their attitude to Jesus was evidenced by devotion, self-sacrifice and a sense of obligation to Him . . . and they had a message concerning this same Jesus which they proceeded to proclaim with enthusiasm and amazing success" (*Encyclopaedia Britannica*, 1956, p. 15).

Life Application

Hebrews 13:8 says Jesus is the same today and can transform your life.

1. How can your life be different if you allow Jesus to transform it? _____

_____

2. How do you think His "resurrection life" can be seen in you on a daily basis? _____

_____

_____

3. How would your life be different from what it is if Jesus had not risen from the dead? _____

_____

Thomas Arnold, for 14 years the renowned headmaster of Rugby, author of the famous three-volume *History of Rome*, and a man appointed to the chair of Modern History at Oxford, gave the following testimony to his own persuasion of the historic trustworthiness of the resurrection narrative:

"The evidence for our Lord's life and death and resurrection may be, and often has been, shown to be satisfactory; it is good according to the common rules for distinguishing good evidence from bad. Thousands and tens of thousands of persons have gone through it piece by piece, as carefully as every judge summing up a most important case. I have myself done it many times over, not to persuade others but to satisfy myself. I have been used for many years to study the histories of other times, and to examine and weigh the evidence of those who have written about them, and I know of no one fact in the history of mankind which is proved by better and fuller evidence of every sort, to the understanding of a fair inquirer, than the great sign which God hath given us that Christ died and rose again from the dead."

Suggested Closing Prayer

(Give opportunity for those present to pray silently, asking Christ to become their personal Savior. Encourage those who already know Him as Savior to give Him pre-eminence in their lives, asking Him — in silent prayer — to take control. Close with:) Thank You, Father, for hearing and answering our prayers.

ADDITIONAL BACKGROUND MATERIAL

According to H. W. H. Knott in the *Dictionary of American Biography, Vol. II*, Simon Greenleaf (1783-1853) is credited with being in a large degree responsible for the rise of the Harvard Law School to its eminent position among the legal schools of the United States. In 1842, Greenleaf had written A Treatise on the Law of Evidence which Wilbur M. Smith said became "the greatest single authority on evidence in the entire literature of legal procedure," and Smith added that Greenleaf "was the one who, by his legal works, was quoted thousands of times in the great court battles of our country, for three-quarters of a century" *(Therefore Stand)*.

Then in 1846 Greenleaf wrote *An examination of the Testimony of the Four Evangelists by the Rules of Evidence Administered in Courts of Justice*. In that work he said concerning Jesus Christ and His resurrection:

"The great truths which the apostles declared were that Christ had risen from the dead, and that only through repentance from sin, and faith in Him, could men hope for salvation. This doctrine they asserted . . . in the face of the most appalling terrors that can be presented to the mind of man. Their master had recently perished as a malefactor, by the sentence of a public tribunal . . . The interests and passions of all the rulers and great men in the world were against them . . . Propagating this new faith, even in the most inoffensive and peaceful manner, they could expect nothing but contempt . . . bitter persecutions . . . and deaths. Yet this faith they zealously did propagate; and all these miseries they endured undismayed, nay rejoicing. As one after another was put to a miserable death, the survivors only prosecuted their work with increased vigor and resolution . . . They had every possible motive to review carefully the grounds of their faith . . . and these motives were pressed upon their attention with the most melancholy and terrific frequency. *It was therefore impossible that they could have persisted in affirming the truths they have narrated, had not Jesus actually risen from the dead, and had they not known this fact as certainly as they knew any other fact* . . .

"They possessed the ordinary constitution of our common nature . . . swayed by the same motives, animated by the same fears, and subject to the same passions, temptations, and infirmities . . . If then their testimony was not true, there was no possible motive for its fabrication."

JESUS CHRIST LIVING IN THE CHRISTIAN

Teacher's Objective: To demonstrate to students that a person cannot live the Christian life by his own power and resources, that Christ alone can make a life of victory and power a reality, and to motivate the students toward absolute surrender to Christ.

Teacher's Enrichment: (May be shared with class if time permits.)

The Fact That Jesus Christ Lives in the Christian

"Here is the great principle of life which sets forth the potential of all Christian living; namely, Christ lives in the believer. His resources are our resources. His power is most surely at our disposal."

— William Culbertson

Additional Scriptures which teach this fact and explain the purpose for which Christ lives within:

Colossians 1:27 — Relationship to eternal life.

John 14:20-23 — Jesus introduces the fact.

Matthew 28:20 — Fact of His presence and empowerment.

1 John 3:24 — Fact is communicated by the Spirit.

1 John 4:13, 15, 16 — Relationship between God and man through Christ.

1 John 5:11, 12 — "He who does not have the Son of God does not have the life."

2 Corinthians 13:5 — "Do you not recognize . . . that Jesus Christ is in you?"

CLASS TIME

Suggested Opening Prayer

Dear God, show us today how important it is that we understand what the Christian life really is and how we can live it. Then open our minds and hearts to appropriate this truth to our lives. We thank You for answered prayer.

(Introduction: Be sure students understand objective memory work.)

> **Introduction**
>
> OBJECTIVE: To show the importance of total surrender to Christ.
>
> TO MEMORIZE: Revelation 3:20.

Discussion Starter

Name at least one person you believe is living "the Christian life," and tell what makes you think they are. (Get responses from several students.)

Lesson Development

(Have the class share these paragraphs in any of the ways suggested on page 19 of the Instructions for Teaching.)

Note that Chapters 2 and 3 of Revelation are addressed to churches. This serves to emphasize the fact that merely to be a church member offers no guarantee of a right relationship with Jesus Christ. Notice in Revelation 3:20 that the reference is to individuals, not to a group as a whole. "If *anyone* hears, I will come in to *him*, and eat with *him*, and *he* with Me."

When you invite Jesus Christ to come into your heart and life to be your Savior and Lord, confessing your sin and need of forgiveness, He answers your prayer. He enters your heart and life. Why?

One of the main reasons is so that He can empower you. The Christian life is more than difficult; it is humanly impossible. Jesus Christ alone can live it. When He is within you, He wants to live the Christian life that only He can live through you. He wants to think with your mind, express Himself through your emotions, and speak through your voice, though you may be unconscious of it.

Thus the Christian life is not the Christian trying to imitate Christ. It is Christ imparting His life to and living His life through the Christian. The Christian life is not what you do for Christ; it is what He does for and through you. The Christ-controlled life always produces the fruit of the Spirit as listed in Galatians 5:22-23.

- Love
- Joy
- Peace
- Patience
- Kindness
- Faithfulness
- Goodness

- Christ centered
- Empowered by H.S.
- Introduces others to Christ
- Effective prayer life
- Understands God's Word
- Trusts God
- Obeys God

"Jesus Christ does not want to be our helper; He wants to be our life. He does not want us to work for Him. He wants us to let Him do His work through us, using us as we use a pencil to write with — better

---

Bible Study

A. *The need for Jesus Christ to live in the Christian:*

1. What do you think Jesus was not willing to entrust to men and why not (John 2:24, 25)? Himself--who & what He was. He knew man was evil and wouldn't under-stand.

2. What kinds of things are in our hearts (Mark 7:21, 22)? Evil thoughts and wicked deeds--fornications, thefts, murders, coveting, deceit, price, etc.

3. How did the apostle Paul, one of the world's greatest Christians, evaluate his human nature (Romans 7:18)? "Nothing good dwells in me, that is, in my flesh."

4. What is our condition apart from Jesus Christ (John 15:4, 5)? "Apart from Me you can do nothing."

---

still, using us as one of the fingers on His hand. When our life is not only Christ's but *Christ,* our life will be a winning life; for He cannot fail. And a winning life is a fruit-bearing life, a serving life . . . This fruit-bearing and service, habitual and constant, must all be by faith in Him; our works are the RESULT of His life in us; not the condition or the secret or the cause of the Life" — Charles Trumbull.

B. *The fact that Jesus Christ lives in the Christian:*

1. Paraphrase Revelation 3:20 (restate in your own words):

_____

_____

NOTE: The word "sup" in some translations is Old English for "eat" or "dine" — hence the idea of "fellowship" in its original meaning.

2. What guarantee does Jesus Christ give in this verse, and how can we believe Him? *"If anyone...opens the door, I will come in."*

3. How do you know that Jesus Christ has entered your life?

_____

Christ must be truly at home in your heart.

When you invited Jesus Christ to come into your life as Savior and Lord, He heard and answered your prayer. When He came in you were then born spiritually (John 3:3, 6), becoming a child of God (John 1:12). However, the New Testament teaches that now Christ must be allowed to direct and guide your life. Ephesians 3:17 expresses the prayer that "Christ may dwell in your hearts through faith."

In the *Amplified New Testament* this Scripture is translated: "May Christ through your faith (actually) dwell — settle down, abide, make His permanent home in your hearts."

4. How do you know Jesus Christ will never leave you, even if you sin (Hebrews 13:5)? *He Himself has said,"I will never desert you, nor will I ever forsake you."*

5. But if you do sin, how can you renew your fellowship with Him (1 John 1:9)? *If we confess our sins, He will forgive and restore us to His fellowship.*

NOTE: *Salvation* differs from *fellowship*. Salvation is being forgiven of sins and having eternal life. Fellowship with Christ is our daily relationship, or communion with Him. Through sin we may often lose our fellowship. In the same way, a child may lose fellowship with his father through disobedience, but he does not lose his relationship as a son. See also John 10:27-29.

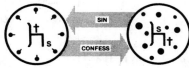

Conclusion and Application

"The conditions of thus receiving Christ as the fullness of the life are simply two — after, of course, our personal acceptance of Christ as our Savior . . .

C. *Jesus Christ at home within the Christian:*

When Jesus Christ is within us, what can He do as we face the following problems:

1. Emptiness (John 6:35)? *He will fill us--we will not hunger or thirst.*

2. Anxiety (John 14:27)? *"My peace I give to you."*

3. Unhappiness (John 15:11)? *He will give us His full joy if we are abiding in Him.*

4. Lack of power (Philippians 4:13)? *"I can do all things through Him who strengthens me."*

"1. Surrender absolutely and unconditionally to Christ as Master of all that we are and all that we have, telling God that we are now ready to have His whole will done in our entire life . . .

"2. Believe that God has set us wholly free from the law of sin (Romans 8:2) — Not WILL do this, but HAS done it.

"Upon this second step, the quiet act of faith, all now depends. Faith must believe God in entire absence of any feeling or evidence . . . We are to say, in blind, cold faith if need be, 'I KNOW that my Lord Jesus IS meeting ALL my needs NOW' "—Charles Trumbull.

Life Application

1. What must we do so that He can live His victorious life through us (Romans 6:13; 12:1, 3)? *Present our bodies to God as instruments of righteousness.*

2. Read and meditate on John 3:16. On the basis of this verse, why do you think we should give control of our lives to God? _____

_____

Galatians 2:20 says, "I have been crucified with Christ and it is no longer I who live, but Christ lives in me."

"Christ was not only crucified for me. He does not live in heaven to intercede for me. No! *Christ liveth in me.* He Himself said that even as His Father dwelt and worked in Him, even so He dwells and works in us" — Andrew Murray.

As non-Christians or carnal Christians examine their lives, they find that they are filled with many areas of activity — studies, finances, social life, home life, business, travel — but with no real purpose or meaning. The reason is that such individuals control these areas themselves, instead of allowing Jesus Christ to control them.

There is a throne in each life (see diagram). Until Jesus Christ comes into a life, the self, or the person's own ego, is on the throne. But when Jesus comes in, He wants to assume His place of authority on this throne. You must step down and relinquish the authority of your life to Him. As you can see from the diagram, when Christ becomes the controller of your life, He becomes Lord of every activity, and that results in purpose and harmony.

Suggested Closing Prayer

(Invite those present to pray silently, surrendering their lives totally to God, believing the fact that He has set them free from the law of sin. Invite non-Christians present to receive Christ into their lives, to save and guide them in an abundant life with Him. Then you close in verbal prayer.)

ADDITIONAL BACKGROUND MATERIAL

"We think of the Christian life as a 'changed life' but it is not that. God offers us an 'exchanged life,' a 'substituted life,' and Christ is our substitute within. 'I live; and yet no longer I, but Christ liveth in me.' This life is not something which we ourselves have to produce. It is Christ's own life reproduced in us. How many Christians believe in 'reproduction' in this sense, as something more than regeneration? Regeneration means that the life of Christ is planted in us by the Holy Spirit at our new birth. 'Reproduction' goes further: it means that that new life grows and becomes manifest progressively in us, until the very likeness of Christ begins to be reproduced in our lives. That is what Paul means when he speaks of his travail for the Galatians 'until Christ be formed in you' (Galatians 4:9).

"Let me illustrate . . . I once arrived in America in the home of a saved couple who requested me to pray for them. I inquired the cause of the trouble. 'Oh, Mr. Nee, we have been in a bad way lately,' they confessed. 'We are so easily irritated by the children, and during the past few weeks we have both lost our tempers several times a day. We are really dishonoring the Lord. Will you ask Him to give us patience?' 'That is the one thing I cannot do,' I said. 'What do you mean?' they asked. 'I mean that one thing is certain,' I answered, 'and that is that God is not going to answer your prayer.' At that they said in amazement, 'Do you mean to tell us we have gone so far that God is not willing to hear us when we ask Him to make us patient?' 'No, I do not mean quite that, but I would like to ask you if you have ever prayed in this respect. You have. But did God answer? No! Do you know why? Because you have no need of patience.' Then the eyes of the wife blazed up. She said, 'What do you mean? We do not need patience, and yet we get irritated the whole day long! What do you mean?' 'It is not patience you have need of,' I answered, 'it is Christ.'

"God will not give me humility or patience or holiness or love as separate gifts of His grace. He is not a retailer dispensing grace to us in doses, measuring out some patience to the impatient, some love to the unloving, some meekness to the proud, in quantities that we take and work on as a kind of capital . . .

"It is a blessed thing to discover the difference between Christian graces and Christ: to know the difference between meekness and Christ, between patience and Christ, between love and Christ . . . He is the answer to every need. That is why Paul speaks of 'the fruit of the Spirit' as one (Galatians 5:22) and not of 'fruits' as separate items. God has given us His Holy Spirit, and when love is needed the fruit of the Spirit is love; when joy is needed the fruit of the Spirit is joy . . . It does not matter what your personal deficiency, or whether it is a hundred and one different things, God has one sufficient answer — His Son Jesus Christ, and He is the answer to every human need" (Watchman Nee, *The Normal Christian Life,* pp. 169-172).

LESSON SIX

THE CHURCH OF JESUS CHRIST

Teacher's Objective: To teach the students about the church (universal and local) and help them appreciate its purpose and importance; to lead them to commitment of service in a local church.

Teacher's Enrichment: (May be shared with class if time permits.)

About the Church

● Definition: The mightiest body of fellowship ever to exist upon the earth is composed of members around the world — that is, every individual who is regenerated by the Holy Spirit, redeemed by the blood of Christ (Ephesians 1:22, 23; 5:24, 25; Colossians 1:18), including those of all ages, in heaven or upon the earth. This company is known as the Body or Bride of Christ, or the church.

● How one becomes a member of the church: When you receive Jesus Christ into your heart and life, you become a child of God (John 1:12; 1 John 5:11, 12), and automatically become a member of the universal church. This is explained as being baptized into the body of Christ (1 Corinthians 12:12, 13), which is the church (Colossians 1:24).

● Illustrations of the relationship between Christ and the members of His church:

1. Vine and branches, emphasizing sustenance and growth — John 15.

In what is perhaps the last opportunity Jesus had to teach his disciples formally, He told them the relationship between Himself and them was that of a vine and its branches, "I am the vine . . . ye are the branches . . . abide in Me . . ." He warns that no one can bear fruit unless he continues to abide in Him, the giver of life. A branch not receiving this life withers and dies. All of the branches abiding in a vine are united with one another, and if we are in Christ, we are united in one body — the body of Christ.

2. Chief cornerstone and building, emphasizing growth — Ephesians 2:20-22; 1 Peter 2:5.

Paul tells the members of the church at Corinth that they are God's building, with Jesus Christ as the foundation which was first laid (1 Corinthians 3:9-11).

3. Head and body, emphasizing headship and unity — 1 Corinthians 12:12,13; Colossians 1:24.

In Ephesians 2 we read that our Lord Jesus Christ has had everything put beneath His feet and that He is head over all things to the church, here stated to be His body, and His fullness. The headship of Christ is again stated in Ephesians 4:15,16. He is described as the one from whom the whole body grows as a unit, unto maturity. See also Colossians 2:19.

4. Bridegroom and bride, emphasizing headship of Christ — Ephesians 5:23-30.

A parallel is drawn between Christ as the Head of the church and Savior of the body, and the husband as head of the wife. Here, we read that the church is subject to Christ, who loved it and gave Himself for it in order that He might cleanse it, making it holy and without blemish.

5. Priesthood of believers, emphasizing our position in Christ — 1 Peter 2:9.

Christians are called a royal priesthood by Peter, and in Revelation 1:6 John says, "He has made us to be . . . priests." Our priesthood is by decree of the Father, and our High Priest is Christ Jesus (1 Timothy 2:5; Hebrews 8:10) through whom every individual is invited to make his requests known unto God.

CLASS TIME

Suggested Opening Prayer

Our Father, thank You for establishing a means whereby we can worship You and fellowship together and learn in order to experience spiritual growth. Help us to understand the importance of Your church and of our responsibility to it.

(Introduction: Be sure students understand objective memory work.)

> **Introduction**
>
> OBJECTIVE: To show the importance of the church in the Christian's life.
>
> TO MEMORIZE: Hebrews 10:25.

Discussion Starter

(Teacher, it would be extremely effective if you could secure four copies of a world map, color them as indicated and use them as visual aids at this point.)

Have you ever considered the changes that have taken place in those parts of the world where the Christian message has gone?

Let us consider four world maps:

On the first, areas of short life expectancy, low sanitary conditions, low literacy, few or no hospitals, no women's suffrage, little concern for children and very little value placed upon human life.

On the second, the areas where the Christian message has not been taken or has not been received. Notice that the same areas of the world have been pictured on each map.

Now, on the third, those areas where a higher standard of living exists, a greater value is placed on human life, schools, hospitals and other similar institutions abound for the benefit of all.

Finally, a fourth map where the Gospel of Jesus Christ has gone, been received and practiced. What do maps three and four tell us?

Lesson Development

The basic New Testament word which is used in reference to the church is a moderately common one, appearing at least 135 times

in our New Testament. The word is *soma*. Translated "body," the word refers to: the body of men or animals, a dead body, or corpse; a living body; the glorified body which Christ now has in heaven; flesh, the instrument of the soul; or celestial bodies. It can refer to a slave, or to an object which casts a shadow. A final usage refers to a "number (large or small) of people closely united into one society, or family, as it were; an ethical, mystical body; so is the New Testament view of the church."

"There is one body," writes Paul in Ephesians 4, even as there is one Lord,

> A. *The universal church*
>   1. Paul frequently compares the church to a body.
>   Who is the only head (Ephesians 5:23)? *Christ.*
>   Who are the members (1 Corinthians 12:27)? *Individual Christians.*
>   2. How does Christ see the church (1 Corinthians 12:12, 13)? *As many members united in one body.*

one Spirit, one faith, one baptism, one God and Father of all. To list the "one body" together with these other great truths places the utmost emphasis upon the fact of the importance of the one body "fitly joined together."

In Romans 12:4,5 Paul makes the reader clearly aware of the unity which exists among the members of the Body of Christ. Here, it is plainly stated that "We, who are many, are one body in Christ, and individually members one of another."

Scripture states expressly that there should be no division or jealousy in the

> 3. As members of His body, how should we feel toward each other (1 Corinthians 12:25, 26)? *Care for one another, suffering and rejoicing together.*
>
> Name some specific ways we can express these feelings.
> _____
> _____

body — if one member suffers, all of the other members suffer with it, and if one member is honored, all of the other members rejoice with the honored member.

No member of the body can say to another, "I do not need you," for God has arranged the body in such a way that all the members are interdependent.

> 4. Read carefully Acts 1:5-11.
>   According to verse 8, what is to be the church's great concern? *To be Christ's witnesses locally and worldwide.*

Where does the Bible say Jesus went physically (v. 9)? *He was lifted up and a cloud received Him.*

Describe in your own words how Jesus will come again for His church (verse 11). _____

Who knows when that will be (verse 7)? (See also Mark 12:32, 33). *Only the Father.*

Within the great company of believers known as the *universal* church, there are included a great number of *local* churches, individual groups of believers. The apostle Paul made many references

The Bible teaches that though Jesus is spiritually present in our hearts, He is also with God the Father in heaven. In the future, He will return to judge the world and rule the nations (Matthew 25:31, 32; 24:36). In the meantime, the church is to be His witness on earth and bring as many people as possible into a living relationship with Him.

5. In light of this, what should be one of your main purposes while here on earth? _____

to churches in particular geographic locations (Romans 16:1; 1 Corinthians 1:2; Galatians 1:2, 22; 1 Thessalonians 1:1, and others). The book of Revelation speaks specifically to seven churches in Asia (chapters 2 and 3).

B. *The local church*

1. What are Christians *not* to do (Hebrews 10:25)? *Not forsake our own assembling together.*

NOTE: The "assembling of ourselves together" refers to the regular meeting of the local church. The Bible *commands* Christians to attend church regularly.

The term "church" means "an assembly of called-out ones," not an *edifice* or building, but *people*. Believers are the "called-out ones" who should gather together for instruction and worship. The significance of the local church is made obvious throughout the book of Acts — everywhere Paul went, local assemblies of believers were established.

(Ask students:) What would a community be like without a church? Would you like to live there? What would you do? (Discuss possible actions.)

Why should church attendance not be neglected? Hebrews 10:25 was written to show the need of Christian fellowship and exhortation. It is a command of God. What would the implications be if we violate this command?

Reasons for Church Membership

It is important for us to realize the real reason for joining a church. Many people who are spiritually blind join a church as a means of salvation. Others join one for social prestige or for other personal purposes. Joining a church does not make one a Christian, but when we are true believers and Christ is our Savior and Lord, *we need the church for a number of reasons.* What would you say they are? (Discuss answers. Then add as needed:)

For *fellowship* with God's children. Dr. Henry Brandt, a Christian psychologist, has said that we need others who see us as we often do not see ourselves, and who can, in Christian love, help us to become strong where we are weak. A group of

logs burn brightly when they are burning together — take one aside and its flame
goes out. This illustration can be applied to our Christian lives.

For our own spiritual *help and growth.* James 5:16 says, "Confess your sins to one
another, and pray for one another."

One excuse given for not becoming a church member is that there are
hypocrites in the church. Actually the church is not an organization of perfect
individuals, but a group of people who desire to be like Christ. It is like a hospital,
helping to make repairs when we break down spiritually.

Could Peter have been called a hypocrite when he said, "All may deny Christ
but I won't"? His heart's desire was to be loyal to the end, but he failed. Then
Christ forgave him and gave him power, and Peter later became a great preacher
of the gospel.

In *remembrance* of the Savior and His death, resurrection and ascension.

To *follow* Christ's command.

Purposes of the Local Church

The purposes for which the local church was established include:

To *glorify* Christ — Ephesians 3:20,21.

To *instruct believers* so that they are equipped to minister to other believers and
to non-believers — 2 Timothy 4:2. Many epistles were written as instruction to
local churches — Ephesians 4:12,13.

To *witness of Christ* — Acts 1:8; 13:1-4; Revelation 1:20; John 15:16.

Baptism was instituted
by the Lord, by example
as well as by command-
ment (Mark 1:9).

> 2. We are saved by faith. But the church has two simple, yet
> meaningful, ordinances we are to observe — baptism and
> communion.
>
> According to Matthew 28:18, 19, why should we be
> baptized? *It is a testimony, or confession*
> *of faith, and a step of obedience to Christ.*

The significance of baptism is correctly interpreted only when we keep in mind
that one must be a regenerated believer before he can truly partake of the
ordinance. Baptism then symbolizes the cleansing from sin which has taken place,
by the figure of death and burial, and resurrection into newness of life
(Romans 6:3-8; Galatians 3:27).

The Lord's Supper was
instituted by our Lord
Jesus Christ at the feast

> What is the purpose of the communion service (1 Corin-
> thians 11:23-26)? *A commemoration--we look back*
> *to Christ's death on Calvary, and ahead to His*
> *return.*

of the Passover, on the night preceding His arrest and trial (Matthew 26:19-29).
The *bread* symbolized the body of the Lord, given in death, the sacrifice for all sin.
The *wine* symbolized the blood of Christ, shed "for many for forgiveness of sins"
(Matthew 26:28).

Some people say they can be Christians and not attend church. That is true, but one cannot be a *dedicated* Christian and not take time to worship God with others and to participate in the ordinances.

Varying degrees of commitment in the lives of Christians were evident in the days of the early church just as they are now, and these differing levels of dedication were reflected in the character of the churches to which those Christians belonged. Some of the churches are described in the New Testament.

(Have students look up verses indicated and discuss their findings as to character of these churches.)

3. Write your own one-sentence description of each of the following local churches:

The church in Jerusalem (Acts 4:32, 33) _____

_____

_____

The church in Thessalonica (1 Thessalonians 1:6-10) ____

_____

_____

The church in Laodicea (Revelation 3:14-17) _____

_____

_____

**Conclusion
and Application:**

Spiritual qualities which are expected in believers in Jesus Christ (Hebrews 10:22-25);

As this shows, some New Testament churches were dynamic; others powerless. So it is today. Not all churches are vital churches, and great variety exists even within a single denomination. In order to stimulate your Christian growth, you should attend a church that exalts Christ, teaches the Bible, explains clearly what a Christian is and how to become one, and provides vital fellowship.

1. Draw near to God.
2. Strengthen our faith, and hold fast without wavering.
3. Declare our faith.
4. Be of help to others (verse 24 — see the *Amplified New Testament*).
5. Assemble ourselves together, as believers.
6. Encourage one another.

It is interesting to note the difference in the attitudes of an individual toward church and what he gains from it now as compared to his attitudes before knowing Christ as Savior. What was meaningless before, now takes on real meaning.

Some suggestions that will make your church worship more meaningful:

1. Bow for silent prayer before the service begins. Pray for yourself, the minister, those taking part and those worshiping, asking that Christ will be very real to them, and that those who do not know Christ may come to know and trust Him.

2. Take your Bible to church with you. Underline portions that are made especially meaningful by the sermon.

3. Meditate upon the words of the hymns.

4. Take notes on the sermon. Review them later in the day and apply what you learned to your daily living.

Life Application

1. Give at least two reasons it is important for us to be a part of a local church. _____

_____

2. If you are not now involved in a local church, what kind of church will you seek and when will you begin attending?

_____

(Special Note to Teacher:

1. Encourage students to participate in the ministry of a local church, to go to the pastor and offer their services.

2. Recommend to those who now know Christ that they become members of a local church since they are already members of the universal church.

3. Caution new converts to avoid criticism of other Christians, churches and pastors who appear to be less zealous than they. "Judge not," is a command of God.

Because a person received Christ does not mean he is perfect, although he is changed. When a caterpillar becomes a butterfly it no longer crawls in the dust. It may light there for a time but does not stay. For the one who truly knows Christ as his personal Savior, the "old life" does not satisfy. He may slip for a time but as soon as he confesses he "soars in the heavens" again.)

Suggested Closing Prayer

Dear Father, thank You for what we have learned today about the Body of Christ and what our relationship is with it. Show each one of us right now if You are pleased with our present involvement in a local church, and if not, what You would have us do about it. We desire to be obedient to You in the fullest way possible and are trusting Your Spirit to lead us.

LESSON SEVEN

RECAP

Teacher's Objective: To be sure students have a full and well-grounded understanding of the person of Jesus Christ; to lead them into any commitments appropriate at this point.

Teacher's Enrichment: (May be shared with class if time permits.)

Christ is either all He claimed to be or He is a liar – an impostor – and in a moral universe a lie then has done more good than any truth.

C. S. Lewis says, "On the one side clear, definite, moral teaching. On the other, claims, which, if not true, are those of a megalomaniac, compared with whom Hitler was the most sane and humble of men. There is no half-way house, and there is no parallel in other religions.

"If you had gone to Buddha and asked him, 'Are you the son of Bramah?' he would have said, 'My son, you are still in the vale of illusion.' If you had gone to Socrates and asked, 'Are you Zeus?' he would have laughed at you. If you had gone to Mohammed and asked, 'Are you Allah?' he would first have rent his clothes and then cut your head off. If you had asked Confucius, 'Are you Heaven?' I think he would have probably replied, 'Remarks which are not in accordance with nature are in bad taste.'

"The idea of a great moral teacher saying what Christ said is out of the question. In my opinion, the only person who can say that sort of thing is either God or a complete lunatic suffering from that form of delusion which undermines the whole mind of man."

Does it not make sense that the person who is regarded as the greatest teacher, the greatest example and the greatest leader the world has ever known would be, as He Himself claimed to be and as the Bible tells us, the one person who could bridge this chasm between God and man?

You remember in Romans 6:23 we read, "For the wages of sin is death, but the free gift of God is eternal life in Christ Jesus our Lord." If you were to study the religions and philosophies of the world, you would find no provision for man's sin apart from the sacrificial death of Christ. The Bible says that without the shedding of blood there is no remission (or forgiveness) of sin.

CLASS TIME

Suggested Opening Prayer

Our Father, we thank You for what we have learned from this introductory portion of the *Ten Basic Steps Toward Christian Maturity*. We pray as we recap these truths today that they will become even more clear and precious to us and that we will be able to appropriate them more fully for our lives.

(Introduction:

Student's objective is simply to review what has been learned in the study of this Introductory Step. Memory work is also to be reviewed and impressed more deeply upon the mind.)

(No Discussion Starter necessary.)

Lesson Development

(Ask for and discuss any questions which those who have completed the studies may still have.)

(Talk about Recap questions and students' answers, also questions included here for additional consideration.)

> What do you think is the most important way in which Jesus Christ is different from other people? _____
> _____

> Who is Jesus Christ to you? _____

What did Jesus say of Himself (John 14:6)?

> Why do you suppose Jesus' enemies did not want to believe His claims about who He was? _____
>
> What does it mean to you now to have Jesus living within you?
> _____
>
> How does your present relationship with Christ correspond to your present relationship with your local church? _____
>
> How should it? _____

Conclusion and Application:

God has a plan for our lives. He did not intend for man to live in a negative, miserable, defeated existence. The Bible tells us that God meant for man to live life to the fullest, a life of abundant living. Jesus said, "I came that they might have life, and might have it abundantly" (John 10:10).

Every man is seeking happiness. The Bible says that there is only one way to know true happiness and this is through God's plan in a personal relationship with Jesus Christ.

Do you know Him as your Savior? Would you like to know Him?

As we close in prayer, if you are not sure that Christ is in your heart, won't you ask Him to come in? (Repeat Revelation 3:20 and John 1:12). Let me first read for you the prayer I will pray. (Read it.) Now, as I pray this prayer, you may want to make it your own. If so, just repeat it, in your heart, after me.

"Lord Jesus, I ask You to come into my heart, to take over my life, to forgive my sins and to show me Your plan for my life."

If you have done this, where is Christ right now? (Give assurance.) As you leave the room today (tonight), won't you come and tell me that you have made this decision? (You might have them sign a piece of paper or make an appointment for further discussion.)

ADDITIONAL BACKGROUND MATERIAL

Here are some parallel Scripture passages for the following subjects:

Trinity: Genesis 1:26, "Let *us* make man in *our* image."

Prophecy: Isaiah 9:6, written 700 years before Christ's coming, tells how He will come.

Why Christ came: Hebrews 1:1-3.

Christ's authority: Matthew 7:29; John 12:49,50.

Lamb sacrifice: Exodus 12.

Lamb of God: John 1:29; Romans 5:10.

Christ is coming again: John 14:3; Mark 13:32; Matthew 24:36.

Christ, a free gift: Romans 5:18.

God's direction: Proverbs 3:5,6; Psalm 37:23.

Attitude when we take communion: 1 Corinthians 11:28-33.

SUMMARY LESSON PLAN

THE UNIQUENESS OF JESUS

Teacher's Objective: To assist students to establish and be assured of their position in Christ and of His power within them; to lead students to whatever appropriation and commitment is needed.

Teacher's Enrichment: (See Teacher's Enrichment sections in each of the preceding lessons of this Step, and share with the class as time permits.)

CLASS TIME

Suggested Opening Prayer

Dear Father, as we begin our studies in this series, we ask that You will open our hearts and minds to the truths You have for us. Help us understand them and appropriate them to our lives. We thank You for the opportunities we are looking forward to and for each person who is interested enough in his or her Christian growth to attend the Bible study. Now help us with this particular lesson as we are introduced to Jesus Christ and as we learn who He is, what He wants to do for us, and what He expects of us.

(Introduction:

STUDENT'S OBJECTIVE: To establish and be assured of his position in Christ and of Christ's power within the student; to make whatever appropriation and commitment necessary for the student as he is led by the Holy Spirit.

TO MEMORIZE: John 1:12.)

Discussion Starter

In what ways do men seek happiness? List some of them. Are these really satisfying? Why or why not? Let's look up John 4:13,14.

Lesson Development

A. Who is Jesus Christ? *(from Lesson 1).*

(The article, "The Uniqueness of Jesus Christ," which appears on pages 27-42 of the *Handbook for Christian Maturity,* and at the beginning of the individual introductory booklet of the *Ten Basic Steps Toward Christian Maturity,* should be read by both teacher and students.)

1. Who did Jesus say He was (John 10:30; 14:6)?

    2. Who did others say He was (Matthew 16:16; John 10:33)?

    3. Who do you say He is? Why? (Discuss students' ideas.)

B. The Earthly Life of Jesus Christ *(from Lesson 2).*

    1. What kind of birth did Jesus have (Matthew 1:18-23)?

    2. How would you describe His character (Mark 1:41; Luke 23:34; John 2:15-17)?

    3. What did he require of His followers (Mark 8:38; Matthew 9:9; Luke 9:23)?

C. The Death of Jesus Christ *(from Lesson 3).*

    1. Why was the death of Jesus Christ necessary (1 Peter 3:18))?

    2. What is sin (Romans 8:7)?

    3. What has Jesus' death done for you?

D. The Resurrection of Jesus Christ *(from Lesson 4).*

    1. How do we know Jesus actually rose from the dead (4 ways)? (1. He said He would, Luke 18:31-33. 2. The tomb was empty, Mark 16:6. 3. He appeared to many, 1 Corinthians 15:4-8. 4. The church was established, Acts 2:32,33,41.)

    2. What is the result of the resurrection of Christ (Romans 1:4; Philippians 3:21)?

E. Jesus Christ Living in the Christian *(from Lesson 5).*

    1. How does Jesus Christ take up residence in a person (Revelation 3:20)?

    2. Why is it necessary for Jesus to be in us (John 15:4,5)?

    3. What will be the results (Galatians 5:22-23)?

F. The Church of Jesus Christ *(from Lesson 6).*

    1. How does Christ see the church 1 Corinthians 12:12,13)?

    2. What is to be the church's greatest concern (Acts 1:8)?

The Bible describes the church in two senses: (1) as the *universal* church, which refers to all true Christians, and (2) as the *local* church, which is an individual group of Christians who gather for worship, instruction and mutual encouragement.

    3. Paul referred to what kind of churches in Romans 16:1, 1 Corinthians 1:2 and Galatians 1:2? (Individual, local churches.)

    4. What is God's commandment regarding the church (Hebrews 10:25)?

    5. Why is it important that we be a part of the church? (For fellowship, help and growth, obedience. Discuss students' responses.)

    6. What are the purposes of the local church? (To glorify Christ, Ephesians 3:20,21; to instruct believers, 2 Timothy 4:2 and Ephesians 4:12,13; to witness of Christ, John 15:16.)

7. The two ordinances of the local church are *baptism* and *communion.*
   a. Why should we be baptized (Matthew 28:18,19)?
   b. What is the purpose of the communion service (1 Corinthians 11:23-26)?

Conclusion and Application

God has a plan for our lives. He did not intend for man to live a negative, miserable, defeated existence. The Bible tells us that God meant for man to live life to the fullest, a life of abundant living. Jesus said, "I came that they might have life, and might have it abundantly" (John 10:10).

Every man is seeking happiness. The Bible says that there is only one way to know true happiness and this is through God's plan in a personal relationship with Jesus Christ.

Do you know Him as your Savior? Would you like to know Him?

As we close in prayer, if you are not sure that Christ is in your heart, won't you ask Him to come in? (Repeat Revelation 3:20 and John 1:12). Let me first read for you the prayer I will pray. (Read it.) Now, as I pray this prayer, you may want to make it your own. If so, just repeat it, in your heart, after me.

"Lord Jesus, I ask You to come into my heart, to take over my life, to forgive my sins and to show me Your plan for my life."

If you have done this, where is Christ right now? (Give assurance.) As you leave the room today (tonight), won't you come and tell me that you have made this decision? (You might have them sign a piece of paper or make an appointment for further discussion.)

Suggested Closing Prayer

Father, we thank You for making our understanding of the person and work of Jesus Christ more full and complete than it has ever been. We praise You for who Jesus is and for loving us enough to send Him to pay for our sins. We pray You will help us to continue to grow in our appreciation of our Savior in our service to You.

The Christian Adventure

THE CHRISTIAN ADVENTURE WITH JESUS CHRIST

With all due respect to the leaders of various religions, it should be noted that Jesus is the only one who ever claimed to be God. Mohammed claimed to be a prophet of God. His body, like that of any mortal being, remains in the grave. So do the bodies of Buddha, Confucius, Zoroaster and the founders and leaders of other religions.

Jesus of Nazareth is unique in many ways. Minute details of His life were foretold by Old Testament prophets hundreds of years before His birth. In life and in example, He remains without a peer. Crucified because He claimed to be God, He confirmed His claims by His resurrection. History supports the fact of His resurrection.

He is recognized as the greatest figure of history by everyone who knows the facts, and He is alive!

What does all this mean to you today? The practical benefits of the resurrection of Jesus Christ are obvious. If you have trusted Him, He has taken up residence in your life, wants you to yield complete control to Him and to invite Him to be the Lord of every area of your life.

The Bible tells us in Colossians 1:15,16 that "He (Christ) is the image of the invisible God, the first-born of all creation. For in Him all things were created, both in the heavens and on earth, visible and invisible, whether thrones or dominions or rulers or authorities — all things have been created through Him and for Him." This creative act included man.

Since we were created by Jesus Christ, God the Son, He alone holds the answer to the basic questions of life: Where did I come from? Why am I here? Where am I going?

With the One who created you in control of your life, you will receive a new quality of life, *His resurrection life*. In exchange for your life of defeat and frustration, Christ will give you His life of victory, purpose and power, You will no longer be a creature of chance. You will be a child of God.

To many people, Christianity is something to be endured in anticipation of heaven. But this is not the way our Lord intended it. He meant for your Christian life to be victorious, fruitful and exciting. To know Jesus Christ personally as Savior and Lord is the greatest privilege and adventure that man can ever experience.

LESSON ONE

THE CHRISTIAN'S CERTAINTY

Teacher's Objective: To lead Christians, both new and older, to assurance of their eternal lives and to awareness of the presence of Jesus Christ in their lives.

Teacher's Enrichment: (May be shared with class if time permits.)

• The Pacific Ocean exists regardless of whether we see it or experience it. The fog may shroud it from view so that even those who live nearby cannot see it — yet it is just as much there as at any other time, because it is an unchanging fact. Eternal life is also an unchanging fact regardless of whether we feel it or not. The Christian is assured beyond a doubt in 1 John 5:12 that he has eternal life. It is impossible to have Christ and not have this life. That assurance is based on our acceptance of God's gift, His only begotten Son, and on our trust in God's promise, not on feelings or experiences. We may feel discouraged and distant from God, but if we have received Christ this cannot affect our possession of eternal life.

There are only two classes of human beings — those who have Christ and eternal life and those who do not. There is *no neutral class.* Notice how many kinds of men are listed in the verse mentioned above.

Everyone in the world is either an American citizen or he is not. There is no in-between class. Regardless of whether you live in Canada, right next to the border, or in Australia, thousands of miles away, you are not an American citizen unless you were born one or have become naturalized. Regardless of how much one admires Christ or would like to believe in Him, he is just as much a non-Christian as the most hardened atheist until he accepts Christ.

• Alexander Maclaren says concerning Revelation 3:20, "Who knocks? The exalted Christ. What is the door? This closed heart of man. What does He desire? Entrance. What are His knockings and His voice? . . . whatsoever sways our hearts to yield to Him and enthrone Him."

The Abingdon Bible Commentary states: "How courteous for the Lord of the world to *stand at the door* not presuming to enter until he is invited. 'God is always courteous' said Francis of Assisi, 'and does not invade the privacy of the human soul.' He who hearkens and opens will find Christ both guest and host, yes, and a feast too (John 6:54). The common meal is the symbol of the Oriental for confidence and affection . . ."

Think about what you have to do to keep Christ from coming in. The answer is *nothing.* He only comes in when we act and open the door.

When someone knocks at the door of your room or home, you can do one of three things: (1) open the door and invite him in; (2) ignore him in the hope he will go away; (3) tell him to go away. Which response have you made to Christ? Which response have your students made?

CLASS TIME

Suggested Opening Prayer

Our Father, we ask that Your Holy Spirit will enlighten our minds and hearts to this truth that You have for us today. Help us to believe and accept the assurance of the eternal life we possess and of the presence of our Savior who is with us always.

(Introduction: Be sure
students understand
    objective
    memory work
    reading assignment.)

> **Introduction**
>
> OBJECTIVE: To give assurance to the new Christian of eternal
>   life and Christ's presence in his life.
>
> TO MEMORIZE: 1 John 5:13.
>
> TO READ: John 3:1-20 and 1 John 5:9-15.

Discussion Starter

(Ask the class:) If someone told you he thought he had accepted Christ and had become a Christian, but was not really sure of it, what would you tell him? (Try to get some different answers and allow a few minutes of discussion. Do NOT give any answer yourself at this time.)

Lesson Development

(Have the class share this
material in any of the ways
suggested in the Instructions
for Teaching on page 21.)

Believers of Old Testament times looked forward to the coming of their Messiah. New Testament believers look back to the cross and the resurrection. Both of these events are culminated in the unique life of Jesus Christ which is the basis for Christian confidence.

Jesus' death on the cross and His bodily resurrection from the dead prove that He was God's promised Messiah of the Old Testament, the Savior of the world.

To believe in Jesus Christ as the Savior of the world is to believe in a living person. People often ask, "What is the meaning of belief?" The Amplified New Testament expresses the full meaning of the term "believe" as "adhere to, trust in and rely on." The Gospel of John has been called the "Gospel of Belief." The word "believe" occurs many times in the book of John. Chapter 20, verse 31, expresses the purpose of that book: "But these have been written, that you may believe that Jesus is the Christ, the Son of God; and that believing you may have life in His name."

(For the Bible Study,
assign each question to
someone in the class. After
each answer, promote dis-
cussion with further
questions, insights and illustrations given.)

(Ask the class:) What does it mean to receive Christ?

> **Bible Study**
>
> A. *Christian certainty*
>
> 1. What must one do to become a Christian (John 1:12)?
>   *Receive Him--Jesus Christ.*

It means "the same thing that it means to receive a gift someone offers us — we put forth our hand and take the proffered gift." — Donald Gray Barnhouse. Compare Romans 6:23, "The *gift* of God is eternal life through Jesus Christ our Lord." "To believe on His name" is an expression which means "to have faith in all that He is." By deciding to have personal faith in Jesus Christ we become Christians.

> 2. To be a son of God is to be born of whom (John 1:13)?
>   *God.*

John 1:13 talks about the family of God. (Ask the class:) Isn't everyone God's child?

The answer is no. Everyone is a creature of God, but only those who have received His Son are members of His family.

A carpenter once said to a minister, "I believe that God created all men, therefore all men must be His children."

The minister replied, "Have you ever made a table?"

"Why, of course," said the carpenter, "scores of them."

"Do you believe the tables are your children because you made them?"

"Oh, no," said the carpenter.

"Why not?" said the minister.

"Well, because they don't have my life in them."

"Exactly," said the minister — "do you have God's life in you?"

This is what is means to be God's child — you must have God's life in you, and this comes only by receiving Christ.

> 3. To believe in Jesus Christ is to possess *Eternal life* and to be free from *judgment* (John 5:24).

Phillips translates this Scripture, "I solemnly assure you that the man who hears what I have to say and believes in the One who has sent Me, has eternal life. He does not have to face judgment; he has already passed from death into life."

(Ask the class:) When do you get eternal (everlasting) life?

What is eternal life?

According to this verse we receive eternal life *when we believe*. Christianity is not "pie in the sky when I die"; it brings new life here and now. Eternal life "is not reserved to be entered on in the blessed future, but is a present possession . . . heaven is not different in kind and circumstance from the Christian life on earth, but differs mainly in degree and circumstance" — Alexander Maclaren. But what is eternal life? It is not endless existence, for all men, Christian or non-Christian, have this according to Matthew 25:46. It is a rich, abundant, full life, centered about God and in vital contact with Him, which no non-Christian has (cf. John 10:10).

Phillips again has a good translation of these verses,

> 4. What did Christ do with our sins (1 Peter 2:24, 25)? _____
> *Bore them in His body on the cross.*
>
> How should this affect your life? _____

"And He personally bore our sins in His own body on the cross, so that we might be dead to sin and be alive to all that is good. It was the suffering that He bore which has healed you. You had wandered away like so many sheep, but now you have returned to the shepherd and guardian of your soul."

Suppose you get a traffic ticket for speeding, but when you show up in court your own father is the judge. Because you are his son, would it be fair for him to fine everyone else who has a ticket, but excuse you? Of course not. Suppose, then, he fines you thirty dollars or thirty days in jail. Since you do not have the thirty dollars, you must spend thirty days in jail. But because he loves you, your father steps down off the judge's bench, and holds out thirty dollars. Justice is satisfied, yet you go free. The only condition is that you accept your father's payment. Similarly, we have violated God's laws and justice demands the penalty be paid. But because of His love for us, God has paid it for us in the person of His Son. We must accept this payment to be forgiven.

The background for these verses is the shepherd life in biblical countries. After watering and resting his sheep, the shepherd calls them to go to another

> 5. What three things characterize Jesus' sheep (John 10:27)? *"...hear My voice, and I know them, and they follow Me."*
>
> 6. What is your relationship with Christ, as He Himself states in John 10:28-30? *Have eternal life, shall never perish, and no one can snatch us out of the Father's hand.*

feeding ground. "At the first sound of his call, which is usually a peculiar gutteral sound, hard to imitate, the flock follow off . . . Even should two shepherds call their flocks at the same time and the sheep be intermingled, they never mistake their own master's voice . . ." Note that John 10:28-30 teaches that a Christian can *never* be lost. He may sin and lose his fellowship, or communication with God, but he can never lose his salvation.

What does it mean to be born again? Notice: (1) It does not mean that we

> 7. What are the implications of failing to believe the testimony that God has given regarding His Son (1 John 5:10, 11)? *We make God a liar.*

"turn over a new leaf," for
it is a far more radical
change than that. (2) It
applies to good as well as
bad people. Nicodemus, to

> **B.** *New life*
>
> 1. In John 3:3, 7, what did Jesus tell Nicodemus about seeing and entering the kingdom of God? ___*A person*___ *must be born again to see or enter the kingdom of God.*

whom Jesus spoke these words, was a Pharisee, a ruler of the Jews, one of the great
religious leaders of his day. He was moral and ethical, prayed seven times a day and
worshipped at the synagogue faithfully — a good man. But Jesus said he "must be
born again."

Birth gives life. A new birth means that a new life must be given to us. This
new life is the eternal life which comes when we receive Christ.

A caterpillar crawling in the dust is an ugly, hairy worm. But one day this worm
weaves about its body a cocoon. Out of this cocoon emerges a beautiful butterfly.
We do not understand fully what has taken place. We realize only that where once
a worm has crawled in the dust, now a butterfly soars in the heavens. So it is in the
life of a Christian. Where once we lived on the lowest level as sinful egocentric
man, we now dwell on the highest plane, experiencing a full and abundant life as
children of God. An individual becomes a Christian through spiritual birth.

> 2. At physical birth one receives many things of which he is not aware; e.g., family name, privileges, wealth, love, care and protection. At spiritual birth one becomes a son of God, receives eternal life, a divine inheritance and God's love, care and protection. God has given us these definite things because of His great love. God's gifts are never based on man's changing emotions, but on His unchanging Word.
>
> In your own words describe what you have, according to these verses:
>
> Ephesians 1:7 ___*redemption, forgiveness*___
> Romans 5:1 ___*Peace with God*___
> Romans 3:22 ___*righteousness of God*___
> Colossians 1:27b ___*"Christ in you, the hope of glory."*___

The four verses listed
here describe some of the
results of accepting Christ.
According to these passages
we have:

(1) *Forgiveness.* All of
our disobedience to God is
eternally forgiven. Christianity alone offers a solution
to the guilt problem.

(2) *Peace.* According to the Bible, the very best non-Christians are at war with
God. Peace comes only through accepting Christ. When the United States was at
war with Japan there was no friendly contact, little communication, only active
hostility between the two. This was not changed until the peace treaty was signed
in Tokyo Bay.

Similarly, all non-Christians, whether they know it or not, are at war with God
and have no hope for communication or friendship with Him until they make
peace through Christ.

(3) *Righteousness.* This is not the personal righteousness of everyday life, but the
righteousness of God ascribed to us when we accept Christ. God has ascribed to us
Christ's righteousness and ascribed to Christ our sins, as He suffered on the cross.

(4) *Christ in you.* Though God forgives us, makes peace with us and clothes us

with Christ's righteousness, this would do us little good in this life unless Christ came to live in our hearts. Because He is in our hearts, we have a new strength from Him, and are able to keep His commandments.

You are always the son (or daughter) of your mother and father — this never changes. Yet you may argue with your parents and

> 3. As you begin to live the Christian life, what three evidences in your life will assure you that you know Jesus Christ?
>
> _"...if we keep His commandments."_ (1 John 2:3).
>
> _"...love the brethren."_ (1 John 3:14).
>
> _"The Spirit...bears witness..."_ (Romans 8:16).

not even be on speaking terms. You would still be their child, but you would have no fellowship with them. We are *always* God's children, if we are Christians; even if we lose our fellowship with Him through sin.

Conclusion and Application

What is the result of being sure we have accepted Christ and knowing He has given us eternal life? Basically, it is that we are now set free from fear and doubt and we can begin to enjoy God and the life of purpose and meaning He has for us.

The Christian who does not have assurance looks at God fearfully, never knowing whether the Father has received him or not. He usually is defeated and miserable.

But the Christian who has assurance can be joyful because he belongs to God, and instead of always regarding Him with fear, he will learn to love Him and serve Him.

(Allow students time to answer these questions privately and give them an opportunity to share their answers if they desire.)

Suggested Closing Prayer

Dear Father, we thank You for the understanding of this basic, glorious truth of eternal life which we have just learned about.

> **Life Application**
>
> On the basis of Lesson One:
> 1. Who is Jesus Christ to you? _____
> 2. What is your relationship to God? _____
> 3. What kind of life do you now possess? _____
> 4. What about your sins? _____
> 5. Why are you sure (or doubtful) of your salvation? _____
> _____
> 6. What changes in your life do you believe have taken place because of Christ? _____
> _____

We pray You will keep us aware of the fact that we are really members of Your family and that we always will be. We thank You for the love and joy we may experience in that knowledge.

LESSON TWO

THE PERSON OF JESUS CHRIST

Teacher's Objective: To confirm the incarnation and to show students through biblical evidence that Jesus Christ is God in human form; to lead students to a life-changing appreciation of their relationship with Him, and to motivate them to prepare for His second coming.

Teacher's Enrichment: (May be shared with class if time permits.)

The Second Coming of Christ

● At some particular time in the future, a time known only to God, the church of the Lord Jesus Christ will be caught up to meet Him in the air. This is known as the "rapture" of the church and is described in 1 Thessalonians 4:13-18.

At this time, according to 1 Corinthians 15:51-56, believers will receive new physical bodies which will be perfect and glorious. "As the believer then passes into a condition of glory, his body must be altered for the new conditions . . . it becomes a 'spiritual' body belonging to the realm of the spirit" (International Standard Bible Encyclopedia.)

This great event will happen suddenly and all believers will be included. Some devout scholars feel it will take place before Christ comes to earth, others feel it will occur at the same time. Though the Bible does not clearly indicate when it will be accomplished, without doubt it will be one of the most marvelous acts God has ever performed.

The Great Tribulation, to take place during the last seven years of history before Christ comes again, is described in Mark 13:14-23, Revelation 6-18, and in other passages. At this time calamity and evil will sweep over the world in an unprecedented manner. A great world leader known as the Anti-Christ will come to power, and he will outdistance all perpetrators of cruelty who ever came before him. At the end of this dreadful period Christ will return to earth to deliver His people and set up His kingdom. If the rapture occurs before Christ's return, Christians living then will not have to go through the Great Tribulation.

● Our knowledge of the second coming of Christ should motivate us to live for Him.

1. We are warned to watch and to be ready. "Take heed, keep on the alert; for you do not know when the appointed time is" (Mark 13:33).

2. We must be extremely careful to maintain a worthy character. The hope of His coming should motivate us to holy living (see 1 John 3:1-3).

3. We are to carry out the terms of the Great Commission (Matthew 28:18-20). We must do our utmost to see that the world is evangelized.

CLASS TIME

Suggested Opening Prayer

Our Father, we thank You for another opportunity to learn of Your Son, and we pray that you will help our understanding of His deity and His personality. And we ask that You will move our hearts to purify ourselves in preparation for His return.

(Introduction: Be sure
students understand
    objective
    memory work*
    reading assignment.)

> **Introduction**
>
> OBJECTIVE: To confirm through biblical evidence that Christ is deity — God in human form.
>
> TO MEMORIZE: John 1:18.
>
> TO READ: Philippians 2:5-11.

(*Students should check each other briefly in pairs. Then have one student explain the meaning to the entire class.)

Discussion Starter

(Ask the class:) Who do you think Jesus Christ is, and why do you think so? (Allow a few minutes for discussion, then proceed into the Lesson Development.)

Lesson Development

(Have the class share this material in any of the ways suggested in the Instructions for Teaching on page 21.)

The Bible explains that God Himself became a man to give mankind a concrete, definite and tangible idea of *what kind of person God is.* "Christ is the image of the invisible God" (Colossians 1:15). (See also John 1:18). Jesus was God incarnate — God in human form. Perhaps the most succinct statement about the deity and humanity of Christ was made by Byron, the poet, when he said, "If ever a man were God or God were man, Jesus was both."

"At the beginning God expressed Himself. That personal expression, that Word, was with God, and was God, and He existed with God from the beginning. All creation took place through Him, and none took place without Him. In Him appeared life and this life was the light of mankind. The light still shines in the darkness and the darkness has never put it out.

"A man called John was sent by God as a witness to the light, so that any man who heard his testimony might believe in the light. This man was not himself the light: he was sent simply as a personal witness to that light. That was the true light which shines upon every man as He comes into the world. He came into the world — the world He had created — and the world failed to recognize Him.

"He came into His own creation, and His own people would not accept Him. Yet, wherever men did accept Him, He gave them the power to become sons of God. These were the men who truly believed in Him, and their birth depended not on the course of nature nor on any impulse or plan of man, but on God. So the Word of God became a human being and lived among us. We saw His splendor (the splendor as of a father's only son), full of grace and truth" (John 1:1-15, Phillips).

> "For God has allowed us to know the secret of His plan, and it
> is this: He purposes in His sovereign will that all human history
> shall be consummated in Christ, that everything that exists in
> heaven or earth shall find its perfection and fulfillment in Him.
> And here is the staggering thing — that in all which will one day
> belong to Him, we have been promised a share" (Ephesians
> 1:9-11, Phillips).

Jesus claims that He and
God are the same —
John 10:30; 14:9. Notice
in John 10:31-32 the crowd
attempts to kill Him for this
claim. They understood
perfectly what He
was saying.

Bible Study

A. *The claims of Christ*

  1. What did Jesus claim for Himself in the following verses?

    Mark 14:61, 62 *He is God's son, sits at His*
    right hand, will return to earth,
    John 6:38; 8:42, 58 *Sent by God, is "I am."*

He claims to be the most powerful authority in the whole universe, not just in
the world — Matthew 28:18.

He claims to be the only way to God the Father. In John 14:6 He says He is *the*
way, not *a* way.

Jesus makes many other claims similar to these. All His claims must be either
true or false. If true, we should worship and serve Him all of our lives.

If false, we can come to one of two conclusions about Jesus: (1) He knew these
claims were false, which makes Him one of the world's greatest impostors
and liars. (2) He did not know they were false, which makes Him insane.

If your roommate made just one of the claims listed above, and really believed
it, his family and friends would quickly see that he was put in a
mental institution.

C. S. Lewis, Professor at Oxford University and a former agnostic, confirmed
the facts mentioned above when he said, "A man who was merely a man and said
the sort of things Jesus said wouldn't be a great moral teacher. He'd either be a
lunatic — on a level with the man who says he's a poached egg — or else he'd be
the Devil of Hell. You must make your choice. Either this man was, and is, the Son
of God, or else a mad-man or something worse. You can shut Him up for a fool,
you can spit at and kill Him as a demon; or you can fall at His feet and call Him
Lord and God. But don't let us come with any patronizing nonsense about His
being a great human teacher. He hasn't left that open to us."

(Teacher, ask the class:) Which of these three choices — liar, lunatic, or Son of
God — seems most logical to you? Why? (Give them opportunity to answer, and
then elaborate as follows, if appropriate.)

The obvious answer is that Jesus is the Son of God. How could the greatest
moral example ever known, admired by Christian and non-Christian alike, be an
unprincipled deceiver? And why would He and His followers die for what they
knew was a lie? Or how could the sanest, most well-balanced figure ever known,

whose teachings serve as a basis for mental health, himself be a psychopath? Those who deny the deity of Christ are faced with these insuperable difficulties.

2. What did Jesus claim to do in the following verses?

John 5:22 _Has been given all judgment by God._

Matthew 9:6 _Has authority to forgive sins._

John 6:47 _Gives eternal life._

3. What did Jesus predict in the following verses?

Mark 9:31 _His death and resurrection._

Luke 18:31-33 _His death and resurrections._

John 14:1-3 _His ascension and return._

B. Contemporary opinions about Christ

1. His enemies

Pilate (Matthew 27:24) _Did not want to crucify Him._

Judas (Matthew 27:4) _Jesus was of "innocent blood."_

The Roman soldier (Matthew 27:54) _Jesus was "the son of God."_

2. His friends

John the Baptist (John 1:29) _"...Lamb of God..."_

Peter (1 Peter 2:22) _"Who committed no sin..."_

Paul (2 Corinthians 5:21) _"...knew no sin..."_

Disciples (Matthew 8:27) _"What kind of a man is this, that even the winds and the sea obey Him?"_

Thomas, who was skeptical and unbelieving, acknowledged Jesus as "My Lord and my God."

Regardless of whether they believed in Him, those who had the best opportunity to observe Him admitted openly that there was something absolutely unique about Jesus.

And this has been the consensus of many of the greatest leaders and thinkers in history. Napoleon, for example, acknowledged, "I know men; and I tell you that Jesus Christ is not a man. Superficial minds see a resemblance between Christ and the founders of empires . . . That resemblance does not exist . . . He is truly a Being by Himself . . . Alexander, Caesar, Charlemagne and myself founded empires. But on what . . . ? Upon force. Jesus Christ alone founded His empire upon love; and at this hour, millions of men would die for Him."

C. The deity of Christ

1. In John 5:17, 18, whom did Jesus Christ claim to be? _The Son of God._

2. Paul described Jesus as _God and Savior_ (Titus 2:13).

3. In the following verses, what characteristics of Jesus are attributes of an omnipotent God?

John 2:24 _"...He knew all men."_

Matthew 8:26, 27 _Power over nature._

John 11:43-45 _Able to raise the dead._

4. What was the most significant sign of Christ's deity (1 Corinthians 15:3-8)? _His resurrection from death._

D. *The compassion of Christ*

   1. How does Jesus' attitude contrast with the attitude of His contemporaries toward:

     adults (Matthew 14:15-21)? *Disciples: send people away to buy food. Jesus: feed them.*

     children (Mark 10:13-16)? *Disciples rebuked children. Jesus said, "Permit (them) to come to Me."*

     those who offend (Luke 9:51-56)? *Messengers: destroy men's lives; Jesus: save them.*

   2. Why did the following people love Christ?

     The widow of Nain (Luke 7:11-15)? *He raised her so from the dead and gave him back to her.*

     The sinful woman (Luke 7:47) *He forgave her many sins.*

     Mary and Martha (John 11:33-44) *Jesus raised thei brother Lazarus from the dead.*

     The disciples (John 14:1-3, 27; 16:24) *Jesus promised a place in heaven, He would return and receive them, they would be with Him, they would have peace, answer prayer, and full joy.*

   3. How do you feel about Him and why? _____

E. *The death of Christ*

   1. Describe the purpose of Christ's death as it is related in 1 Peter 2:24. *"that we might die to sin and live to righteousness."*

   2. How did Christ's death affect your relationship with God (Colossians 1:21, 22; Romans 5:10, 11)? *We are reconciled to God.*

   3. Describe the effect of Christ's death with respect to God's holiness (Romans 3:25; 1 John 2:2; 4:10). *Jesus became the propitiation for our sins.*

F. *The resurrection of Christ*

   1. What event did Jesus Christ predict in John 2:19-21? Summarize the details. *His death and resurrection. (Have students summarize details in their own words.)*

   2. Three days after Christ's death, of what were the disciples reminded (Luke 24:6)? (Read Luke 24:1-9.) *He had told of His coming death and resurrection.*

   3. According to the apostle Paul, where was it recorded that Christ would rise from the dead on the third day (1 Corinthians 15:4)? *In the Scriptures.*

(More information on the subject, "Appearances of the Resurrected Christ" will be found in the Additional Background Material on page 79 and may be included here if time permits.)

> 4. For a period of six weeks after His resurrection, Jesus Christ walked and talked with many individuals and groups. As recorded in 1 Corinthians 15:5-8, who saw Him? List them here.
>
> | | |
> |---|---|
> | *Cephas* | *James* |
> | *the twelve* | *all the apostles* |
> | *five hundred brethren* | *Paul, himself* |
>
> 5. Read 1 Corinthians 15:12-26 and state how it would affect your life if Christ were not resurrected. _____
>
> G. *The visible return of Christ*
>
> After spending approximately six weeks giving His disciples final instructions, Christ ascended into heaven (Acts 1:1-9).
>
> 1. Describe the way in which Christ will return to earth (Matthew 24:30; Acts 1:11). *On the clouds, the same as the disciples saw Him go.*

What is meant by Christ returning "in just the same way as you have watched Him go into heaven"?

(Answer:) How did Christ go into heaven? He went *physically* and *visibly*. Therefore, He will return the same way. Compare Revelation 1:7, "every eye shall see Him." Old and New Testament writers frequently speak of such a coming of Christ (cf. Daniel 7:14; Titus 2:13), and Jesus Christ himself repeatedly refers to this kind of second coming (Mark 13:24-27). Therefore, unless the Bible is mistaken, Jesus Himself deluded, and Christianity a hoax, he will certainly come again physically and visibly.

> 2. How does this compare with the first time Christ came to the earth? *(Students should answer in their own words.)*

At His first coming Christ entered human history humbly and obscurely, being virgin-born into the poor Jewish family of Joseph and Mary. He imposed human limitations on Himself, such as the need for food and rest. Then He concluded His earthly sojourn by allowing Himself to be crucified by the world He came to save.

But at His second coming He will suddenly descend out of heaven with great power and glory (Mark 13:24-27), conquer His enemies and assume rulership of the world (Matthew 25:31-32). Human history is not wandering on aimlessly; it is heading inescapably toward this goal.

> 3. What will happen to the Christian when Christ comes for him (1 Corinthians 15:51, 52; Philippians 3:20, 21)? _Chris tians will be changed, transformed "...into conformity with the body of His glory..."_
>
> 4. According to Matthew 24:6-8, what will be the condition of the earth when Christ returns? _Wars and rumors of wars, nations against nation, famines earth - quakes._

Christ specifically states world conditions will worsen and become critical before He comes (Matthew 24:6-8; 2 Timothy 3:1-5). This is in accord with historical trends in the twentieth century. All hopes that mankind will eventually solve its problems or reform itself are doomed to failure. Christians should attempt to reform evils in society whenever possible, but their main task is to call men to Christ out of a world headed toward destruction.

D. L. Moody, the famous evangelist, once stated, "God has not told me to reform the whole world. The world is like a sinking ship which cannot be kept from going down. But God has given me a life boat and said, 'Moody, save everyone off that ship you can.' Our chief task is to save everyone we can."

> 5. What did Jesus say will happen to those who are not Christians when He returns (2 Thessalonians 1:7-9)? _Retribution to be dealt out, they will pay the penalty of eternal destruction, away from God._
>
> 6. How does this motivate your present life, as you wait expectantly for His visible return (1 John 3:2, 3)? _We should purify ourselves, as He is pure._

Conclusion and Application

During the fall of every year, hurricanes frequently strike the Southeast and Texas gulf coasts of the United States. Many hours before the hurricane strikes, the weather bureau issues warnings to areas likely to be devastated. As the storm approaches, tides and wind begin to rise and the weather grows more ominous. During this time people board up windows, move boats, store food and water and make every preparation for the winds, rain and high tides. Only a fool would not prepare for the storm because so many signs of its approach are apparent.

In the same way, the signs of our age indicate that Christ's coming is drawing near. In light of this the Christian who refuses to prepare for Christ's coming is unbelievably foolish.

In what ways can we purify and prepare ourselves? (Have students list ways.)

Life Application

1. Contrast your relationship to Christ with your relationship to any other human being. _____

_____

_____

2. Compare man's use of profanity to God's honored use of the name of Jesus in Philippians 2:9-11. _____

_____

3. Write a brief statement answering, "In what way does this study of the deity of Christ make me appreciate my relationship with Him more deeply?" _____

_____

Suggested Closing Prayer

Our Father, we thank You for Your presence today and for the reliability of Your Word. Through it we realize that Jesus Christ is God in human form, that He died for our sins, that He is risen, and that He is now in heaven, and we are anxiously awaiting the time of His return. Help us to be prepared properly for that return, and give us a burden to take the message to those who do not yet know Jesus and to show them how to be prepared also.

ADDITIONAL BACKGROUND MATERIAL

Appearances of the Resurrected Christ

(Ask the class:) What is the significance of so many different appearances of the risen Christ to so many different people?

(The answer is that it is one of the strongest confirmations that Christ actually did rise from the dead.)

Certainly the abundance of witnesses destroys any theory that this was a vision or hallucination. Floyd E. Hamilton states: "Now it is perfectly possible for one man to have an hallucination, and two men might have the same hallucination by a singular coincidence, but that eleven men of intelligence, whose characters and writings indicate their sanity in other respects, or that five hundred men in a body should have seen the *same* hallucination and at the *same* time, stretches the law of probability to the breaking point!"

In 1 Corinthians 15:12-26 Paul shows that Christianity stands or falls with the resurrection of Jesus Christ:

(1) The Christian faith is in vain if Christ is not risen, v. 14.

(2) The leaders of the early church, including Paul himself, are liars and Christianity a hoax, v. 15.

(3) The Christian believer individually is unforgiven and his faith is in vain, v. 15.

(4) The Christian has no hope of a future life, and the many trials which the early church and Christians through the ages endured are therefore to no avail, v. 19.

Many have attempted to explain away the resurrection by various theories, but with no real success. Some of these theories include:

(1) The *swoon theory* — Jesus never actually died, but only fainted and was removed from the cross still alive. Afterward, when He revived, His followers thought He was resurrected. The objections to this are (a) Jesus could never have moved the stone or escaped from the guards in His weakened condition, and (b) the soldiers judged He was dead and pierced his side to make sure, and blood and water, a sign of death, flowed out.

(2) The *vision* or *hallucination theory* — Jesus' followers saw an hallucination or a vision of Him because of their disturbed mental condition at this time. See the quote by Hamilton, above, for a refutation of this. This theory also fails to explain why Jesus' enemies did not produce His body when the disciples began to preach the resurrection. It would have soon ended the Christian movement.

(3) The *stolen body theory* — Jesus' body was stolen by either His followers or His enemies. This theory quickly falls apart when we realize (a) His enemies had no reason to steal the body, since they did not want to give credence to a belief in His resurrection. And even if they had stolen the body they would have produced it when His disciples began to preach resurrection. (b) His friends were too weak and scattered to steal the body if they wished, since Roman soldiers guarded the tomb. And if they had stolen the body they would not have preached His resurrection at the risk of their lives when there was nothing to gain and they knew it was a lie. Men are not in the habit of sacrificing their lives, which many of these early Christians did, for what they know is a deception.

We conclude, therefore, that in 1 Corinthians 15 Paul is expressing his belief in the resurrection for the simple reason that he had actually seen it (verses 7 and 8). He and the other early Christians were willing to stake their lives on it — the leaders of the early church fearlessly preached it — they had all seen it. The resurrection really happened!

Comparative Scriptures on the Person of Jesus Christ

A. The claims of Christ

1. Son of God — Matthew 11:27 (Luke 10:22).

2. Came from heaven — John 5:17-18.

3. Same reverence as God — John 5:23.

4. Never failed to please God, never sinned — John 8:45.

B. Contemporary opinions

1. Philip — John 1:45.

2. Nathaniel — John 1:49.

3. Centurion and soldiers — Matthew 27:54.

C. His deity — John 1:14; Colossians 2:9; Hebrews 1:3; John 1:12.

    1. Lord — Philippians 2:11; 1 Timothy 6:14-15; Ephesians 1:20-21.

    2. Son of God — Hebrews 1:1-2; 1 John 4:9,15.

    3. Messiah — Matthew 1:23; John 1:41.

D. His compassion — Matthew 20:30-34; Mark 1:41; Luke 19:41.

E. His death — 1 Corinthians 15:3; 2 Corinthians 5:14-15; 1 John 3:16; Ephesians 1:7.

F. His resurrection — Acts 2:24, 32-33; Romans 1:4; Ephesians 1:20.

G. His visible return to earth — Matthew 24-27; Acts 1:11; Revelation 1:7.

LESSON THREE

THE CHRIST-CONTROLLED LIFE

Teacher's Objective; To demonstrate the difference between the carnal Christian and the one who is Christ-controlled; to show that the Christian life is maintained by the power and life of the indwelling Christ and not by our own efforts; to motivate students to yield their lives to Christ's control.

Teacher's Enrichment: (May be shared with class if time permits.)

The Fruit of the Spirit

Kenneth Wuest says this about Galatians 5:22-23: "The choice of (the word) 'fruit' here instead of 'works' is due probably to the conception of the Christian experience as the product of a new and divine life implanted in the saint . . . The word "fruit' is singular, which fact serves to show that all of the elements of character spoken of in these verses are a unity, making for a well-rounded and complete Christian life."

Note the individual elements of the fruit:

Love — The divine love which only God can give and which exceeds normal human love.

Joy — Happiness.

Peace — The tranquility of mind which comes from a right relationship with God; freedom from anxiety.

Patience — patient endurance under wrong or ill-treatment without anger or thought of revenge.

Kindness.

Goodness — Moral uprightness.

Faithfulness — Trustworthiness, dependability.

Gentleness — Concerning this word, W. E. Vine says, "The meaning . . . is not readily expressed in English, for the terms . . . commonly used, suggest weakness whereas the Greek word does nothing of the kind . . . meekness is the opposite to self-assertiveness and self-interest; it is equanimity of spirit that is neither elated nor cast down simply because it is not occupied with self at all."

Self-control — The word refers to a mastery of one's own desires or impulses. Christians who lose control of themselves in any area — sex, money, studies, etc. — are not spiritual Christians.

The Deeds of the Flesh

Galatians 5:19-21 lists practices which result from letting our old sinful nature rule us instead of Jesus Christ.

Sins in the realm of sex (v. 19).

Immorality — any kind of sexual impurity.

Impurity — extreme immorality, "dirty" jokes or thoughts.
Sensuality — open indecency.

Sins in the realm of religion (v. 20).

Idolatry — allowing something else, family, a friend, good grades, a job, etc., to become more important than God; also false religion.

Sorcery — use of magic, common in the ancient world. It includes such modern day phenomena as astrology, fortune telling, seances, etc.

Sins in the realm of personal relationship (v. 20-21).

Enmities — the opposite of love; hostility toward others.
Strife — quarreling, fighting.
Jealousy.
Anger — outbursts of wrath; losing one's temper.
Disputes — factiousness; inability to get along with others.
Dissensions — divisions; one group against another.
Factions — "self-willed opinions" which lead to division.
Envying — desiring to take away from another what is his.

Sins in the realm of self-control (v. 21).

Drunkenness — a problem in that time as today.
Carousing — drunken, lewd parties; orgies.

CLASS TIME

Suggested Opening Prayer

Dear Father, we pray that today You will make our hearts and minds especially receptive to the important truths You have for us. We need to be reminded continually of just what the Christ-controlled life involves and how that life may be lived.

(Introduction: Be sure
students understand
   objective
   memory work
   reading assignment.)

Introduction

OBJECTIVE: To show how the indwelling life of Christ, not our own efforts, is the key to the Christian life.

TO MEMORIZE: Philippians 4:13.

TO READ: 1 Corinthians 2:11 - 3:5; Galatians 5:16-24.

Discussion Starter

(Ask the class:) What do we mean when we talk about Jesus Christ controlling our lives?

Is the Christ-controlled life a perfect life?

If Christ controlled every area of your life, would you lose your individual personality?

Lesson Development

(Have one of the students read this section aloud.)

There are many misconceptions concerning the Christian life. Some feel that once they have admitted Jesus Christ into their lives by faith, it is up to them to try their best to live a life that is pleasing to God. Others feel that Christ has entered their lives to help them live and work for God's glory. Perhaps these two ideas of Christian living look good on the surface, but there is a basic weakness in each concept that actually undermines the basis of vital Christian living.

In light of Romans 7:18, Galatians 2:20 and Romans 1:17, what do you think the basic approach should be, rather than trying or seeking help?

_____

_____

(Take time here for students to look up Scriptures, determine an answer and record it.)

(Continue with the reading.)

It has been said, "The Christian life is not hard; it is impossible." Only one person has ever lived the Christian life, and that was Jesus Christ. He desires to go on today living His life through Christians whom He indwells. J. B. Phillips, in the preface (p. xiv) to his translation of part of the New Testament, *Letters to Young Churches,* said:

"The great difference between present-day Christianity and that of which we read in these letters is that to us it is primarily a performance; to them it was a real experience. We are apt to reduce the Christian religion to a code, or at best a rule of heart and life. To those men it is quite plainly the invasion of their lives by a new quality of life altogether. They do not hesitate to describe this as Christ 'living in' them."

Prior to his death, Christ told His disciples that it was best for Him to leave them in order that the Spirit of God might come to dwell in each of them (John 14:16-20; 16:7). In other words, Christ was physically departing from His disciples in order that He might always be present spiritually within each of them.

Today when a person places his faith in Christ, Christ comes to dwell within him by means of the Holy Spirit (Romans 8:9). His purpose for dwelling in us is that *He might live His life through us.* Many Christians are trying to operate on their own finite power when there is an infinite power available.

One may ask, "How can I experience the victorious life of Christ?" In this lesson we will examine the three types of persons in the world today — the non-Christian (natural man), the spiritual Christian and the carnal Christian.

Bible Study

A. *The non-Christian or natural man*

This first circle represents the life of the person who has never received Christ as Lord and Savior. Christ stands outside the door of the life, seeking entrance (Revelation 3:20).

(Discuss Scripture and diagram.)

SELF-DIRECTED LIFE
S - Self is on the throne
† - Christ is outside the life
• - Interests are directed by self, often resulting in discord and frustration

> 1. What adjective do you think best describes the man who does not understand the things of the Spirit of God (1 Corinthians 2:14)? *(Students should use their own terminology.)*

(Ask:) What does this Scripture mean when it says the natural man does not receive the things of the Spirit of God? Can you give us a good illustration? (Teacher, if students don't have illustrations, you might supply some from your own witnessing experiences.)

Note that the non-Christian can intellectually understand the Bible, but until he becomes converted he cannot respond to its truth.

"Not that the natural faculty of discerning is lost, but evil inclinations and wicked principles render the man unwilling to enter the mind of God, in spiritual matters of His kingdom, and to yield to their force and power." — Matthew Henry.

Bertrand Russell, great philosopher, a versatile and brilliant scholar, and winner of the 1950 Nobel Prize for literature, was consistently antagonistic toward Christianity. One of his works was entitled *Why I am not a Christian*. He obviously was capable of intellectually understanding the Bible, but not of receiving its truth.

> 2. What terms describe "self" in the following verses?
> Romans 6:6 _____ *body of sin.*
> Galatians 5:16, 17 _____ *the flesh.*
> 3. List at least three characteristics of the man without Christ, as described in Ephesians 2:1-3. *dead in trespasses and sins, sons of disobedience, children of wrath.*

Every man without Christ is under Satan's dominion. The phrase "prince of the power of the air" is a description of Satan. The Greek word for "air" here means "the lower denser atmosphere."

"The kingdom of Satan is in this lower atmosphere where we human beings are . . . The unsaved order their behavior according to his dictates and those of his demons" — Kenneth Wuest.

> 4. What is the condition of the heart of the natural man (Jeremiah 17:9)? *"The heart is more deceitful than all else and is desperately sick, who can understand it?"*
> 5. List the 13 sins that Jesus said come from the heart of man (Mark 7:20-23). *evil thoughts, fornication, thefts, murders, adulteries, coveting, wickedness, deceit, sensuality, envy, slander, pride, foolishness.*
> 6. Summarize the relationship between God and the non-Christian (John 3:36). *(Students should answer in their own words.)*

Matthew Henry comments on John 3:36, "He that believeth not the Son is undone . . . They cannot be happy in this world nor that to come."

How can we explain that some non-Christians have much higher standards than others, if all are under Satan's control?

John Calvin says, "For in all ages there have been some persons, who . . . have devoted their whole lives to the pursuit of virtue . . . amidst this corruption of nature there is some room for Divine grace . . . For should the Lord permit the minds of all men to give up the reins to every lawless passion, there certainly would not be an individual in the world, whose actions would not evince all the crimes for which Paul condemns human nature in general."

> 7. How, then, does one become a Christian (John 1:12; Revelation 3:20)? _Receive Him, open the door, invite Him into one's heart and life._

B. The spiritual or Christ-controlled Christian
This second circle represents the life of the person who has

- Love
- Joy
- Peace
- Patience
- Kindness
- Faithfulness
- Goodness

- Christ centered
- Empowered by H.S.
- Introduces others to Christ
- Effective prayer life
- Understands God's Word
- Trusts God
- Obeys God

invited Jesus Christ to come into his life and who is allowing Him to control and empower his life. Christ is occupying His rightful place on the throne of the life. Self has been dethroned.

Galatians 2:20 clearly explains that the Christ-controlled life is Christ living through the Christian. "Instead of attempting to live his life in obedience to . . . the Mosaic law, Paul now yields to the indwelling Holy Spirit and cooperates with Him in the

1. List the characteristics of a life controlled by the Spirit of God (Galatians 5:22, 23). _Love, joy, peace, patience kindness, goodness, faithfulness, gentleness, self control._

2. In what sense could the Spirit-controlled life be called the "exchanged life" (Galatians 2:20)? _"crucified with Christ,...no longer I who live, but Christ who lives in me."_

production of a life pleasing to God" — Kenneth Wuest.

The Christ-controlled life does not mean our individual personality is abolished. Christ expresses Himself through _me_ — my own personality with its peculiarities — though He may knock off some rough edges in the process. Paul was a logical thinker before conversion and God used this element so that he could write logical treatises like the Epistle to the Romans. John thought more mystically, on the other hand, and God used this element in his personality to write the Gospel of John. God did not totally change their personalities — He used them as His instruments.

Alexander Maclaren comments on Philippians 4:13,

> 3. Where does the Christian receive the power to live this otherwise impossible life (Philippians 4:13)? _"Him (Christ) who strengthens me."_

"Stoicism breaks down because it tries to make men apart from God sufficient for themselves, which no man is . . . A godless life has a weakness at the heart of its loneliness, but Christ and I are always in the majority."

"The man whose mind . . . shares the thoughts of

> 4. What does the spiritual Christian have that will enable him to understand the things of God (1 Corinthians 2:14-16)? *the mind of Christ.*

Christ . . . is beyond natural man's assessment. The mere humanist is no more competent in the spiritual sphere than one who is tone-deaf is capable of criticizing music, or a man who is color-blind is qualified to discuss a painting" — Abingdon Bible Commentary.

"Men of intellectual gifts who are ignorant of the things of Christ talk learnedly and patronizingly about things of which they are grossly ignorant. The spiritual man is superior to all this false knowledge" — A. T. Robertson.

This is the difference that the indwelling Holy Spirit can make in one's life.

(A question for the class:) What does "carnal" mean?

(The dictionary says: worldly or earthly; not spiritual; not holy or sanctified.)

> C. The carnal Christian and the solution to carnality
>
> In 1 Corinthians 3:1-3, the apostle Paul addresses the Christians as "carnal" (self-centered), rather than "spiritual" (Christ-centered). The following diagram represents a life in which ego has asserted itself. It has usurped the throne of the life, and Christ has stepped down. The result is the loss of the individual's fellowship with God though he is still a Christian.
>
> • LEGALISTIC ATTITUDE   • IGNORANCE OF HIS
> • IMPURE THOUGHTS   SPIRITUAL HERITAGE
> • JEALOUSY   • UNBELIEF
> • GUILT   • DISOBEDIENCE
> • WORRY   • LOSS OF LOVE FOR
> • DISCOURAGEMENT   GOD AND FOR OTHERS
> • CRITICAL SPIRIT   • POOR PRAYER
> • FRUSTATION   • NO DESIRE FOR
> • AIMLESSNESS   BIBLE STUDY

The "carnal mind," i.e., our self-centered ego, is opposed to God and could not be subject to Him even if it wanted to. Our own ego naturally "rebels against His authority, thwarts His design, opposes His interest, spits in His face" — Matthew Henry.

Ruth Paxson says of the carnal man, "Christ has *a* place in his heart but not *the*

> 1. Describe the carnal Christian as presented in 1 Corinthians 3:1-3. *A man of flesh, a babe in Christ, still fleshly, with jealousy and strife, walking like mere men.*

place of supremacy and pre-eminence . . . He, the carnal man, attempts to live in two spheres, the heavenly and the earthly — and he fails in both."

The first part of 1 John 1:9 should never be read without looking at the last part. God openly and freely forgives us because Christ has died for us.

> Name five or six practices that result from carnality (Galatians 5:19-21). *Immorality, impurity, sensuality, idolatry, sorcery, enmities, strife, jealousy, anger, disputes, dissensions, factions, envying, drunkeness, carousing.*
>
> Summarize in your own words the relationship between the carnal mind and God, as described in Romans 8:7. *Hostile toward God, does not subject itself to the law of God, not even able to.*
>
> 2. The solution to carnality (the self-controlled life) is threefold:
>
> We must confess our sins — recognize that we have been rulers of our own lives. When we do confess them, what will God do (1 John 1:9)? *forgive us our sins and cleanse us from all unrighteousness.*
>
> Read Proverbs 28:13. What is the result of not admitting sin? *The person will not prosper.*
>
> What is the result of admitting sin? *The person will find compassion.*

We must confess all *known* sins. "The word confess is *homologeo*, from *homos*, 'the same,' and *lego*, 'to say,' thus 'to say the same thing as another,' or to 'agree with another' . . . means therefore to say the same thing that God does about that sin, to agree with God as to all the implications of that sin" — Kenneth Wuest.

> We must *surrender* or yield the throne to Christ. State in your own words how Paul describes the act of presenting ourselves to God in Romans 12:1, 2. _____

(Ask the question:) What is "surrender"?

Surrender is the "deliberate, voluntary transference of the . . . whole being, spirit, soul and body from self to Christ, to whom it rightfully belongs by creation and by purchase . . . The question is not, 'Do I belong to God?' but 'Have I yielded to God that which already belongs to Him?' " — James McConkey.

> By *faith* we must recognize that Christ assumed control of our lives upon our invitation.
>
> How can you be sure that if you ask Jesus Christ to assume His rightful place on the throne of your life, He will do so (1 John 5:14, 15)? *"if we ask anything according to His will...we have the requests."*

(Another question to ask the class:) Why do some Christians surrender to Christ but fail to experience victory?

(The answer:) Lack of faith. "Surrender opens the door; faith believes that Christ enters, fills, abides."

The two elements of faith are:

Knowledge — "Faith is not ignorance; it is not closing one's eyes to the facts. Faith is never afraid to look truth squarely in the face. Man is not saved by knowledge, but he cannot be saved without it" — Lindsell and Woodbridge.

We have a knowledge that God will take over control of our lives because it is His will (1 John 5:14-15) and we must give a rational assent to the truth to be believed.

Personal appropriation — "Mental assent is not enough. The will must be exercised and a decision must be made" — Lindsell and Woodbridge.

As we must have sufficient trust in another person to commit ourselves in a marriage, it is only after we commit ourselves to Christ in faith, believing He will control our lives, that His control becomes a reality.

Do you really want Him to take control of your life?
_____

We receive the Lord Jesus Christ by faith. How then do we allow Him to control our lives moment by moment (Colossians 2:6)? *We walk in Christ.* _____
_____

Give three reasons faith is so important (Hebrews 11:6; Romans 14:23; Romans 1:17)? *Without faith it is impossible to please Him, whatever is not from faith is sin; the righteous shall live by faith; faith becomes our way of life.*

Conclusion and Application

(Give students a sheet of paper and briefly go over these suggestions with them. Then allow a quiet time for the students to think through this material and do the writing.)

Life Application

The secret of the abundant life is to allow Jesus Christ to control one's life moment by moment. When one realizes he has sinned, he should confess his sin immediately, thank God for forgiving him and continue to walk in fellowship with God.

1. List areas of your life that you feel should be brought under the control of Jesus Christ: _____
_____
_____
_____

2. To make 1 John 1:9 meaningful in your life:
Make a list of your sins and failures on a separate sheet of paper.
Claim 1 John 1:9 for your own life by writing the words of the verse over the list.
Thank God for His forgiveness and cleansing, and then destroy the list.

(After 5 or 10 minutes, have the students write the words of the verse over their lists and then lead them in a closing prayer of thanksgiving for forgiveness and cleansing. Teacher, you might benefit by taking part in this exercise, too.)

Suggested Closing Prayer

Our Father, You see the lists which we have made of our sins and failures, and we see in Your Word that You have already forgiven us of every one of them. Jesus has cleansed us of them all with His blood, and we are so grateful to You. We thank You. And we ask You to take firmer control of every area of our lives.

ADDITIONAL BACKGROUND MATERIAL

Parallel Scripture passages for:
> The non-Christian or natural man: Romans 3:9-20; Titus 3:3; John 5:19.
> The spiritual or Christ-controlled Christian: John 15:1-7; the book of Acts; Ephesians 3:16-19; Colossians 1:10,11.
> The carnal Christian: Romans 7:15,17,18,21,24; 8:7; 1 Corinthians 3:1-7.

LESSON FOUR

THE FIVE PRINCIPLES OF GROWTH

Teacher's Objective: To teach the students principles essential to spiritual growth and to motivate them to begin to practice those principles in their everyday lives.

Teacher's Enrichment: (May be shared with class if time permits.)

STUDY OF GOD'S WORD

Why is it necessary to study the Bible in order to grow?

The answer is that the Bible, being the Word of God, does the following for us:

1. It causes our faith to grow. Romans 10:17 tells us faith comes from hearing the Word of God. You may pray all you want for more faith, but you will only get it by reading God's Word.

2. It convicts us of sin. Hebrews 4:12-13 shows that the Word of God reveals our inmost self to us. Without this correcting influence, we soon wander away.

3. It helps keep us from committing sin. Psalm 119:11 teaches that the Word of God holds us back from sins we might otherwise commit.

4. It gives us a standard by which we can guide our lives. 2 Timothy 3:16-17 emphasizes that the Bible is inspired by God and therefore practical in everyday life. It gives guidance in the difficult areas of life — studies, social life, family life, career, etc.

WITNESSING

What is witnessing? It has been aptly described as, "One beggar telling another where to get bread." Some reasons we should witness are:

1. Jesus Christ commanded it — Matthew 28:18-20.

2. Non-Christians may not know how to receive Christ unless someone witnesses to them — Romans 10:17.

3. Our own Christian experience will become more vital — John 4:27-34.

4. God has prepared a large number who are ready to accept Christ — John 4:35.

5. Jesus Christ will be with us as we do it — Matthew 28:20.

CLASS TIME

Suggested Opening Prayer

Dear Father, we thank You for another opportunity to open your Word and study it, and we pray You will enlighten our hearts and minds to what You have for us today. Help us understand the principles we will be examining and help us apply them to our lives in a way that will be according to Your will.

(Introduction: Go over with
students

   objective,
   memory work.)

> **Introduction**
>
> OBJECTIVE: To understand the essentials of Christian growth
> and put them into practice.
>
> TO MEMORIZE: 2 Timothy 2:15.

Discussion Starter

(Read the following excerpt to the class:) "I do not consider myself to have 'arrived,' spiritually, nor do I consider myself already perfect. But I keep on, grasping ever more firmly that purpose for which Christ grasped me . . . But I do concentrate on this: I leave the past behind and . . . go straight for the goal — my reward the honor of being called by God in Christ."

(Then ask:) Who wrote this? Do you have any idea how long he had been a Christian when he wrote it?

(Answer:) The excerpt is from Philippians 3:12-14 in the Phillips translation. These verses were written by Paul, probably the greatest Christian of all time, *at least 25 years* after his conversion! If he still needed to grow, we certainly need to even more, don't we? The way we grow is by practicing what is set forth in this lesson.

Deciding to receive Jesus Christ as one's personal Lord and Savior is the most important choice a person will ever make. It is an act of faith which starts a whole new life. Just as physical life requires, air, food, rest and exercise, so does spiritual life require certain things for growth and development. This lesson deals with five principles of growth. If these are followed, one can know that he will grow toward spiritual maturity in Christ.

Lesson Development

These verses compare the Bible to physical food.

Matthew Henry remarks, "A new life requires suitable food. They, being newly born (spiritually), must desire the milk of the

Bible Study

A. *Principle one: we must study God's Word*

Read James 1:18-27.

One would not think of going without physical food for a week or for even a day. It is necessary for physical life. Without food, one becomes weakened and eventually may become ill. Lack of spiritual food produces the same results in our spiritual lives.

1. What is the food of the young Christian (1 Peter 2:2)?
   "...the Word..."

word. Infants desire common milk, and their desires toward it are fervent and frequent."

2. Jesus said, "Man shall not live by bread alone." How did He say that we should live and be nourished (Matthew 4:4)? *"...on every word that proceeds out of the mouth of God."*

Phillips translates
2 Timothy 2:15, "For
yourself, concentrate on
winning God's approval,

> 3. List the two characteristics of the workman of whom God approves, according to 2 Timothy 2:15. _Does not need to be ashamed; handles accurately the Word of truth._

being a workman with nothing to be ashamed of, and who knows how to use the word to best advantage." Matthew Henry comments on this verse, "Workmen that are unskillful or unfaithful, or lazy, have need to be ashamed; but those who mind their business, and keep to their work, are workmen that need not be ashamed. And what is their work? . . . Not to invent a new gospel, but rightly to divide the gospel that is committed to their trust."

> 4. What did Jesus say about those who read and believe God's Word (John 8:31)? _"...you are truly disciples of Mine."_
>
> 5. When does the man who is spiritually mature meditate on the Word of God (Psalm 1:2, 3)? _Day and night_
>
> 6. In what specific ways do you expect God's Word to affect you? _____

Notable sayings about
the Bible:

"It is impossible rightly
to govern the world without God and the Bible" — George Washington.

"I am profitably engaged in reading the Bible. Take all of this book . . . and you will live and die a better man" — Abraham Lincoln.

"The vigor of our spiritual life will be in exact proportion to the place held by the Bible in our life and thoughts." — George Mueller.

"I prayed for faith . . . But faith did not seem to come. One day I read in the tenth chapter of Romans, 'Now faith cometh by hearing, and hearing by the Word of God.' I had closed my Bible and prayed for faith. I now opened my Bible and began to study, and faith has been growing ever since" — D. L. Moody.

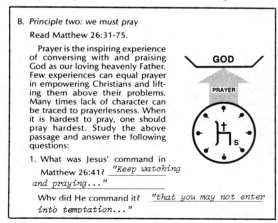

> B. *Principle two: we must pray*
>
> Read Matthew 26:31-75.
>
> Prayer is the inspiring experience of conversing with and praising God as our loving heavenly Father. Few experiences can equal prayer in empowering Christians and lifting them above their problems. Many times lack of character can be traced to prayerlessness. When it is hardest to pray, one should pray hardest. Study the above passage and answer the following questions:
>
> 1. What was Jesus' command in Matthew 26:41? _"Keep watching and praying..."_
>
> Why did He command it? _"that you may not enter into temptation..."_

Jesus commanded His
disciples to "watch and
pray." The word "watch"
means to "be wide awake,
"alert."

"Watchfulness and
prayer are inseparable. The one discerns dangers, the other arms against them"
— Alexander Maclaren.

> 2. Why did Peter fail to resist temptation? *His flesh was weak because of prayerlessness.*
>
> 3. What was the most serious result of Peter's prayerlessness? *He denied Jesus three times.*

A major cause of Peter's failure was prayerlessness.

(Ask the class:) Why do you think Peter failed to pray?

(Answer:) Apparently he did not feel sufficient need of it. He would rather sleep. When physically exhausted, sleep is undoubtedly more important than prayer, but at this crisis moment Peter should have prayed. A further look at the chapter reveals why Peter felt so little need of prayer and why he failed so tragically. Matthew 26:33,35 shows that Peter had too much confidence in himself.

On these verses Matthew Henry says, "He fancied himself better armed against temptation than anyone else, and this was his weakness and folly."

> 4. Why did Christ experience inner power to face the severest test of His life? *Because He spent so much time in concentrated prayer.*
>
> 5. How often are we to pray (1 Thessalonians 5:17)? _____ *"Pray without ceasing."*
>
> Prayer without ceasing involves conversing with our heavenly Father in a simple and free way throughout the day. Our prayer life should be such that we come to know the Lord Jesus in a personal way. Our prayer life becomes effective as our relationship with Christ becomes more intimate.
>
> "And I will do — I Myself will grant — whatever you may ask in My name (presenting all I AM) so that the Father may be glorified and extolled in (through) the Son. (Yes) I will grant — will do for you — whatever you shall ask in My name (presenting all I AM)" John 14:13, 14, Amplified New Testament.

Notable sayings about prayer:

"Prayer took much of the time and strength of Jesus. One who does not spend much time in prayer cannot properly be called a follower of Jesus Christ" — R. A. Torrey.

"I never prayed sincerely for anything but it came, at some time . . . somehow, in some shape" — Adoniram Judson.

C. *Principle three: we must fellowship with other Christians*

Read 1 Corinthians 12:12-27.

Fellowship is spending time and doing things with others who love Christ. Just as several logs burn brightly together,

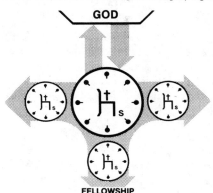

Notable sayings about the church:

"It is the will of Christ that his followers should assemble together . . . The communion of the saints is a great help and privilege, and a good means of steadiness and perseverance" — Matthew Henry.

but the fire goes out of one placed alone on the cold hearth, so do Christians need to work together or the fire of enthusiasm will go out. Fellowship is vital for Christian growth. That is why church attendance is important.

1. As God's children, what should we not neglect (Hebrews 10:23-25)? *Our own assembling together.*

"Every true follower of Christ should be identified in some way with the Christian community. The church needs men, but more than this, men need the church" — Lindsell and Woodbridge.

Think of a group you may belong to — a frater-

2. According to the above verses, what should we do for one another? *"...stimulate...to love and good deeds...encouraging on another..."*

nity or sorority, a political group, a social club of some kind, etc. Now suppose the members of this group never came together at any time and most of them did not even know each other. All business was transacted by mail. How much would this group mean to its members? How much enthusiasm would they have for it? How much good would it do them? Very little.

So Christians, having little to do with each other, and never coming together in a group, can accomplish nothing. If the early Christians had not assembled for mutual encouragement and common worship, Christianity never could have survived and we would not know Christ today!

This Scripture pictures the Christian church right

3. The new believers in Acts 2:42 continued steadfastly in what four things? *The apostles' teaching, fellowship, breaking of bread and prayer.*

after it came into being. Its four characteristics were: (1) Adherence to the apostles' doctrines, which are now contained for us in the New Testament. We should select a church where the Bible is explained and preached. (2) Fellowship — this indicates the Christians regularly met together for fellowship and mutual encouragement. (3) Breaking of bread, which was the communion service. Since Christians had no church buildings then, this was done in homes. Usually they ate a meal also, which was known as the "love feast." It was a time of very close fellowship. (4) Prayers — "Systematic, definite, positive praying, not as individuals only, but in connection with one another."

Note in verse 43 the effect such a new society had upon the outside world. These early Christians had a closeness, a fellowship, a vitality which many churches lack today.

(A questions for the class to consider:) What do you think the practices of the church in verse 42 had to do with its effectiveness?

In contrast to the closeness of the early Christians, A. B. Bruce has compared many churches today to a restaurant, "Where all kinds of people meet for a short space, sit down together . . . then part, neither knowing or caring anything about each other."

> 4. If you spend 90% of your time with non-Christians and 10% with Christians, you know which group will have the greater influence on your life.

Fellowship means more than mere friendship. The Greek word for fellowship is *koinonia,* which means "sharing in common." We desperately need to share our Christian experience with others who believe and likewise allow them to share with us. The church, where we can meet other Christians and hear the word of God preached, is God's appointed place for Christians to meet in fellowship, though meetings on campus, at work, in homes and other places are also extremely helpful.

> How can you increase your own time of fellowship with other Christians? _____
>
> _____
>
> 5. In what ways do you profit from Christian fellowship?
>
> _____

(Some suggested answers for question 5:)

We can profit from other's experiences.

We receive mutual encouragement.

We have the opportunity for group prayer. God especially honors united prayer (Matthew 18:19).

We can learn what others have discovered in the Bible.

We can be involved in planning and teamwork for reaching others with the message of Christ.

D. *Principle four: we must witness for Christ*

WITNESSING

Read Acts 26:12-29.

A witness is a person who tells what he has seen and heard. heard. He shares his own personal experience. Anyone who has a vital personal relationship with Christ can be a witness for Him. Witnessing is the overflow of the Christian life. As our lives are filled with the presence of the Lord Jesus, we cannot help but share Him with those with whom we come in contact. A vital Christian life is contagious.

1. What is the greatest thing that has ever happened to you?

   _____

   What, then, is the greatest thing you can do for another person? _____

2. In Romans 1:14-16, Paul tells us his own attitude concerning the matter of sharing the gospel with others. Using his three "I am's" as the keys to the passage, describe his attitude in your own words.

   "I am under obligation both to Greeks and to barbarians...I am eager to preach the gospel ...I am not ashamed of the gospel..."

   _____
   _____
   _____

3. Compare your own attitude concerning witnessing with that of Paul's. _____
   _____

Paul's three great 'I am's':

"I am a debtor" — The Greeks Paul refers to here were those versed in Greek language and culture. The barbarians were not necessarily savages, they were merely those not associated with Greek culture — generally the more ignorant and backward. The wise were the morally wise. The foolish were those who were of low morals. So in this verse Paul makes clear that our obligation is to all kinds of people, cultured and crude, good and bad — we have a universal debt.

"I am ready" — The Greek word for ready is literally "of a forward mind," hence, willing and eager. Paul did not witness out of sheer duty; he was eager to so serve His Lord. God should not have to force us to witness. Cf. 2 Corinthians 5:14.

"I am not ashamed" — There was a great deal in the gospel which might tempt Paul to be ashamed, for it centered about a man who was crucified. It had little appeal to the scholars of the day, and its followers were persecuted and despised. But Paul was not ashamed. James Denney notes, "The conception of the gospel as a force . . . is demonstrated, not by argument, but by what it does; and looking to what it can do, Paul is proud to preach it anywhere."

4. What did Peter tell us we should always be ready to do (1 Peter 3:15)? *"...to make a defense...for the hope that is in you..."*

5. What was Jesus' promise in Acts 1:8? *"shall receive power..shall be my witnesses..."*

6. Name at least three people to whom you can witness in the power of Christ. _____

_____

Some helpful suggestions in witnessing:

Combine aggressiveness with tact. People will not always come to you. Often you

It is the privilege and responsibility of every Christian to reach "his world" with the message of Christ. (If you would like to receive information regarding how to witness effectively for Christ, write to Campus Crusade for Christ, Arrowhead Springs, San Bernardino, Ca 92414. Ask for speciallly prepared materials concerning witnessing for Christ.

must go to them and make your own openings for presenting the gospel. But *always* use love and tact. Irreparable damage can be done by those who witness in an offensive manner. If you are driving people away rather than winning them, you should change your methods.

Make use of a good plan of presentation, such as "The Four Spiritual Laws" which can be obtained from Campus Crusade. This will make your witnessing more organized, concise and effective.

Avoid arguments. They never win people and usually drive them away. If the person wants to argue don't feel obliged to continue witnessing.

Expect people to trust Christ. In John 15:5,8, Jesus promises us much fruit if we follow Him. In Matthew 9:37-38, He says the harvest is great and the laborers few. Multitudes are waiting to hear the gospel, so you need have no fear in approaching people. If some do not accept, do not be discouraged, because sooner or later others will.

(Teacher: Share with the class one of your own witnessing experiences.)

Some reasons we should obey God:

Because we love Him — John 14:21.

Because we are not our own — 1 Corinthians 6:20.

Because we cannot

E. *Principle five: we must obey God*

Read Romans 6:14-23.

The key to rapid growth in the Christian life is instantaneous obedience to the will of God. Knowing the principles of growth is of no value unless we actually apply them to our lives. This is why obedience is a basic necessity to all Christian growth. To be disobedient to the One who loves us and who alone knows what is really best for us would be sheer folly. Remember that He is even more desirous than you are that you have an abundant life.

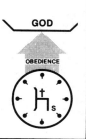

possibly benefit in the long run by disobedience — Job 9:4; Galatians 6:7,8.

Before his conversion,
Paul was convinced
Christianity was a fraud

1. What did Christ teach concerning the possibility of serving more than one master (Matthew 6:24)? *It is impossible to serve or love or hold to two masters.*

and a heresy so he went to all ends to stamp it out. After his conversion, when he realized his mistake, he began to serve God with all his heart. He was either for or against Christianity, but he never made the mistake of trying to be neutral. Revelation 3:16 says God counts lukewarmness and neutrality a greater sin toward Christ than active opposition to Him!

Matthew Henry further comments on Matthew 6:24, "Our Lord Jesus here exposes . . . those . . . who think to divide between God and the world, to have a treasure on earth and a treasure in heaven too . . . He does not say we must not or we should not, but we cannot serve God and mammon."

"Our love of God must
be a sincere love, and not in

2. How much are you to love the Lord (Matthew 22:37)? *Completely, with all our heart, soul and mind.*

word and tongue only, as theirs is who say they love Him, but their hearts are not with Him . . . All the powers of the soul must be engaged for Him, and carried out toward Him. This is the first and great commandment" — Matthew Henry.

3. How can you prove that you love Him (John 14:21)? *Keep His commandments.*

4. What will be the result of keeping Christ's commandments (John 15:10-11)? *We will abide in His love our joy will be full.*

5. What would you say God's standard life is for those who say they are abiding in Christ (1 John 2:6)? *To walk as Christ walked.*

6. Where do we get the power to obey God (Philippians 2:13)? *God is at work in us.*

7. In light of Christ's illustration in Luke 6:46-49, why do you think obedience to Christ is imperative for your life? *Students should answer in their own words.*

Conclusion and Application

"If Christ be God, and died for me, there is nothing too great that I can do for Him" — C. T. Studd, missionary to Africa, who gave up fame, fortune and family to be spent for God on a primitive continent.

Life Application

We may look at these five principles of growth in the following way: The first two relate to our *vertical* relationship with God. Through the Bible, God communicates — reveals Himself — to us. Through prayer we communicate with Him. The next two principles relate to our *horizontal* relationship with men. In fellowship, we Christians communicate with each other concerning our Savior and the bond that He gives us with one another. In witnessing, we communicate with non-Christians concerning our Savior, what He has done for us, and what He desires to do for them.

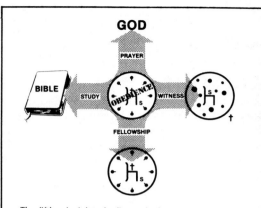

The fifth principle, *obedience*, is the catalyst for growth. As you obey Christ, you will experience increasing joy, peace and fellowship with Him, and you will become increasingly mature in the Christian life.

"Have this attitude in yourselves which was also in Christ Jesus, who . . . (became) *obedient* to the point of death, even death on a cross" (Philippians 2:5-8).

Suggested Closing Prayer

Heavenly Father, we thank You for these five principles of Christian growth and we pray You will teach us to be faithful in Bible study and prayer. Show us the way to walk hand in hand with Christ every moment of every day

CHART

On this chart, list the five key principles of Christian growth, a key verse relating to each one, and at least one way you can apply each principle to your own life.

PRINCIPLE	KEY VERSE	HOW TO APPLY

of our lives. Give us an enthusiasm for fellowship and power for witnessing, and we thank You for giving the person of Your Son through whom we may be obedient to You.

ADDITIONAL BACKGROUND MATERIAL

Parallel Scriptures supporting each principle of growth:

We must read the Bible — Matthew 22:29; Romans 15:4; 1 Peter 1:25; Psalm 119:30.

We must pray — 1 Chronicles 16:11; Daniel 6:10; Luke 18:1; Psalm 55:17.

We must fellowship with other Christians — Matthew 18:20; 2 Corinthians 6:14; Galatians 6:2; Proverbs 13:20.

We must witness for Christ — Matthew 4:19; Acts 5:20; 18:9,10; Psalm 107:2.

We must obey God — Matthew 12:50; John 7:17; Romans 14:12,13; 1 John 2:6.

LESSON FIVE

THE CHRISTIAN'S AUTHORITY

Teacher's Objective: To demonstrate the dependability and authority of the Bible, and to motivate students to study it and apply it to their lives.

Teacher's Enrichment: (May be shared with class if time permits.)

ADDITIONAL PASSAGES REGARDING
THE AUTHORITY OF THE SCRIPTURES

Old Testament claims: Exodus 32:16; 34:27,32; Isaiah 59:21; Jeremiah 30:2; 36:1.
Jesus Christ's claims: Matthew 7:23ff; Mark 13:31; John 7:16; 12:48,48.
Paul's views: Acts 28:25ff; Ephesians 6:17; 2 Timothy 3:16.
Peter's views: Acts 1:16; 2 Peter 1:20,21.

CLASS TIME

Suggested Opening Prayer

Dear Father, we give this lesson time to You now and trust You to enlighten our understanding regarding the source of our authority — Your Word. We ask You to help each of us in our own particular, individual needs.

(Introduction: Be sure
students understand
    objective
    memory work
    reading assignment.)

> **Introduction**
>
> OBJECTIVE: To understand the role and the power of the Bible in our daily Christian lives.
>
> TO MEMORIZE: 1 Thessalonians 2:13.
>
> TO READ: Psalm 119:97-104.

Discussion Starter

A biographer of General Douglas MacArthur records that one evening before a major battle in the Pacific, feeling uneasy, the general picked up his Bible and read until he felt at peace. Then he went to bed and slept soundly, even though the battle the next day would play a major part in the course of World War II. Why the Bible? Why not Shakespeare, or some great novel, or some discourse on philosophy?

(Answer: Because of its authority as God's Word to man, it has the power to bring peace, happiness and comfort as no other book in the world can do.)

Lesson Development

(Have one of the students read these three paragraphs and then proceed to the Bible Study.)

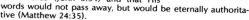

Ultimately our views of the authority of the Bible and of the incarnation of Christ are related. For instance, in John 10:34-36, Christ taught that the Old Testament was totally accurate. In Matthew 4:4-7, 10, He quoted it as being authoritative. Furthermore, He taught His followers that He was speaking God's own words (John 3:34) and that His words would not pass away, but would be eternally authoritative (Matthew 24:35).

He even said that the Holy Spirit would bring to mind what He said so that the disciples would preach and write accurately, not depending only upon memory and human understanding (John 16:12-15). Obviously, then, high views of the incarnation and of the inspiration of the Old and New Testaments are related.

A high view of inspiration should be related to personal Bible study and meditation. Even though you believe in the Bible as a unique, written message from God, you would defeat the purpose of God if you failed to apply biblical truths to your life.

Bible Study

A. *Biblical claims of authority*

   1. What were the attitudes of the following prophets concerning their writings?

   Isaiah 43:1-12   *"thus says the Lord, your Creator"*

   Jeremiah 23:1-8   *"declares the Lord"*

   Ezekiel 36:32-38   *"thus says the Lord God"*

(After discussing this question and its answers, ask:) Why has the Bible met man's basic need? (Answer:) It is an authoritative message from God, who knows the human heart as no one else can, so it naturally meets the needs of the human heart as nothing else can.

Carl F. H. Henry states concerning the Old Testament prophets, "Both in speech and writing they are marked off by their unswerving assurance that they were spokesmen for the living God . . . The constantly repeated formula, 'thus saith the Lord,' is so characteristic of the prophets as to leave no doubt that they considered themselves chosen agents of the divine self-communication."

   2. What were the attitudes of the following authors toward other writers of Scripture?

   Paul (Romans 3:1, 2)   *"were entrusted with the oracles of God"*

   Peter (2 Peter 1:19-21)   *"men moved by the Holy Spirit"*

   The writer of Hebrews (1:1)   *"God spoke... to the fathers"*

New Testament writers likewise viewed Old Testament Scripture as being inspired of God. Toward their own writings, "they extended the traditional claim of divine inspiration. Jesus . . . spoke of a further ministry of teaching by the Spirit (John 14:26; 16:13). The apostles assert confidently that they thus speak by the Spirit (1 Peter 1:12) . . . They not only assume a divine authority (1 Thessalonians 4:2,15; 2 Thessalonians 3:6,12), but they make acceptance of their written commands a test of spiritual obedience (1 Corinthians 14:37)" — Carl F. H. Henry.

Either these men were deluded or the Bible is from God. But this greatest and most influential book of all time does not give evidence of being the product of deluded men. The power of the Bible rather is evidence that it does come from God.

B. *Purpose of personal Bible study*

1. Name some practical results of a thorough study of the word of God (2 Timothy 3:15-17). *Gives wisdom, knowledge of salvation, is profitable for teaching, reproof, correction, training in righteousness, equips men of God for every good work.*

Additional results of Bible study are found in: John 15:3,7; Romans 15:4; 1 Peter 2:2,3.

2. In Acts 20:32, Paul says that the Word of God is able to do what two things?
   1. *"Build you up"* 2. *"Give you inheritance among all those who are sanctified"*

3. What should be the effect upon your own life of reading the Bible (James 1:22-25)? *Reveals what we really are, helps us remember how to be obedient, promises blessings when we do obey God's Word.*

One who hears and studies God's Word without doing anything about it is like a man who looks in a mirror, sees that his face is dirty and unshaven, yet goes away without washing and shaving it.

"The great aim of education is not knowledge but action" — Herbert Spencer.

"It is only when we obey God's laws that we can be quite sure that we really know Him. The man who claims to know God but does not obey His laws is not only a liar but lives in self-delusion. In practice, the more a man learns to obey God's laws, the more truly and fully does he express his love for Him. Obedience is the test of whether we really live 'in God' or not" (1 John 2:4-6, Phillips translation).

C. *Preparations for personal Bible study*

1. Set aside a definite time.
   When did Moses meet with God (Exodus 34:2-4)? _____

   When did Christ meet with God (Mark 1:35)? *In the early morning before dawn.*

   When is the best time for you? _____

2. Find a definite place.
   Where did Christ pray (Mark 1:35)? *In a lonely place.*
   What is the value of being alone? *No distractions.*

3. Employ these tools:
   Modern translation of the Bible.
   Notebook and pen.
   Dictionary.

Bible Study Exercise

(If time permits, go over the procedure, then have the class take two sheets of paper, preferably 8½ x 11. Make two columns on one sheet. Over the first column write "observation"; over the second, "interpretation." On the other sheet write "application." Now have the class divide into groups and spend twenty minutes or so studying Luke 19:1-10, recording their findings on their papers.

Then come together and share the results.

This is inductive Bible study, and a sample might look like this:)

OBSERVATION   INTERPRETATION   APPLICATION

D. *Procedure for personal Bible study*

Three major steps to methodical Bible study.

1. Observation: "What does the passage say?"
   Read quickly for content.
   Read again carefully, underlining key words and phrases.
2. Interpretation: "What does the passage mean?"
   Ask God to give you understanding of the passage.
   Consult a dictionary or modern translation for the precise meaning of words.
   Ask: Who? What? Where? When? Why? How?
3. Application: Ask yourself, "What does the passage mean to me and how can it be applied to my life?"

Make a list of:
Attitudes to be changed   Sins to confess and forsake
Actions to take or avoid   Examples to follow
Promises to claim   Other personal applications

OBSERVATION

Vv. 1-2 — Zacchaeus was *chief* among the publicans and *very* rich.

Vv. 3-4 — Zacchaeus *ran* ahead of the crowd and climbed a sycamore tree to see Jesus.

Vv. 5-6 — Jesus saw Zacchaeus and invited Himself to stay at his house. Zacchaeus responded by receiving Jesus *joyfully.*

V. 7 — The crowd murmured against Jesus because He stayed with a man of bad reputation rather than with one of the religious rulers.

INTERPRETATION

Publicans were tax collectors, often cruel and dishonest. Zacchaeus had probably been unscrupulous in acquiring his riches.

He must have been extremely anxious to see Jesus to go to so much trouble. His behavior was even more remarkable considering his wealth and high position.

Jesus had evidently observed Zacchaeus' behavior and detected a hungry soul, thus He had no reservations about His boldness.

The crowd must have been very self-righteous. They should have been overjoyed that such a man as Zacchaeus would be interested in Jesus.

Vv. 8-9 — Zacchaeus now publicly announced that he would give half of his fortune to the poor, and offered to restore *four* times as much as he may have cheated any individual. Jesus responded by announcing that *this day* Zacchaeus had acquired salvation, and that he was a true descendant of Abraham.

Zacchaeus offered proof of a conversion experience. Before this time money had probably been his god, but he gave up what he had considered most dear for something worth much more. Jesus' response showed how willing God is to forget past sins when we give evidence of true repentance.

V. 10 — Jesus stated that He came specifically to save the lost.

This is apparently the whole point of the story. Zacchaeus was lost, and now was found. The crowd was also lost, but did not know it, and hence remained lost.

APPLICATION

(through first seven verses)

Vv. 1-4: (1) Among even the least likely classes there are those ready to receive God. Do I have friends who are outwardly sinful and godless, but *inwardly* as anxious as Zacchaeus to know Christ? (2) God responds immediately to a seeking heart. Zacchaeus did not have to wait to find salvation. I do not have to wait to find God in my daily experience either. I can know Him *now.*

Vv. 5-6: (1) Jesus knows who will respond to Him and who will not — if I am led by Him, I will come into contact with hungry souls just as He did. (2) Jesus was bold in inviting Himself to stay with Zacchaeus. If I meet one who is hungry for God, can I be bold with him too?

V. 7: (1) How easy it is to be snobbish. Do I purposely steer clear of others just because they don't measure up to my standards? (2) How easy it is to be self-righteous. Zacchaeus *knew* he needed Jesus — the crowd did not. Do I feel I am pretty good, and do not need Jesus as much as others?

(Teacher, have students continue application of other verses on their own.)

NOTE: This is a sample of observation, interpretation, and application. Undoubtedly as you study Luke 19:1-10, you will observe, interpret and apply things not mentioned here, as will others in the class. You should follow a procedure similar to this frequently in your private devotions.

Conclusion
and Application

(These questions and the answers may be discussed in the group.)

(If you didn't have time to do this Bible study in class, encourage the students to do it at home.)

Life Application

1. What has been your view of the Bible before this? _____

_____

_____

_____

2. Study Luke 19:1-10 and apply the Bible study method you have just learned.

What does the passage say? _____

_____

What does it mean? _____

How does this apply to you? _____

Can you now use this method of Bible study for other Scripture passages? _____

3. What changes in your life do you expect as you proceed with more in-depth Bible study? _____

_____

Suggested Closing Prayer

Father in heaven, we thank You for showing us the absolute authority of Your Word as the source of our power. Help each one of us choose the right definite time and specific place for our individual Bible study, and we pray You will guide us as we make this important procedure a regular part of our lives.

ADDITIONAL BACKGROUND MATERIAL

Taken from "Mr. Steak Has a Rare Chairman of the Board," *Worldwide Challenge,* May, 1978, pp. 9-11.

James A. Mather is founder and Chairman of the Board of Mr. Steak, a nationwide chain of family restaurants with nearly 300 franchises in the United States and Canada.

" . . . He served on the Board of Directors of the International Franchise Association; he is on the Board of Trustees for Rockmont College and Youth for Christ Foundation, as well as the Board of Business and Industrial Advisors for the University of Wisconsin. He also chairs the curriculum committee as a member of the Board of New York University School for the Study of Foodservice Management.

"Mather came to the Lord on a rainy night in June, 1956. He and his wife attended the funeral for Dawson Trotman, founder of The Navigators. Jim admits that he didn't even know who Dawson Trotman was at the time. He had just come to hear Billy Graham, one of the Christian leaders who spoke that night.

"Although he was an usher and adult church school teacher, Mather had never accepted Christ. 'Jesus had always been my hero,' he says. 'I believed everything that I had heard about the Bible and about Jesus Christ. I just never remember anyone telling me that I had to make a personal decision to invite Him into my heart.'

"Jim received Christ as Savior that night and later was discipled by Bob Glockner, a man who worked with the Navigators. One morning a week they would get together to study and memorize the Scriptures.

"The Scriptures, then so new, have become familiar ground to him. It is evident from the way he frequently refers to specific verses and tells how God has taught him principles of business and principles of life through them."

In 1975, on the occasion of a radio interview in Canada, Mather was asked what he would most like to talk about. "The most important thing in my life is my relationship with the Lord Jesus Christ," Mather responded.

LESSON SIX

THE CHURCH

Teacher's Objective: To demonstrate to the students the importance of the church and to encourage them to be active in it.

Teacher's Enrichment: (May be shared with class if time permits.)

● Why did Jesus Christ found the local church?

Through the years the church has been widely criticized and often subject to failure. Many have suggested it is an outmoded institution which Christianity could well do without. When the church is not true to Christ and not fulfilling its mission, this is undoubtedly true; but when the church does the task He assigned to it, it is absolutely essential, not only to the growth and progress of Christianity, but to the spiritual welfare of the believer as well.

Some reasons why Jesus Christ founded the local church:

1. For the Christian movement to succeed, some form of organization was necessary. If Jesus had left only a loose association of followers, Christianity might well have died out within a few years. Powerful movements (such as Communism) depend on organized local groups for their success.

2. The church provides a place of fellowship and mutual encouragement for Christians.

3. The church provides a place of instruction — here the doctrines contained in the Word of God are explained to us.

4. The church provides a place of worship — here we can join together in worship of the risen Lord.

5. The church provides a place of service — here we can put our talents at His disposal so that we may help others.

● Some parallel passages on the church:

1. Christ the Head of the church — Ephesians 5:23; Colossians 1:18.

2. The universal church — 2 Corinthians 16:1; Galatians 1:2; 1 Thessalonians 2:14.

3. The local church — Acts 5:11; 11:26; 1 Corinthians 11:18; 14:19,28,34; Romans 16:4.

4. Marks of a church — 2 John 9; Matthew 18:19; Acts 2:42; 1 Corinthians 5:1-5 (discipline); 11:18; 14:19,28,5.

CLASS TIME

Suggested Opening Prayer

Our Father, we thank You for Your promise that where two or three are gathered together in Your name, You are with them, and we thank You for being with us now. We pray You will open our minds and our hearts and let us see the church as You would have us see it. Help us understand its importance because of its relationship with our Savior Jesus Christ.

(Introduction: Be sure students understand
    objective
    memory work
    reading assignment.)

> **Introduction**
>
> OBJECTIVE: To realize the importance of involvement in a local church.
>
> TO MEMORIZE: Colossians 1:18.
>
> TO READ: Acts 2:41-47.

Discussion Starter

(Ask the class:) Why do you think Jesus Christ founded the local church? (Have students list as many reasons as possible.)

Lesson Development

(Have someone read opening paragraphs, then discuss study answers.)

> In the Greek New Testament the word for church is *ecclesia*, which comes from two Greek words with the root meaning of "to call out." In usage, the meaning was "assembly," and was adopted in New Testament times to refer to the church in two ways. One refers to the local assembly or congregation of Christians meeting together for worship, Bible study, teaching and service. The other is the universal church composed of every believer in Jesus Christ.
>
> **Bible Study**
>
> A. *Composition of the church*
>
> 1. What did the early Christians do that we should do also?
>
> Acts 2:41, 42 _Were baptized, added to church._
>
> Acts 4:31, 8:4 _Prayed, were filled with Holy Spirit, preached the Word._
>
> Acts 5:41, 42 _Rejoiced, taught, preached Jesus as Christ._

The early Christians also studied the Bible, had fellowship with each other, celebrated the communion service, witnessed fearlessly and preached Christ in every place possible.

Concerning the early church, which we read about in the Book of Acts and the New Testament Epistles, J. B. Phillips says, "The great difference between present-day Christianity and that of which we read in these letters is that to us it is primarily a performance, to them it was a real experience . . . the invasion of their lives by a new quality of life altogether."

The Bible *commands*
Christians to assemble

> 2. As God's children, how do we obey the instruction given in Hebrews 10:25? *Assemble together, share in worship, fellowship, church activities, witnessing,.*

regularly. "The Christian life is not just our own private affair. If we have been born again into God's family, not only has He become our Father but every other Christian believer in the world . . . has become our brother or sister in Christ . . . Every Christian's place is in a local church" — John R. Stott.

Matthew Henry says
about the church as the
body of Christ, "Each
(Christian) stands related
to the body as a part of
it . . . Mutual indifference

> 3. The entire church is compared to a _body_ of which Christ is the _head_ and the individual believers are the _members_ (Colossians 1:18; 1 Corinthians 12:27).
>
> 4. Read 1 Thessalonians 1:1-10, then list some qualities God desires for members of any church. *Work of faith, labor of love, steadfastness of hope, imitators of Paul and Lord, example to all believers, good reputation, turn to God from idols, wait for Jesus' return.*

. . . contempt, and hatred, and envy, and strife, are very unnatural in Christians. It is like the members of the same body being destitute of all concern for one another.

> B. Ordinances of the church
>
> 1. What do you believe baptism accomplishes (Matthew 28:19)? *Is act of obedience, public proclamation of faith, announcement to world of identification with Christ and His cause.*
> Who is eligible for baptism? *Those who are discipled.*
> What was the significance of your baptism? _____

Baptism was an initiatory
rite practiced by the Jews in
the time of Jesus to signify
that an individual was

identifying himself with Judaism as a convert, or with a particular movement within Judaism, such as that led by John the Baptist. The early church took over this rite so that Christians could make a public proclamation of their faith and announce to the world that they had identified themselves with Christ and His cause.

To all churches, baptism is essential to an obedient walk with the Lord.

(Ask the class members
to share their understanding
of the meaning of the communion service. Point

> 2. What is the meaning of the communion service (1 Corinthians 11:23-26)? *(An act of obedience, time of facing Jesus' death, time to examine our lives.*
> How do you prepare to observe the Lord's Supper?
> _____

out again that this specifically was given to the disciples to be incorporated into their remembrance of Him. It is important to note that participation in this act also is essential to the obedient walk of the believer.)

C. Purposes of the church
1. What should be one of the basic purposes of a church (2 Timothy 4:2)? _Preach the Word of God._

"The preacher must present, not book reviews, not politics, not economics, not current topics of the day, not a philosophy of life denying the Bible and based upon unproven theories of science, but the Word. The preacher . . . cannot choose his message. He is given a message to proclaim by his Sovereign. If he will not proclaim that, let him step down from his exalted position" — Kenneth Wuest.

2. List several of your own reasons for joining a church.
_____
_____
_____

3. What should the church believe about Christ?
His birth (Matthew 1:23) _He was virgin-born._
His deity (John 1:14) _The Word (God) became flesh._
His death (1 Peter 2:24) _For our sins._
His resurrection (1 Corinthians 15:3, 4) _A fact._
His second coming (1 Thessalonians 4:16, 17) _Will occur._

About the five basic things a church should believe (among others):
1. The virgin birth — "Practically every person who denies the doctrine rejects the supernatural as such . . . (and that denial) deprives us of knowledge as to the manner in which He entered the world. It seriously weakens, if it does not destroy, the doctrine of the incarnation (God manifest in the flesh) upon which our confidence rests and without which the Christian faith cannot survive" — Lindsell and Woodbridge.

2. The deity of Christ — "Unfortunately some believe that His deity is of little importance and . . . that the Christian faith is coherent, sufficient, and satisfactory even if Jesus is not God . . . If Jesus is not God, then He bore false witness. He was a liar and thus a sinner Himself . . . The Bible itself would be an unreliable witness . . . founded on error . . . leads to a denial of the supernatural in general . . . eliminates the Virgin Birth of Christ, His physical resurrection, and His miracles" — Ibid.

3. The death of Christ — "Man separates himself from God by sin, and death is the natural result . . . But it was not that way that Jesus became subject to death, since He had no personal sin . . . Death is . . . above all the judicially imposed and inflicted punishment of sin . . . It is from this . . . point of view that the death of Christ must be considered" — Louis Berkhof. When Christ died, God punished *Him* for *our* sins.

4. The resurrection of Christ — "The resurrection of our Lord teaches three important lessons: (1) It showed that His work of atonement was completed and

was stamped with the Divine approval; (2) It showed Him to be Lord of all and gave the one sufficient external proof of Christianity; (3) It furnished the ground and pledge of our own resurrection, and thus 'brought life and immortality to light' (2 Timothy 1:10)" (Strong, A. H., *Systematic Theology*, p. 131).

(For further study on the resurrection of Christ, see *The Resurrection Factor* by Josh McDowell, published by Here's Life Publishers, 1981.)

5. Second coming of Christ — "The faith in a second coming of Christ has lost its hold upon many Christians in our day. But it still serves to stimulate and admonish the great body, and we can never dispense with its solemn and mighty influence" — A. H. Strong.

> 4. Whom did God give, besides prophets and apostles, to strengthen the church members (Ephesians 4:11, 12)?
> _Evangelists, pastors and teachers._

Of those whom God has given to the church:

(1) Evangelists — those who present the gospel to the lost. Billy Graham, foreign missionaries, and many laymen effective in winning others to Christ have been given the gift of evangelism. We are all to witness, but it seems, since certain people are so effective in this area, that God has given this special gift to them.

(2) Pastors and teachers — The original Greek makes clear that these are one and the same (pastor-teacher). The term "pastor" originally meant "a feeder of sheep," and it came to be applied to Christians who teach. Ministers are, of course, pastors, but many who never enter the ministry also have this gift and are expected to exercise it.

Many gifts given to the church are not listed here — but undoubtedly God has gifted you in some special area. He expects you to develop it and use it for His glory. Some ways in which God can gift us that we can use for Him:

Superior intellect — you can use this to gain a deeper understanding of the Scriptures and teach others.

Leadership and administrative abilities — You should help to organize and oversee some of the Christian activities on your campus, in your community or in your church.

Maybe, as you evaluate yourself, you feel you are only average. Do not be discouraged. You undoubtedly have hidden talents which God will develop as you follow His will. You must never forget that many average people in the Bible accomplished great feats because they trusted in a great God. Study Hebrews 11.

Conclusion and Application

Writing for the Ladies' Home Journal, in an article called, "Shall We Do Away with the Church?" President Theodore Roosevelt once said, "In the pioneer days of the West, we found it an unfailing rule that after a community had existed for a certain length of time, either a church was built or

> **Life Application**
> 1. If you are not already in a local church, prayerfully list two or three you will visit in the next month, with the purpose of planning to join one. _____
> _____
> _____

else the community began
to go downhill."

> 2. Suggestions for making your church worship more meaningful:
>   Bow for silent prayer before the service begins. Pray — for yourself, for the minister, for those taking part in the service and for those worshipping — that Christ will be very real to all, and that those who do not know Christ may come to know Him.
>   Always take your Bible. Underline portions that are made especially meaningful by the sermons.
>   Meditate upon the words of the hymns.
>   Take notes on the sermon and apply them to your life.
>   Can you list some other ways? _____
>   _____
>   _____
>
> 3. If you are a part of a local church, ask God to show you ways in which you can be more used by Him by being of service in the church. List the ways He reveals to you. _____
>   _____

Suggested Closing Prayer

Thank You, Father, for Your Word and for the way You have instructed us regarding Your church. We have seen its importance and now want to commit ourselves to serving You more fully and to being more obedient than we have been before. In these moments we ask You to reveal to each of us how You would like to work individually through us in Your church. (Observe a few moments of silence for each person to listen to the inner voice of God as he instructs that person in his relationship with his own church and to give that person an opportunity to make that commitment. Then continue:) We thank You, Father, and we do surrender ourselves for that particular service. Give us the measure of faith we need to obey You.

ADDITIONAL BACKGROUND MATERIAL

Some further remarks by President Theodore Roosevelt in the Ladies' Home Journal article: "On Sunday go to church. Yes — I know all the excuses: I know that one can worship the Creator and dedicate oneself to good living in a grove of trees or by a running brook or in one's own house just as well as in a church, but I also know that as a matter of cold fact the average man does not worship or thus dedicate himself. If he stays away from church he does not spend his time in good works or in lofty meditation . . . He may not hear a good sermon at church, but unless he is very unfortunate he will hear a sermon by a good man.

"Besides, even if he does not hear a good sermon, the probabilities are that he will listen to and take part in reading some beautiful passage from the Bible, and if he is not familiar with the Bible, he has suffered a loss which he had better make all possible haste to correct. He will meet and nod to or speak to good, quiet neighbors. If he doesn't think about himself too much, he will benefit himself very much, especially as he begins to think chiefly of others."

The five basic things a church should believe are at the heart and core of the Christian faith — they are the traditional doctrines as enunciated in the New Testament. We should seek to worship in churches which affirm these doctrines.

How can you know if a church is true to Christ and to His doctrines? Ask yourself these questions:

1. Do the sermons make clear as a rule, that we become Christians by accepting Christ personally, or do they leave a vague impression that a Christian is just a good moral person?

2. Do the church members seem to be those who have had a true conversion experience, or those who are just coming to church for social reasons?

3. Is the Bible really taught, or does the minister spend most of his time preaching his own opinions, political issues, etc.? Remember, good oratory is no substitute for the clear preaching of God's Word!

LESSON SEVEN

RECAP

Teacher's Objective: To impress more deeply upon the hearts of the students the Christian principles and truths presented in the six previous lessons, and to lead the students to any further commitments needed.

CLASS TIME

Suggested Opening Prayer

Our Father, as we study this Recap and review the past six lessons today, we pray You will reveal to us the areas we should think more deeply about and the commitments we need to make at this time. Thank You for Your promise of forgiveness of sins and spiritual growth when we obey Your commands.

(Introduction: This review lesson does not have a new student's objective, previous memory work is to be reviewed, and some of the earlier reading assignments are repeated. Now would be a good time for students to do any reading that was missed during the study of these lessons.)

> Review verses memorized.
> Reread: John 3:1-20; 1 John 5:9-15; Romans 6:14-23.

Discussion Starter

(The first question in the students' books may be used to start the discussion of this lesson.)

> 1. Assurance of salvation:
> Suppose you have just made the great discovery of knowing Jesus Christ personally and you know you have eternal life. In your enthusiasm you tell your roommate you have become a Christian and have eternal life. He replies, "That is mere presumption on your part. No one can know he has eternal life." How would you answer him? What verse would you use as your authority? *Possible: John 1:12; 3:16, 36 10:28-30; 1 John 5:12; and others.*

Lesson Development

(Any Teacher's Enrichment or Additional Background Material that you were not able to use in the previous lessons could be utilized at this time and any point which you feel was not sufficiently covered, or which the students do not understand completely, can

> 2. How may a Christian be restored to fellowship after he has sinned? What Scripture reference is your authority? _____
> *Confess and accept forgiveness. 1 John 1:9.*

115

be dealt with now too.

Going over the Recap material will benefit both the students and you by making these truths a more active part of your subconscious, habitual way of life.

(Answers below.)

3. Name some of the qualities of a Christ-controlled life.
Love, joy, peace, patience, kindness, goodness, faithfulness, gentleness, self-control, Christ-centered, empowered by Holy Spirit, witnessing, effective prayer life, trusting and obeying God.

4. List the five principles of growth.
Bible study, prayer, fellowship, witnessing and obedience.

5. What are the three major steps in methodical Bible study?
Observation: What does it say?
Interpretation: What does it mean?
Application: How does it apply to my life?

6. List at least three ways Scripture may be applied to your life.
Attitudes to be changed; sins to confess and forsake; actions to take or avoid; examples to follow; promises to claim.

7. Name some characteristics of a New Testament church.
Preaches Word of God; believes in virgin birth and deity of Christ, atoning death and resurrection, second coming.

8. Match the titles with the appropriate references:

The humiliation and exaltation of Christ	Philippians 2:5-11
The meaning of the resurrection for us	Acts 2:41-47
The value of the Word of God to us	1 Corinthians 2:11; 3:5
The fruit of the Spirit	Psalm 119:97-104
The spiritual and carnal Christians	Psalm 63
Reading the Bible for growth	Galatians 5:16-24
A psalm relating to prayer	James 1:18-27
The early church	1 Corinthians 15:12-26

The humiliation and exaltation of Christ . . . . Philippians 2:5-11
The meaning of the resurrection for us . . . . 1 Corinthians 15:12-26
The value of the Word of God to us . . . . Psalm 119:97-104
The fruit of the Spirit . . . . Galatians 5:16-24
The spiritual and carnal Christians . . . . 1 Corinthians 2:11; 3:5
Reading the Bible for growth . . . . James 1:18-27
A psalm relating to prayer . . . . Psalm 63
The early Church . . . . Acts 2:41-47

Conclusion and Application

(Give students a minute
or two to think about the
Life Application questions
and then discuss their
answers.)

Life Application

Ask yourself these questions and write the answers. "In what specific ways is my life different now from what it was when I began this study about the Christian adventure?" _____

_____

_____

"In what areas do I need to obey Scripture more?" _____

_____

Suggested Closing Prayer

(Start with a short time of silent prayer for personal, private commitments to be made. Then pray aloud:) We thank You, God, for accepting our commitments today, as You have refreshed our minds with these truths.

We thank You for the life which is eternal; we thank You for forgiveness of sins; we thank You for the promise of eternal fruit and power through Your Holy Spirit; we thank You for Your Word and for how it teaches us and we thank You for the church in which we find fellowship and spiritual blessings and a place to serve You. We thank You for answered prayer. But most of all we thank You for the gift of Your Son and pray that we may come to know Him better and that we may be conformed to His image as we grow in Him.

SUMMARY LESSON PLAN
THE CHRISTIAN ADVENTURE

Teacher's Objective: To ground the new convert in some of the most basic doctrines and areas of Christian living, and to lead him to full commitment to Jesus Christ.

Teacher's Enrichment: (See Teacher's Enrichment sections in each of the preceding lessons of this Step, and share with the class as time permits.)

CLASS TIME

Suggested Opening Prayer

Our Father, we ask that Your Holy Spirit will enlighten our minds and hearts to the truths You have for us today. Help us believe and accept the assurance of eternal life and help us to learn how to grow therein as we obey Your commands.

(Introduction:

Student's Objective: To understand eternal life, how to grow in Christ, and how Christ dwelling in us, the power of the Bible and the importance of the church all contribute to the adventure of being a Christian.

To Memorize: 1 John 5:13 and Philippians 4:13.

Reading Assignment: John 3:1-20; 1 John 5:9-15; Romans 6:14-23.)

Discussion Starter

(Ask the class:) What do you think are some of the things you need to know before you can successfully live the Christian life? (Get several answers, then mention what you consider the most important areas, drawing them from the subject of each lesson.)

Lesson Development

(Use the Recap — Lesson 7. Go over each question with the group and supplement your answers from the material in this teacher's manual for each lesson. The questions refer to the lessons as follows:)

Lesson 1

1. Assurance of salvation:
Suppose you have just made the great discovery of knowing Jesus Christ personally and you know you have eternal life. In your enthusiasm you tell your roommate you have become a Christian and have eternal life. He replies, "That is mere presumption on your part. No one can know he has eternal life." How would you answer him? What verse would you use as your authority? _Possible: John 1:12; 3:16, 36 10:28-30; 1 John 5:12; and others._

Lesson 3 (Solution to carnality.)

2. How may a Christian be restored to fellowship after he has sinned? What Scripture reference is your authority? _Confess and accept forgiveness; 1 John 1:9._

Lesson 3 (The Spiritual, or Christ-controlled Christian.)

3. Name some of the qualities of a Christ-controlled life.
Love, joy, peace, patience, kindness, goodness, faithfulness, gentleness, self-control, Christ-centered, empowered by Holy Spirit, witnessing, effective prayer life, trusting and obeying God.

Love is the great proof we are Christ's disciples.

"The qualities which should characterize the love we are to manifest toward our fellow-men are beautifully set forth in 1 Corinthians 13. It is patient and without envy; it is not proud or self-elated; neither does it behave discourteously; it does not cherish evil, but keeps good account of the good; it rejoices not at the downfall of any enemy or competitor, but gladly hails his success; it is hopeful, trustful, and forbearing — for such there is no law, for they need none; they have fulfilled the law" — William Evans.

Lesson 4

4. List the five principles of growth.
Bible study, prayer, fellowship, witnessing, and obedience.

Lesson 5

5. What are the three major steps in methodical Bible study?
Observation--what does it say?
Interpretation--what does it mean?
Application--how does it apply to my life?

Regarding the impact of the Bible on history:

John Richard Green, English historian, and author of the *Short History of the English People,* notes: "England became the people of a book, and that book was the Bible . . . familiar to every Englishman. It was read in churches, it was read at home, and everywhere its words, as they fell on ears which custom had not deadened to their force and beauty, kindled a startling enthusiasm . . . Elizabeth might silence or tune the pulpits, but it was impossible for her to silence or tune the great preachers of justice and mercy and truth, who spoke from the book which the Lord again opened to the people . . . The effect of the Bible in this way was simply amazing. The whole temper of the nation was changed. A new conception of life and of man superseded the old. A new moral and religious impulse spread through every class . . . Theology rules there, said Grotius of England, only ten years after Elizabeth's death. The whole nation, in fact, became a church."

A friend of Rufus Choate, in looking over the large library of that outstanding lawyer and United States Senator, remarked banteringly, "Seven editions of the New Testament and not a copy of the Constitution!" To which Choate replied, "Ah, my friend, you forget that the Constitution of my country is in them all."

Lincoln's imperishable phrase, "Government of the people, by the people, and for the people," the essence of democracy, comes from the introduction to Wycliffe's Bible, the first English Version of the Holy Scripture. Here is the preface to that pioneer translation: "The Bible will make possible a Government of people, by people, and for people."

Ernst Haekel, the noted German scientist and philosopher who was an untiring protagonist of atheistic rationalism, admitted the world-transforming power of the Bible when he said: "Beyond all doubt the present degree of human culture owes, in great part, its perfection to the propagation of the Christian system of morals and its ennobling influence."

Lesson 5

> 6. List at least three ways Scripture may be applied to your life.
> *Attitudes to be changed; sins to confess and forsake; actions to take or avoid; examples to follow; promises to claim.*

Lesson 6

> 7. Name some characteristics of a New Testament church.
> *Preaches Word of God; believes in virgin birth. deity of Christ, atoning death, resurrection, second coming.*

All the lessons

> 8. Match the titles with the appropriate references:
>
> | | |
> |---|---|
> | The humiliation and exaltation of Christ | Philippians 2:5-11 |
> | The meaning of the resurrection for us | Acts 2:41-47 |
> | The value of the Word of God to us | 1 Corinthians 2:11; 3:5 |
> | The fruit of the Spirit | Psalm 119:97-104 |
> | The spiritual and carnal Christians | Psalm 63 |
> | Reading the Bible for growth | Galatians 5:16-24 |
> | A psalm relating to prayer | James 1:18-27 |
> | The early church | 1 Corinthians 15:12-26 |

Answers to question 8:

The humiliation and exaltation of Christ. . . . . Philippians 2:5-11
The meaning of the resurrection for us. . . . . 1 Corinthians 15:12-26
The value of the Word of God to us. . . . . Psalm 119:97-104
The fruit of the Spirit . . . . Galatians 5:16-24
The spiritual and carnal Christians . . . . 1 Corinthians 2:11; 3:5
Reading the Bible for growth . . . . James 1:18-27
A psalm relating to prayer. . . . . Psalm 63
The early Church. . . . . Acts 2:41-47

Conclusion and Application

(Give students a minute
or two to think about the
Life Application questions
and then discuss their
answers.)

Life Application

Ask yourself these questions and write the answers. "In what
specific ways is my life different now from what it was when I
began this study about the Christian adventure?" _____

_____

_____

"In what areas do I need to obey Scripture more?" _____

_____

_____

Suggested Closing Prayer

(Encourage the class to commit themselves totally to Jesus Christ. Start with a
short time of silent prayer for personal, private commitments to be made. Then
pray aloud:) We thank You, God, for accepting our commitments today, as You
have taught us these truths. We thank You for eternal life, for forgiveness of sins,
for the promise of eternal fruit and for power through Your Holy Spirit. We thank
You for Your Word and for how it teaches us and we thank You for the church in
which we find fellowship and spiritual blessings and a place to serve You. And we
thank You for answering prayer. Most of all we thank You for the gift of Your Son
and pray that we may come to know Him better and that we may be conformed to
His image as we grow in Him.

The Christian
and the Abundant Life

The Christian life is a life of victory, joy, peace and purposeful living. Jesus said, "I came that they might have life, and might have it abundantly" (John 10:10). True, there are many professing Christians who are defeated and discouraged, but this is not the New Testament norm. Picture the apostle Paul and Silas imprisoned in Philippi. They were beaten and cast into the inner prison where their feet were locked in the stocks. Yet they prayed and sang praises unto God. Their confidence was not in themselves. Their confidence and trust were in the true living God whom they loved, worshipped and served.

Picture the disciples and thousands of other first-century Christians singing praises to God as they were burned at the stake, crucified or fed to the lions. They faced horrible deaths with courage and joy because of their vital, personal relationship with Christ, remembering that "the servant is not greater than his Lord." Such dedication to Christ is not limited to the disciples and early Christians. Down through the centuries, there have been — and still are — many thousands of Christians who have dedicated their very lives to Christ. They are living the abundant life which Christ promised. You may not find it necessary to die for Christ, but are you willing to live for Him?

Referring to the world crises of his time, Sir Winston Churchill once said, "This generation may well live to see the end of what we now call civilization." As civilization stands on the brink of extermination, *the desperate need of this hour is men and women who are utterly abandoned to Jesus Christ — Christians who are willing to serve Him at any cost.*

"The more I think of and pray about the state of religion in this country, and all over the world, the deeper my conviction becomes that the low state of the spiritual life of Christians is due to the fact that they do not realize that the aim and object of conversion is to bring the soul, even here on earth, to a daily fellowship with the Father in heaven. When once this truth has been accepted, the believer will perceive how indispensable it is to the spiritual life of a Christian to take time each day with God's Word and in prayer to wait upon God for His presence and His love to be revealed.

"It is not enough at conversion to accept forgiveness of sins, or even to surrender to God. That is only a beginning. The young believer must understand that he has no power of his own to maintain his spiritual life. No, he needs each day to receive new grace from heaven through fellowship with the Lord Jesus. This cannot be obtained by a hasty prayer, nor a superficial reading of a few verses from God's Word. He must take time quietly and deliberately to come into God's presence, to feel his own weakness and his need, and to wait upon God through His Holy Spirit, to renew the heavenly light and life in his heart. Then he may rightly expect to be kept by the power of Christ throughout the day, and all its temptations.

"Many of God's children long for a better life, but do not realize the need of giving God time day by day in their inner chamber through His Spirit to renew and sanctify their lives.

"Meditate on this thought: The feeble state of my spiritual life is mainly due to the lack of time day by day in fellowship with God."

— Andrew Murray

LESSON ONE

WHAT IS THE CHRISTIAN LIFE?

Teacher's Objective: To explain to the new Christian the difference between his new life in Christ and his old life; to lead the student to whichever commitment is necessary — new birth, or deeper awareness of his new life.

Teacher's Enrichment: (May be shared with the class as time permits.)

• "As many as received Him, to them (only) He gave the right to become children of God" (John 1:12). The Christian life can be lived only by first receiving Christ as your Savior.

If you haven't already done so, why not ask Him into your heart and thank Him for so graciously forgiving your sins and becoming your Lord and Savior.

Look at Romans 10:9-10 (Amplified).

This new birth results in an entirely new kind of life. Basically it changes one's perspective, or point of view. One sees things now from God's point of view. It also gives him the power of spiritual life just as in the natural birth he is given the power of natural life. "Therefore if any man is in Christ, he is a new creature; the old things passed away; behold, new things have come" (2 Corinthians 5:17). When we receive Christ, everything is different.

• Because of His interest in our lives, we can yield our lives totally to Him without fear.

"Casting the whole of your care — all your anxieties, all your worries, all your concerns, once and for all — on Him; for He cares for you affectionately, and cares about you watchfully" (1 Peter 5:7, Amplified Version).

So many people console themselves with, "God causes all things to work together for good" (Romans 8:28). Note the verse explains, "to those who love God, to those who are called according to His purpose." This is a relationship to be cherished. Spend time in prayer with God; get to know Him above all others.

CLASS TIME

Suggested Opening Prayer

Lord, may we understand what it means to be a new creature in Christ, and may we respond to what we learn today.

(Introduction: Be sure students understand
    objective
    memory work
    reading assignment.)

Introduction

OBJECTIVE: To show the difference between our new life in Christ, and the old life.

TO MEMORIZE: 2 Corinthians 5:17.

TO READ: John 1-3.

(Review 2 Corinthians 5:17 together. Devote about five minutes to this, allowing each one in the group to recite audibly. Assign next week's memory verse. *Care should be given to continue to emphasize the importance of memorizing Scripture.*)

Discussion Starter

(Ask the class:) What would you expect in the life of a person who had been made a new creation? (Get a number of responses.)

Lesson Development

(One suggested method for studying this lesson: Divide entire class into four groups. Count off in fours as follows:

> Group 1 — A New Creation
> Group 2 — A New Relationship With God
> Group 3 — A New Motivation
> Group 4 — A New Relationship to Mankind

Request each group to discuss and review each verse under its chosen topic. The small groups should then reconvene and summarize their conclusions to the entire group.)

To experience "Christ living in you" involves the new birth. Life in the physical realm requires a physical birth at a particular time and in a certain place, and you receive a name. It is the same in the Christian life. There is a definite time when you personally receive Jesus Christ, there is a place,

The Christian life begins with spiritual birth (John 3:6) through faith in the Lord Jesus Christ (Ephesians 2:8, 9). The Christian life is a personal, daily relationship between the believer and Christ. This life is lived by faith. *Faith is trust. We trust our lives to Christ's keeping because He has proven Himself trustworthy by His life, His death, H. His abiding presence.*

Bible Study

A. *A new creation*

1. On the basis of 2 Corinthians 5:17, what has happened to you? _A new creature._

   What are some evidences in your life of new things having come, and old things having passed away? _____

   _____

   _____

2. To what does the Bible compare this experience of newness (John 3:3)? _____ _A new birth._

and you receive a name — Christian. There are many genuine Christians, however, who cannot identify the time or place of their conversion yet who know with certainty that Jesus Christ lives within them.

In John 1:13 we read,
"Not of blood (we cannot

> 3. How was your new birth accomplished (John 3:16; 1:12, 13)? *We believe in the Son, receive Him, and thus are born of the will of God.*

inherit it), nor of the will of the flesh (we cannot earn the right), nor of the will of man (we cannot be voted into it), but of God!"

We are told that we have the *right* (Greek word means "authority") to call ourselves members of His family. We are called

> 4. According to Ephesians 2:8, 9, what did you do to merit this gift? *Nothing except receive it as a gift.*
>
> B. A new relationship with God
>   1. What are you called (1 Peter 2:2)? *Newborn babes.* What should be your desire? *Pure milk of the Word.*
>   2. What is your new relationship with God (John 1:12)? *We are His children.*

"babes" and as such we must immediately receive nourishment. Therefore, as soon as we accept Christ or become by birth a new member of God's family, it is essential that we immediately begin studying the Word of God and also begin having fellowship with other members of God's family — in church and in other Christian groups.

God imparts His nature

> 3. What does it mean to you to be a partaker of the divine nature (2 Peter 1:4)? _____

to us immediately at birth. The evidence of God's nature is more apparent in some people than in others. *If we give Him our all, He can accomplish more quickly that which He wills for us.* This means a total yielding of our lives to God.

God reveals Himself in each life in such a way that

> 4. How do you know that you are God's child (Galatians 4:6; Romans 8:16)? *His Holy Spirit dwells within us and witnesses to our spirits.*

each person knows or has the assurance of his salvation. The way He reveals Himself may be completely different in each case. The important thing is that you *know*. See John 5:11-13 for further assurance that God gives us.

Christ lives in you. He loves, acts, talks through you. Your entire life becomes different because you are no longer living your life but Christ is living it (Galatians 2:20)! His motives are yours. As you

C. *A new motivation*

1. How does the love of Christ motivate you (2 Corinthians 5:14)? *Controlled by His love.*

2. What has replaced self as the most important factor (verse 15)? *He died and rose again on our behalf.*

3. Two things have happened in your life to give you new motivation, according to Colossians 3:1-3:

What has happened to your old life according to verse 2? *It is dead.*

What will motivate you to seek those things which are above, according to verse 1? *We have been raised up with Christ.*

study the Bible you will see how He moved among men, how He had a heart for those around Him. As you "let Jesus live" through you, you will be amazed at your reason for doing things — "for the glory of God." (Teacher, encourage your

students to read Matthew 6:19-34 at their first opportunity to become acquainted with the mind of God regarding this.)

D. *A new relationship to mankind*

1. What is new about your relationship to people (1 John 3:11, 14)? *"We should love one another."*

2. How can you show that you are a follower of Christ (John 13:35)? *"Have love for one another."*

3. Read 2 Corinthians 5:18-21. What ministry has been given to you (verse 18)? *Reconciliation.*
We are called *ambassadors* for Christ (verse 20).

4. As an ambassador for Christ, what is the greatest thing that you can do (Matthew 4:19)? *Follow Jesus--He will make us fishers of men.*
Name at least three ways you can do that in your own life.

5. How can your friends benefit from the message you, as an ambassador for Christ, deliver to them (1 John 1:3, 4)? *They will have fellowship with us and with Father, and our joy will be full.*

Through the Christians, Christ comforts lonely hearts, instructs and teaches, seeks and saves the lost, and can again walk among men and tell them of His love and sacrifice for their sin. He chooses to do this through *you.* God loves the world, not just a little section where you are now. Your concern becomes the world. You want others to know the Lord as you do because Jesus Christ died for the world. Your relationship now to man is world-wide and your responsibility is to let Jesus Christ live in you to reconcile the world to Him.

Conclusion and Application

The Christian life begins with a new birth. It is a personal daily relationship with Christ. It is simply — Christ living in you!

Life Application

1. What is the greatest change you have seen in your life since you became a new creation in Christ Jesus? _____

2. In your new relationship with God, what now can be your response toward problems, disappointments and frustrations (1 Peter 5:7; Romans 8:28)? _____

3. How will your goals be changed as a result of your new motivation? _____

4. What now is your responsibility to other men and women, and how will you carry it out? _____

5. List two changes you would like to see in your life now that you are a Christian, and ask God to bring those changes about. _____

Suggested Closing Prayer

(Read the following prayers and give those representing each group an opportunity to pray a similar prayer:)

(Salvation:) Lord Jesus, come into my life, forgive my sin and change my life. Give me a new life — Your life. I exchange my life for Yours.

(New life:) Thank You, Lord, for giving me a new life. Make me more conscious of Your presence in my life and I pray others will see the change in my life and want to come to know You too.

(After a period of silence the leader should close with a brief appropriate prayer.)

ADDITIONAL BACKGROUND MATERIAL

Parallel Scripture passages which may be considered:
Old Testament provision of a new heart: Ezekial 36:26.
New Testament contrasts between old and new life: Titus 3:3-4;
    Ephesians 2:1-13; Galatians 5:19-23.

LESSON TWO

AN APPRAISAL OF
YOUR OWN SPIRITUAL LIFE

Teacher's Objective: To help each student evaluate his or her personal relationship with Christ.

CLASS TIME

Suggested Opening Prayer

(Teacher, say to students:) This lesson is a very personal one in that God and you are the only ones that know your heart. As we study this lesson let it be as if you alone were with Christ that day He gave this parable. Ask Him to show you on which ground you stand and be willing to take action on that which He reveals to you. (After a minute or two of silent prayer, you should pray aloud very briefly:) Lord make us willing to respond positively to what You show us today.

(Introduction: Be sure
students understand
    objective
    memory work*
    reading assignment.)

Introduction
OBJECTIVE: To evaluate your relationship with Christ.
TO MEMORIZE: Galatians 6:7.
TO READ: John 4-6.

(*Have the group members count off by two's to determine partners, and then have the partners say the verse and check it with each other.)

Discussion Starter

(Have the students take out a piece of paper and write their answers to this True-False test as you read the statements:

1.	All good soil produces the same amount of fruit.	F
2.	Stony ground refers to an unreceptive heart.	F
3.	Thorny soil includes the deceitfulness of riches.	T
4.	Every Christian should be fruitful.	T
5.	This parable refers only to people in college.	F
6.	Patience comes through the trying of our faith.	T
7.	God's Word offers the solution to every "care" in life.	T
8.	My life would be different if I learned God's solutions and applied them.	T

(Read the answers and let each person correct his own paper. Stress the need to know these truths.)

Lesson Development

(Choose one of the references of the parable of the sower — Matthew 13:1-23, Mark 4:3-20 or Luke 8:4-15 — and have your group read aloud either in unison or go around the group with each person reading one verse until completed. Then discuss answers to the questions.)

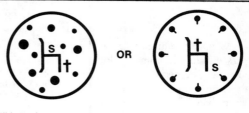

OR

Bible Study

Meditate upon each question as, well as upon the answer. Make this a personal appraisal of your spiritual condition.

A. *Types of soil*

Read the parable of the sower in Matthew 13:1-23; Mark 4:3-20; Luke 8:4-15.

1. To what does the seed refer (Mark 4:14)? _The Word._

2. What are the four kinds of soil referred to in Matthew 13:4-8? _Roadside, rocky, thorny, good._

B. *Making soil productive*

1. What does each kind of soil represent?

Compare verse 4 with 18, 19. _Roadside--hard, unreceptive heart, no germination, Satan takes seed._

Roadside soil: a life on which the Word of God has fallen but where Satan, by creating a hard heart or a lack of receptiveness, has snatched away the seed.

Compare verses 5, 6 with 20, 21 _Rocky—receives with joy, falls in affliction, weak roots._

Description of seed sown in *rocky soil:* those who, when they have heard the Word, immediately receive it with gladness and follow Christ for a time, but when difficulty or persecution arises are not rooted enough to stand.

Compare verse 7 with 22. _Thorny--worries of world, deceitfulness of riches choke the Word._

Seed sown on *thorny soil:* cares of the world can be any burden, problem, or decision that is carried by self instead of casting it on the Lord — grades, boyfriend or girlfriend, husband or wife, job, future, health, etc. Deceitfulness of riches refers to allowing things to give you a false sense of security — believing that this is what brings security and happiness — for instance, a rich, successful man who ends his life in suicide. Lusts are great, driving, fleshly desires, and they apply to all of life including possessions, ambitions, etc.

Compare verse 8 with 23. _Good--hears Word, under-_
stands, bears fruit to varying degrees.

2. What must happen for the roadside soil to be changed
(Hebrews 3:15)? _Hearts must not be hardened, but_
must be made receptive.(See also Romans 10:17)

3. How can unproductive, rocky ground be made productive?
(See 1 Corinthians 10:13 and Proverbs 29:25). _Look for_
God's provision for endurance/escape; trust
Him.

We are promised that persecution will come. "No man may be disturbed by these afflictions, for you yourselves know that we have been destined for this" (1 Thessalonians 3:3). "For you have been called for this purpose, since Christ also suffered for you, leaving you an example for you to follow in His steps" (1 Peter 2:21). Yet 1 Corinthians 10:13 tells us God has promised us nothing too great to bear, and Romans 8:28 reminds us that "God causes all things to work together for good to those who love God, to those who are called according to His purpose."

For God's answers to:
ridicule from the world — see John 15:18-21.
persecution from Satan — see Revelation 2:10
strife from within — see Romans 7:15-25.

4. How can individuals described as thorny soil become vital and effective Christians (1 Peter 5:7, Matthew 6:19-21)? _Cast all anxiety upon Him._

In the Amplifed Version of the Bible, 1 Peter 5:7 says, "Casting the whole of your care — all your anxieties, all your worries, all your concerns, once and for all — on Him; for He cares for you affectionately, and cares about you watchfully." See also Psalm 37:1-7.

For further scriptural help in the area of deceitfulness of riches, see Matthew 6:19-21; and for lust, see 1 John 2:15-17 and 1 Corinthians 6:18.

Determine to be a single-minded person. James 1:8 refers to "a double-minded man, unstable in all his ways." James 4:8 says, "Draw near to God, and He will draw near to you. Cleanse your hands, you sinners; and purify your hearts, you double minded."

C. Result of dwelling in good soil
1. What condition in a Christian results in abundance of fruit (Mark 4:20; Luke 8:15)? _Hear the Word and_
accept it.

To live the victorious life is to live on *good ground* and to *abide* in Christ. John 15:5, "I am the vine, you are the branches; he who abides in Me, and I in him, he bears much fruit; for apart from Me you can do nothing."

In the Amplified Version, Galatians 5:22-23 gives us the fruit of the Spirit this way: "The fruit of the (Holy) Spirit, (the work which His presence within accomplishes) is love, joy (gladness), peace, patience (an even temper, forbearance), kindness, goodness (benevolence), faithfulness; meekness (humility), gentleness, self-control (self-restraint, continence). Against such things there is no law (that can bring a charge)."

We are instructed in 2 Peter 1:5 to have faith, moral excellence, knowledge, self-control, perseverance, godliness, brotherly kindness and love in order not to be unfruitful. In John 15:16, Jesus tells us about fruit that will remain — new Christians.

---

2. What type of soil do most of the professing Christians whom you know represent? (_____

_____

3. What type of soil would you say your life now represents?

_____

4. What type of soil do you want your life to represent?

_____

Conclusion and Application

Only good soil brings forth fruit: some thirty-fold, some sixty, some one hundred. This is referred to in John 15 as fruit, more fruit, much fruit:

On the one hand	On the other hand
1. Neglect the Word	1. Hear the Word
2. Fear of man	2. Trust in the Lord
3. Satan's snares	3. God's victory
4. Flesh pleased	4. Spirit fed
5. Burdened	5. Carefree
6. Materialistic	6. Spiritual
7. Worldly	7. Heavenly
8. Fruitless	8. Fruitful

Life Application

1. How must the soil of your life be changed to become good ground or to increase in its fruitfulness? _____

_____

_____

2. What can you do? _____

3. What must you trust Christ to do? _____

_____

Suggested Closing Prayer

Father, give us a true sense of values. May we say, as did Joshua, "As for me I will serve the Lord." Also with Paul, "Lord, what wilt Thou have me to do?"

LESSON THREE

ABUNDANT LIVING

Teacher's Objective: To show that the abundant life is possible in practical, everyday life and to provide guidance in how students can live the abundant life.

Teacher's Enrichment: (May be shared with class as time permits.)

Read Romans 7:14-24, stressing the personal pronouns — I, me, my, etc.

Then read Romans 8:1-17, stressing God, Spirit, Son, Christ, etc. Determine what you think makes the difference in the life described in Romans 7 (defeat) and Romans 8 (victory).

CLASS TIME

Suggested Opening Prayer

Lord, help us to see that the abundant life is a life of faith in what Jesus Christ has accomplished and can accomplish in our lives.

(Introduction: Be sure
students understand
   objective
   memory work
   reading assignment.)

> **Introduction**
>
> OBJECTIVE: To learn how practical the "abundant life" is.
> 'TO MEMORIZE: John 10:10.
> TO READ: John 7-9.

Discussion Starter

(Go around the group and have each person take one word from the memory verse — begin with "I" and continue through "abundantly" — and explain what that word means.)

Lesson Development

> Jesus said, "I came that they might have life, and might have it abundantly" (John 10:10b).
> "As you therefore have received Christ Jesus the Lord so walk in Him" (Colossians 2:6). *We have received Christ by faith and we are admonished to live by faith.*
> YOU HAVE BEEN SAVED FROM THE PENALTY OF SIN (John 3:18; Ephesians 2:8).
> YOU ARE BEING SAVED FROM THE POWER OF SIN (Jude 24, 25; 2 Thessalonians 3:3).
> YOU SHALL BE SAVED FROM THE PRESENCE OF SIN (1 John 3:2; Philippians 3:21; 1 Corinthians 15:51, 52).
> You have trusted God for payment of your penalty for sin and for eternal life. Why not trust Him now for power over sin? Remember that you received Christ by faith, so you should now walk in faith.

At the moment you became a Christian, God not only forgave all your sins, but also gave you all you need to live a victorious

Christian life. *God does not need to do something new — He has already done all that needs to be done.* You need only to take hold of this provision by faith, just as you took hold of forgiveness of sins by faith.

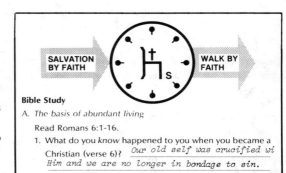

Bible Study

A. *The basis of abundant living*

Read Romans 6:1-16.

1. What do you *know* happened to you when you became a Christian (verse 6)? *Our old self was crucified wi Him and we are no longer in bondage to sin.*

Romans 6:3 says all who have received Jesus Christ were "baptized into His death." This does not refer to water baptism. The word means primarily to dip, immerse or sink. Here it stresses that we were immersed in Christ. We became part of Him, indissolubly joined to Him. In John 15:1-6 Jesus pictures this union with Him as being like the union of a vine and its branches. In 1 Corinthians 12 Paul pictures it as being like the union of a body with its members.

(Ask the group:) What does this spiritual union to Jesus Christ mean? (Discuss their answers, then elaborate as appropriate:) It means that when Christ died, we took part in His death. He paid the penalty for sin and satisfied all of God's demands and sin has no claim on Him whatsoever. Since we were in Him, this now becomes true of us. Sin can make no demands on us. We are free from it just as Christ is.

Since Christ rose from the dead and lives in a resurrected life, this is also true of all who are in Him. We have risen and can now live a resurrected life, a life of victory over sin. "For if we have become united with Him in the likeness of His death, certainly we shall be also in the likeness of His resurrection" (Romans 6:5).

All who are in Christ should live the life which overcomes sin. Christ has paid for your sins; you are free from them. You can live in victory over them through His power. Know these facts from God's Word!

> 2. According to verse 11, what must you do? *Consider ourselves dead to sin but alive to God in Christ.*

Consider yourself dead to sin. Count upon that fact. You are dead to sin and its control. But you say, 'I do not *feel* dead to sin. Sin seems as strong as ever in me." Paul does not say *feel*, he says *consider*. Count upon it in spite of feelings because *you actually* are! Even if you never count on it, you are still dead to sin. You are like a man who has a bank account of thousands of dollars and nevers uses it. It is still his whether he uses it or not.

Victory is not fighting down your wrong desires or concealing your wrong feelings — that is counterfeit. Victorious living is a gift of God. Acknowledge it and thank Him for it.

Consider yourself to be alive to Jesus Christ. A dead man is no good to anyone. Take hold by faith of the fact that you are now alive to Jesus Christ and do not fool yourself into thinking you must help Him accomplish His will in your life.

> 3. What does verse 13 tell you your responsibility is? _____
> *Present--yield--bodies not to sin but to God for*
> *righteousness.*

Have you ever considered why God asks for your "members," that is, your physical body? In Romans 12:1-2 you will find an exhortation similar to this one in verse 13. *The Lord Jesus needs a body prepared for Him now, just as He did while He was on earth.* Our bodies are the only ones He can possess. Galatians 2:20 becomes true in your life, "I have been crucified with Christ; and it is no longer I who live, but Christ."

The only thing that keeps the Lord from operating in your life at 100 percent potential is you. The Lord does not want you to try to live the Christian life. He wants to live it through and for you.

> 4. According to verse 16, man is either a servant of sin or of righteousness.
> What determines his allegiance? *To whomever he*
> *yields himself: to sin or to obedience.*
> What is your choice? _____

We need a proper perspective on life. We must not forfeit the lasting good for the immediate pleasure which passes so quickly. We must count the cost! The Bible says, "Whatever a man sows, this he will also reap" (Galatians 6:7).

There are two powers in the world: God and Satan. Many times we fool ourselves into thinking we are our own rulers when actually we are controlled by Satan. He tries to blind our eyes to the truth, as he has been doing since the creation, and we often are not smart enough to recognize him.

We are to obey God from the heart. You may say, "But my heart is deceitful." When you yield yourself to God, He says He will "give you a new heart . . . and cause you to walk in My statutes" (Ezekiel 36:26-27). Obeying God will become a natural thing, the abundant life for which you were created. If you do these things, "sin shall not be master over you" (Romans 6:14).

> Review Romans 6:6, 11, 13 and 16 and note the progression: *Know* that you have been crucified with Christ; *reckon* yourself dead to sin and alive to Jesus Christ; *yield* yourself unto God; *obey* God. (See Directory of Terms.)
>
> B. *The practice of abundant living*
>   Read Psalm 37:1-7, 34.
>
> 1. What is to be your attitude toward worry (verse 1)? _____
>   *Fret not.*

God wants us to trust Him in all things. When we worry, we show the Lord that we do not believe God really causes "all things to work together for good to those who love God, to those who are called according to His purpose." The saying, "Why pray when you can be sorry?" may be true in many lives, but it is not pleasing to God.

"In everything give thanks, for this is God's will for you in Christ Jesus" (1 Thessalonians 5:18). Try thanking the Lord instead of worrying. Your whole attitude will be changed.

Trust. What does it mean
to trust? The Amplified

2. What is to be your attitude toward the Lord (verse 3)?
   Trust in the Lord.

New Testament defines it as, "confidence in His power, wisdom, and goodness." If
you have confidence in God, you know that His way is best and that He is in
control of your life.

In the Lord. It is one thing to trust someone who is not trustworthy, but quite
another to trust a God who has never, ever failed or let one of His children down.
We can trust because the One in whom we trust is worthy of it. See also
Hebrews 13:5.

Most Christians think if
they just serve God, they'll

3. What must you do to receive the desires of your heart
   (verse 4)? *Delight yourself in the Lord.*

get all they want. But this verse puts first things first. Delight in the Lord *first, then*
He will give you the desires of your heart. You cannot fool God. He "looks upon
the heart" and He knows whether you are "delighting" yourself in Him for
Himself, or for what you can get from Him.

This goes back to "obeying from the heart." God makes it possible when you
yield, or present yourself to Him to delight yourself in Him — making His every
wish your command.

Jesus Christ came to do
the Father's will. When we

4. Why is it necessary to consider verse 5 when you plan
   your future? *God knows beginning and end and
   what's best for us.*

let Jesus Christ live in and through us, He does His will in and through us and God
is glorified in us. This is the greatest privilege we can have in life.

Rest in the Lord. What
can you do when you do

5. How will you comply with the admonishment in verse 7?

not know what God's will is in a certain matter? Rest in Him. Take advantage of
the time of indecision by being with Him. Learn His ways. Memorize His
promises. Do not waste this precious time when you could be learning so much
from Him. Leave the situation in His hands and He will work it out and will always
tell you the answer in time to do what he wants you to do (Hebrews 2:3).

Wait patiently for Him. "Be anxious for nothing, but in everything by prayer and
supplication with thanksgiving let your requests be made known to God"
(Philippians 4:6). Lack of patience is lack of trust and God will often not let you
know His will until you trust His judgment of time as well as will.

6. What does verse 34 mean to you? _____

Now, review each of the above references and note the progression: *Fret not* thyself, *trust* in the Lord, *delight* thyself in the Lord, *commit* thy way unto the Lord, *rest* in the Lord, *wait* on the Lord. (See Directory of Terms.)

The secret of the abundant life is contained in these words: *know, reckon, yield, obey, fret not, trust, delight, commit, rest* and *wait*. (Underline these key words in your Bible in Romans 6 and in Psalm 37.)

Directory of terms:

Know — To be fully assured of a fact.

Reckon — To act upon a fact, to consider it, to depend upon it instead of upon feelings.

Yield — To give up, to surrender, to submit.

Obey — To put instructions into effect, to comply with, to trust.

Trust — To rely on wholeheartedly.

Delight — To take great pleasure or joy.

Commit — To place in trust or charge, to entrust.

Wait — To anticipate with confident expectancy.

Conclusion and Application

God does not call us to a life of victory and abundance and then leave us to find our own victory. He has provided everything we need in His Son Jesus Christ.

Life Application

1. In the chart below, list which key words of the abundant life you are now applying, and which you need to begin to apply, through the power of Christ:

KEY WORDS	APPLYING NOW	NEED TO APPLY
KNOW		
RECKON		
YIELD		
OBEY		
TRUST		
DELIGHT		
COMMIT		
WAIT		

2. How do you plan to go about applying these? Be specific.

_____

_____

Suggested Closing Prayer

Father, we rest in what You have done for us in and through the Lord Jesus Christ. Now we enter by faith into the abundant life which You have provided for us in Him. We are trusting in Him and in His faithfulness alone, not ours.

LESSON FOUR

THE ABIDING LIFE

Teacher's Objective: To bring students to an understanding of the principle of abiding in Christ and of how they can abide in Him more consistently.

Teacher's Enrichment: (May be shared with class as time permits.)

Persecution. Along with all the blessings received from abiding in Christ is another blessing in disguise, persecution. Outward pressures propel us closer to the heart of God if we are abiding in Him.

"All who desire to live godly in Christ Jesus will be persecuted" (2 Timothy 3:12). This is a promise and we should thank the Lord for being able to suffer with Him. Don't look for trouble, but if it comes, accept it as from the Father's hand. Rest in the promise of Romans 8:28 and practice 1 Thessalonians 5:18.

CLASS TIME

Suggested Opening Prayer

Dear Lord, how we long to be conscious of Your presence with us constantly! Teach us today the true meaning of abiding in Christ and the results of such a life.

(Introduction: Be sure students understand
   objective
   memory work
   reading assignment.)

Introduction

OBJECTIVE: To understand and begin *abiding* in Christ.

TO MEMORIZE: John 15:7, 16.

TO READ: John 10-12.

Discussion Starter

(Ask the class:) Have you ever wondered about your life, why there are times when you are not happy and the Lord seems far away? Why do you think that is?

(After a few minutes of discussion, continue with:) There are many keys in Scripture which unlock great experiences. Today we will discuss the key that unlocks joy, real joy, which is full and which remains.

The abiding life is one of the most significant phases of the Christian life. To have real abiding joy, we must learn to abide in Christ constantly. Many people never find the secret to a joyous life; consequently they feel the Lord has let them down. The Christian who is not enjoying his Christian experience should be taught the truth of God's Word. "These things have I spoken unto you that My joy might remain in you, and that your joy

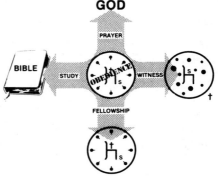

might be full." The abiding life brings lasting joy. Abiding in Christ also makes our lives fruitful; our prayers are answered. We are obedient to Him because He lives in and through us.

Lesson Development

(Have a class member read the above paragraph in the student's book, and then you may want to discuss the diagram briefly.

Have another student read this paragraph at the beginning of the Bible Study and proceed to the questions and answers.)

Bible Study

A. *The abiding life explained*

To abide in Christ is to live in conscious dependence upon Him, recognizing that it is His life, His power, His wisdom, His resources, His strength and His ability, operating through you, which enable you to live according to His will. "I can do all things" through Him who strengthens me," but apart from Him I can do nothing (Philippians 4:13; John 15:5). The Christian believes, "I am strong enough for all things, due to Christ's strength."

1. Jesus referred to Himself as the _vine_ and Christians as the _branches_ in John 15:5. What is the relationship between Christ and you, as illustrated in that verse? _____

2. Why does Jesus prune every branch that bears fruit (John 15:2)? _That is may bear more fruit._

When we abide in the vine, we bear fruit. A branch never worries about fruit bearing. The only thing that can prevent the branch bearing fruit is an obstruction that keeps the sap from flowing through the branch.

Sin obstructs the flow of life through us from the Lord Jesus. God has to prune our lives so as to keep them free from obstruction.

The branch does nothing of its own will, but only what the vine does through it. We as Christians cannot produce in our own strength, but only as we let the life of the vine accomplish His purpose through us.

> What are some experiences that have constituted "pruning" in your life as a Christian? (See Hebrews 12:6; Romans 5:3-5.) _____
> _____

We must abide in Christ to have our prayers answered, as this is how we know the Father's will. Also, we must be in the place of answered

> B. The results of abiding in Christ
> 1. Read John 15:7-11.
>   List two necessary qualifications for effective prayer according to verse 7. _We must abide in Christ, and His words must abide in us._

prayer — abiding in Christ — to receive the answers (John 15:7).

His words must abide in us so that we might know what is in accordance with His will when we pray. He cannot answer any prayer which is contrary to His Word.

> 2. Jesus glorified God. Can you glorify God? How (verse 8)?
>   _By bearing much fruit._

Andrew Murray says, "The most heavily laden branches bow the lowest."

It is with this same infinite, eternal love that Christ invites you to abide

> 3. Christ commands us to continue in His love. How great do you believe this love to be (verse 9)? _As great as the Father's love for Him._

in Him. "I have loved you with an everlasting love" (Jeremiah 31:3). It is a perfect love. It gives all, and holds nothing back. When it was needed, He sacrificed His throne and crown for you. It is an unchangeable love. "Jesus Christ is the same yesterday and today, yes and forever" (Hebrews 13:8).

> How are we to abide in Christ's love (verse 10)? _Keep His commandments._

Faith in His love will enable us to continue in

His love. Let His love permeate your being. By abiding in His love you will learn to trust Him in all circumstances. Meditate upon His love and His care for you as an individual.

A life of overflowing happiness results from abiding in Christ as He

> How do you think the result promised in verse 11 will be revealed in your life today? *Students answer from own present life situations.*

gains more complete possession of every aspect of a person.

The reason many Christians are not joyful is they are not abiding. Those who yield themselves unreservedly to abiding in Christ have a bright and blessed life; their faith comes true — the joy of the Lord is theirs.

Jesus Christ's command

> 4. What has Christ chosen us to do (John 15:16)? *Go and bear fruit.*
>
> What is meant by "fruit"? *Souls of men and women.*

to Peter was, "Follow Me and I will make you to become fishers of men" (Matthew 4:19).

The great blessing of offering to others that which will bless and trans-

> 5. Will you be able to do what Christ expects of you? _____
>
> How do you know? _____

form their lives becomes the lot of the abiding one. We need to have only one care: to abide closely, fully, wholly. God will give the fruit.

As you grow more closely united to Christ, the passion for souls which urged Him to Calvary compels you more and more to devote your life to win the souls Christ teaches you to love, and for whom He died.

> 6. Why do you think Jesus chose this particular way to illustrate our abiding in Him? _____

Conclusion and Application

It takes time to accomplish maturity through growth. Do not expect to abide in Christ unless you give Him that time. You need to meet with Him day by day — to put yourself into living contact with the living Jesus. Fill your heart with His Word; pray at every spare moment acknowledging His presence with and in you.

Confide in Him; live and
dwell in Him. Rely only
upon Him in all circum-
stances of your life. Learn
the secret of the abiding life,
then share it with others that
all Christians may know the
joy of the Christian life.

Life Application

1. Write briefly what you need to do to begin abiding in Christ
   more consistently. _____
   _____

2. What do you think He will do as a result? _____
   _____
   _____

"Abiding is the key to Christian experience by which the
divine attributes are transplanted into human soil, to the trans-
forming of character and conduct."

— Norman B. Harrison

Suggested Closing Prayer

(Give opportunity for
those who have never trusted
Christ, to pray, placing
their faith in Him to come
into their lives and forgive their sin, and live through them from this moment on.

Then for Christians the prayer may be:) Lord, let each of us yield ourselves
wholly to the grace and power of our Savior. Keep us united with Him so that we
will grow. Give us an ever-stronger desire to seek to win others to know Him and
grow in Him also that we may together experience the joy of the Christian life.

ADDITIONAL BACKGROUND MATERIAL

Scofield's definition of abiding in Christ:

> To abide in Christ is, on the one hand, to have no known sin unjudged
> and unconfessed, no interest into which He is not brought, no life
> which He cannot share. On the other hand, the abiding one takes all
> burdens to Him, and draws all wisdom, life and strength from Him.

Notes on above:

"No known sin unjudged or unconfessed" — No one can abide in Christ until
his sin has been forgiven and he has received the righteousness of God by accepting
the Lord Jesus Christ as his personal Savior. Then, as a believer, he must confess sin
as the Holy Spirit makes him aware of it and claim the forgiveness of God through
the blood of Christ.

"No interest into which He is not brought" — This includes every activity in
which you participate. Christ is the sinless Savior and limits Himself exclusively to

doing the will of God. You can only abide in Christ when there is no activity or interest in your life which hinders Him from living His life and doing God's will through you.

"No life which He cannot share" — This refers to any relationship which Christ Himself does not have. Joining yourself to someone who is not abiding in Christ causes Him to be joined to one with whom He cannot have fellowship. He has told us not to be united with lawlessness (2 Corinthians 6:14-18), for then He cannot live His life through us because we have cut off the source of power by sin (disobedience). In order for us to have fellowship with the Lord, *every* relationship we have must be shared by Him. We are *in* the world but we must follow our Savior's example and not be *of* the world. We are to be witnesses to those of the non-Christian world but we are to avoid entangling alliances with them.

"The abiding one takes all burdens to Him" — That person does not carry his burdens for himself. Jesus Christ lives completely in and through him, taking all responsibility on Himself. Next time you find yourself carrying your own burdens, just remind yourself that you are abiding in Christ. He wants to live His life through you and He cannot as long as you are doing anything — even carrying your own burdens.

"Draws all wisdom, life and strength from Him" — To abide in Christ is to receive all the power to live the Christian life from Him. Let Him teach you from His Word. Your life comes from God; your life is His. Let Him live! Even your strength comes from Him. The times when you feel you cannot go on, He says, "Let me be your strength." See 2 Corinthians 12:9.

LESSON FIVE

THE CLEANSED LIFE

Teacher's Objective: To teach the reality of moment-by-moment cleansing from sin (forgiveness) through immediate confession.

Teacher's Enrichment: (May be shared with class as time permits.)

Some of the benefits of fellowship with God are pardon, purpose, peace, joy, power, fruitfulness, etc. Some of the penalties of sin in the life are separation from God, frustration, insecurity, no power, no joy, no peace, no fruit. The value of constant cleansing rests in fellowship with Christ and Christians, according to 1 John 1:15-10.

God uses only those vessels which are cleansed and filled. The smallest sin will break fellowship with God and thus render us impotent and unfruitful for Christ. We must immediately confess our sins to Him. We must set our affections on things above. It is not enough to empty our lives of former practices which we feel are not pleasing to God; we must let Him fill our lives with His presence and with friends and deeds which are pleasing to Him. We must saturate ourselves with Him if we desire to be faithful Christians.

CLASS TIME

Suggested Opening Prayer

Lord, we ask You today to teach us how to abide moment by moment in Your presence.

(Introduction: Be sure students understand objective memory work* reading assignment.)

> **Introduction**
>
> OBJECTIVE: To learn the importance and means of living a cleansed life, moment by moment.
>
> TO MEMORIZE: 1 John 1:9.
>
> TO READ: John 13-15.

(*Go around the group having each person take one word of the verse and explain.)

Discussion Starter

The Christian life on earth is a victorious life, but we are not perfect. When we became Christians, God united us with Christ, made us new creatures, gave us His Holy Spirit, but He also left us with the same sin nature we had before we accepted Christ. When Christ comes again we will receive a new body and at last lose our sin nature, but until then it will be constantly with us. We see in 1 John 1:8, "If we say that we have no sin, we are deceiving ourselves, and the truth is not in us." Why do you think God has not taken it away?

(Allow a few minutes for students to talk about this, then proceed as appropriate:) Let's look at 2 Corinthians 4:7. It tells us, "We have this treasure in earthen vessels, that the surpassing greatness of the power may be of God, and not of us." God has left us with these "earthen vessels" for a short while that we might live and walk by faith and demonstrate His power. It would be nothing for Him to use strong, well-equipped vessels to do great tasks. But to use weak, sinful vessels like us to accomplish great works is more to His glory, and the "power is of Him and not of us."

Lesson Development

(Have someone in the group read the paragraph just above the diagram in the student's book.)

God does not fill a dirty vessel with His power and love. Cleansing precedes filling. We often yearn for spiritual power and do not have it because of impure motives, double motives or unconfessed sin. To be filled vessels, we must be cleansed vessels.

This lesson explains how your life can have power. The first step is to be cleansed from sin and filled with the Spirit of God.

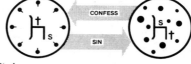

Bible Study

A. *Being "out of fellowship" with God*

Study the diagram at the beginning of this lesson:

1. What characterizes a person who is not in fellowship with God (James 1:8)? *He is double minded, unstable.*

Instability is a result of being double minded. A person who is trying to serve two gods, who sits on the fence, and who compromises to fit each situation in which he finds himself, is unstable.

In 1 Kings 18:21, Elijah said, "How long will you hesitate between two opinions? If the Lord is God, follow Him; but if Baal, follow him." *Don't be double minded!*

2. Read Isaiah 59:2. What is the result of sin in one's life? *Separation from God, God's face hidden, God does not hear person's prayers.*

Even the smallest sin denies us the joy of fellowship with our Lord.

As an illustration, suppose you are dating someone and a minor problem comes up. You know how it goes — a little thing can come between you and if it's not dealt with, it soon builds a big wall and you can't get through to each other. There is no fellowship, no communication.

The Lord does not answer our prayers when we have sin in our lives. "If I regard wickedness in my heart, the Lord will not hear" (Psalm 66:18).

The more sin we allow in our lives, the more miserable we are. God feels all of this with us and longs for us to come immediately for cleansing that we might walk together as before.

3. Do you think sin in your life has affected your relationship with God? _____ How? _____
_____
_____

B. *How to be cleansed*

1. What is the condition for cleansing and forgiveness (1 John 1:9)? _____

The word "confess" means to "say the same thing as another — to agree with God." When God brings to your attention the fact that something you have done is sin, you are to confess — agree with God — say the same thing that God says about it. Do not just say, "I have sinned," but state what the sin was and agree with God, looking at it from His viewpoint. Then determine that you will put it out of your life and will not do it again.

A man who had been a wonderful Christian for many years was telling another man that he had never known an hour of defeat in his fifty years of Christian life. "What!" said the other man in astonishment, "You have never known any defeat in your Christian life?"

"No, I didn't put it that way," said the first man. "I've known *moments* of defeat, but never an hour. I always get back into fellowship immediately by confessing my sin and claiming a promise from God's Word — 1 John 1:9."

2. What two things did the psalmist do about his sin in Psalm 32:5? *Acknowledged and confessed it; acknowledged God's forgiveness.*

It is impossible to hide our sin from God. He is aware of all that we do. Someone may ask, "Then why do we have to confess to Him, if He already knows?" The answer is that, in God's mercy, He provided for our forgiveness because we could never make up for the sins we commit. It takes faith in His provision to believe that He cleanses us, completely apart from anything we can do. God is glorified by our acknowledging His forgiveness.

We in our own strength cannot "forsake" our sins. By faith we must accept from Christ our victory over temptation. Christ is faithful, and it is His responsibility to accomplish this miracle in our lives as we confess and abide in Him. He is always true to His responsibility toward us.

According to Proverbs 28:13, what is the result of not admitting sin? *The person will not prosper.*

Of admitting sin? *Will find compassion.*

C. *Living "in fellowship" with God*

1. Notice in the diagram that, when we confess our sins, God restores us to fellowship. Walking in fellowship with the Father and the Son is referred to as "walking in the light." Read 1 John 1:7 and list two results promised: *Fellowship with one another; cleansing from sin.*

Purpose, peace, power and joy are the result of being in fellowship with God. Inner stability and all the qualities of Christ become ours because we are in Him.

Almighty God Himself lives, moves and has His being in and through us.

All power in heaven and in earth is ours. We have a life that has power because it is cleansed and filled with the Holy Spirit of God.

2. When we are in fellowship with God, some things are happening within us. According to Philippians 2:13 and 4:13 what are they? *God is at work in us; He wills and works for His good pleasure; we can do all things because He strengthens us.*

3. What is this power within us and what is its result (Romans 8:9; Galatians 5:22, 23)? *Spirit of God—Spirit of Christ—Holy Spirit; spiritual fruit.*

4. What should be our attitude when temptations come (Romans 6:11-13)? *Students discuss.*

Why (Colossians 3:3)? _____

What responses does that make possible? _____

Jesus manifests Himself to those who are obedient to His comands (John 14:21).

Conclusion and Application

Confession of sin means agreeing with God concerning our sin, recognizing His opinion of the sin. Confession suggests a willingness to repent, to turn from going our way to going God's way. We name the sin to God, and we want it dealt with now. As we continue to claim 1 John 1:9, we are going to do one of two things. Either we will stop that sin, or we will stop praying.

Life Application

1. In your own words write what you will do when you find anything that breaks the fellowship between you and the Lord. _____

2. Summarize the reasons it is so important to confess sin as soon as you are aware of it. _____

3. List any sin in your life right now which needs to be confessed. Then, confess the sin, and thank God for His complete forgiveness. _____

Suggested Closing Prayer

Lord teach us that, because of the price You paid on Calvary, we can have forgiveness moment by moment and can abide in You. May our lives show forth the victory of the Lord Jesus and we pray our every act will be in accordance with Your will.

(Say to the class:) Perhaps you have never appropriated the cleansing power of the blood of Jesus Christ. Maybe you have never asked Him to forgive your sin, to come into your life and live in and through you. Wouldn't you like to invite Him to come into your life now?

On the authority of Revelation 3:20, He promises to come into your life. Isaiah 1:18 says, "Though your sins are as scarlet they will be as white as snow; though they are red like crimson, they will be like wool." Won't you accept His forgiveness for your sin now?

(Allow time for a brief silent prayer.) Did you ask Christ to come into your heart and cleanse you of your sin? If you were sincere, you may be sure that He came in and you have been forgiven. Now, thank Him for what He has done for you. And come and tell me what you have done that I may rejoice with you and help you in your Christian growth.

ADDITIONAL BACKGROUND MATERIAL

Some parallel passages of Scripture which will help in the study of the cleansed life:

James 1:14-15 — form in which sin begins.

1 Corinthians 10:13 — no excuse for succumbing.

Psalm 24:3-4 — must be cleansed to glorify God.

Isaiah 53:5 — price paid for forgiveness of sin.

Galatians 6:7-8 — future result of sin in life now.

Psalm 32:1-5 — example of David in sin.

SUGGESTED SUPPLEMENTARY READING

Full Surrender — J. Edwin Orr
Victory in Christ — Charles G. Trumbull

LESSON SIX

THE CHRISTIAN ARMOR AND WARFARE

Teacher's Objective: To bring students to an awareness of spiritual warfare, and to teach them how to use the armor God has provided.

CLASS TIME

Suggested Opening Prayer

Lord, open our eyes to the real issues of life and help us to understand how we can be more than conquerors through Christ.

(Introduction: Be sure students understand
  objective
  memory work
  reading assignment.)

> **Introduction**
>
> OBJECTIVE: To learn of spiritual warfare and how to use the things God has provided for the battle.
>
> TO MEMORIZE: Ephesians 6:10-12.
>
> TO READ: John 16-18.

Discussion Starter

(Have students read Ephesians 6:10-18. Then have them close their Bibles and study books. Give them paper and pencils and have them write down all the pieces of armor they can remember.)

Lesson Development

The Bible teaches very clearly that the Christian life is not only a walk, but also a warfare. Many Christians do not realize this. They think living the Christian life means escaping all trials, difficulties and temptations, and they expect to glide through their years on earth with scarcely a problem.

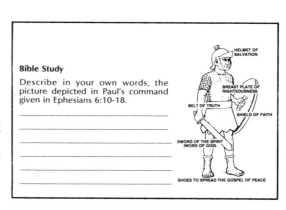

Bible Study

Describe in your own words, the picture depicted in Paul's command given in Ephesians 6:10-18.

_____
_____
_____
_____
_____
_____
_____

HELMET OF SALVATION

BREAST PLATE OF RIGHTEOUSNESS

BELT OF TRUTH

SHIELD OF FAITH

SWORD OF THE SPIRIT (WORD OF GOD)

SHOES TO SPREAD THE GOSPEL OF PEACE

The truth is, though, that we are strangers and pilgrims on this earth
(1 Peter 2:11), living in a world ruled by Satan, and we repeatedly face opposition
and difficulty. The Christian life should be a victorious one, but it is not always
easy. We continually must be strengthened "in the Lord and in the strength of His
might" (Ephesians 6:10).

(Assign to each student present one question relative to the Christian spiritual
warfare and allow time for each to look up his passage and find the answer. Then
give each student an opportunity to answer his assigned question at the
appropriate time.)

There are so many
philosophies, false doctrines,
etc., that would mislead us.
Our only defense is to put

> A. *We are on the battlefield*
> 1. What two things will putting on the whole armor of God
>   help you to do (verses 11-13)? _Stand firm against_
>   _the schemes of the devil; resist in the_
>   _evil day._

on the whole armor of God. Each piece, as we study them later in the lesson, must
be in place before we can expect the Lord Jesus to fight for us.

The *world* consists of all
non-Christian humanity. It
is ruled by Satan. It will
ridicule us and try to get us

> 2. Christians are engaged in warfare.
>
> | Who are the enemies? | | How should you respond to these enemies? | |
> |---|---|---|---|
> | James 4:4 | _World_ | Romans 12:2 | _Don't conform_ |
> | Galatians 5:17 | _Flesh_ | Galatians 5:16 | _Walk in Spirit_ |
> | 1 Peter 5:8 | _Devil_ | James 4:7 | _Resist_ |

to live by its standards. But the Bible says, "Set your mind on the things above, not
on the things that are on earth" (Colossians 3:2). The Christian must not be
conformed to this world (Romans 12:2), and he is not to love the world
(1 John 2:15). The world, with all its pleasures and allurements, will pass away. The
Christian is living with eternal values in mind, not temporary ones. Why live for
that which you won't be able to enjoy for more than a few years? Why waste your
time and energy on that which is fleeting, old and hollow?

The *flesh* is our old sin nature. God has left it with us and it is always hostile
toward Him (Romans 8:7). Paul said that nothing good dwelt in his flesh
(Romans 7:18). Our sin nature will always tempt us, always assert itself, always try
to entice us away from God. We can never trust it, not even for a moment. But we
can have victory over it. Romans 6:11 says we must consider ourselves, that is,
count upon the fact, that we are dead to sin. When we realize that God judged the
flesh on the cross, and that it no longer has control over us, we can overcome it.
We are to rest in the victory God gave at the cross.

Satan, or the *devil,* our third enemy, is the strongest power in the universe next
to God. Satan is alive and active, but he is nevertheless a defeated foe. John 12:31
tells us he was defeated at the cross although he continually tries to frighten the
Christian. We conquer him by being strong *in the Lord.*

We have no strength ourselves to match his, no cunning, no wisdom by which we can outwit him. He will defeat us every time. But when we trust in God and not ourselves, when we rely on God's strength and not our own, we have victory. No Christian need ever fear the devil.

Whenever Satan attacks, we are to resist him in God's strength and he must flee (James 4:7). When we pray, we should claim God's victory over him at the cross, and he will be driven out. The Christian, in the name of Jesus Christ, has the right and privilege of trampling the devil, with all his power, underfoot. Christ defeated Satan at the cross — victory has already been announced with the resurrection of Jesus Christ from the dead. The need is to act upon these facts, and by faith claim the victory in the name of Christ.

Loins girded with truth — In New Testament times, soldiers used a 6-8 inch belt

> 3. Name the five protective pieces of armor God provides and expects you to wear (Ephesians 6:14-17). _____
> _____ *See diagram*

to gather up their flowing garments and as a foundation upon which to hang their swords and other weapons. The belt facilitated movement for the soldier in battle. Truth (Jesus Christ) is the Christian's belt that facilitates movement in the Christian's warfare. Knowing the truth frees us from sin and allows us to obey the call of our new Captain, Jesus Christ, in this great battle in which we are engaged. See John 14:6, 8:32 and 8:36.

Breastplate of Righteousness — Jesus frees us from the penalty of our sin. We can fight the good fight because He is our righteousness. See 2 Corinthians 5:21 and Romans 3:22.

Feet shod with the Gospel of Peace — We were at war with God but now are reconciled to Him and at peace. We are free from condemnation. This is the message we should take with us wherever we go. Every step you take should bear the news — the Gospel of Peace. See 1 Corinthians 15:1 and 3-4, Philippians 4:7, and Romans 5:1.

Shield of Faith — We take the faith of Jesus Christ which is free from doubt. He is always faithful. We fight in His strength, knowing "The battle is the Lord's" (2 Chronicles 20:15). See also Galatians 2:20 and 2 Timothy 2:13.

Helmet of Salvation — Jesus Christ Himself becomes our salvation. Being assured of our salvation gives us the confidence we need to fight the battle. See Acts 15:11 and 2 Peter 1:10.

Sword of the Spirit — This is the weapon that the Holy Spirit uses to convict the hearts of men and

> 4. How can you employ the sword of God's Word (verse 17) for defense against temptation (Psalm 119:9, 11)? *Keep one's way according to Word, treasure it in heart; OR memorize it and live it.*

women, not our brilliant oratory, our persuasiveness, etc., but the Word of God. Learn it from cover to cover. Learn the answer to every problem you face by searching its pages. This is your only offense. Use it always!

Which is the Word of God — We can expect no conviction of sin or awareness of the need for the Savior apart from the Word — the *Spirit* uses the sword. He does not say to us, "See how good *you* are."

> 5. List some ways the sword of God's Word can be used in an offensive action (2 Timothy 3:16, 17). *Teaching, reproof, correction, training in righteousness.*

Teaching — The sword of God's Word is the Christian's source of teaching or doctrine. The victorious Christian knows the Word of God and applies it to everyday experiences.

Reproof — To reprove is to rebuke a person for wrong words or actions. We should always use the Word of God when showing someone that a part of his life is displeasing to the Lord. It should not be just our opinion.

Correction — Through the Word of God we can correct errors of doctrine taught by others. If we give our own opinion, theirs is as good as ours. Always use the Word of God to correct error.

Instruction in Righteousness — The Bible is the *Holy* Bible. It alone has the perfect standard of righteousness. Someone has well said, "God's Word will keep you from sin, or sin will keep you from God's Word."

> 6. How can you stay alert and always be prepared (Ephesians 6:18; Colossians 4:2)? *By being always in prayer.*

That does not mean we must be always on our knees but we can be continually in an attitude of prayer. The battle is fought by the Lord Jesus Christ, but we allow Him to fight through us by yielding ourselves to Him in prayer.

Then we must watch for the enemy and the opportunities for offensive attack. We must "keep on keeping on." Be aware of the battle, and be constant in your prayer to Him who fights for you.

> B. We are more than conquerors through Christ!
> 1. When you consider the pieces of armor and weapons provided, who can you conclude is really fighting the battle (Ephesians 6:10)? *The Lord.*

Jesus Christ, the "captain of our salvation," is fighting our battle and he has already won the victory. We fight *from* victory, not *toward* victory.

When you take over and fight in your own strength, you cannot win the battle. If you lose, you know that you have taken over. God ordained that you "stand and see the salvation of the *Lord* on your behalf" (2 Chronicles 20:17).

Not from any merit or
ability on our part do we

> 2. Why can you always expect God to be the winner (1 John
> 4:4)? *"Greater is He (Holy Spirit) who is in*
> *you than he who is in the world."*

win in this battle, but through the strength of the Lord. He defeated Satan at the
cross, and has given us all we need to be "more than conquerors." We are to
march forward, as soldiers of Christ, claiming victory by His strength and His
power. See 1 John 5:4.

> 3. What does Romans 8:31 suggest to you regarding your
> attitude toward adversity and temptation? *If God is*
> *for us, no one can win against us.*

Conclusion and Application

What a thrill to be in the army of the Living God! Great men and women of
the past have died on the battlefield for the Lord Jesus Christ. Today we find few
who are willing to live for
Him. You can believe Him
for the victory in the battles
of your life right now. He
has the power to overcome
any habit or problem in
your life.

> **Life Application**
> 1. Describe a specific situation in your life right now in which
>   you need to employ a spiritual "weapon." _____
>   _____
> 2. Which weapon(s) will you use and how? _____
> 3. What result(s) do you expect? _____
>   _____

Suggested Closing Prayer

Oh God, make us aware that we are on the battlefield for You. Discipline us in
our stewardship of the armor and the weapons You have given us, that we may
have victory over the world, over our own flesh, and over Satan. Make us more
than conquerors through our Lord Jesus Christ.

SUPPLEMENTARY READING

Bone of His Bone — Huegel
Fox's Book of Martyrs

LESSON SEVEN

ATTITUDE

Teacher's Objective: To show students how to look at life from God's perspective and to lead them to begin trusting God and thanking Him for all situations.

Teacher's Enrichment: Read 1 Samuel 17:31-58 for the account of David as an example of trusting God in a potentially frightening situation.

Read Job 1:1-22; 13:15; 42:12a for an example of learning to trust God in extreme suffering and to see things from God's point of view.

CLASS TIME

Suggested Opening Prayer

Lord, we thank You for making it possible for us to look at our circumstances through Your eyes. Enable us by Your grace always to possess Your divine point of view concerning the issues of our lives.

(Introduction: Be sure students understand
  objective
  memory work
  reading assignment.)

> **Introduction**
>
> OBJECTIVE: To begin to look at life consistently from God's perspective.
>
> TO MEMORIZE: 2 Corinthians 1:3, 4.
>
> TO READ: John 19-21.

Discussion Starter

(Use this question from the student's book to start the discussion today.)

> **W**hen two Christians face the same tragedy, one may become depressed and defeated while the other is drawn closer to God. What do you think is the reason for this? _____
> _____
> _____

Lesson Development

Victory or defeat occurs in the mind before it occurs any place else. God has

> In this study you will learn about unrecognized blessings. Sometimes Christians feel that God has let them down when they find themselves without money, health, prestige, or in severe straits. Such an attitude leads to coldness of heart, prayerlessness, distrust, worry and selfish living. Attitude makes the difference.

called on us to win the battle of maintaining a correct mental attitude first. See Proverbs 23:7.

The Bible tells us "perfect love casts out fear" (1 John 4:18). If the Israelites had loved God

Bible Study

A. *God's people in trouble*

In Exodus 14:1-4, the Israelites experienced an unrecognized blessing. As you read, notice the human viewpoint of the people and God's viewpoint as seen in Moses.

1. How did the Israelites react to apparent danger (Exodus 14:10-12)? *They became very frightened.*

sincerely they would have trusted Him and not been seized with fear.

Their fear led to torment. They began to gripe — to Moses and to the Lord. They were discontented because they were not still in Egypt where they had been in bondage. How true this is to human nature. We remember the good of the past, but not the bad.

Moses was in the same situation as the others, but he trusted God while they

2. Notice how Moses reacted. Why do you think he commanded the people as he did (Exodus 14:13, 14)? *Discuss students' ideas.*

doubted. He gave the glory to God! He told the people to watch what God would do. God was Moses' only hope. And He did not let him down!

The people were allowed to see God in action! It is so thrilling to be present when God does a mighty work.

3. State the blessings God wrought in their hearts and minds through this experience (Exodus 14:31). *They learned to fear and believe God and to believe Moses.*

God must teach us to trust Him, it is not a part of our nature. When everything is going well, we often do not credit God, but our own ingenuity. He has to bring us to the place where we recognize that we cannot do anything in our own wisdom and strength — then He moves in and works. See Psalm 37:5 and 1 Peter 5:7.

We often think we are enduring something no one else ever has. Yet we can learn important lessons and gain real comfort from others who have been through the same trial.

That we will not be tempted above what we are

4. List some ways God has worked through difficulties in your life, and has shown these difficulties really to be blessings. _____

B. *Taking the proper attitude*

1. List some things the Bible guarantees when you are tempted or tested (1 Corinthians 10:13). *Our temptation is common to all. God won't let it be too great for us; He will provide a way of escape; we will be able to endure it.*

able to withstand is a fact written by God. It is never right to think we cannot endure the temptation. If we had not been able to resist a particular thing, God would not have allowed us to be tempted in that way.

To find the way to escape, the Christian should immediately go to God's word. When we do not seek His answer to the problem, we fall deeper into the temptation.

God promises that we will be able to bear it. Always remember that we can "do all things through Him who strengthens" us (Philippians 4:13). All power in heaven and earth is ours. We have all the resources we will ever need in Jesus Christ.

(Ask the group:) Does Romans 8:28 refer to everyone?

> 2. How can the Bible's guarantee in Romans 8:28 about *everything* you will experience be true? _____
>
> _____

(After giving them a chance to respond, continue as appropriate:) It is qualified to include those "who love God." Love for God brings trust. Therefore you know that whatever comes is under the Father's control.

The second qualification is "those who are called according to His purpose." God's purpose is fulfilled in those who are yielded to Him. Until we come to the point in our lives where we can accept His will, we will not see His perfect will being accomplished.

Why do suffering, heartbreak and tragedy come into a Christian's life? Philippians 1:29 says, "It has been granted for Christ's sake, not only to believe in Him, but also to suffer for His sake." These things come *to accomplish God's*

> 3. What response to tribulation does God expect from you according to Romans 5:3-5? _____
>   _____ *We are to exult in them.*
>
>   What are the results of tribulations? (See also James 1:3.)
>   *Perseverance and endurance, proven*
>   _____ *character, hope.*
>
> 4. Give the Bible's explanation of the purpose of unrecognized blessings in:
>   2 Corinthians 1:3, 4 _ *So we can comfort others.*
>   Hebrews 12:6-11 *That we may share His holiness,*
>   *be trained by the discipline, receive the*
>   *peaceful fruit of righteousness.*

divine purpose. All sunshine and no rain creates a desert. *To mold our Christian character,* God must not only give us times of blessing and encouragement, but also allow times of trouble and difficulty. Most of us feel these are to be escaped at all costs, but God does not always intend for us to escape.

In times of trial we *learn to trust God and draw close to Him.* We learn of the comfort He can give; we learn of the provision He can make; and we learn how weak and self-centered we really are. We learn to see God's power in a new way.

Suffering sometimes comes *to expose a rebellious attitude.* The world can see no meaning in suffering, no purpose for it; but for the Christian it is the hand of a loving God, who is tenderly disciplining His children, sending a blessing in disguise. Learn to accept God's victory in suffering and difficulties.

What is the advantage in "giving thanks in all things"? First of all, we acknowledge

> 5. Read 1 Thessalonians 5:18 and Hebrews 13:15.
> What response does God command in *all* situations?
> <u>Give thanks.</u>
> _____

God's authority in our lives. We show our trust in His faithfulness. As Moses did, we see the glory of God manifested, and enjoy it because we look for His way out rather than our own.

Then, we understand more clearly when we think from God's point of view, Thanking Him reminds us that He is in control of the situation. We don't have to fall apart trying to manufacture an answer.

The person who is looking for the good is always quicker to find it.

> How can you rejoice and give thanks when sorrow and tragedy come? _____
> _____
>
> Describe how this contrasts with the attitude of the Israelites in Exodus 14:1-12. _____
> _____

Conclusion and Application

This is one of the greatest lessons we can learn in the Christian life — to give thanks in all things — and it can change the course of our lives. We need to stay in such close fellowship with the Lord that we will have His mind in all circumstances.

> **Life Application**
>
> 1. List the methods by which an attitude of trust can become a reality for you. (See Ephesians 5:18; Galatians 5:16; 1 Thessalonians 5:17; Romans 10:17.) <u>Be filled with the Spirit, walk by the Spirit, pray without ceasing, study God's Word.</u>
>
> 2. With what trial in your life do you need to trust God right now? _____
> _____
>
> 3. What do you think the unrecognized blessings in that trial could be? _____
> _____
> _____
>
> 4. How can you appropriate those blessings? _____
> _____

Suggested Closing Prayer

Lord, teach us Your viewpoint concerning all things in our lives. Help us look at them as You do. Make our witness positive every moment because we are trusting You, and let the world see the steadfastness and faith of a real believer as we trust Your love in testings and sufferings.

LESSON EIGHT

RECAP

Teacher's Objective: To review the concept of the Christian life being one that can be lived successfully only by allowing Christ to live in the believer, to intensify the individual students' appreciation of that life and to go over again the methods involved in attaining that life of victory and joy; to be sure the students understand the facts of these lessons, the new versus the old life, the meaning of the four kinds of soil, how to be cleansed of sin and filled with power, the Christian's armor and how to use it for victory over the world, the flesh and the devil.

CLASS TIME

Suggested Opening Prayer

Father, we thank You for what You have taught us in this study on the Christian and the abundant life. As we go through the Recap today, we pray that these truths will become an important part of our lives and that we will have the power to live victoriously no matter what the circumstances. Help us to realize anew and to remember that the power comes only from You.

(Introduction:

Students' objective is to review and understand what has been learned, and to appropriate it to their own lives according to their needs.

Memory work: Be sure every person in the group knows and understands John 10:10b.

Encourage members to reread the passages indicated.)

> Review verses memorized.
>
> Reread: Luke 8:4-5; Romans 6:1-16; John 15:1-17; 1 John 1:1-9.

Discussion Starter

(Ask for and discuss any questions group members may have about any of the material covered in the previous seven lessons.)

Lesson Development

(Talk about the Recap and the students' responses to the questions included.)

> In your own words, what does the abundant Christian life involve? _____
> _____
> _____
> _____

159

Envision the abundant life you desire for yourself and describe
it. _____

_____

_____

_____

How do you know your picture of the abundant life is consistent
with God's view? _____

_____

_____

**Conclusion
and Application**

What specific steps do you still need to take to make that life a
reality for you? _____

A careful, prayerful,
sincere study of these great

_____

truths will, if claimed in

_____

faith, change your life so
that you will never be the
same. These are the keys which unlock the door to a full and abundant Christian
life. A key is no good unless it is used. Search the Scriptures diligently and make
these great doctrines true in your everyday experience.

Suggested Closing Prayer

God, make us willing to take the time to apply these great truths from Your
Word to our lives. May we enter the abundant life to give glory to You.

(Invite non-Christians to receive Christ, stressing His Lordship.)

THE CHRISTIAN AND THE ABUNDANT LIFE
SUMMARY LESSON PLAN

Teacher's Objective: To introduce students to the concept of the abundant Christian life which is possible only by allowing Christ to live within the believer; to awaken the individual student's appreciation of that life and to present methods involved in attaining a life of victory and joy; to motivate the students toward making the commitments necessary in order to have that abundant life.

Teacher's Enrichment: (See Teacher's Enrichment sections in each of the lessons of this Step, and share that material with the class as time permits.)

CLASS TIME

Suggested Opening Prayer

Father, we thank You for meeting with us today. We pray that as we study these truths about the Christian and the abundant life, they will become an important part of our lives and we will have the power to live victoriously no matter what the circumstances. Help us to realize and to remember that the power comes only from You.

(Introduction:

STUDENTS' OBJECTIVE: To understand the abundant life and how it is available to the individual, and to make the commitments that are necessary to live that life of victory.

TO MEMORIZE: John 10:10b and 2 Corinthians 5:17.

READING ASSIGNMENT: Luke 8:4-5; Romans 6:1-16; John 15:1-11; 1 John 1:9.)

Discussion Starter

(Ask the group members for their answers to these two questions:) How would you define a person who is living an abundant Christian life? What qualities would that person have?

Lesson Development

To be in Christ is to have new life. It is God's desire, according to John 10:10, for everyone who has this new life to have it in abundance. There are many professing Christians who are defeated and discouraged, but this is not what God desires for us. What is the secret? How do we have that abundant life? What is involved in it? These are the things our study will cover today.

A. The nature of the new life in Christ as described in 2 Corinthians 5:17 *(from Lesson 1)*.

    1. How is it obtained (John 3:3)? (Through the new birth.)

    2. How is this accomplished (John 3:6 and 1:12-13)? (Through the Spirit and according to the will of God.)

    3. What can you do to earn this new birth (Ephesians 2:8-9)? (Nothing but receive it.)

B. The four types of soil *(from Lesson 2)*. Read Luke 8:4-15. (Also found in Matthew 13:1-23 and Mark 4:3-20.)

    1. Describe each of the four types of soil and what they refer to:

        (1) Roadside soil — unreceptive heart, Satan takes seed away.

        (2) Rocky — receives Word with joy, but is weak, easily destroyed by affliction.

        (3) Thorny — hears and accepts Word and continues for a while, but is choked out by cares of the world.

        (4) Good — hears Word, understands, perseveres to fruit-bearing.

    2. Which of these best describes your life?

C. The secret of abundant life *(from Lesson 3)*. Read Romans 6:1-16.

At the moment you became a Christian, God not only forgave all your sins, but also gave you all you need to live a victorious Christian life. *God does not need to do something new — He has already done all that needs to be done.* You need only to take hold of this provision by faith, just as you took hold of forgiveness of sins by faith.

When Christ died, we took part in His death. He paid the penalty for sin and satisfied all of God's demands and sin has no claim on Him whatsoever. Since we are in Him, this now becomes true of us. Sin can make no demands on us. We are free from it just as Christ is.

Christ rose from the dead and lives in a resurrected life, so this is also true of all who are in Him. We can now live a life of victory over sin. "For if we have become united with Him in the likeness of His death, certainly we shall be also in the likeness of His resurrection" (Romans 6:5).

Consider yourself dead to sin. Count upon that fact. You are dead to sin and its control.

D. The abiding life *(from Lesson 4)*. Read John 15:1-11.

    1. Jesus referred to Himself as the *(vine)* and Christians as the *(branches)* in John 15:5.

When we abide in the vine, we bear fruit. A branch never worries about fruit bearing. The only thing that can prevent the branch bearing fruit is an obstruction that keeps the sap from flowing through the branch. Sin obstructs the flow of life through us from the Lord Jesus. God has to prune our lives so as to keep them free from obstruction.

The branch does nothing of its own will, but only what the vine does through it. We as Christians cannot produce in our own strength, but only as we let the life of the vine accomplish His purpose through us.

2. What two qualifications are necessary for effective prayer according to verse 7? (1. We must abide in Christ. 2. His words must abide in us.)

3. How do we abide in Him (verse 10)? (Keep His commandments.)

E. The cleansed life *(from Lesson 5)*.

1. What is the result of sin in one's life (Isaiah 59:2)? (Separation from God; His face hidden; He does not hear the prayers.)

2. How are we to be cleansed of sin (1 John 1:9)? (Confess.)

It is impossible to hide our sin from God. He is aware of all that we do. Someone may ask, "Then why do we have to confess to Him, if He already knows?"

> The word "confess" means to "say the same thing as another — to agree with God." When God brings to your attention the fact that something you have done is sin, you are to confess — agree with God — say the same thing that God says about it. Do not just say, "I have sinned," but state what the sin was and agree with God, looking at it from His viewpoint. Then determine that you will put it out of your life and will not do it again.

The answer is that, in God's mercy, He provided for our forgiveness because we could never make up for the sins we commit. It takes faith in His provision to believe that He cleanses us, completely apart from anything we can do. God is glorified by our acknowledging His forgiveness.

3. What would be the result of cleansing from sin?

(1 John 1:7 — fellowship with God; Galatians 5:16 — we would be walking by the Spirit; Galatians 5:22,23 — we would produce the fruit of the Spirit.)

F. The Christian's Armor *(from Lesson 6)*. Read Ephesians 6:10-18.

The Bible teaches that the Christian life is not only a walk, but also a warfare. We are living in a world ruled by Satan, and we repeatedly face opposition and difficulty. The Christian life should be victorious, but that is not always easy.

1. Who are our enemies?

(James 4:4 — the world; Galatians 5:17 — the flesh; 1 Peter 5:8 — the devil.

2. How do we overcome them? (By applying these Scriptures to our lives: the world — Romans 12:2; the flesh — Romans 6:11 and Galatians 5:16; the devil — James 4:7.)

3. Name the five protective pieces of armour and the weapon God provides and expects you to wear and use as listed in Ephesians 6:10-18.

G. Attitudes *(from Lesson 7)*.

1. How do we usually instinctively react to danger? (In fear.)

     How can we be victorious over that attitude of fear (1 John 4:18 and 1 Peter 5:7)?

2. How does 1 Corinthians 10:13 teach us we can handle temptations? (We can trust God's judgment in what He allows and look to Him for our way of escape.)

3. What are some of the results of tribulations when we are trusting God? (James 1:3 — development of perseverance, endurance, character, hope; 2 Corinthians 1:3,4 — ability to comfort others; Hebrews 12:10 — share His holiness, trained by discipline, receive the peaceful fruit of righteousness.)

Conclusion and Application

A careful, prayerful, sincere study of these great truths will, if claimed in faith, change your life so that you will never be the same. These are the keys which unlock the door to a full and abundant Christian life. A key is no good unless it is used. Search the Scriptures diligently and make these great doctrines true in your everyday experience.

(Discuss as appropriate these questions which appear in the Recap in the student's handbook.)

> In your own words, what does the abundant Christian life involve? _____
> _____
> _____
> What specific steps do you still need to take to make that life a reality for you? _____
> _____
> _____

Suggested Closing Prayer

God, make us willing to take the time to apply these great truths from Your Word to our lives. May we enter the abundant life to give glory to You.

(Invite non-Christians to receive Christ, stressing especially His Lordship.)

STEP THREE

The Christian
and the Holy Spirit

TEACHER: The article, "You Shall Receive Power," appearing in the opening pages of the Step Three booklet *(The Christian and the Holy Spirit)* of the *Ten Basic Steps Toward Christian Maturity* and beginning on page 127 of the *Handbook for Christian Maturity,* presents a thorough teaching on the person and work of the Holy Spirit and His relationship with the Christian. Students should be instructed to read this article thoughtfully and prayerfully before coming to class.

LESSON ONE

WHO IS THE HOLY SPIRIT
AND WHY DID HE COME?

Teacher's Objective: To introduce students to the ministry of the Holy Spirit, and to lead them to submit at least one area of their lives to His control.

Teacher's Enrichment: (May be shared with students if time permits.)

● Members of the early church and succeeding generations of the church believed the Holy Spirit to be equal with God the Father and God the Son.

Nicene Creed, 325 A.D. (1600 years old):
I believe in the Holy Ghost, the Lord and Giver of life, which proceedeth from the Father and the Son, and with the Father and the Son together is worshipped and glorified.

Athanasian Creed (1300 years old):
Such as the Father is, such is the Son, and such is the Holy Ghost.

● Hymn writers of all ages attribute Him with deity:
"Holy Ghost with light divine, Shine upon this heart of mine.
Holy Ghost with power divine, Cleanse this guilty heart of mine."

(From "Holy Ghost With Light Divine" by L. Gottschalk and Andrew Reed.)
(Written 100 years ago. Who could cleanse a guilty heart but God?)

● Webster's Dictionary defines the Holy Spirit as the third person of the Trinity.

CLASS TIME

Suggested Opening Prayer

Dear Father, we ask that Your Holy Spirit will open our minds and hearts to an understanding of His person, His ministry and His work in our lives as we study about Him in this lesson.

(You may want to give students time to read "You Shall Receive Power," the Holy Spirit article starting on page 127 in the student's book if they have not done so before.)

(Introduction: Be sure
students understand
　　objective
　　memory work
　　reading assignment.)

BE SURE YOU HAVE READ THE ARTICLE ABOUT THE HOLY
SPIRIT BEFORE YOU START THIS LESSON.

Introduction

OBJECTIVE: To become acquainted
　　　　　　with the Holy Spirit and to
　　　　　　understand His mission.

TO MEMORIZE: John 16:13, 14.

TO READ: John 3:1-8; Romans 8.

Discussion Starter

(Teacher, hold up a candle and ask someone to read Proverbs 20:27, "The Spirit
of man is the lamp [*candle* in the King James version] of the Lord." Then say:)

Until the Holy Spirit of God lights the candle of man's spiritual life, he cannot
see and know God. Man is spiritually dead (unlighted candle), but when the Holy
Spirit takes up residence at the time of spiritual birth (John 3:3,6), he becomes
spiritually alive (light candle). What differences do you think that would make in a
person's life?

(After considering responses from group members, continue as appropriate:)
The majority of Christians know very little about the Holy Spirit. All of us have
heard sermons on God the Father, and many on God the Son, but a sermon of God
the Holy Spirit is rare. The Holy Spirit is equal in every way with God the Father
and God the Son. He vitally affects our lives as Christians. In fact, His presence or
absence in a person's life makes the difference between life and death spiritually.
We are born spiritually through the ministry of the Holy Spirit according to
John 3:1-8.

Lesson Development

(Have someone read
"Who the Holy Spirit is"
from student's book.)

Bible Study

A. *Who the Holy Spirit is*

The Holy Spirit is a person, the third person of the Trinity:
Father, Son and Holy Spirit. He is not some vague, ethereal
shadow, nor an impersonal force. He is a person equal in
every way with the Father and the Son. All of the divine
attributes ascribed to the Father and the Son are equally
ascribed to the Holy Spirit.

Would you consider God a person (a personality)? Why?

1. Personality (a person) is composed of intellect, emotions
   and will. In 1 Corinthians 2:11, what indicates that the
   Holy Spirit has intellect? _He knows thoughts of a man._

   What evidence is there in Romans 15:30 that the Holy
   Spirit has emotion? _Love of the Spirit._

   How do you see the Holy Spirit exercising His will in
   1 Corinthians 12:11? _Works, distributes as He
   wills._

The Holy Spirit is the
Spirit of God. "For this
reason, I bow my knees
before the Father, from
whom every family in
heaven and on earth derives its name, that He would grant you according to the
riches of His glory, to be strengthened with power through His Spirit in the inner
man" (Ephesians 3:14-16).

What is the particular ministry of the Holy Spirit mentioned here in Paul's prayer?

(Read verses 17 through 19.) How are the other persons of the Trinity mentioned?

The work of the Holy Spirit in the Old Testament:

Creation: Job 26:13; Psalm 104:30; Genesis 1:2,3.

Revelation: 2 Peter 1:21; 2 Timothy 3:16.

> 2. What do you understand about the nature of the Holy Spirit from the following references?
> Romans 8:2   *He is the Spirit of life.*
> John 16:13   *He is the Spirit of truth.*
> Hebrews 10:29 *He is the Spirit of grace,*
> Romans 1:4   *He is the Spirit of holiness.*
> 3. What about His function or His role?
> John 14:26   *To teach, bring to remembrance.*
> 1 Corinthians 3:16   *To dwell in the believer.*
> John 16:13, 14   *To guide to all truth, disclose things of Christ.*

Power for service: 1 Samuel 16:13; 2 Chronicles 15:1,2; Judges 14:5-7; 15:9-14.

The work of the Holy Spirit in Jesus' ministry:

Incarnation: Matthew 1:18-20; Luke 1:30-35.

Baptism: John 1:32.

Miracles: Matthew 12:28.

Message of new birth: John 3:5,6.

Resurrection: 1 Peter 3:18; Romans 8:11.

The life of the Lord Jesus and the ministry of the disciples depended upon the Holy Spirit. We must depend upon Him even more.

Why would the Holy Spirit seek to glorify Christ? (Answer: Because He is "the Way" (John 14:5), and He came "to seek and save that which was lost" (Luke 19:10).

> B. Why He came
> 1. What is the chief reason the Holy Spirit came (John 16:14)? _ *To glorify Christ.*
> 2. What will be a logical result when the Holy Spirit controls your life? _____

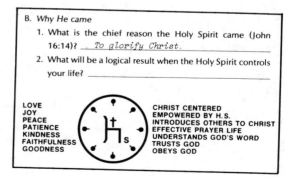

> LOVE
> JOY
> PEACE
> PATIENCE
> KINDNESS
> FAITHFULNESS
> GOODNESS
>
> CHRIST CENTERED
> EMPOWERED BY H.S.
> INTRODUCES OTHERS TO CHRIST
> EFFECTIVE PRAYER LIFE
> UNDERSTANDS GOD'S WORD
> TRUSTS GOD
> OBEYS GOD

Conclusion and Application

People often give the impression that God is an impersonal force which may be exploited for a life of well-being. This is wrong. God is a person, and through His

Spirit He wants to control
and use us for His own
glory and our own good.
We do not use God — He
uses us.

Life Application
Write one new insight you have gained from this lesson concerning the Holy Spirit: _____
_____
_____
In what area of your life do you believe the Holy Spirit needs to be more in control? _____
_____
What will be the result when He is? _____
_____
_____

Suggested Closing Prayer

Dear Father, I want to allow the Holy Spirit to control my life each moment of every day in order that I may always know and do Your perfect will. And today I want to submit ___(area of life)___ to Your complete control. Thank You for Your assurance of answered prayer.

ADDITIONAL BACKGROUND MATERIAL

The disciples were gathered in the upper room with Jesus for the Last Supper. During the meal, He announced He would have to die. They became very sorrowful.

For three years they had been His closest companions. They had seen Him heal the sick, the deaf and the blind. They had watched Him feed five thousand people with only five small loaves and two fishes. They had listened to His words and determined with others, "Never did a man speak the way this man speaks." They even saw Him raise the dead. With such conclusive evidence that Jesus was the promised Messiah, the Redeemer, they had forsaken all and followed Him. Imagine their dismay and grief when they realized their beloved Master would have to die.

But Jesus spoke words of comfort to them as He said, "It is to your advantage that I go away: for if I go not away the Helper shall not come to you; but if I go, I will send Him to you" (John 16:7).

In other words, Jesus said it was necessary for Him to go away, to die, that they might benefit. But He would send someone else to replace Him. Notice He did not say He would send His help, but the Helper, a person.

In John 14:16, Jesus said He would send "another Helper" who would be with them forever. There are two words for "another" in the Greek: *allos* — another, but similar (another of the same kind); *heteros* — another as distinguished from (qualitative difference). Jesus said He would send *allos,* another who was to be just like Himself!

LESSON TWO

WHAT IS THE HOLY SPIRIT'S RELATIONSHIP WITH EVERY CHRISTIAN?

Teacher's Objective: To show that the relationship of the Holy Spirit to Christianity is His being within us, that successful Christian living is based upon His control of our lives and to lead students to allow that relationship to be vitally real in their daily lives.

Teacher's Enrichment: (May be shared with students as time permits.)

The work of the Holy Spirit includes the following:

● He *regenerates,* John 3:5. "Generation is impartation of physical life; regeneration is impartation of spiritual (divine) life."

Men are spiritually dead until regenerated. Romans 6:23, "The wages of sin *is* death." See also Ephesians 2:1.

There is only one thing a dead man needs, and that is life. See John 14:6, 5:24 and 11:25.

● He *indwells,* 1 Corinthians 3:16; 6:19; John 14:16-17.

Is there a contradiction when we say that Jesus comes into our hearts, and we also say the Holy Spirit lives in us? See John 14:17-20; 15:5; 17:18-23,26; Romans 8:9; Ephesians 3:17; Philippians 1:19-21. *The Holy Spirit is the Spirit of Christ.*

Every believer, no matter how weak and imperfect, has the indwelling Holy Spirit. The best references on the indwelling Spirit, 1 Corinthians 3:16 and 6:19, were written to the weak, carnal Christians at Corinth.

● He *assures* us of our salvation, Romans 8:16.

"Jesus Christ wanted to take religion out of the external and make it internal and put it on the same level as life itself, so that a man knows he knows God the same as he knows he is himself and not someone else . . . Only the Holy Spirit can do that. The Holy Spirit came to carry the evidence of Christianity from the Bible . . . into the human heart." (A. W. Tozer, *How to be Filled With the Holy Spirit,* p. 13.)

● He *seals* the believer. Ephesians 1:13 (cf. 2 Timothy 2:19) denotes ownership and assurance.

"When Jesus comes again . . . the indwelling Holy Spirit will respond to the shout of the coming Bridegroom (Christ), and will present to Christ His own without spot or wrinkle. It is vital to know one is sealed by the Holy Spirit . . . He is here to prepare for the glorious moment when faith will give way to sight — for the meeting with the Bridegroom face to face" (Harold Wildish, *Did Ye Receive the Holy Ghost?* p. 31).

● The Holy Spirit is the *earnest* of our inheritance, Ephesians 1:14.

When a businessman makes a transaction, he wants some kind of guarantee.

Suppose, for example, you were buying a house. You would have to make a down payment before business could be contracted. This down payment, or guarantee that the rest would be paid, is called the "earnest." The Holy Spirit is our earnest, or guarantee, that the Lord will do all for us that He has promised.

• The Holy Spirit *baptizes* us. The baptism of the believer by the Holy Spirit is found in Acts 1:4,5 and 1 Corinthians 12:13. This is an act of the Holy Spirit in which He, at the moment of the individual's acceptance of Christ in faith, takes the person and places him into the body of Christ (note Romans 6:3).

CLASS TIME

Suggested Opening Prayer

Dear Father, we pray that the Holy Spirit will make Himself real in His relationship with us and that we will allow You to take control of our lives through Your Spirit as we study and understand the truths presented in this lesson.

(Introduction: Be sure
students understand
   objective
   memory work
   reading assignment.)

Introduction
OBJECTIVE: To realize the necessity of being filled with the Holy Spirit in order to live the Christian life.
TO MEMORIZE: Ephesians 5:18.
TO READ: Romans 12:1-8; 1 Corinthians 2.

Discussion Starter

In your estimation, how are God the Father, God the Son and God the Holy Spirit individually related to you, the Christian? (Discuss briefly.)

God the Father — source of life, source of all that is holy and good.

God the Son — God manifest in flesh, our Savior, provides way of salvation.

God the Holy Spirit — regenerates, gives new life, seeks to control us.

Lesson Development

Have you ever heard the story of the three men who all claimed ownership of the same house? The first man was the builder of the house. He planned the whole thing, built it and then put it up for sale. The second man was the buyer who paid the price to buy the house. He owns the house, but there is a third man who now lives in it. So it is with us. God the Father made us, God the Son redeemed us — bought us — with His precious blood at Calvary, and God the Holy Spirit has come to live within us. "Do you not know that you are a temple of God, and that the Spirit of God dwells in you?" (1 Corinthians 3:16). In Christ we are indwelt by the Godhead: Father, Son and Holy Spirit (Colossians 2:9,10).

It is almost inconceivable that God Himself lives in us when we receive Christ, but He does!

Bible Study

A. *The work of the Holy Spirit*

   1. When you become a Christian (i.e., at the time of your spiritual birth), the Holy Spirit does a number of things for and in you. What are they?

     John 3:5 *Gives spiritual life.*

     1 Corinthians 3:16 *Indwells.*

     Ephesians 4:30 *Seals.*

     1 Corinthians 12:13 *Baptizes into body of Christ.*

     2 Corinthians 5:5 *Becomes God's pledge-- guarantee.*

   2. Explain in your own words what the Holy Spirit does for the Christian according to:

     Romans 8:16 *Bears witness with our spirit that we are children of God.*

     Romans 8:26, 27 *Helps our praying, intercedes for us according to God's will.*

B. *The results of being filled with the Holy Spirit*

   1. Can a person be a Christian and not have the Holy Spirit dwelling in Him (Romans 8:9)? Explain. *No. Being in the Spirit depends on Spirit of God dwelling in us.*

   2. What is the main reason to be filled with the Spirit (Acts 1:8; 4:29, 31)? *To have power for witnessing and be able to speak with boldness.*

   3. What work of the Holy Spirit is necessary for successful Christian living and service (Ephesians 5:18)? *He must fill us.*

The Holy Spirit initiates the new life and then wants to fill (control) the believer.

(Teacher: Any part of the material from the "Teacher's Enrichment" section may be shared at this point if you feel it is appropriate.

Then continue discussion of questions and answers.)

Dr. R. A. Torrey once said, "There is not one single passage in the Bible, either in the Old Testament or the New Testament, where the filling with the Holy Spirit is spoken of, where it is not concerned with testimony for service."

Paul certainly was Spirit-filled and his message was powerful. Note his testimony in 1 Corinthians 2:4-5. How did he speak? What does he contrast this with? (Demonstration of the Spirit and of power versus man's wisdom.)

How can one have this boldness and power?

Conclusion and Application

It is evident that the Holy Spirit plays a major role in the life of the Christian. God carries out His purpose in the life of the Christian through the control of the

Holy Spirit. To be a
successful Christian, one
must yield to His control.

(Discuss possible ways
students can fill out the
"Life Application" chart.)

Life Application

Fill in the chart below:

"How I viewed the Holy   "How I view Him now"
 Spirit in the past"

_____

_____

_____

_____

Do you really desire to be filled with the Holy Spirit? _____
Why? _____

_____

_____

(Students should write
their answers to the last
two questions privately. Encourage them to be honest.)

Suggested Closing Prayer

Dear God, teach me to live in the reality of my relationship with the Holy
Spirit. Reveal to me the areas in my life which I must yield to your control, and
make my life a channel for His power to the end that the Lord Jesus Christ may
always be glorified.

LESSON THREE

WHY ARE SO FEW CHRISTIANS FILLED WITH THE HOLY SPIRIT?

Teacher's Objective: To guide students in understanding the barriers to living a Spirit-filled life, to help the students identify those barriers in their own lives, and to lead them to surrender those barriers to God.

Teacher's Enrichment:

Galatians 5:16-17 points out to us that there is a battlefield within the heart of the Christian:

Physical Life ————— versus ————— Spiritual Life

The works of the
flesh are described
in Galatians 5:19-21.

The fruit of the
Spirit is described
in Galatians 5:22-24.

To think about: Is the issue "our doing" of these things or "our surrender" to the controlling principle which produces either the works of the flesh or the fruit of the Spirit?

CLASS TIME

Suggested Opening Prayer

Dear Father, help us all to understand the barriers to living the victorious, Spirit-filled, Christian life and reveal to us those barriers which are present in each of our own lives. Help us to trust You now as we seek truths from Your Word.

(Introduction: Be sure students understand
   objective
   memory work
   reading assignment.)

Introduction

OBJECTIVE: To understand the barriers to a Spirit-filled life.

TO MEMORIZE: 1 John 2:15-17.

TO READ: Galatians 5 and 6; Acts 5:1-11.

Discussion Starter

(Ask each member of the group to write out four or five things which he feels would keep an individual from experiencing the control of the Holy Spirit and living a Spirit-filled life. Discuss those things together.)

Galatians 5:25 says, "If we live by the Spirit, let us also walk by the Spirit." What does Paul mean when he speaks of "living" as opposed to "walking"?

Lesson Development

The battle is fought within the heart of the Christian.

> **Bible Study**
>
> A. *The heart's battlefield*
>
> 1. How does Paul describe himself in Romans 7:19-24? _Not in control, wicked, evil, prisoner of law of sin, wants to do good but cannot._
>
>   What kind of feeling does that description arouse in you?
>   _____
>
> 2. State in your own words why there are so many unhappy Christians, according to Galatians 5:16, 17. _Flesh and Spirit oppose each other creating conflict._

A key reason many Christians are not controlled by the Holy Spirit, and the battle for a Spirit-filled life is lost, is a lack of knowledge of the Word of God.

"Suppose a young Christian who loved the Lord Jesus Christ and wanted to serve Him was very eager to get married. This Christian boy was in the Armed Forces in France. He became very fond of two French girls — he just didn't know which one he liked better — he liked them both. He really wanted to get married, but he didn't know which girl to ask. As a man who believed in God, he walked into a big church in France and sat down in one of the pews. He asked God to guide him, and then looking up at the stained glass windows, he seemed to see two words that guided him: 'Ave Maria.' Strangely enough the name of one of the French girls was Maria. He thought, 'Have Maria, have Maria! I'll ask her to be my wife.' But, sad to say, that girl was not a Christian.

"If that boy had been reading God's Word diligently, and if he had read and digested that phrase in 2 Corinthians 6:14 which says, 'Be ye not unequally yoked together with unbelievers,' he would never have looked to a stained glass window for guidance. If the word of God was dwelling in him richly, the Spirit of God would have shown him clearly that he could not ask an unsaved girl to be his wife. The Spirit-filled life is tremendously practical" (Wildish, p. 57).

> B. *Why the battle is often lost*
>
> 1. Read the following Scriptures and state what you think they teach are the reasons so few Christians are filled with the Holy Spirit.
>   Psalm 119:105   _Don't use the lamp—the Word._
>   Proverbs 16:18   _Pride_

Pride was also the sin of Satan, Isaiah 14:12-14. Pride was the first sin of man as Adam and Eve wanted to be something they were not, Genesis 3:5. The self-centered Christian cannot have fellowship with God, "for God is opposed to the proud, but gives grace to the humble" (1 Peter 5:5).

> Proverbs 29:25   *Fear of man.*

One of the greatest
tragedies of our day is the difficulty of telling a Christian from a non-Christian
(generally speaking). We are not to be "conformed to this world, but be
transformed" (Romans 12:1-2). The world should know we are different.

All around us are people with hungry hearts who would respond if some
Christian would be brave enough to let people know where he stands.

Dr. Henrietta Mears said that a Christian should be like a lifeguard at a beach.
Everyone knows who he is, but pays him scant attention. But when someone swims
too far and begins to drown, he remembers the lifeguard and calls for him to help.
If we will let it be known what we stand for, someone is bound to come to us when
he gets in trouble and really needs help.

> Luke 9:26   *Ashamed of Christ.*

"Martin Luther, the great
Protestant reformer, stood fearlessly before the Holy Roman Emperor and the Diet
of Worms as an Archbishop questioned him about his writings. Luther replied,
'The books are all mine, and I have written more.'

" 'Do you defend them all, or do you reject a part?' asked the Archbishop.
Luther replied aloud, 'This touches God and His Word. This affects the salvation
of souls. Of this Christ said, "He who denies me before men, him will I deny
before my Father." '

"Luther was given a day to think it over and asked the next day to recant his
statements. Luther replied, 'Unless I am convicted by Scripture and plain reason —
I do not accept the authority of popes and councils, for they have contradicted each
other — my conscience is captive to the Word of God. I cannot and I will not
recant anything, for to go against conscience is neither right nor safe. Here I stand,
I cannot do otherwise. God help me.' "

— Bainton, *Here I Stand, A Life of Martin Luther*, p. 144.

> 2. What is another thing that will put a block between you
> and the Lord and keep you from being filled with the
> Spirit (Psalm 66:18)?   *"If I regard wickedness in*
> *my heart, the Lord will not hear."*

God will not fill an
unclean or unyielded vessel.
He wants you to confess all known sin, and make restitution where you can. See
1 John 1:9; Exodus 22:3,5-6,12.

> What about 1 John 2:15-17?   *Love of the world.*

Love for material things
and desire to conform to a secular society is the spiritual disease of many
Christians. Every Christian should make careful and frequent evaluation of how he
invests his time, talent and treasures in order to accomplish the most for Christ.

3. Lack of trust in God also will keep you from being filled with the Holy Spirit. Read John 3:16 again. Do you feel that *you* could trust a God like this? _____

Why? (Romans 8:32 and 1 John 3:16 can help you with your answer.) _____

_____

_____

Basically, the reason most Christians are not filled with the Holy Spirit is that they are *unwilling to surrender their wills to God.*

- LEGALISTIC ATTITUDE
- IMPURE THOUGHTS
- JEALOUSY
- GUILT
- WORRY
- DISCOURAGEMENT
- CRITICAL SPIRIT
- FRUSTRATION
- AIMLESSNESS

- IGNORANCE OF HIS SPIRITUAL HERITAGE
- UNBELIEF
- DISOBEDIENCE
- LOSS OF LOVE FOR GOD AND FOR OTHERS
- POOR PRAYER
- NO DESIRE FOR BIBLE STUDY

Some people are afraid that if they surrender to God's will He will take something away from them or make them unhappy. Nothing could be further from the truth. When a person chooses to do God's will, that person will:

Find the inner longings of his own heart gratified — *selfward:* Psalm 23:5; 16:11; 63:5; John 4:13,14; 7:37,38.

Glorify God — *Godward:* John 15:8; Matthew 5:16; 1 Corinthians 6:20; Ephesians 1:6.

Bring salvation and blessing to others — *manward:* Acts 4:13; 9:15; 1 Corinthians 4:9; 2 Corinthians 4:10,11; Galatians 1:16; Philippians 1:20; Luke 24:47,48.

Conclusion and Application

The most unhappy people in the world are not the unbelievers, but Christians who resist the will of God for their lives! The Christian who refuses to do the will of God must be prepared to pay the price of disobedience. "As we sow, so shall we reap."

A story was told by a man who resisted the call to ministry in Sweden. He stubbornly resisted God's will even through the death of his wife and daughter. He went into business and prospered, only to be robbed by his own son. In his older years, as he languished with cancer, he said, "I know that I am saved, but Oh, the loss, as I soon will be ushered into His presence only to give an account of a whole life of disobedience."

God is a loving Father, in whom we can trust without reservation, as a son trusts an earthly father who has proven his love. Romans 14:23 says, "Whatever is not from faith is sin." And Hebrews 11:6 says, "Without faith it is impossible to please Him." Many Christians grieve the Holy Spirit because of their unbelief.

Life Application

List any barriers you are aware of now between yourself and God. _____

_____

Prayerfully consider, then answer this question:

"Am *I* willing to surrender my will to God?" _____

_____

_____

Suggested Closing Prayer

Dear God, I recognize _____ as a barrier between myself
and You. I confess it now as sin and with Your help I determine not to allow it to
rule my life any longer. Help me to recognize sin and self-will whenever they
occur and may they never become controlling forces of my life. Help me to yield
continually to the control of the Holy Spirit.

LESSON FOUR

HOW CAN A CHRISTIAN BE FILLED WITH THE HOLY SPIRIT?

Teacher's Objective: To discuss how one is filled with the Holy Spirit and to pray with those who desire to be filled with the Holy Spirit.

Teacher's Enrichment: (May be shared with class as time permits.)

There are two negative and two positive aspects to the filling of the Holy Spirit.

First the negative: "Do not grieve the Holy Spirit of God, by whom you were sealed for the day of redemption" (Ephesians 4:30). We grieve the Spirit of God by committing some sin or breaking one of God's laws. This is called a sin of *commission,* and includes bitterness, wrath, clamor, etc.

Then we are also told, "Do not quench the Spirit" (1 Thessalonians 5:19). When we quench the Spirit, we do not openly break one of God's laws, but we refuse to do something God wants us to do. This is referred to as a sin of *omission.* For example, the still, small voice of God may tell us to speak to a friend about Christ. If we refuse, we have quenched the Spirit.

Then the positive: If we have grieved or quenched the Spirit in our lives, we must *confess* that sin to Him before He will fill us with His power. "If we confess our sins, He is faithful and righteous to forgive us our sins, and to cleanse us from all unrighteousness" (1 John 1:9).

The final step is to *believe* that God has filled you with His Spirit. Every time sin breaks your fellowship with God, confess that sin to Him, and then believe that God has filled you with His Spirit. Colossians 2:6 says, "As you therefore have received Christ Jesus the Lord, so walk in Him." How did you receive Christ? By works or by faith? By faith of course! So you must continue your Christian life by faith.

CLASS TIME

Suggested Opening Prayer

Our Father, we realize this lesson is a vital one in our Christian growth, and we pray You will make it clear to us and lead us to complete obedience.

(Introduction: Be sure students understand
    objective
    memory work
    reading assignment.)

Introduction

OBJECTIVE: To personally appropriate the filling of the Holy Spirit.

TO MEMORIZE: Romans 12:1, 2; 1 John 5:14, 15.

TO READ: Acts 6:8 - 7:60.

179

(Have someone read
the paragraph, "Your
Love for Christ.")

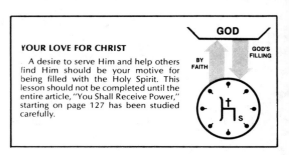

YOUR LOVE FOR CHRIST

A desire to serve Him and help others find Him should be your motive for being filled with the Holy Spirit. This lesson should not be completed until the entire article, "You Shall Receive Power," starting on page 127 has been studied carefully.

Discussion Starter

Suppose you are a counselor. A new Christian comes to you and asks, "Don't you think one's conversion experience and sinful background determine the success in personal witnessing, in Christian work and in Christian growth? I do not have the power 'X' has because he has such a tremendous background." What would you say? What does determine success? (Consider students' ideas.)

Bible Study

A. *What you must know*

    1. What is the admonition found in Ephesians 5:18? *To be filled with the Holy Spirit.*

Lesson Development

To try to live the
Christian life or do service for God apart from His Spirit is like trying to operate a car without gas. It doesn't work!

    2. Why do you need to be filled with the Spirit?

    Galatians 5:22, 23 *To have fruit of Spirit in life;*

    Acts 1:8 *To have power to witness.*

The Holy Spirit was
responsible for our new
birth. We are "born of the
Spirit" (John 3:5,6). The Holy Spirit living in us is what makes us conscious of God's presence and gives us the assurance that we are children of God. "The Spirit Himself bears witness with our spirit, that we are the children of God" (Romans 8:16).

The Holy Spirit guides our lives. "For all who are being led by the Spirit of God, these are sons of God" (Romans 8:14). Our hope of the resurrection lies in the power of the Holy Spirit. "But if the Spirit of Him who raised Jesus from the dead dwells in you, He who raised Christ Jesus from the dead will also give life to your mortal bodies through His Spirit who indwells you" (Romans 8:11).

Since the Holy Spirit inspired the writing of the Bible, we cannot understand its true meaning apart from His control.

We pray with His assistance according to Romans 8:26, and we witness in His power according to Acts 1:8.

The fruit of the Spirit is never an end in itself, but only a means to the end that we win men and women to Christ, which in turn will bring glory and honor to Him (John 15:8).

B. *The one thing you must feel*

What is one prerequisite to being filled with the Spirit, according to Matthew 5:6? *We must hunger and thirst for righteousness; we must desire to be filled.*

The Holy Spirit indwells every believer from the moment he receives Christ. However, He does not continue to control the life in the sense of filling unless we want Him to do so.

C. *What you must do*

1. If your desire to be filled with the Spirit is sincere, what will you do now (Romans 12:1, 2)? *Present body as a living sacrifice; be transformed.*

This means there can be no unconfessed sin in your life. The Holy Spirit cannot fill an unclean vessel. He waits to fill you with His power. Do not resist Him any longer.

Read John 7:37-39. Pick out the verbs in verses 37-38. (Thirst, come, drink, believe.) When one thirsts one must come to Christ,

2. How then are you filled with the Holy Spirit (Matthew 7:7-11; John 7:37)? *Ask.   Come to Jesus.*

drink, and believe. Some come to Christ because they thirst, but they do not believe (trust, rely on, have faith in).

According to John 7:38,39, what can one expect will be the result in coming to Christ, drinking and believing? (An outflow of "rivers of living water.")

3. Will the Holy Spirit fill you if you ask Him? *Yes.*

How do you know (1 John 5:14, 15)? *When we pray according to God's will, He hears and answers.*

Conclusion and Application

The Spirit-filled life is the norm of the Christian life. It is for every Christian. With a Spirit-filled life the Christian will experience the joy and reality of his Christian life; he will have power to witness. The simple prerequisites are confession, cleansing, complete yielding to His will by faith.

Life Application

You can be filled with the Holy Spirit only by faith. However, prayer is one way of expressing your faith. If you truly desire to be filled with the Holy Spirit, you can pray this prayer now:

"Dear Father, I need You. I acknowledge that I have been in control of my life; and that, as a result, I have sinned against You. I thank You that You have forgiven my sins through Christ's death on the cross for me. I now invite Christ to take control of the throne of my life. Fill me with the Holy Spirit as You commanded me to be filled, and as You promised in Your Word that You would do if I asked in faith. I pray this in the name of Jesus. As an expression of my faith, I now thank You for taking control of my life and for filling me with the Holy Spirit."

Would you like to pray this prayer now? (Teacher, lead in praying according to student's book.)

(Continue with discussion
of "Life Application"
questions and answers
as appropriate.)

> What must you do when you have asked Him to fill you (Hebrews 11:6)?   *Believe God has done it.*
>
> If you have asked the Holy Spirit to fill you, *thank Him.* God is dependable; His Word is true. If you are sincere, He has filled you. What should be your attitude from this day forward (1 Thessalonians 5:18)?   *Be thankful for all things.*
>
> Date of filling _____
>
> Your comments: _____
>
> _____
>
> _____

Suggested Closing Prayer

Dear Father, thank You for helping us to understand and appropriate the fullness of Your power and love by faith.

HOW CAN A CHRISTIAN KNOW WHEN HE IS FILLED, AND WHAT ARE THE RESULTS OF BEING FILLED WITH THE SPIRIT?

Teacher's Objective: To give students the assurance of Spirit-filled relationships, encouraging them to continue their walk in the Spirit by faith.

Teacher's Enrichment: (May be shared with class as time permits.)

The Enemy of the Spirit-Filled Life

Satan bitterly opposes the doctrine of the Spirit-filled life. He confuses it, surrounding it with false notions and fears. He does this to keep believers from winning others to Christ and thus taking them from his control.

Be on guard against Satan's temptations, but realize that "greater is He who is in you, than he who is in the world" (1 John 4:4).

What to do About Difficulties

Allow the Holy Spirit to develop within you a new attitude of having "no confidence in the flesh" and check impulses to see if they are of the flesh or of the Spirit. Out of our sinfulness and failures will come a deep sense of the need to abide in Christ, and more and more we will lean on Him.

CLASS TIME

Suggested Opening Prayer

Our Father, we thank You for the Holy Spirit and the power that is ours through His infilling. We pray today that we will come to an even deeper understanding of this truth and that our relationship with Him will grow and will be pleasing to You.

(Introduction: Be sure students understand
    objective
    memory work
    reading assignment.)

Introduction

OBJECTIVE: To experience assurance of the filling of the Holy Spirit.

TO MEMORIZE: Galatians 5:22, 23.

TO READ: Galatians 5:16-26.

(Teacher, it is important to have the students seriously consider these questions. Your continuation of this lesson will depend upon their responses. If some of the students need to go back to Lesson 4, don't hesitate to do so.)

> Did you sincerely follow the steps outlined in Lesson Four? Did you ask the Holy Spirit to fill you? If you did not, Lessons Five and Six will not mean much to you. Go back to Lesson Four and ask God to work in your heart. If He has filled you, you will be anxious to proceed with Lessons Five and Six.

Discussion Starter

(Ask the class:) What do you think Paul meant when he said, "It is no longer I who live, but Christ lives in me" (Galatians 2:20)?

Bible Study

A. *Results of the Spirit-filled life*

1. What will the Holy Spirit demonstrate in and through your life, as a result of His filling you (Galatians 5:22, 23)?
   His fruit--love, joy, peace, etc.

   Which specific fruit of the Spirit are you most in need of?

Lesson Development

Let's look up and talk about these Scriptures: John 4:34 — the motive for living that Jesus had; and

2. Read Acts 1:8. How do you see this power evidenced in your life? _____

   How does John 15:16 apply to you today? *We are chosen to go and bear fruit which will remain.*

John 7:37-39 — an exuberant, abundant life flowing over into the lives of others.

---

3. How do you identify with 1 Corinthians 12:1-11 and Ephesians 4:11? _____

4. What mannerisms, language, activities and inconsistencies in your life do you feel are hindering the Holy Spirit's development of His fruit, power and gifts in you? _____

Check List of Results of Being Filled With the Spirit

_____ I realize my utter dependence on Jesus Christ hour by hour, moment by moment.

_____ I look to Him in all things.

5. What happens as we are occupied with Christ and allow the Holy Spirit to work in us (2 Corinthians 3:18)? *We are transformed into His image.*

B. *Facts, faith and feelings*

1. What is the primary way we know if we have been filled with the Spirit (1 John 5:14, 15)? *We pray according to His will, and He answers our prayers.*

_____ I am slow to speak, to act, to plan, until I have been in touch with Him.

_____ I let Christ live His life through me, instead of trying in my own strength to live my life for Him.

_____ I realize that He is Love.

_____ I have given up self-love and made it a supreme purpose of my life to love others.

_____ I experience boldness in my witness for Christ.

_____ I produce fruit according to Matthew 4:19 and John 15:8.

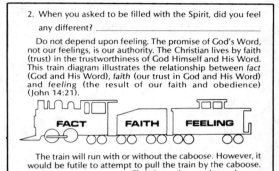

2. When you asked to be filled with the Spirit, did you feel any different? _____

Do not depend upon feeling. The promise of God's Word, not our feelings, is our authority. The Christian lives by faith (trust) in the trustworthiness of God Himself and His Word. This train diagram illustrates the relationship between *fact* (God and His Word), *faith* (our trust in God and His Word) and *feeling* (the result of our faith and obedience) (John 14:21).

FACT   FAITH   FEELING

Why should we make feeling subordinate to fact and faith? (Feeling fluctuates when fact does not change — faith anchors.)

The train will run with or without the caboose. However, it would be futile to attempt to pull the train by the caboose. In the same way, we, as Christians, do not depend upon feelings or emotions, but we place our faith (trust) in the trustworthiness of God and the promise of His Word.

Conclusion and Application

The Christian is filled with the Holy Spirit by *faith*. He continues to be filled and controlled by *faith*. Evidence of a Spirit-controlled life will be a more fruitful witness for Christ, (Matthew 4:19 and John 15:8.)

Life Application

Though you may not be aware of change immediately, with the passing of time there should be some evidence of your being filled with the Spirit. Ask yourself these questions now and in the future from time to time:

1. Do you have a greater love for Christ? _____

2. Do you have a greater love for God's Word? _____

3. Are you more concerned for those who do not know Christ as Savior? _____

4. Are you experiencing a greater boldness, liberty and power in witnessing? _____

If you can answer "yes" truthfully to these questions, you undoubtedly are filled with the Spirit.

What does that knowledge mean to you now? _____

_____

_____

If your answer was "no" to any of those four questions, what do you suppose that indicates? _____

_____

_____

Do you think a person can be filled with the Holy Spirit and not be aware of it? _____ Explain. _____

_____

ADDITIONAL BACKGROUND MATERIAL

If you ask them, a bride and groom will tell you they do not feel very married five minutes after the ceremony. It is all so new and uncertain to them. They have not really begun to experience the marriage relationship although the legal transaction of binding them together has taken place. Ask them a year later, though, if they feel married and you'll get a much different answer.

Likewise, don't be discouraged if you have not had a dramatic change immediately after yielding to the filling of the Holy Spirit. The changes will come. Expect them and prepare for them.

LESSON SIX

HOW CAN A CHRISTIAN CONTINUE TO BE FILLED WITH THE HOLY SPIRIT?

Teacher's Objective: To help each student make the Spirit-filled life a moment-by moment reality.

Teacher's Enrichment: (May be shared with class as time permits.)

That child of God will have the fullest manifestation of the Spirit who adopts as the deliberate purpose and principle of his life *the love of Christ instead of the love of self.*

a. He ceases to grasp all, and begins to give all.

b. He ceases to seek all, and begins to surrender all.

c. He ceases accenting "take care of number one," and begins to accent "let every man take care of the things of others."

d. He no longer seeks the high place, but the lowly one.

e. He seeks to minister, instead of being ministered to.

f. He no longer seeks, but shuns the praise of men.

g. He no longer seeks to save his life, but to lose it for others.

h. He no longer seeks to lay up, enjoy and be at ease, but suffer, and spend and be spent for Christ Himself.

i. He seeks to love as God loves, regardless of his treatment by others. "He is kind to the unthankful and the evil." If some grievous wrong, insult or unkindness goads you from your attitude of love, justify it not, but hasten to confess, and find forgiveness from Him who prayed for those who murdered Him as well as for those who loved Him (James McConkey, *Three-fold Secret of the Holy Spirit,* p. 86).

CLASS TIME

Suggested Opening Prayer

Dear Lord, we pray that You will open our hearts and minds to the necessity for a moment-by-moment filling of Your Spirit in order to experience the victorious Christian life. Help us to understand and appropriate what You have for us today.

(Introduction: Be sure
students understand
  objective
  memory work
  reading assignment.)

Introduction
OBJECTIVE: To make the Spirit-filled life a moment-by-moment reality.
TO MEMORIZE: John 14:21 or John 15:10.
TO READ: Acts 10.

Discussion Starter

(*An experiment in role play:* This is an excellent means to help members of the group identify their problems. Have three individuals briefly play the roles of:

1. A Christian who has not confessed sin, and lacks faith to claim 1 John 1:9 and the refilling of the Holy Spirit — 1 John 5:14-15.

2. A Christian who has been defeated by sin, but is now using 1 John 1:9 to rebound. Discuss how long a Christian has to remain defeated — only until he realizes his need for confession and cleansing.

3. A Christian just returning from meeting a friend to whom he has successfully witnessed. Discuss what a witnessing Christian indicates — that he is Spirit-filled and controlled.

Discuss the roles played and why they reacted as they did.)

We have become so used to depending on feelings instead of facts in the Christian walk that we tend to doubt God's Word and inwardly question whether He will do what His Word says He will. Many of you have come to realize that you have been living a powerless Christian life and you honestly asked the Holy Spirit to fill you. Now, a few days later, you may be doubting the validity of this filling because there has been no big emotional reaction or drastic change.

Remember this, what God says is fact and whether your response be calm assurance, excited enthusiasm, or no definite emotional reaction at all, you can be positive that the Spirit has filled you if you've met the qualifications we discussed in Lesson 4, surrendered your will to Christ, asked in faith and expected Him to fill you.

Lesson Development

There are three basic steps necessary for a person to take to be Spirit-filled:

1. *Confess* sin and receive cleansing from self-life — 1 John 1:9.

2. *Claim* God's will and purpose which is the filling of the Holy Spirit — Ephesians 5:17,18; Romans 12:1-2; Acts 1:8. This is done through prayer — 1 John 5:14-15.

3. *Believe* God's promise and act in faith — Hebrews 11:5 and James 1:5.

Bible Study

How to be filled continually

Read Ephesians 5:18. In the original Greek, "be filled" means "keep on being filled constantly and continually."

1. In prayer you must not only pray for yourself, but *Pray for others.* _____ (Ephesians 6:18 and 1 Samuel 12:23).

   What person have you stopped praying for recently who still needs your prayers? _____

2. You must *examine the Scripture.* daily (Acts 17:11).

   What does the Word of God do for you (Psalm 119:11)? *Keep us from sinning.* _____

3. You must abide in Christ. How can you do that? (John 14:21 and John 15:10)? *Keep His commandments.* Which two commandments do you think are the most important? _____

_____

Abiding in the Spirit is not only communion but ministry *expressed* in love — 1 John 3:23. God who is love, can manifest Himself only to those who are willing to love others. See John 3:16; 1 John 3:16; 3:1; 4:8; 4:19; John 13:1; 15:9.

4. Read Ephesians 4:25-32. How do you grieve the Holy Spirit? _____

   Which commandment in that list do you need to pay special attention to? _____

5. How can you get rid of sin in your life (1 John 1:9)? *Confess it and accept forgiveness and cleansing.*

6. What do you think Romans 8:13 teaches that the Holy Spirit wants to do for you? *Put to death the deeds of the body.*

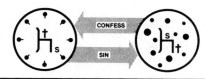

Conclusion and Application

To have a continuous, day-by-day Spirit-filled life is God's norm for the Christian and results from cleansing, and uncompromising faith which believes God and claims His promises to be truth *each day*, moment by moment.

Life Application

The Spirit-filled life is an obedient and abiding life. It can be experienced daily as you:

Begin each day by asking God to cleanse your life, according to 1 John 1:9.

Present your body to the Holy Spirit according to Romans 12:1, 2 and ask Him to keep you filled with His power.

Ask the Holy Spirit to lead you to men who are lost. Be sensitive to His leading.

Expect others to come to Christ through your witness. Do not quench the Spirit by failing to respond.

Rejoice in all things, praising God even in adversity (1 Thessalonians 5:18; Romans 8:28).

1. What sin do you need to confess today? _____

2. Have you realized today victory over a sin you confessed yesterday? _____

Suggested Closing Prayer

(Observe a moment of silent prayer time to give students an opportunity to confess sin and appropriate God's forgiveness. Then pray aloud:) Our Father, we thank You for what You are going to do in each life that is yielded to You.

ADDITIONAL BACKGROUND MATERIAL

Results of the Spirit-filled life, in addition to the fruit listed in Galatians 5:22,23, include the following:

You will have the same motive for living that Jesus had — John 4:34.

You will have an exuberant, abundant life flowing over into the lives of others — John 7:37-39.

You will have power for witnessing and aggressive spiritual warfare — Acts 1:8; Philippians 4:18; John 14:12.

You will live a life of constant prayer and intercession because you have the inmost self of Christ in you. (Only the Holy Spirit can teach you to pray — Romans 8:26,27.)

You will have the character of Christ, the fruit of the Spirit. (It is not my trying to live like Christ, but letting Him live His life in me — Galatians 2:20.)

You will have a greater understanding of Scripture — 1 Corinthians 2:9-13; John 14:26.

LESSON SEVEN
RECAP

Teacher's Objective: To impress more deeply upon the minds and hearts of the students the importance of being filled with the Holy Spirit; to be sure the students understand who the Holy Spirit is, why He came, what His relationship is with each Christian; to refresh the students' minds as to the reasons a Christian might not be Spirit-filled; to be sure they understand how to be filled and how to walk continually in the Spirit; and to lead any of them in steps of appropriation as the need is indicated.

Teacher's Enrichment: This is the time to share any Teacher's Enrichment material of the previous six lessons which you were not able to share earlier.

CLASS TIME

Suggested Opening Prayer

Father, we thank You for what You have taught us about the Holy Spirit, and we pray that You will now deepen our understanding of who and what He is and what He wants to do for us.

(Introduction:

Student's objective is to review what has been learned and to fill in any gaps in the understanding of the ministry of the Holy Spirit.

Memory work: Students should especially be able to quote Ephesians 5:18 and

Review verses memorized.
Read: John 14:16-26; John 16:7-15.

should learn 1 John 1:9 and 1 John 5:14,15 if they have not already done so.)

Discussion Starter

(Ask for and discuss any questions anyone in the group may have about the teaching of the Holy Spirit as presented in the previous six lessons.)

Lesson Development

(Talk about the Recap and the students' responses to the questions included.)

Is the Holy Spirit a personality or an impersonal force? *He is a personality* How do you know? *He has intellect, emotions and will.*

What is the chief reason the Holy Spirit has come? *To glorify Christ.*

What is the command of Ephesians 5:18? *To be filled with the Holy Spirit.*

Name as many reasons as you can that Christians are not filled with the Holy Spirit. *They don't know the Word of God, are proud, feel fear of man, are ashamed of Christ, regard wickedness in their hearts, do not trust in God, and have a love of the world.*

What should be your motives for being filled with the Spirit? *To manifest fruit of Spirit and have power to witness.*

How can a Christian be filled with the Spirit? *Desire filling confess sin, ask for and receive filling by faith.*

How do you know you are filled with the Holy Spirit? *Your life shows His fruit and witnessing becomes a joy.*

How can you continue to be filled with and to walk in the Spirit? *Confess sin in prayer, Claim cleansing, examine Word daily, believe God's promise, act in faith.*

Conclusion and Application

Every day can be an exciting adventure for the Christian who knows the reality of being filled with the Holy Spirit and living constantly, moment by moment, under His gracious control. God commands every Christian to be filled with the Holy Spirit. Not to be filled and controlled by the Spirit is an act of disobedience.

(If anyone has not yet prayed for the filling of the Holy spirit and indicates a desire to do so, you should lead them in the appropriation prayer of Lesson 4.)

Suggested Closing Prayer

Our Father, we are so grateful for Your love and care for us. We appreciate Your provision of the indwelling Holy Spirit and the abundant life which we can have as He empowers us. Again, we pray You will live Your life through us and accomplish Your will in us.

SUMMARY LESSON

THE CHRISTIAN AND THE HOLY SPIRIT

NOTE: Each student should read the article, "You Shall Receive Power," beginning on page 127 of the *Handbook for Christian Maturity*, before this lesson is begun.

Teacher's Objective: To present the ministry of the Holy Spirit and to lead students to an appropriation of His filling.

Teacher's Enrichment: (See Teacher's Enrichment sections in each of the preceding lessons of this Step, and share with the class as time permits.)

CLASS TIME

Suggested Opening Prayer

Dear Father, we pray that the Holy Spirit will make Himself real in His relationship with us and that we will allow You to take control of our lives through Your Spirit as we study and understand the truths presented in this lesson.

• (Introduction:

STUDENTS'S OBJECTIVE: To become acquainted with the Holy Spirit — who He is and what His relationship is with each Christian; to become aware of some of the reasons Christians are not Spirit-filled; and to learn how to be filled and how to walk continually in the Spirit.

TO MEMORIZE: Ephesians 5:18; 1 John 1:9; 1 John 5:14,15.

READING ASSIGNMENT: John 3:1-8; Romans 8:1-17; Galatians 5:16-26; John 14:16-26; 16:7-15. This is quite a long reading assignment, but it is extremely important as the Christian's entire life is determined by his understanding of the ministry of the Holy Spirit.)

Discussion Starter

(Ask the class:) What differences would you expect to see between a Christian who was filled with the Holy Spirit of God and one who was not?

Lesson Development

A. In order to understand the ministry of the Holy Spirit, there are some things we must know about Him. *(from Lesson 1.)*

1. Who the Holy Spirit is. (Have someone read the paragraph from page 151 of student's book.)

2. What is the chief reason the Holy Spirit came (John 16:14)? (To glorify Christ.)

> **Bible Study**
>
> A. *Who the Holy Spirit is*
>
> The Holy Spirit is a person, the third person of the Trinity: Father, Son and Holy Spirit. He is not some vague, ethereal shadow, nor an impersonal force. He is a person equal in every way with the Father and the Son. All of the divine attributes ascribed to the Father and the Son are equally ascribed to the Holy Spirit.

3. What are some of the things the Holy Spirit wants to do for us? *(From Lesson 2.)* (John 14:26 — teach; 1 Corinthians 3:16 — indwells us; Romans 8:16 — gives us assurance; Romans 8:26,27 — helps our praying.)

B. We also need to understand some reasons why many Christians are not filled with the Holy Spirit. *(From Lesson 2.)*

1. They lack knowledge of God's Word (Psalm 119:105).

2. They are proud (Proverbs 16:18).

3. They fear what man might say or do (Proverbs 29:25).

4. They have sin in their lives (Psalm 66:18).

5. They love the world (1 John 2:15-17).

6. They do not trust in God (Romans 8:32,38,29).

Basically the reason most Christians are not filled with the Holy Spirit is that they are *unwilling to surrender their wills to God.*

C. How to be filled with the Spirit of God. *(From Lesson 3.)*

1. What is the most important thing you must know about the admonition, the command of God, found in Ephesians 5:18? (To be filled with the Holy Spirit.)

2. Why do we need to be filled with the Spirit according to Galatians 5:22,23? (To have fruit of the Spirit in our lives.) According to Acts 1:8? (To have power for witnessing.)

3. What is one prerequisite to being filled with the Spirit, one thing you must feel, according to Matthew 5:6? (Must hunger and thirst for righteousness — must desire to be filled.)

4. What must you do:

    a. *confess* sin — 1 John 1:9 — and accept God's forgiveness and cleansing;

b. *claim* by faith the fullness of the Holy Spirit as God's will for your life — Ephesians 5:18;

c. *believe* God's promise — 1 John 5:14,15 — that he will always answer when you pray according to His will.

(Teacher, you may lead class members in this prayer of faith to appropriate the fullness of the Holy Spirit.)

> "Dear Father, I need You. I acknowledge that I have been in control of my life; and that, as a result, I have sinned against You. I thank You that You have forgiven my sins through Christ's death on the cross for me. I now invite Christ to take control of the throne of my life. Fill me with the Holy Spirit as You commanded me to be filled, and as You promised in Your Word that You would do if I asked in faith. I pray this in the name of Jesus. As an expression of my faith, I now thank You for taking control of my life and for filling me with the Holy Spirit."

D. How can you know you are filled with the Spirit of God? *(From Lesson 5.)* (When you see results — you evidence the fruit of the Spirit in your life and you have power for witnessing.) (Teacher, if time permits, refer students to check-list in Lesson 5.)

E. In the original Greek, "be filled" in Ephesians 5:18 means "keep on being filled constantly and continually." How is this possible? What must we do, according to the following Scriptures? *(From Lesson 6.)*

Ephesians 6:18 and 1 Samuel 12:23 (pray for others);
Acts 17:11 (examine the Scriptures daily);
Psalm 119:11 (study God's Word to keep from sinning);
John 14:21 and 15:10 (keep His commandments);
1 John 1:9 (when we sin, confess it and accept forgiveness);
Romans 12:1,2 (present our bodies to the Holy Spirit and ask Him to keep us filled with power)
Galatians 5:16 (walk in the Spirit);
Hebrews 11:5 and James 1:5 (act in faith).

Conclusion and Application

The Bible commands us to be filled constantly and continually, moment by moment. Do not expect a dramatic once-and-for-all-time ecstatic experience. Feelings are a by-product of faith. To disobey a command of God is sin. Therefore, it is sin not to be filled with the Spirit.

But God can only fill a cleansed vessel. Sin in our lives keeps us from being filled. We must confess sin the moment it occurs. We must present ourselves to God in a decisive dedication of our lives, our wills, our bodies and our total personalities. Once sin is confessed, and the control of our lives is surrendered to Him, we are cleansed. We then simply thank God for filling us and *believe* Him, on the basis of His Word, that we are filled.

Suggested Closing Prayer

Our Father, we thank You for what we have learned today and for what you are going to do in each life that is yielded to You.

STEP FOUR

The Christian and Prayer

THE WORD AND PRAYER

"Revive me, O Lord, according to Thy Word" — Psalm 119:107.

"Prayer and the Word of God are inseparable, and should always go together in the quiet time of the inner chamber. *In His Word God speaks to me; in prayer I speak to God.* If there is to be true communication, God and I must both take part. If I simply pray, without using God's Word, I am apt to use my own words and thoughts. This really gives prayer its power, that I take God's thoughts from His Word, and present them before Him. Then I am enabled to pray according to God's Word. How indispensable God's Word is for all true prayer!

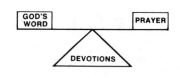

"When I pray, I must seek to know God aright. It is through the Word that the Holy Spirit gives me right thoughts of Him. The Word will also teach me how wretched and sinful I am. It reveals to me all the wonders that God will do for me, and the strength He will give to me to do His will. The Word teaches me how to pray — with strong desire, with a firm faith, and with constant perseverance. The Word teaches me not only what I am, but what I may become through God's grace. And above all, it reminds me each day that Christ is the great Intercessor, and allows me to pray in His name.

"O Christian, learn this great lesson, to renew your strength each day in God's Word, and so pray according to His will. Then we turn to the other side — prayer. We need prayer when we read God's Word — prayer to be taught of God to understand His Word, prayer that through the Holy Spirit I may rightly know and use God's Word — prayer that I may see in the Word that Christ is all in all, and will be all in me.

"(In my) blessed inner chamber — where I may approach God in Christ through the Word and prayer — I may offer myself to God and His service, and be strengthened by the Holy Spirit, so that His love may be shed abroad in my heart, and I may daily walk in that love."

— Andrew Murray

"If you abide in Me, and My words abide in you, ask whatever you wish, and it shall be done for you" (John 15:7).

"And this is the confidence which we have before Him, that, if we ask anything according to His will, He hears us. And if we know that He hears us in whatever we ask, we know that we have the requests which we desired from Him" (1 John 5:14,15).

Prayer is communion with God. This is the way our heavenly Father has ordained for His children to communicate with Him.

Often prayer is misunderstood. It is thought of as a vague, mystical element in one's relationship to a holy, awesome God. The Word of God does not teach this; rather it teaches that God our Father desires the fellowship of His children.

Our relationship with God, our heavenly Father, should be a relationship of complete trust, faith and obedience. We, as children, should approach our Father in love and gratitude. Our prayer to God should be an expression of our complete trust that He will hear us, according to John 15:7 and 1 John 5:14,15. If prayer is anything less than this, it is not prayer. Prayer is more than words; it is an attitude and an expression of the heart toward God.

The prayer life of the Christian is essential. His source of spiritual life is God in Christ. The Christian who does not utilize his resource of prayer fails, for the Christians life is an impossibility except it be lived in and through the Lord Jesus Christ.

As you study carefully the following lessons, it is our sincere desire that you will see the importance of prayer and that you will begin immediately to spend definite time daily in such fellowship with our heavenly Father. Remember, Jesus said, ". . . I am the way, and the truth, and the life; no one comes to the Father, but through Me . . . And whatever you ask in My name, that I will do, that the Father may be glorified in the Son. If you ask Me anything in My name, I will do it" (John 14:6,13,14).

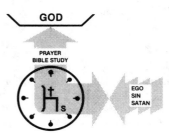

POWER THROUGH PRAYER

"No amount of money, genius, or culture can move things for God. Holiness energizing the soul, the whole man aflame with love, with desire for more faith, more prayer, more zeal, more consecration — this is the secret of power. These we need and must have, and men must be the incarnation of this God-inflamed devotedness. God's advance has been stayed, His cause crippled, His name dishonored for their lack. Genius (though the loftiest and most gifted), education (though the most learned and refined), position, dignity, place, honored names, cannot move this chariot of our God. It is a fiery one, and fiery forces only can move it. The genius of a Milton fails. The imperial strength of a Leo fails. But Brainerd's spirit could move it. Brainerd's spirit was on fire for God, on fire for souls. Nothing earthly, worldly, selfish came in to abate in the least the intensity of this all-impelling and all consuming force and flame.

"Prayer is the creator as well as the channel of devotion. The spirit of devotion is the spirit of prayer. Prayer and devotion are united as soul and body are united, as life and heart are united. There is no real prayer without devotion, no devotion without prayer."

"The Church is looking for better methods; God is looking for better men . . . What the Church needs today is not more or better machinery, not new organizations or more and novel methods, but men whom the Holy Ghost can use — men of prayer, men mighty in prayer. The Holy Ghost does not flow through methods, but through men. He does not come on machinery, but on men. He does not anoint plans, but men — men of prayer."

— E. M. Bounds

John Quincy Adams, President of the United States, noted in his journal, in connection with his custom of studying the Bible each morning: "It seems to me the most suitable manner of beginning the day."

"Beginning the day with a devotional Bible study and prayer equips a man for the day's fight with self and sin and Satan."

— John R. Mott

LESSON ONE

DEVOTIONAL BIBLE STUDY AND PRAYER

Teacher's Objective: To explain the meaning of devotional time and its importance as a daily practice; to lead group members to determine individually a specific time and place for having devotions and actually to begin doing it.

Teacher's Enrichment: (May be shared with class members as time allows.)

"Yet those who wait for the Lord will gain new strength; They will mount up with wings like eagles, they will run and not get tired, they will walk and not become weary" (Isaiah 40:31 NASV). "Wait for the Lord": to look to and expect help from Him. This, of course, is an attitude we should have constantly, but it is something we especially need in our devotional time. Daily waiting for the Lord means being alone with Him in prayer and meditation for a specific period every day.

The result of daily waiting for the Lord: strength to live the Christian life — strength we would not otherwise have. Note the context of Isaiah 40:31. Verse 30 has just told us that even the young and strong shall faint and collapse under strain, but those who wait upon God shall gain new strength for the tasks at hand.

Mounting up "with wings like eagles," running without being weary and walking without fainting: a picture of the strength we gain from daily waiting for God. We are able to begin what God has for us with zeal and enthusiasm, as an eagle — with great power — is suddenly able to rise in flight. We are able to continue at what God wants us to do over a long period, as one who walks a great distance without becoming weary.

CLASS TIME

Suggested Opening Prayer

Our Father, help us today to understand the importance of a daily time alone with You in Your Word and in prayer. Teach us as we study Your Word now.

(Introduction: Be sure students understand
    objective
    memory work
    reading assignment.)

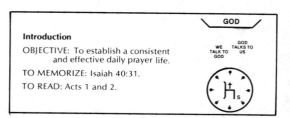

Introduction

OBJECTIVE: To establish a consistent and effective daily prayer life.

TO MEMORIZE: Isaiah 40:31.

TO READ: Acts 1 and 2.

GOD

WE TALK TO GOD   GOD TALKS TO US

Discussion Starter

Many young Christians know almost nothing about devotional time, and many older Christians are very lax in their practice of this foundational element of an effective Christian life. How do you think it could make a difference in your life?

Lesson Development

(Have the class share this material in any of the ways suggested in the Instructions for Teaching on page 21.)

Jesus Christ, the very Son of God, found it necessary to have definite and extended periods of fellowship alone with His Father. Who could be busier than He? His day was filled from morning to night, speaking to crowds, healing, holding private interviews, traveling and training His disciples; yet He found it necessary to have time alone with God.

Down through the years the biographies and writings of men of God who have done great things for God testify to the necessity of having a devotional time. John Wesley, who shook the world for God and founded the Methodist Church, is representative of other such great spiritual leaders. He thought prayer, more than anything else, to be his business.

Just as a child needs food to grow physically, so we need food to grow spiritually. We can miss a meal, and not feel any ill effects, but, if we don't eat for a week, we begin to weaken physically. So it is in our spiritual lives. The study of the Word of God and the practice of prayer are vitally important for spiritual growth. We may miss a day without feeding on the Word of God or praying and not feel any apparent ill effects in our lives, but if we continue this practice, we shall lose the power to live the victorious Christian life.

The Christian life might be compared to a soldier in battle. He is out on the front lines but is connected with his commanding officer by radio. He calls and tells of the conditions and problems he is facing. Then his commanding officer, who from his vantage point can see the entire battle area, relays instructions. In like manner the Christian shares his joys and sorrows, his victories and defeats, and his needs, as God instructs and guides him through His Word.

It is our heavenly Father who directs our battle of life. He knows the steps we should take. We must take time to go to Him for guidance.

(Have one of the group members read this paragraph in the student's book and have another one look up and read the two Scriptures.)

Bible Study

A. *Establish a definite time*

A daily devotional time in which Christians seek fellowship with the Lord Jesus Christ for the purpose of nourishing their spiritual lives should be set aside for personal worship and meditation. Once begun, this fellowship is continued throughout the day (Psalm 119:97; 1 Thessalonians 5:17).

1. In obedience to Christ's command, what did His disciples do (Acts 1:13, 14)? *Gathered for prayer--prayed continually..*

2. Although different individuals' schedules will vary, many people prefer the morning hours, before the responsibilities of the day begin.

    David was called a man after God's own heart. What time did he set aside to communicate with God (Psalm 5:3)? *The morning.*

    How often do you think it was? _____

The important thing to note here is that we should meet regularly with God. It cannot be haphazard or intermittent if we are to have sound spiritual health.

In this instance, Jesus had just finished an

> Name two characteristics of the devotional life of Jesus
> (Mark 1:35). *In the early morning, a lonely place*

extremely busy day. He was worn out, but not too tired to get up and pray. Why? Because He recognized that the effectiveness of His ministry depended on time alone with God. *A man or woman too busy for time with God is too busy.*

Suppose that for every day you spent at least twenty minutes in prayer,

> 3. When is your best devotional time? _____
> No one can say that he does not have time for prayer and Bible study. We can all do anything that we really want to do. Whether the period is long or short, set aside some time.

someone would give you at least a thousand dollars. Would you be more diligent and faithful in your prayer life than you are now? Is it possible that you and I would be willing to do for money what we would not be willing to do for God just because He is God and has given us access to Himself?

> 4. Make your devotional time unhurried.
>   Do not think about your next responsibility. Concentrate on your fellowship with the Lord. A definite time every day will do much to help.
>   An air of expectancy should pervade our devotional times. Anticipate meeting God.
>   A brief period with concentration is better than a long devotional time with your mind on many things.
>
>   How many minutes can you set aside daily for your time with God? _____
>
> B. *Choose a definite place*
>   Avoid distraction by finding a quiet, private place of worship. If privacy is impossible, you will need to learn to concentrate. If you cannot have a devotional time in your own room, perhaps one of the following places will be suitable:
>   A nearby chapel
>   A corner of the school library
>   The library of your house

In Mark 1:35 Christ selected a place where he could be alone and without distraction. This is essential in the devotional time. We must be able to turn all of our time and attention to God. If possible, select a place of beauty, such as a

church, or some place surrounded by the beauties of nature. Sometimes, if this is impossible, you can sing a hymn to yourself or play one on a record and your devotional time is transformed to a time of real worship. You can enjoy it as much as you do any other time of the day.

> Name three other places you might find appropriate for your private prayer and Bible study.
>
> _____
>
> _____
>
> _____

Two things are important in the devotional time: (a) First and foremost, God should get something from it. It should be God-

> C. *Goal and content of the devotional time*
>
> 1. We should have a purpose, goal or reason for everything we do. "Aim at nothing and you will surely hit it." Our purpose for prayer should be fellowship with God and the meeting of our own spiritual needs.

centered, a time to praise and worship Him, a time when we show our love for Him. (b) Also, we should get something out of it. From reading the Bible we should learn more about God. From praying we should find our burdens lifted and gain strength and help for the activities of the day.

Remember, you cannot lead anyone higher than you yourself have gone. You cannot enrich anyone beyond your own actual experience of God, hence, the absolute necessity of the Bible in the devotional time.

> During the devotional time we should be concerned with learning where we have failed and with rededicating ourselves to the task before us. We should use the time to regroup our forces after the battles of the previous day, and plan for the next day's attack.
>
> What particular spiritual need do you feel today? _____
>
> _____
>
> What battles did you have yesterday? _____
>
> 2. The devotional time should include Bible study, prayer, personal worship and quiet meditation. All phases of the devotional time are so closely related that one can actually engage in all at one time. For example: Begin by reading a psalm of thanksgiving or praise. As you read, your heart actually responds and you continue to praise and worship God from a grateful heart. Turn now to another portion of Scripture, such as Romans 8. Interrupt your reading to thank God for each truth that applies to you as a Christian. You will be amazed at how much you have to praise and thank God for, once you get started.

Prayer is one of the most important disciplines of the Christian life. In John 4:23 it says the Father *seeks* those who worship Him in prayer.

> After you have read and prayed for a while, remain in an attitude of quiet, listening for instructions from God. Write down on a piece of paper any reluctant thoughts that come to mind and pray about these.
>
> Supplementary content may include memorizing Scripture or reading from a devotional book or hymnal.
>
> Which of these do you have available to use? _____
>
> _____
>
> 3. Study Matthew 6:9-13. Paraphrase this prayer in your own words, using expressions meaningful to you. _____
>
> _____
>
> _____
>
> _____

Conclusion and Application

In conclusion, once again, we need to see the strategic importance of the devotional time in the life of the Christian:

"There is no true, deep conversion, no true, deep holiness . . . no abiding peace or joy, without being daily alone with God. There is no path to holiness but in being much and long alone with God.

"What an inestimable privilege is the institution of daily secret prayer to begin every morning. Let it be the one thing our hearts are set on, seeking, and finding, and meeting God" (Andrew Murray, *God's Best Secrets*).

Life Application

Fill in the blank spaces:

1. I have set aside the following definite time in the day for my devotional time: _____

2. I have decided on the following definite place: _____
   _____

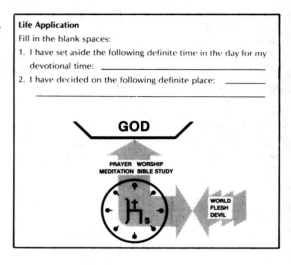

Suggested Closing Prayer

(Read Psalm 145 as a prayer of praise, then spend several minutes letting each group member who wishes pray briefly. You, as the leader, may finish with an appropriate closing.)

LESSON TWO

PURPOSE OF PRAYER

Teacher's Objective: To give students an understanding of the basis for scripturally sound and meaningful prayer.

CLASS TIME

Suggested Opening Prayer

Dear God, we pray today that You will give us a clear understanding of the scriptural basis for prayer both from our own standpoint and from Yours.

(Introduction: Be sure students understand
    objective
    memory work*
    reading assignment.)

(*Review verses, phrase by phrase, to facilitate learning.)   (Read.)

> **Introduction**
>
> OBJECTIVE: To understand the reasons for prayer.
> TO MEMORIZE: 1 John 5:14, 15.
> TO READ: Acts 3 and 4.
>
>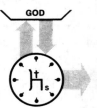
>
> Someone has wisely said, "Satan laughs at our toiling, mocks at our wisdom, but trembles when he sees the weakest saint on his knees." Prayer is God's appointed way of doing God's work.

Discussion Starter

(Ask class members for their responses to these two questions:) Why do you pray? Why do you think we should pray?

Lesson Development

Prayer is not an "escape hatch" to get us out of trouble. It is not merely something to make life easy for us. It is a means of glorifying God, whatever the cost may be to us. Prayer that moves God is prayer that seeks first the kingdom of God and His

> **Bible Study**
>
> A. *The apostles' motive*
>
> 1. On the basis of Acts 4, what was the problem which faced the apostles? <u>*Persecution and threats--result*</u> *of preaching death, burial, resurrection of Christ.*
>
> 2. Did they pray for God to remove the persecution? <u>*No.*</u> Why not? <u>*They were not concerned about per-*</u> *sonal safety and ease.*
>
> 3. For what did they pray (Acts 4:29)? <u>*That they might*</u> *speak God's Word with all confidence--courage.*
>
> 4. What was their real motive (John 14:13)? _____ *To glorify the Father.*

righteousness. In Acts 4:31 God answered the prayer of the apostles by filling them with the Spirit so that they could speak the Word boldly.

Other reasons for prayer which we might list — communion with God, adoration, confession,

> **B. Your motives**
>
> On the basis of your personal experience, list four (or more) reasons you pray.
>
> _____
>
> _____

thanksgiving, supplication — are united by the common purpose of glorifying God. If we pray merely for personal pleasure, and not to glorify God, we pray, for the most part, in vain.

It is important to realize, as we pray, that prayer is a spiritual activity, an activity which must be motivated and carried out by the Holy

> **C. God's motives in teaching us about prayer**
>
> 1. Read John 4:23, 24 and John 3:5-8.
>   What form does God take? _That of a Spirit._
>   What must happen to man before he can fellowship with God? _He must be born again--of the Spirit._
>   What kind of worship does God desire? _That which is in spirit and in truth._

Spirit. The person who is not a Christian is a "natural man" (1 Corinthians 2:14). He "does not accept the things of the Spirit of God; for they are foolishness to him, and he cannot understand them, because they are spiritually appraised." This is why so much of prayer is an empty experience for the person who is not a Christian. This is also the reason it can be a dead and dull experience for one who is a Christian.

> What is God's delight (Proverbs 15:8)? _The prayer of the upright._
>
> 2. List some purposes of prayer from each of the following Scripture references:
>   Matthew 7:7 _To seek God's supply._
>   Matthew 26:41 _Not to enter into temptation._
>   Luke 18:1 _Not to be afraid._
>
> 3. From your understanding of the above Scriptures, what do you think God wants you to realize about Him? _____
>
> _____

Qualifications for effective prayer are wrapped up in two phrases taken from John 15:7: "If you abide in me" and "My words abide in you." Abiding in Christ means total dependence on Him.

There are at least three ways to cross the Pacific Ocean. You can swim, which would be total dependence on your own strength. In this case you would go a few miles at the most, and drown. You can paddle, in a canoe, which would be partial dependence on your own strength, and you might get several miles farther, but the first strong wind would overturn you. Finally you could travel on an ocean liner, which would be the total committing of yourself to another to do what you could not do. This would guarantee you a safe trip, even through storms and gales.

In the same way, abiding in Christ means total dependence on the strength, power and ability of another. We do not trust ourselves even in part. Lack of abiding — laboring in our own strength, being out of fellowship with God — makes our prayer lives empty and vain.

Christ's words also must abide in us. His words must rest in our hearts and control our lives. In the military a soldier who refuses to obey instructions can be court-martialed. An employee who refuses to obey instructions is fired. A student who does not obey instructions may fail the course. The Christian who, whether from ignorance or unwillingness, does not obey God's instructions in the Bible, will see his whole life suffer — especially his prayer life.

Right living means right praying.

D. *Prayer meets the heart's needs*

1. According to 2 Corinthians 3:5, what is the source of the Christian's sufficiency? <u>God.</u>

   How do you tap into that source? <u>*Through prayer.*</u>

2. Read Psalm 63. Note the elements of human worship and write the word or phrase below with references (e.g., My soul thirsts for Thee — Psalm 63:1).
   <u>*"My flesh yearns for Thee...my lips will*</u>
   <u>*praise Thee...I will bless Thee...I will lift*</u>
   <u>*up my hands in Thy name. My soul is satisfied...*</u>
   <u>*my mouth offers praises...I remember Thee on*</u>
   <u>*my bed, I meditate on Thee...I sing for joy.*</u>
   <u>*My soul clings to Thee."*</u>

Prayer satisfies the longings of our hearts. One reason for prayerlessness is lack of desire to seek God. Do we seek God for Himself alone — apart from all He can give us? Exodus 33:12-17 records Moses' pleas for the presence of God after Israel's sin with the golden calf. In verse 15 Moses said, "If Thy presence does not go with us, do not lead us up from here." God had said He would send an angel, but this was not enough for Moses. Moses wanted the best — God's presence with him.

Conclusion and Application

The Christian's fellowship with the Father is two-fold:

1. God speaks to us in His holy Word. The Bible is the Father's message to His children.

2. We have the privilege of speaking directly to God in prayer. Prayer can

be the Christian's constant delight, his refuge in the moment of distress, his recourse in time of struggle, his solace in the hour of need.

Life Application

1. What conclusions can you now make concerning your relationship with God in prayer? _____
_____
_____

2. Begin a prayer list. Keep a record of the things for which you pray.

DATE	REQUESTS	DATE ANSWERED

Suggested Closing Prayer

(Have each person pray silently that God will reveal unconfessed sin so it may be confessed and not hinder the future effectiveness of his prayer. Prayer session should be closed by a brief prayer by leader.)

LESSON THREE

PRIVILEGE OF PRAYER

Teacher's Objective: To show the divine operation of the Father, Son and Holy Spirit in our prayers and to help students have a deeper appreciation of the great privilege of prayer.

CLASS TIME

Suggested Opening Prayer

Father, we ask You for a realization of the great privilege we have in being able to come to You in prayer. Help us understand the part that God the Son and God the Holy Spirit have in this activity of our lives.

(Introduction: Be sure students understand
  objective
  memory work
  reading assignment.)

Introduction

OBJECTIVE: To understand the roles of the Father, Son and Holy Spirit in prayer.

TO MEMORIZE: Philippians 4:6, 7.

TO READ: Acts 5 and 6.

The God who created us and loved us so much that He sent His only begotten Son to die for us, the God who in spite of our sin and lack of love for Him has done everything for us, now waits anxiously for us to come to Him in prayer. We would think nothing of waiting hours at the White House to have a short appointment with the President, and it would be unthinkable to keep the President waiting even a little while.

How can we keep our great God waiting for us, as unimportant as we are? What a privilege for us to come to our heavenly Father, just as a child comes to his father, and know that He will meet our needs and that He *desires* our fellowship (John 4:23).

Discussion Starter

(Have each group member take a pencil and paper and list these four names: Jesus, God, Holy Spirit and you. Now assign one or two of the Scripture passages listed to each person and have him or her relate the Scripture verse to the proper name:)

Hebrews 4:14-16	1 Timothy 2:5	Isaiah 59:2
Ephesians 6:18	Matthew 6:9	Romans 8:26
John 14:6	1 John 3:22-23	Jude 20

(Ask the group:) What do these Scripture verses show about how the Father, the Son and the Holy Spirit are involved in prayer?

Lesson Development

Bible Study

A. *To whom do we pray?*

1. To whom are our prayers to be directed (Matthew 6:9)? *Our Father who is in heaven.*

> "But some will say, 'Is not all prayer unto God?' No. Very much so-called prayer, both public and private, is not unto God. In order that a prayer should be really unto God, there must a definite and conscious approach to God when we pray; we must have a definite and vivid realization that God is bending over us and listening as we pray. In much of our prayer there is little thought of God. Our mind is not taken up with the thought of the mighty and loving Father... We are occupied neither with the need nor with the One to Whom we are praying but our mind is wandering here and there throughout the world . . . When we really come into God's presence, really meet Him face to face in the place of prayer, really seek the things that we desire *from Him*, then there is power."
>
> — R. A. Torrey, *How to Pray*

(Have group members discuss this, then write.)

2. Rewrite in your own words the description of God in 1 Chronicles 29:11, 12. _____

_____

_____

_____

_____

B. *Through whom do we pray?*

Read John 14:6.

1. How many mediators are there between God and man (1 Timothy 2:5)? *One.*

Who is the mediator? *The man Christ Jesus.*

A college student at an eastern university was once invited by a friend to go with him to Washington, D.C. The college student had no idea that anything out of the ordinary would happen, but when they arrived in Washington, his friend took him to the White House. Here they spent the day with the President and his wife, as their guests.

It turned out that the friend had known the President for years, and through him the college student was able to spend a day he would never forget. This would have been impossible on his own initiative, but when an acquaintance of the President opened the way for him, he received a priceless privilege.

The way to God is opened for us through Christ and our relationship with Him.

2. On the basis of Hebrews 4:14-16, describe the qualifications of our great high priest. _He can sympathize with our weaknesses, has been tempted in all things as we are, yet without sin._

3. What are the requirements for prayer relationship according to 1 John 3:22, 23? _Keep His commandments; believe in Jesus Christ; love one another._

We are to pray *in the Spirit.* This has already been discussed in earlier lessons, but we should note again that unless our prayer is in the Spirit it can never be

4. What does unconfessed sin in our lives do to our prayer fellowship with God (Psalm 66:18)? _The Lord will not hear when we cry to Him._

C. *In whom do we pray?*
   Read Ephesians 6:18 and Jude 20.

effective before God. Only the filling of the Holy Spirit can produce vital, believing prayer. No matter how we may work up our emotions, no matter what our feelings, no matter how great our desperation — unless God the Holy Spirit is behind our praying, it is fleshly, self-centered powerless prayer.

1. According to Romans 8:26, 27, why does the Holy Spirit need to help us pray? _We don't know how to pray as we should._
   How does He help us pray? _Intercedes for us._
   Why does God answer the prayers of the Holy Spirit? _He intercedes according to the will of God._

2. What, then, should be our relationship to the Holy Spirit (Ephesians 5:18)? _We should be filled with the Holy Spirit._

We cannot afford to neglect this priceless privilege. No wonder prayer accomplishes so much; no wonder it does what nothing else can do.

C. H. Spurgeon said years ago: "You have no

3. As we exercise the privilege of prayer, what does God then do about anxiety (Philippians 4:6, 7)? _(He gives us His peace which surpasses all comprehension.)_

4. Why can we cast our troubles on Him (1 Peter 5:7)? _Because He care for us._

place in which to pour your troubles except into the ear of God. If you tell them to your friends, you but put your troubles out for a moment, and they will return again. Roll your burden onto the Lord, through prayer, and you have rolled it into a great deep out of which it will never by any possibility rise. Cast your trouble where you cast your sins; you have cast your sins into the depths of the sea, *there* cast your troubles also. Never keep a trouble half an hour before you tell it to God in prayer. As soon as the trouble comes, quick, the first thing, tell it to your Father in prayer."

Continual prayer means continual freedom from burdens and anxieties. It is the only way to be a happy Christian.

Conclusion and Application

That God *desires* our fellowship is, perhaps, one of the most amazing facts conveyed to us through the Scriptures. This fact is so staggering that it is extremely difficult for us to grasp its significance.

That God should allow His creatures to have fellowship with Himself is wonder enough; but that He can desire it, that it gives Him satisfaction and joy and pleasure, is almost too much for understanding.

"The Father seeketh such to worship Him . . ." This reflection will inspire us with a passionate desire to seek His face. The usual concept — that we read our Bibles and say our prayers for our own benefit and satisfaction — will fade into insignificance. Let this simple thought of His desire for our fellowship obsess us morning by morning and day by day. It will carry us through times of darkness and give us patience to persevere when we remember that He is waiting to be gracious to us, waiting for us to come to Him.

Life Application

1. List any new insights into prayer you have gained from this lesson. _____

_____

_____

2. Write down one new way in which you want to apply prayer in your life right now. _____

_____

_____

Suggested Closing Prayer

Our Father, we thank You for the precious privilege of prayer and for how You the Father, how God the Son, and how God the Holy Spirit all have a part in it. Help us to live always praying in the Spirit.

ADDITIONAL BACKGROUND MATERIAL

Some additional passages of Scripture on the privilege of prayer:

A. The mediator between God and man:
    Romans 5:15.
    1 Corinthians 8:6.

B. How we should pray:
    Without display — Matthew 6:5.
    In faith, believing — James 1:6.
    Fervently — James 5:16.
    In line with God's will — 1 John 5:14-15.
    Unceasingly — 1 Thessalonians 5:17.

LESSON FOUR

PROCEDURE IN PRAYER

Teacher's Objective: To teach students a simple guide to use in their daily prayer times.

Teacher's Enrichment: (Share with students as time permits.)

The ACTS Plan of Prayer

The acronym, ACTS is an easy pattern to help us remember the things we usually want to include during our praying time: A for adoration, C for confession, T for thanksgiving and S for supplication.

- A —Adoration (Praise) gives honor to God because of His omnipotent and sovereign rule in all of life — Romans 8:28; Habakkuk 3:17-19; Psalm 113.

- C —Confession presents a clean vessel to God — Psalm 51:6, 16-17; 32; Ezra 9:5-15.

- T —Thanksgiving indicates appreciation to God as the supplier of all our needs — Psalm 107:1, 2; Luke 17:11-19.

- S — Supplication refers to requests made of God — Philippians 4:6-7; Ephesians 6:18-20.

     The prayers of supplication fall into two classifications:

     (1) intercession, prayer for non-Christians — 1 Timothy 2:1-4.

     (2) petition, prayer for ourselves.

     Things that hinder our prayers include doubt — James 1:6-8; and pride — Psalm 66:18.

     Things we should realize to have successful prayer include God's willingness to give — Romans 8:32; and that right living means right praying — Psalm 84:11-12.

CLASS TIME

Suggested Opening Prayer

Dear Father, we ask today that You will teach us how to pray. Help us understand the various things involved in effective prayer, and as the disciples asked Jesus so long ago, teach us TO pray.

(Introduction: Be sure
students understand
   objective
   memory work
   reading assignment.)

Introduction

OBJECTIVE: To apply a simple guide to your daily prayer time.

TO MEMORIZE: 1 Corinthians 14:40.

TO READ: Acts 7 and 8.

GOD

ADORATION
CONFESSION
THANKSGIVING
SUPPLICATION

    There are many procedures one may follow in prayer. It is good to follow a simple procedure but never to become bound to a ritual. God is more interested in our hearts than in our words. John Bunyan, author of *Pilgrim's Progress*, said, "In prayer it is better to have a heart without words than words without a heart." In this lesson we will consider a simple guide that you may use in your daily devotional time. It is:

    Adoration, Confession, Thanksgiving, Supplication.

    This order can be easily remembered by the first letter of each word — ACTS.

Discussion Starter

(Ask students to define: adoration, confession, thanksgiving, supplication. Then proceed with:) We may categorize this prayer pattern in two phases: giving to God (adoration, confession, thanksgiving) and receiving from God (supplication).

Lesson Development

Adoration: Act of paying honor to a divine being; to regard with fervent devotion and affection.

Bible Study

A. *Adoration*

  1. Why should we praise God?

    Jeremiah 32:17   *He made heaven and earth; nothing too hard.*

    1 John 4:10   *He loved us and sent His Son.*

    Philippians 1:6   *He began a good work and will perfect it.*

  2. What is the best way for you to show your gratitude toward, and your faith and trust in God in all circumstances (Philippians 4:6)? *"In everything by prayer... with thanksgiving let your requests be made known"*

    What would you conclude that God expects of us (1 Thessalonians 5:16-18)? *"Rejoice always; pray without ceasing; in everything give thanks."*

    If you sometimes find it hard to praise God, read some of the Psalms (Psalms 146-150 in particular).

B. *Confession*

  1. Read Isaiah 59:1, 2.

    What will hinder fellowship with God? *Iniquities, sins.*

  2. Psalm 51 was David's prayer after he had fallen out of fellowship with God. What did David conclude that God wanted of him (Psalm 51:6, 16, 17)? *Truth, broken spirit, contrite heart.*

  3. What should you do when and if you find your fellowship with God is broken (1 John 1:9)? *Confess sin, accept forgiveness.*

Confession: To make confession of one's faults, especially to confess one's sins. The Greek word means "say the same thing with." We agree with God about our sins.

In confession of sin, note these principles:

(1) We do not need to feel "spiritual" to confess our sins. If we have sin that

we need to confess, it is a sign we are not spiritual at that moment anyway. But the time to confess it is immediately when we realize we have sinned.

(2) Confession should be honest, but beware of torturous self-examination or unhealthy extremes of introspection. Lord Wariston, a devout young man of the 17th century, describes himself in his diary as being God's "poor, naughty, wretched, useless, passionate, humorous, vain, proud [man] . . . the unworthiest, filthiest, passionatest, deceitfulest, crookedest, . . . of all thy servants." However true, this cataloging of sins seems tainted with a bit of pride in the thoroughness of his self-condemnation.

(3) We must be willing to accept God's forgiveness and then change behavior appropriately. When some confess their sins they still retain their guilt feelings and self-pity because they do not want to accept the fact God cleanses from all unrighteousness.

C. *Thanksgiving*

Let us never be guilty of being ungrateful to God.

1. How often should we give thanks (Hebrews 13:15)?
   Continually.

   What for (Ephesians 5:20)? _*For all things.*_
   Why (1 Thessalonians 5:18)? _*God's will for us in Christ.*_
2. What about a situation that seems adverse? _____

Thanksgiving: Act of rendering thanks, especially to God. A prayer expressing gratitude.

To fail to give thanks *in* all things is to sin against God, just the same as violating the Ten Commandments is sin against God. After Job had lost his money and his family, he worshiped God and said, "Blessed be the name of the Lord" Job 1:21. If, in the next twenty-four hours, you were to lose your whole family and every cent you have, what would your attitude be? If you were filled with God's Holy Spirit and recognized that He controls all things, it could be one of praise and thanksgiving.

D. *Supplication*

1. Intercession.

   An example of intercession is provided in Colossians1:3,9
   What was Paul's prayer for the Christians of Colossae?
   *They may be filled with knowledge of his will.*

   Many times our efforts in leading people to Christ are fruitless because we forget the necessary preparation for witnessing. The divine order is first to talk to God about men, and *then* to talk to men about God. If we follow this formula, we shall see results. Prayer is really the place where people are won to Christ; service is just gathering in the results of our prayer.

Supplication: To implore God. A humble petition, entreaty.

Christians often do not realize the importance of intercession. Paul continually prayed for his converts, as the first chapters of almost all his epistles show. He also asked them to pray for Him (Romans 15:30-31, etc.).

> As you meditate on the above, list the requests you can make to God for Christians and non-Christians. _____
> _____

Early in your Christian life, you should try to form prayer partnerships with your friends. This will bring you closer together and will profoundly affect your life. (Teacher, discuss this with your group and try to motivate them to form prayer partnerships whether with one another, or with others.)

> 2. Petition.
>
> Why should we expect God to answer our prayers (John 3:16; Romans 8:32)? *Because of His great love*
> *for us and His willingness to give.*
>
> What part does belief have in our prayers (Mark 11:24)?
> *To receive, we must believe that we have*
> *received.*
> Faith is necessary for answered prayers. What else is necessary (1 John 5:14, 15)? *We must ask according*
> *to God's will.*
>
> Why will God not answer some prayers (James 4:3)?
> *We ask with wrong motives.*
>
> According to Psalm 84:11, 12, what has God promised to do? *He will not with hold any good thing.*
>
> 3. Explain 2 Corinthians 12:7-10 in light of Romans 8:28.
> _____
> _____
>
> What does this passage teach us about apparently unanswered prayer? _____
> _____

Conclusion and Application

Once again we are faced with the importance of prayer. We can be careful to use these methods and procedures, but they in themselves will not make us great prayer warriors. To learn to use these things effectively, we must pray.

> **Life Application**
>
> 1. Add other requests to the prayer list you began at the end of Lesson Two.
>
> 2. Select one prayer request from your prayer request list and before you make the request, apply A-C-T. Then make the request, which completes the procedure: (S = Supplication).

Suggested Closing Prayer

Father, we thank You for the things we have learned today. Thank You for the simple plan of prayer, of using the word ACTS as a guide which includes adoration, confession, thanksgiving and supplication. Help us to submit to the leading of Your Spirit and to be effective in our praying.

ADDITIONAL BACKGROUND MATERIAL

THE PLACE OF PRAYER

There is a place where thou canst touch the eyes
Of blinded men to instant, perfect sight;

There is a place where thou canst say, "Arise"
To dying captives, bound in chains of night;

There is a place where thou canst reach the store
Of hoarded gold and free it for the Lord;

There is a place — upon some distant shore —
Where thou canst send the worker and the Word.

Where is that secret place — dost thou ask, "Where?"
O soul, it is the secret place of prayer!

— Alfred Lord Tennyson

LESSON FIVE

POWER IN PRAYER

Teacher's Objective: To lead students to an awareness of the great power available through prayer and to help them discover how to use that power.

CLASS TIME

Suggested Opening Prayer

Our Father, we thank You for meeting with us today, and for the opportunity we have to learn more about You and Your Word. We ask that You will teach us how our prayers can be powerful enough for us to see results.

(Introduction: Be sure students understand
   objective
   memory work
   reading assignment.)

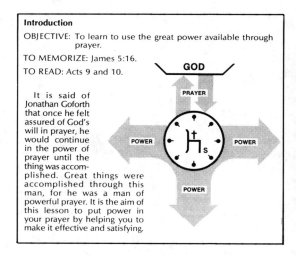

Introduction

OBJECTIVE: To learn to use the great power available through prayer.

TO MEMORIZE: James 5:16.

TO READ: Acts 9 and 10.

It is said of Jonathan Goforth that once he felt assured of God's will in prayer, he would continue in the power of prayer until the thing was accomplished. Great things were accomplished through this man, for he was a man of powerful prayer. It is the aim of this lesson to put power in your prayer by helping you to make it effective and satisfying.

Discussion Starter

(Ask the group members this question:) What are some of the things you can do to be sure your prayers get answered?

Lesson Development

There was a serious problem here out of which

Bible Study

A. *Power for answered prayer*
   Read Acts 12:5-18.

there was no conceivable escape. Peter was an important leader in the early church and his death might have meant catastrophe for the early church at this time. James had already been killed, and it looked as if Peter would be also.

> 1. How did Peter's fellow Christians respond to his imprison-
> ment (Acts 12:5)? *"Prayer for him was being made*
> *fervently by the church of God."*
>
> What was God's answer to their prayer (Acts 12:6-11)?
> *He was miraculously released from prison.*
>
> What was their response to God's answer (Acts 12:13-16)?
> *Disbelief.*

We should not despair when prayer is the only way out, for prayer is more effective than anything else we can use.

> 2. What do the following Scripture references tell you about the qualities God demands in a person for powerful prayer?
> Hebrews 11:1, 6 *Faith.*
> Romans 12:1, 2 *Yieldedness.*
> 1 Corinthians 15:58 *Steadfastness, abounding in God's work.*
> 1 John 3:22 *Keep His commandments.*
> Ephesians 5:18 *The filling of the Spirit.*

Answered prayer is not just automatic. It is the experience of those who only truly want to live for God and put Him in first place. If your prayers are powerless before God, perhaps the difficulty is not just in your prayers, but in your life. Perhaps you are not surrendered in some area. Perhaps some sin is hindering you.

R. A. Torrey tells the story of a woman who came to him and said she did not believe in the Bible any more. When he asked her why, she replied, "Because I have tried its promises and found them untrue." "The Bible says," she continued, " 'Whatsoever ye ask believing, ye shall receive.' Well, I fully expected to get things from God in prayer, but I did not receive them, so the promise failed." Dr. Torrey then turned her to 1 John 3:22 — "Whatsoever we ask, we receive of Him, because we keep His commandments, and do those things that are pleasing in His sight." Then he said, "Were you keeping His commandments and doing those things pleasing in His sight?" She confessed she was not. Her trouble was not the Bible's promises; it was her own disobedience.

> B. Conditions to answered prayer
> 1. Why is it necessary to ask in accordance with the will of God 1 John 5:14, 15? *God will not answer contrary to His will.*

Would God really be doing the best thing for us if He answered prayers which were not His will? A baby playing in the kitchen might see a shining steel knife and want it. Yet his mother, knowing the danger of giving it to him, keeps it from his grasp. Many times things we want with all our hearts are things which will ultimately bring misery and spiritual weakness to our lives and are outside of God's will.

220 THE CHRISTIAN AND PRAYER

> 2. Write out John 15:7 in your own words and state what it teaches about conditions to answered prayer. _____
> _____
> _____

Why is it necessary to abide in Christ, and allow His Word to abide in us, that prayer may be answered? We noted above that we must pray *in the will of God.* But the important question is, how do I know the will of God when I pray? The answer is first of all, through God's Word. This lays down the general principles of Christian living. Many times we pray outside the will of God because we do not know the Word of God.

"My words must abide in you." John 16:13 says, "He will guide you into all truth." If we put all our dependence on Christ, He will guide our prayers by the Holy Spirit. This experience becomes true in our lives as we walk close to God and spend much time in prayer with Him.

> 3. What is the value of several Christians praying for something as opposed to just one (Matthew 18:19)? _____
> *It increases our power in prayer.*
> _____

There are times, of course, when God answers the prayer of just one individual. But when several share the burden of a prayer, the Scripture teaches that there are greater results. Paul requested others to pray for him (Ephesians 6:18-19).

When many pray, many have a chance to witness God's power instead of one. When many pray, a closer fellowship both with God and with one another results. Seek a prayer partner and share your prayer burdens. Christians in the same living group, work crew, class or school, family, etc. should meet together for prayer. There is *power* in united prayer. (See Additional Background Material for suggestions for group praying if time allows.)

> C. *Prevailing prayer*
> 1. Example of prevailing prayer: During his lifetime, George Mueller recorded more than 50,000 answers to prayer. He prayed for two men daily for more than 60 years. One of these men was converted shortly before Mueller's death and the other about a year later. As in Mueller's experience, we do not always see the answer to our prayers. We must leave the results to God.
> One of the great needs of the present day is for men and women who will begin to pray for things and then pray on and on until they obtain that which they seek from the Lord.
> How long do you think we should pray for someone or something? (Read Luke 18:1-8; Matthew 15:21-28.)
> _____
> Why do you think God honors prevailing prayer? _____
> _____

Many Christians become impatient in waiting for a prayer to be answered. They want to see results immediately. But one aspect of the fruit of the Spirit is patience.

God waited many years before He sent Christ. He may wait many more years before He sends Him the second time. He waited patiently for years while some of us lived without knowing or wanting to know Him. Even today He bears patiently with all kinds of weaknesses and rebellious attitudes. So, if He requires us to wait days, weeks, even years before prayers are answered, we should have no complaints. Through waiting patiently our faith grows and our characters are refined.

> 2. What did the following men accomplish through prayer?
>
> Moses (Exodus 15:23-25) _He made bitter water_ _sweet._
>
> Samson (Judges 16:28-30) _He killed more Philist-_ _ines at his death than he did in his life._
>
> Peter (Acts 9:36-41) _Raised Tabitha from the dead._
>
> Elijah (James 5:17, 18) _Prayed that it might not_ _rain--it didn't for 3½ years; then prayed_ _for rain and "the sky poured rain."_
>
> 3. In what way are all of these examples alike? _____

Conclusion and Application

R. A. Torrey says, "Prayer is the great problem-solver. Yet even the church found it hard to believe prayer would work (Acts 12:15). 'Power belongeth unto God,' but all that belongs to God we can have for the asking. God holds out His hands and says, 'Ask and it shall be given you . . .' The powerlessness and poverty of the average Christian finds its explanation in the words of the apostle James, 'Ye have not because ye ask not.' "

> **Life Application**
>
> 1. Do you pray for results? _____
>   Do you really believe and trust God when you pray? _____
>
> 2. Write down one prayer request for which you are having to exercise "prevailing prayer." _____
>
> 3. List two verses of Scripture you can claim in relation to this prayer request. _____

Suggested Closing Prayer

Dear Father, we thank You for all the examples of powerful prayer You have given us in Your Word, and we thank You for showing us how we can have answered prayer. We are trusting Your leadership through Your Holy Spirit and expect to see changes in our lives which will be pleasing to You.

ADDITIONAL BACKGROUND MATERIAL

Some practical suggestions for group praying:

Make your prayers sentence prayers.

Wait in silence until the Spirit impresses you to pray about something specific.

Feel free to pray more than once about different individuals and circumstances.

Be thankful for the silences between prayers. Let God speak to your heart at that time.

Be specific — avoid the over-use of general words like "bless" and "help." Ask God not just to bless in a general way, but to bless in specific ways.

Make praise and thanksgiving an important part of your time of prayer.

(NOTE: The article, "The Praying Christian" by Andrew Murray, which appears on page 187 of the student's book, may be read and discussed in class if time allows.)

LESSON SIX

PROMISE OF PRAYER

Teacher's Objective: To show the student that God answers prayer in every area of life, and to lead him to a more active appropriation of His promises.

Teacher's Enrichment: In Detroit, Michigan, an old couple was taken to the hospital suffering from malnutrition and starvation. After they went to the hospital, police began to search through their rubbish-cluttered home, and they discovered $40,000 stored away. The husband said he was not even aware that he possessed over a thousand dollars.

This is exactly the plight of most Christians in relation to prayer. "You do not have because you do not ask" (James 4:2). "He who did not spare His own Son, but delivered Him up for us all, how will He not also with Him freely give us all things?" (Romans 8:32). God does not expect us to live like spiritual misers, suffering malnutrition in our Christian life, when He has vast treasures of blessings ready to give us only on the condition that we come in believing prayer. Ask yourself if you are really appropriating His blessings.

CLASS TIME

Suggested Opening Prayer

Dear Lord, we thank You for the opportunity to meet today and to learn more of Your Word. As we study these promises of prayer, we ask You to help us understand that You desire to meet the needs in every area of our lives if we will only come to You.

(Introduction: Be sure students understand
    objective
    memory work
    reading assignment.)

Introduction
OBJECTIVE: To claim God's promises for us about and in prayer.
TO MEMORIZE: Jeremiah 33:3.
TO READ: Acts 11 and 12.

Discussion Starter

Think about the statement, "God helps him who helps himself." Is there a false conviction underlying this statement? What is it that allows God to help you?

Lesson Development

Bible Study

It is estimated that there are more than 5,000 personal promises in the Bible. However, to many Christians, these promises mean little or nothing. Why (Hebrews 4:2)? _The Word was not "united by faith."_

GOD

TALK 1

TALK 2

MAN

Bags of cement sitting in a warehouse will never become concrete until they are mixed with sand, gravel and water. Even so, God's promises will never become concrete unless they are mixed with faith and action. You must make them yours by believing them and putting your faith to work.

A. *What God has promised concerning prayer*

1. Jeremiah 33:3

   Condition: _"Call to Me."_

   Promise: _Will answer, tell great and mighty things._

At the time God made this promise, Jeremiah was being held captive by the unbelieving rulers of Israel. Israel had strayed far from God. They were a nation given to idolatry, and the horrible judgment by Babylonian captivity was about to descend on them. God showed Jeremiah (in the rest of chapter 33) that a day was coming when He would utterly transform and change this idolatrous nation. What a marvelous revelation, what an encouragement to the heart of God's prophet!

Often, we are so governed by earthly circumstances we lose the heavenly vision. We need to take our eyes off the discouragement of self and circumstance. We need to realize God has "great and mighty" things to show us about our individual relationships to Him and what He can do for and through us. We need only call upon Him to receive these things.

Matthew 21:22

Condition: _Ask, believe._

Promise: _Shall receive._

"Without faith it is impossible to please Him" (Hebrews 11:6). This is a stumbling block for most of us because we are tempted by Satan to doubt God's love and willingness to make provision for us. The first sin entered the human race because Eve began to doubt God's Word (Genesis 3:1-6).

We cannot believe God for just anything, however, for sometimes it is not His will to do just the things we ask. We must therefore ask God to lead us to ask for the right things, and when He does this, along with it He will give us the faith to believe.

The problem is not that
God refuses to answer

> **1 John 5:14, 15**
> Condition: _Ask according to His will._
> Promise: _We have the requests._

prayer, or is ungenerous; the problem is that we do not ask according to His will.
How can we know His will?

(1) By studying the Word of God.

(2) By thinking carefully about whether our prayer is for the glory of God and
according to His will, or just something to gratify selfish desires. "You ask and do
not receive, because you ask with wrong motives, so that you may spend it on your
pleasures" (James 4:3).

(3) By asking the Holy Spirit to lead us. "For all who are being led by the
Spirit of God, these are sons of God" (Romans 8:14).

What does it mean to
ask in the name of Christ?

> **John 14:14**
> Condition: _Ask in Jesus' name._
> Promise: _"I will do it."_

It means far more than saying "in Jesus' name" glibly at the end of a prayer. To ask
in the name of Christ means to ask on the basis of the authority Christ has given to
us. We are to ask in His authority for His glory, so that "the Father may be
glorified in the Son" (John 14:13).

> 2. Which promise do you need most to apply to your own
>   prayer life right now and why? _____
>   _____
>   _____

God says He will supply
your *needs,* not necessarily
your desires. And it is
according to His riches
in glory. If you had a

> B. What God will provide through prayer
>   1. Material needs:
>   In Philippians 4:19? _"All your needs."_
>   In Psalm 84:11? _Withholds no good thing._

benefactor with a million-dollar fortune, would you worry about where
tomorrow's meals were coming from? God's fortune is far greater than a paltry
million, and we need have no worry about His willingness to supply.

God gives only *good* things. Sometimes the things that are good for us in the
long run may not make us happy for the moment. Sometimes it is good for us to go
through testings, and we need to consider these as gifts from God too.

God does not promise to
show us the whole future at

> Guidance:
> In Proverbs 3:5, 6? _He will make your paths straight_
> In Psalm 32:8? _Instruct, teach, counsel._

once, but he does promise to guide us day by day. But this comes only as we "trust in the Lord." Before making any important decision we should always pray for guidance; and in even the little things of life, there should be an attitude of surrender and trust.

These, the greatest needs of life, are things which God alone can satisfy.

> Spiritual needs:
> In Ephesians 1:3? _Every spiritual blessing._
> In Philippians 4:13? _Can do all things through Christ._
> In Isaiah 41:10? _Is with us, strengthens, helps,_

Spiritual needs include happiness and satisfaction in our hearts, victory over sin, and courage to overcome Satan and face trials. The Bible promises God will supply for these generously and in abundance — more so than any other kind of blessing He gives. God does not allow every person on earth to be a material millionaire — some people live in elegant mansions and some live in one-room shanties — but God made *all* Christians spiritual millionaires. What we need to do is possess the possessions He has given us.

> 2. Is God dependable? _upholds_ Can you trust Him? _____
> 3. In what particular circumstance of your life do you presently need to trust Him more and for what? _____
>
> These promises are real — claim them; believe them; live by them.

Conclusion and Application

Through this Bible Study we see again how important prayer is. It is like the pipe which carries water from the great city reservoir into our homes. Though it is but a channel, if the pipe is broken all of the water is held back and nothing comes through. Prayer is our channel to God.

> **Life Application**
> List on this chart at least three things you need to pray for, and a verse for each which promises God's provision.
>
> | NEED | PROMISE |
> |------|---------|
> | | |
> | | |
> | | |

Suggested Closing Prayer

Our Father, give us a heart to pray and to trust You for the answers. Help us appropriate these promises You have shown us, and help us to understand that when we are not appropriating Your blessings the trouble is not with You but with ourselves. Keep us mindful of the importance of looking to You and trusting You to supply all our needs.

LESSON SEVEN
RECAP

Teacher's Objective: To deepen the students' understanding of the importance of prayer and assist them in their resolve to spend definite time daily in fellowship with their heavenly Father.

CLASS TIME

Suggested Opening Prayer

Help us, dear Father, as we review the last six lessons now and increase our understanding and appropriation of Your promises in prayer. Help us appreciate the importance and purpose of prayer, the procedures and power available, and what a great privilege we have to be able to fellowship with You in this way.

(Introduction: This review lesson does not have a new student's objective. Previous memory work is to be reviewed, especially 1 John 5:14,15. The reading assignment involves a continuation of reading the book of Acts, chapters 13 and 14.)

> Review all memorized verses.
> Read Acts 13 and 14.

Discussion Starter

(Ask the group members to share their answers to this question:) How has what you have recently learned about prayer changed your life?

Lesson Development

(Any Teacher's Enrichment or Additional Background Material that you were not able to use in the previous lessons could be utilized at this time and any point which you might feel was not sufficiently covered before, or which the students do not understand completely, can be dealt with now too.

Then go over the Recap questions and answers. This material will benefit both the students and you by

> Have you set aside a specific place and time for daily prayer and devotions? _____ Where and when? _____
> What adjustments do you need to make for it to be more effective (more time, less time, different place, etc.)? _____
>
> Why are you praying? _____

giving you a broader com-
prehension of the scope of
powerful prayer.)

What conditions are you now meeting, which you weren't
before, to be more effective in prayer? _____

Fill in the words to complete the suggested guide for prayer
content:

        A _____
        C _____
        T _____
        S _____

Are you presently following this guide or do you have another?
_____

(Remember, a guide is not mandatory, it is just helpful.)
How has your understanding of power and promises in prayer
been broadened? _____
_____
_____

Conclusion and Application

The world little knows what is accomplished through prayer. It is one of the most important things anyone can do. Through prayer, often prayer alone, men and women can be brought to Christ, Christians can be strengthened, holiness infused into their lives, circumstances altered, tragedies averted, perplexing problems solved, governments and kingdoms overturned, forces of evil defeated and Satan rendered helpless. We have such a great privilege that it would be foolish not to spend time and effort in prayer.

Suggested Closing Prayer

(Allow a short time of silent prayer for personal, private commitments to spend definite time daily in prayer. Then pray aloud:) Thank You, Father, for refreshing our minds regarding the importance of prayer and for leading us in these commitments. We ask that each person's prayer life will be strengthened and deepened because of our studies of this part of Your Word.

SUMMARY LESSON
THE CHRISTIAN AND PRAYER

Teacher's Objective: To lead students to an awareness of the importance of prayer and of the great power available through it and to help them discover how to use that power; to challenge students to a regular and effective prayer life.

Teacher's Enrichment: (See Teacher's Enrichment sections as they occur in the previous lessons of this Step, and share with the class as time permits.)

CLASS TIME

Suggested Opening Prayer

Help us, dear Father, as we study this lesson, to realize the importance of a daily time alone with You and Your Word in prayer. Give us an understanding of the purpose of prayer, the procedures and power available, and give us an appreciation of the great privilege we have to be able to fellowship with You in this way. Help us appropriate your promises regarding prayer.

(Introduction:

STUDENT'S OBJECTIVE: To understand the reasons for prayer, to appreciate God's promises and the power available through prayer, and to begin a consistent and effective daily prayer life.

TO MEMORIZE: 1 John 5:14,15; Isaiah 40:31.

READING ASSIGNMENT: Matthew 15:21-28; John 14:12-14; 16:23-27; Romans 8:26,27; Philippians 4:6,7; James 5:13-18.)

Discussion Starter

(Hand out sheets of paper and ask the students to write down as many reasons as they can think of as to why we should pray. After three or four minutes, have each one read his list. You may then add any of your own and conclude the discussion by pointing out the importance of prayer.)

Lesson Development

A. Devotional Bible study and prayer *(from Lesson 1)*.

(Have one of the students read the opening paragraphs on page 168 of the student's book.)

1. We must establish a definite time if we are to begin regular Bible study. What was the time that David set aside to communicate with God (Psalm 5:3)? What about Jesus (Mark 1:35)? When would your best time be?

2. We must also choose a definite place, preferably a quiet place where we can be alone. Notice again Mark 1:35. What do you see about Jesus' choice of a place?

3. We should have a two-fold purpose, or goal, to be accomplished when we meet with God: 1) fellowship with God, and 2) having our spiritual needs met.

4. The content of our devotional time may include Bible study, prayer, worship and meditation. Additional content may include memorizing Scriptures, reading from a devotional book or a hymnal. How can these be used to accomplish the two-fold purpose of devotions?

B. Purpose of prayer *(from Lesson 2)*.

1. For what did the apostles pray, and why (Acts 4:29; John 14:13)? (They were not concerned with personal safety and ease, but prayed for boldness to witness.)

2. Can you name some other reasons for prayer? (Communion with God, adoration, confession, thanksgiving, supplication — all united by the common purpose of glorifying God.)

3. What is God's motive in teaching us about prayer (John 4:23,24)? (So we can pray in the Spirit. God is a Spirit — see 1 Corinthians 2:14. So our heart's needs may be met — see 2 Corinthians 3:5; Psalm 63, especially verse 1.)

C. Privilege of prayer *(from Lesson 3)*.

1. To whom do we pray (Matthew 6:9)? (Our Father who is in heaven. Much so-called prayer, both public and private, is not unto God. In order that a prayer should be really unto God, we must make a definite and conscious approach to Him; we must realize He is listening.)

2. Through whom do we pray (John 14:6; 1 Timothy 2:5)? (Jesus Christ.) Why (Hebrews 4:14-16)? (He knows our weaknesses, has been tempted in all things as we are, but is without sin. He is worthy. Old Testament saints approached God indirectly through their appointed priests, but now, as our high priest, the one in authority, Jesus by His death and resurrection has gained direct access for us and He instructs us to go boldly to God through Him.)

3. What are the requirements for a proper prayer relationship (1 John 3:22,23; Psalm 66:18)? (Keep His comandments; allow no unconfessed sin in our lives.)

    4. In whom do we pray? (The Holy Spirit.) Why (Romans 8:26,27)? (We don't know how to pray as we should, but the Holy Spirit does.)

D. A suggested procedure for prayer *(from Lesson 4).*

The acronym, A C T S, is an easy pattern to help us remember the things we usually want to include during our praying time:

    A — Adoration: The act of paying honor to a divine being; praise. (See Jeremiah 32:17; 1 John 4:10; 1 Thessalonians 5:16-18.)

    C — Confession: To agree with God about our sins. Note these principles about confession of sin:

        1. We do not need to feel "spiritual" to confess sin. We only need to agree with God that it is sin as soon as we realize it.

        2. Confession should be honest, but without unhealthy introspection or extremes of self-condemnation.

        3. We must be willing to accept God's forgiveness — which we already have upon confession — and change our behavior appropriately.

    T — Thanksgiving: Expression of gratitude to God in prayer. (See Hebrews 13:15; Ephesians 5:20.) To fail to give thanks *in all things* is to sin against God.

    S — Supplication: To implore God; a humble petition or entreaty. An example of Paul's prayers of intercession is found in Colossians 1:3. (See also Romans 15:30-31.) We may expect God to answer our petitions, because of John 3:16 and Romans 8:32.

        (The difference between intercession and petition: intercession is for others; petitions are requests in general.)

E. Power in prayer *(from Lesson 5).*

What are the conditions which must be met in order for a person to be powerful in prayer? Hebrews 11:6 (faith); Romans 12:1,2 (yieldedness); 1 Corinthians 15:58 (steadfastness, abounding in God's work); 1 John 3:22 (keep His commandments); Ephesians 5:18 (be filled with the Spirit); 1 John 5:14,15 (ask in accordance with the will of God); James 4:3 (ask with right motives).

F. Promises of prayer *(from Lesson 6).*

    1. What are the conditions and the promises shown by these Scriptures: Matthew 21:22 (Ask, believe/shall receive.) 1 John 5:14,15 (Ask according to His will/we have the requests.) John 14:14 (Ask in Jesus' name/"I will do it.")

    2. What will God provide according to these Scriptures. Philippians 4:19 (All your needs — *material* needs.) Proverbs 3:5,6 (Make paths straight — need for *guidance.*) Ephesians 1:3 (Every spiritual blessing — *spiritual* needs.)

Conclusion and Application

Through this Bible study we see how important prayer is. It is like the pipe which carries water from the great city reservoir into our homes. Though it is but a channel, if the pipe is broken all of the water is held back and nothing comes through. Prayer is our channel to God.

(Teacher, encourage each student now to set aside a specific time for daily devotional Bible study and prayer, and to choose a particular place. Also refer students to the Life Application on page 174 of the *Handbook* and challenge each student to begin and keep a prayer list as illustrated there.)

Suggested Closing Prayer

(Allow a short time of silent prayer for personal private commitment to these things, then you pray aloud:) Thank You, Father, for what You have taught us about the importance of meeting daily with You for a time of devotions. And we thank You for the great privilege of and the power available in prayer, and for the promises You have made regarding answered prayer. Keep us aware of the things that are involved and guide us toward the goal of effective praying.

STEP FIVE

The Christian and the Bible

GOD'S MEN AND THE WORD OF GOD

"The vigor of our spiritual life will be in exact proportion to the place held by the Bible in our life and thoughts . . . I have read the Bible through 100 times, and always with increasing delight. Each time it seems like a new book to me. Great has been the blessing from consecutive, diligent, daily study. I look upon it as a lost day when I have not had a good time over the Word of God."

— George Mueller

"I prayed for faith, and thought that some day faith would come down and strike me like lightning. But faith did not seem to come. One day I read in the tenth chapter of Romans, 'Now faith comes by hearing, and hearing by the Word of God.' I had closed my Bible and prayed for faith. I now opened my Bible and began to study, and faith has been growing ever since."

— D. L. Moody

"The Bible is truly the Word of God. He is the final and the ultimate Author; the Bible comes from God. Without Him there could have been no Bible. Without men, however, there could have been a Bible. God could have given us His Word in some other manner than that which He actually did choose. As a matter of fact, He did choose to speak through inspired men but He was not compelled to do so. In no sense was he limited. That He employed human writers was an act of grace, and the heart of faith will ever adore and revere Him that He so honored the human race as to employ lost sinners as writers of His pure and Holy Word. While the human authors were true authors, nevertheless they were not the originators of the words and the thoughts that are found in the Bible. They were holy men indeed, but they were holy men who were borne by the Spirit."

— Dr. E. J. Young,
Professor of Old Testament at
Westminster Theological
Seminary: *Thy Word Is Truth*

LESSON ONE
THE BOOK OF BOOKS

Teacher's Objective: To help the students discover the wonders and uniqueness of the Bible and to motivate them to want to know more about it. (NOTE: This is an introductory lesson; study the objective carefully and limit yourself to it. Even if a student is agnostic, the facts regarding the Bible's content and influence should draw his interest and open his mind to want to know more.

Therefore keep off the subject of inspiration; if it comes up, table the topic until Lesson 2. Your object here is to lay a good foundation for teaching the high view of the Bible as God's Word.)

CLASS TIME

Suggested Opening Prayer

Our Father, we pray You will help us discover the wonders of Your book and appreciate its uniqueness as never before.

(Introduction: Be sure
students understand
  objective
  memory work
  reading assignment.)

Introduction

OBJECTIVE: To recognize the unparalleled composition of the
Bible and to become familiar with its structure.

TO MEMORIZE: 2 Timothy 3:16, 17.

TO READ: Acts 15 and 16.

(Have the class share this material in any of the ways suggested in the Instructions for Teaching on page 21.)

**39
O.T.
27
N.T.**

The Bible's Amazing Composition

"The way in which the Bible came into being is nothing short of a miracle.

"Everyone knows that the Bible is made up of 66 individual books. But did you know that about 40 different human authors wrote these books? And that they wrote independently, knowing almost nothing of the others' part? Furthermore, their period of composition extended over 15 long centuries, three languages and on three continents? Yet, as we examine the Book today, it is one Book, not 66. It has a single subject. There is coherence in its content, and progression in its truth.

"To see the weight of this argument, suppose you were to endeavor to assemble a comparable book from various bits of literature written since the first century of the Christian era. Take your material from the ancient papyri, pieces of ostraca, writing of the philosophers, ancient wisdom books of the East or anything you choose. Get some writing from each century, select representative material from men in various walks of life; merchants, laborers, priests, farmers. Gather it all together and bind it into one book. Now, what have you? Why it will be the most ridiculous, contradictory hodgepodge of nonsense you have ever seen.

"The Bible, on the other hand, while like that in compilation, is wholly different in result. Everything about its composition argues against its unity. There's no reason in the world why it should be *one* Book. Yet it is, and no honest inquirer will doubt this, if he will take the time to read it carefully.

"The human writers of the Scriptures had almost nothing in common. Look at their diverse literary qualifications. While Moses may have been somewhat of a man of learning, having been schooled in the best universities of Egypt, Peter certainly was no writer. He was a fisherman, and there is no record that he had any education. Yet the writing of both are saturated with the wisdom of God.

"There's only one satisfactory answer. Using the ability of these men, or overcoming their disability, God *spoke through them,* and caused that they should write the Scriptures to His divine plan."

— William W. Orr
Ten Reasons Why

The Bible: A Book for Important Men

Abraham Lincoln: "I believe the Bible is the best gift God has ever given to man. All the good from the Savior of the world is communicated to us through this Book."

Immanuel Kant: "The existence of the Bible, as a book for people, is the greatest benefit which the human race has ever experienced. Every attempt to belittle it is a crime against humanity."

Sir Isaac Newton: "There are more sure marks of authenticity in the Bible than in any profane history."

Robert E. Lee: "In all my perplexities and distresses, the Bible has never failed to give me light and strength."

Daniel Webster: "If there is anything in my thought or style to commend, the credit is due to my parents for instilling in me early love for the Scriptures."

Discussion Starter

Two claims for the Bible are made in 2 Timothy 3:16,17. What are they? If you were a non-Christian and you wanted seriously to investigate Christianity, how would you evaluate these two claims? What would be your criteria for the first claim? The second?

Lesson Development

Bible Study

A. *Various names of the Bible*

List the various names the Bible is called according to the following references:

1 Corinthians 15:3, 4   *The Scriptures*.

Turn to the Table of

Ephesians 6:17   *Sword of the Spirit; Word of God*.

Contents in your Bible and we shall survey the composition of the whole Book. *Note:* There are two objectives in this survey: (1) to see the practical value of being familiar with Bible books (many students feel lost when asked to look up verses; so inform them of the fact that the Table of Contents is put there to be used — this will save time and embarrassment); (2) to have a better grasp of the argument regarding the amazing composition. (Turn back to the article, "The Bible's Amazing Composition," and discuss it now.)

B. *Construction of the Bible*

To get familiar with your own Bible, leaf through it and look at these divisions and books as you progress through this lesson.

The Bible is comprised of two main sections: the Old Testament, containing 39 books, and the New Testament containing 27 books.

Genesis contains the

The Old Testament can be divided into five parts:

account of the creation of

1. *Pentateuch.* The first five historical books, written by Moses, also are called the books of the Law. List these

the universe and of man. It shows how man was created to have fellowship

books: *Genesis*   *Exodus*   *Leviticus*

       Numbers   *Deuteronomy*

with God, but because of his own stubborn self-will, he chose to go his own independent way and that fellowship was broken. It gives the first promise of the coming Redeemer (3:15), and shows the establishment of the Jewish nation through which He was to come. *Exodus* is the story of Israel's leaving the bondage of Egypt and the beginning of their journey to the promised land. While on their journey, God gives the Law by which His nation is to live. *Leviticus* contains the more detailed instructions of the Law. *Numbers* and *Deuteronomy* tell of Israel's wandering in the wilderness and coming to the promised land.

2. *Historical Books.* The next 12 books tell of the establishment of the kingdom of Israel, of Israel's repeated turning from God to sin, and finally of the Assyrian and Babylonian exile — God's punishment. List these 12 books as follows:

First three (pre-kingdom era) _____

| Joshua | Judges | Ruth |

Next six (duration of the kingdom) _____

| 1 and 2 Samuel |
| 1 and 2 Kings |
| 1 and 2 Chronicles |

Last three (exile and post-exile period) _____

| Ezra | Nehemiah | Esther |

Paul tells us in the New Testament that these narrations of Hebrew history were given to be examples to us.

3. *Poetry.* Of the next five books, Psalms — the Hebrew hymn book — is probably the best known. List the books of poetry:

| Job | Psalms | Proverbs |
| Ecclesiastes | The Song of Solomon | |

4. *Major Prophets.* Written shortly before Israel was taken into captivity and during the exile, these books prophesy the coming Messiah and other world events. They also contain the record of warning of impending disaster if Israel did not turn from her wicked ways. List the five books of the Major Prophets.

| Isaiah | Jeremiah |
| Lamentations | Ezekiel | Daniel |

Some of these prophecies are still to be fulfilled.

5. *Minor Prophets.* These last 12 books of the Old Testament are called minor only because they are shorter, not because they are less important. They mainly concern Israel and the coming Messiah. List all 12: _____

Hosea	Joel	Amos
Obadiah	Jonah	Micah
Nahum	Habakkuk	Zephaniah
Haggai	Zechariah	Malachi

The New Testament can also be divided into five parts.

6. *Gospels*. The first four books of the New Testament tell of Christ's life and ministry. List them here: _____

   Matthew   Mark   Luke   John

   Acts. This history of the early church which also describes the ministries of Peter and Paul consists of only one book.

   For practice, write it here: _____ *Acts*

7. *Pauline Epistles and Hebrews*. Thirteen of the epistles were written by Paul, and named for the church or individual to whom they were sent. Although the author of Hebrews is not identified, many believe Paul also wrote that 14th epistle. List all 14: _____ *Romans*

   1 and 2 Corinthians, Galatians, Ephesians,

   Philippians, Colossians, 1 and 2 Thessaloni-

   ans, 1 and 2 Timothy, Titus, Philemon, Hebrews

8. *General Epistles*. There are seven of them, and they are named not for the recipients, but for the authors. List those here: _____ *1 and 2 Peter*

   1, 2 and 3 John, Jude

9. *Revelation*. The last book of the New Testament is one of prophecy. It describes the end times and the triumph of Christ in His second coming. Write the name of it here:

   _____ *Revelation*

Why do you think the Bible is called the Sword of the Spirit? (After hearing ideas from several group members, explain, as appropriate, how the Holy Spirit uses the Word to teach and convict; and how we need to be familiar with it, so that we are able to use this sword effectively.)

Conclusion and Application

Two arguments for inspiration of the Bible have been touched upon here: (a) the amazing composition of the Bible, its unity and progression despite centuries of differences among authors; (b) the moral uplift and drive of the Bible, its helpful influence and its saving power.

Life Application

1. What new insight about the composition of the Bible have you gained from this study? _____

2. In order to know your Bible well and to be able to find Scripture references quickly, you should memorize the names of the books in the order in which they appear. It is easier if you learn them by division. Master one group and then go on to the next.

   Today, commit to memory the books of the first division, the Pentateuch, and write them again here: 1. _____

   2. _____ 3. _____ 4. _____

   5. _____

3. NOTE: A word about different versions of the Bible:

   In his discussion of the two main texts from which the various versions have been translated, Josh McDowell says, ". . . areas of variation consist in only 10% of the text. There is total agreement between all text types 90% of the time . . . it must always be kept in mind that the same basic story is contained both in the majority text and in the other texts and that no crucial doctrine of the Christian faith rests upon the 10% in dispute" (*Reasons*, San Bernardino: Here's Life Publishers, 1981, p. 48).

Suggested Closing Prayer

We thank You, dear Father, for what we have learned today about the Book of books — how it was written by so many different people and over such a long span of time and yet its message is unified and powerful and it agrees with itself throughout. Thank You for a new appreciation of the wonders of Your Word.

ADDITIONAL BACKGROUND MATERIAL

Some additional quotations regarding the importance of the Bible for important men:

Robert Millikan, past-president of California Institute of Technology and Nobel Prize winner: "I consider an intimate knowledge of the Bible an indispensable quality of a well-educated man."

William Lyon Phelps of Yale: "I thoroughly believe in a university education; (yet) I believe a knowledge of the Bible without a college course is more valuable than a college course without the Bible."

Goethe: "Let mental culture go on advancing, let the natural sciences progress in even greater extent and depth, let the human mind widen itself as much as it desires; beyond the elevation and moral culture of Christianity, as it shines forth in the Gospels, it will not go."

Horace Greeley: "It is impossible to enslave mentally or socially a Bible-reading people. The principles of the Bible are the groundwork of human freedom."

Mark Twain: "The things that bother me in the Bible are not the things which I do not understand, but the things I *do* understand!"

LESSON TWO

CHRIST IS THE CENTRAL PERSON OF THE BIBLE

Teacher's Objective: To show the students that the unity of the Bible lies in one theme, Jesus Christ, and all that he is and has done, and to encourage them to rest in His absolute authority.

Teacher's Enrichment: (This material can be shared with class members as time permits.) During his first Antarctic expedition Admiral Byrd was flown to the Pole itself and spent the six-month-long night there alone. Snow after snow and blast after blast buried his small hut.

Each day he shoveled his way to the surface for exercise. There was enough light to see only a dozen yards or so as he walked the few steps he dared to take. One day he turned to go back, but was shocked to discover that he could not see his stove pipe. Veteran that he was, he controlled any tendency to panic, refusing to move because he knew his danger. To wander about would probably place him farther from the hut.

He drove a stake into the snow, and using it as his center, he walked a large circle around. Not finding the hut, he extended his radius and walked another circle, always with one eye on the stake, the other searching through the blackness. The third time he tried this, the circle was so large that he almost lost his stake. He returned and resolved to make one more attempt, with a still larger circle.

The range of visibility was strained to its limit as he walked keeping contact with his point of reference. He knew that if he were to lose that point of reference, the ice and snow would quickly claim another victim. But it was enough. He walked right into the hut's tunnel.

Some people get lost reading the Bible. But the secret for understanding the Bible is a point of reference, around which one must move. Learn to keep your eyes on Christ, and you will find that as your spiritual eyesight improves and allows you to penetrate the gloom and darkness of this world, you will be able to extend your radius of faith further and further. You will be able to explore more and more of the exciting and adventurous life in Christ while you maintain contact with Him as your point of reference.

Have you ever heard this?

"You Christians provide the best examples of reasoning in a circle. You quote the Bible as God's Word and therefore the final authority, yet when you are challenged as to why one should consider the Bible to be so authoritative, you can only say, 'It claims to be God's Word.' What kind of logic is that? 'It is God's Word because God's Word says it is God's Word.' So does the Koran!"

This is a vital question for any clear-thinking Christian, as well as for the sincere investigator of Christianity. It is important that we grant to the critic the correctness of his logic, and then proceed to explain to him that there are solid facts behind our Christian convictions — facts which elevate the Bible far above all other books — facts which logically point to just one conclusion: the Bible *is* the Word of God. These facts are focused partially on the Bible itself but more on the Bible's central message: God-in-Christ.

Certainly the first Christians did not reason in a circle; they had objective data to work with, namely, Christ Himself — all that He was, and all that He taught. They came to a place of accepting Jesus Christ's authority unconditionally because in Him they were brought face to face with the God who fulfills *heart* and *mind, natural* and *supernatural.*

We live twenty centuries later. Yet the same confrontation is made today. Let us enlarge these four points with modern man in mind.

1. *God in Christ meets the heart's need.* In Him we meet the God who lays claim to our hearts with an unparalleled offer of love, joy and peace. He frees us, on the one hand, from self-centered living with its guilt, anxiety and sensuality, its petty purposes, recurring friction and inevitable loneliness; and He arms us, on the other hand, with power to become creative and redemptive servants — in His image (Nehemiah 8:10b; John 16:33; 2 Timothy 1:7).

2. *God in Christ meets the needs of the mind.* In Him we meet the God who calls for intellectual allegiance to the highest philosophy, a world-view which is "a light for our feet and a lamp for our path" and is "the power of God unto salvation." The realism and discipline of Jesus Christ forces us to confront the drabness and rawness of life in such a radical way that we are transformed in the process — we discover meaning, beauty, purpose, and dynamic energy for our lives and for all mankind (John 8:31-32).

3. *God in Christ accounts for natural phenomena.* In Him we meet face to face the same God who is viewed dimly in nature. His Word and Spirit are found to lie in and through, beneath and above the facts of life, whether known through common experience or through our physical, social and historical sciences.

The divine activity, rooted in nature as well as history, is expressed today in living persons and events. All our sciences touch upon it, some more and some less. And — when stripped of philosophical presuppositions and allowed to be purely scientific instruments — all of them do supplement the Christian revelation, and confirm it; far from contradicting it, they find their ultimate significance in it (John 1:1-5, 10-14, 18; Acts 17:24-29).

4. *God in Christ brings the supernatural to a natural world.* In Him we meet the God who answers our desire for a voice directly from Him to us.

Through fulfilled prophecy and miracles, providential guidance and answered prayer, but pre-eminently in the person of Christ Himself and our experience of His Holy Spirit within us, God personally validates the message of Scripture. Our faith rests confidently in it as His true Word and nothing less (Acts 1:1-5).

We may conclude, therefore, that true Christian thinking does not reason in a circle at all. It begins with objective data. In the mission and message of Jesus we find the deepest harmony of the demands of our own hearts and minds and the facts of life with a sure Word straight from God. The case for the Bible rests fundamentally on the case of Christ, for Christ identified the Bible indissolubly with Himself.

CLASS TIME

Suggested Opening Prayer

Dear Father, we pray that You will open our minds and hearts to the truths presented in this lesson today. Show us Christ as the central point of reference in Your Word and show us how we can understand Your Word so much better by keeping our eyes on Him.

(Introduction: Be sure
students understand
    objective
    memory work
    reading assignment.)

> **Introduction**
>
> OBJECTIVE: To recognize the entire Bible as God's revelation of Jesus Christ to us.
>
> TO MEMORIZE: 1 Corinthians 15:3,4.
>
> TO READ: Acts 17 and 18.
>
>
> O.T.   N.T.

Discussion Starter

Why is Christ the central person of the Bible? (Let each group member think in silence and then talk this over. Refer briefly to the four foundations of our faith in Christ as listed in the Teacher's Enrichment.)

Lesson Development

> **Bible Study**
>
> A. *What Christ said about Himself and the Old Testament*
>
>   1. What did Christ say of the Scriptures in John 5:39? _____
>   *They bear witness of Him.*
>
>   2. Read Luke 24:25-27, 44-48.
>
>   What was Christ's claim concerning the Old Testament teaching about Himself? *That all the Scriptures concerned Him and were written about Him.*
>
>   What parts of the Old Testament did Christ say referred to Him (verse 44)? *All things which were written about Him in the Law of Moses, Prophets, and Psalms.*
>
>   What do you think Christ wants you to understand about the Old Testament from verse 26? _____
>
>   Verses 46, 47? _____

B. *What the apostles said about Christ and the Old Testament.*

1. What does Peter conclude in Acts 3:18? *Christ fulfilled everything that was announced before
hand.*

2. How did the apostle Paul use the Old Testament to show
that it contained the "good news" of Christ (Acts 17:1-3)?
*Reasoned from Scriptures, explaining, giving
evidence.*

3. What three things occurred in Christ's life that Paul said
were taught in the Old Testament (1 Corinthians 15:3, 4)?
His death, burial and resurrection.

4. What does Paul conclude in Romans 15:8, 9 about the
ministry of Christ? *He confirmed promises to
the fathers.*

C. Old Testament prophecies concerning Christ fulfilled in the
New Testament

All of the more than 300 Old Testament prophecies about
the first coming of the Messiah were fulfilled in the life of
Christ. Here are a few of them.

1. Compare these Scripture references and record the
prophecies fulfilled.

COMPARE	WITH	FULFILLMENT
Isaiah 11:1 1 Samuel 16:19	Luke 1:31-33	*Descendant of Jesse/ David, son of Jesse, was "father" of Jesus.*
Genesis 3:15	Galatians 4:4	*Seed of the woman/ God's Son born of a woman.*
Numbers 24:17	Matthew 2:2, 9	*A star from Jacob/ Magi saw star when Jesus was born.*
Isaiah 9:6	Matthew 1:23	*A son to be given/ virgin's Son to be Immanuel--"God with us."*
Isaiah 40:3	Matthew 3:1-3	*A voice crying in the wilderness/John Baptist came crying from wilderness*
Zechariah 9:9	Matthew 21:1-5	*King coming riding on donkey; Jesus entered Jerusalem in triumph on donkey*
Psalm 69:21	Matthew 27: 34, 48	*Gall and vinegar to be given/ gall and vinegar given.*
Psalm 34:20	John 19:33, 36	*No bones to be broken/. no bones broken.*
Job 19:25-27	Galatians 3:13	*Redeemer expected/ Christ is the expected Redeemer.*

One of the many remarkable features of Christianity's foundation is the phenomenon of fulfilled prophecy. Suppose there were only 50 predictions in the Old Testament (instead of approximately 300) concerning the first advent of Christ, giving details of the coming Messiah which meet in the person and work of Jesus. The probability of chance fulfillment is calculated by mathematicians to be less than one in 1,125,000,000,000,000 (1125 x 10^{12}).

2. What is your impression after seeing these Old Testament
prophecies and their New Testament fulfillment? _____

(If time allows, have each of three students read one of the following: Matthew 5:17-18; Luke 4:16-21; John 5:39-40. Discuss briefly.)

D. *Christ, the central person of the New Testament*

  1. The four Gospels are the history books of Christ's ministry. (Read Matthew 1:1; Mark 1:1; Luke 1:1-4; John 20:30, 31).

In what ways did the disciples know Jesus (1 John 1:3)? *They had seen and heard Him.*

(See verse 31.)

Do the four Gospels purport to record all that Jesus did (John 20:30)? *No.*

Why were the historical facts and teachings of Jesus Christ written? *That we might believe Jesus is the Christ and might have life in His name.*

What are we to do with these teachings according to Matthew 28:19-20?

  2. The book of Acts is an historical account of the acts of the Holy Spirit through the apostles.

Who wrote it (Luke 1:1-4 and Acts 1:1)? *(Luke.)*

How do you think the passage in Luke applies to the book of Acts? _____

  3. The Epistles are letters written to show the church the practical outworking of the life of Christ in the lives of those who wrote them. By example, they teach us regarding our membership in the body of Christ, privileges, responsibilities and destiny.

Read Colossians 2:6-8.

What are Christians to do? *Walk in Christ.*

How are we to do it? *Be firmly rooted in faith.*

Of what are we to beware? *Traditions of men.*

What would you say our greatest responsibility is? _____

  4. The book of Revelation is the only New Testament book of prophecy. Read Revelation 1:1-3.

This book is the revelation of whom? *Jesus Christ.*

What is its purpose? *To show things to come.*

Who gave such knowledge, how, and to whom? *God gave it to Christ, Christ gave it to John through His angel.*

How will the book of Revelation affect your life and under what conditions? *Blessed--happy--is he who reads, hears and heeds the things written there.*

What is the warning recording in Revelation 22:18-19?

Conclusion and Application

It is not merely in the isolated predictions which are fulfilled with precision, but it is also in the entirety of the Old Testament that one finds a looking forward to something yet to come, something beyond itself. If that something is not a delusion, it is to be found in the New Testament and in Christ.

Jesus' life and work give a fullness of meaning *to the whole Old Testament* that it could not otherwise have. This total fulfillment provides us with firm ground for the belief that the Old Testament not only *did* lead to Christ, but *was intended*, by the God whose partial revelation it records, to lead to Christ.

Life Application

1. How will recognizing Jesus as the central figure of the entire Bible affect your Old Testament reading? _____

_____

_____

2. What do you see as your individual responsibility in fulfilling the commands of this person presented in the entire Bible? See John 15:16 and Matthew 28:19, 20. _____

_____

3. Memorize the 12 Historical books and write them again here:

Pre-kingdom era (3) _____

Kingdom era (6) _____

_____

_____

_____

Exile and post-exile era (3) _____

Review those learned earlier _____

_____

Suggested Closing Prayer

Our Father, we thank You for showing us how the Old Testament is completely fulfilled in Christ and how the New Testament presents Him as the fullness of everything we need. Help us always to look to Him as the source of authority for the truth of the Bible.

ADDITIONAL BACKGROUND MATERIAL

Each of the Gospels presents different aspects of Jesus' life and ministry:

Matthew, written to the Jews, presents Jesus as the "Messiah" (the "Christ," the "Anointed"), the Law-giver who is far greater than Moses and the Ruler who is far greater than King David, the Son of God who is Authority and Power (Matthew 5:17-18, 21-22, 27-29; 28:18-20).

Mark wrote with the Romans in mind — men of action who built roads and conquered nations. In Mark's Gospel you will find the words "immediately" and "straightway" used over and over again as the writer pictures Jesus with divine power and compassion, constantly serving rather than being served; the Son of God who is the Servant (Mark 10:42-45).

Luke, the only Gentile writer in the New Testament, wrote perhaps for a Greek nobleman with the Greek ideals of the development of fine manhood — "perfect mind," "perfect body," etc. He presents Jesus as the perfect Man, the Son of God who is the Son of Man (Luke 4:16-21; 7:36-50; 14:1-6; 15:1-2).

John, writing years after the other three, provides a deeper perspective than they. From the very first there was an intensity of divine glory in Jesus which human thick-headedness appreciates only partially. After years of contemplation, John saw this more clearly and presents Christ to the world as God incarnate — God became man; the Son of God who is God Himself (John 1:1-18).

LESSON THREE

AUTHORITY OF THE OLD TESTAMENT

Teacher's Objective: To give the students confidence in the authority of the Old Testament.

Teacher's Enrichment: (May be shared with class as time permits.)

Inspiration of the Bible

In evaluating the case for inspiration of the Bible, it is important that we ask: Does inspiration mean that the writers lost their individuality and became stenographers or dictaphones in relation to their own writings?

Critics of the Bible's claim to be divinely inspired often interpret this as meaning that the Book was mechanically dictated by God, that it has no more of the human personality in it than a girl imparts to the letters she types from the dictation of her business employer. This is miles from the truth.

Every author has his own literary style. Each displays his intellectual and emotional characteristics in varying ways and to varying degrees.

Paul's letters, for instance, are so loaded with his own personality that a famed scholar has rightfully asserted that no man of antiquity is better known to us than he. In his letters to Christians whom he had not yet met we are introduced to the apostle's tremendous analytical mind and the depth of his experience with Christ, with sin, with life; and in the letters to his own converts we feel the personal warmth of his great heart. Plainly, there is in the Bible a human element which is magnetic.

Dr. B. B. Warfield, the greatest writer on this subject, has said: "As light passes through the colored glass of a cathedral window, it is light from heaven we are told. So, any word of God which is passed through the mind and soul of a man must come out discolored by the personality through which it is given, and just to that degree ceases to be the pure word of God.

"But what if that personality has itself been formed by God into precisely the personality it is, for the express purpose of communicating to the word given through it just the coloring which it gives it? What if the colors of the stained-glass window have been designed by the Architect for the express purpose of giving to the Light precisely the tone and quality it received from them?"

Intellectual difficulties which some people feel toward the Bible are discarded once they realize that inspiration does not mean that God used writers as though they were dictaphones.

CLASS TIME

Suggested Opening Prayer

Father, we thank You for meeting with us today and we ask You to impress upon our minds the importance of understanding and accepting the authority of the Old Testament.

(Introduction: Be sure students understand
  objective
  memory work
  reading assignment.)

Introduction

OBJECTIVE: To gain assurance of the Bible's trustworthiness by looking at the Old Testament and its validity.

"THUS SAITH THE LORD"
2,000 TIMES IN O.T.

TO MEMORIZE: 2 Peter 1:20, 21.

TO READ: Acts 19 and 20.

Discussion Starter

(Ask the group members:)

What is meant by the inspiration of the Bible?

What part does God play and what part does man play in writing the Bible? (Take time to discuss the questions. Consult 2 Peter 1:21; 2 Timothy 3:16; Hebrews 1:1.)

Lesson Development

Men do not ordinarily maintain their messages when extreme suffering and isolation is their payment. They, rather, trim their talk to suit the listener's applause. Jeremiah 23:16-17 has a good description of the false prophet who lacks God's inspiration and cannot resist conformity.

Bible Study

A. *Testimony of its writers*

The phrase, "Thus saith the Lord," or its equivalent, occurs more than 2,000 times in the Old Testament.

1. Write out the statements concerning inspiration made by the following writers:

  David (2 Samuel 23:2) _____

  _____

  Isaiah (Isaiah 8:1, 5, 11) _____

  _____

  Jeremiah (Jeremiah 1:9) _____

  _____

  Ezekiel (Ezekiel 3:4) _____

The character and veracity of these men provide strong evidences for their divine inspiration:

Isaiah 6:1-8, declares the prophet's consciousness of his own inadequacy to deliver God's message, his unworthiness.

Amos 7:12-14, records the prophet's answer to royal orders, to stop prophesying or get out. (Cf. Peter's response in Acts 4:19-20.)

> 2. What two statements of Moses in Exodus 31:18 and 32:16 show that God actually wrote the Ten Commandments? *"Two tablets of testimony .... written by the finger of God"--"the writing was God's writing engraved on the tablets."*
>
> 3. What statement made by David shows that the pattern for the temple was dictated by God (1 Chronicles 28:19)? *"The Lord made me understand in writing."*

The Old Testament can and should be independently evaluated regarding its claims. Nevertheless, it is inseparably linked to Christ. The final evaluation therefore rests upon the testimony of Christ.

> **B. Testimony of Christ**
>
> The New Testament had not been written during Christ's earthly ministry and His references to the Scriptures refer to the Old Testament writings. He never once denied or made light of Old Testament Scriptures; He related Himself to them as their fulfillment. He said, "He who has seen Me has seen the Father" (John 14:9) and, "I and the Father are one" (John 10:30). "The word which you hear is not Mine, but the Father's who sent Me" (John 14:24). Christ, the God-man said, "Search the Scripture . . . it is these that bear witness of Me" (John 5:39).

> 1. How did Christ see those who did not believe the Old Testament prophecies (Luke 24:25)? *Foolish, slow.*
>
> 2. What did Christ say that unbelief in Him implied (John 5:46, 47)? *They did not believe Moses.*
>
> 3. What do you think Christ indicated was His responsibility concerning Old Testament prophecy (Matthew 5:17, 18)? *He came to fulfill all the Law and The Prophets.*
>
> 4. What was Christ's view of the story of man's creation as recorded in Genesis (Matthew 19:4-6)? *It was fact--God had created male and female.*
>
> 5. What authority did Christ use to answer: Satan (Matthew 4:4, 7, 10)? *"It is written."* Men (Matthew 22:29-32, 43-46)? *The Scriptures.*
>
> 6. In John 18:37b, who did Jesus say He was and what connection did His purpose in coming to earth have to the Old Testament? *He was a king, and was born and came into the world to bear witness to the truth.*
>
> 7. Summarize here Christ's attitude and view of the Old Testament. _____

"Christ's claim to be divine is either true or false. If it is true His Person guarantees the truth of all the rest of His teaching (for a divine person cannot lie or err; therefore, His view of the Old Testament is true). If His claim is false, there is no compelling reason for us to believe anything else that He said. If we accept Christ's claims, therefore, we commit ourselves to believe all that He taught — on His authority. If we refuse to believe some part of what He taught, we are in effect denying Him to be the divine Messiah — on our own authority. The question, 'What think ye of the Old Testament?' resolves the question, 'What think ye of Christ?' " (Packer, James I., *Fundamentalism and the Word of God,* Grand Rapids, MI: Eerdmans, 1958, p. 59).

Historical accuracy is established on three foundations: geography (and topography), ethnology, and chronology. In all three areas modern science has been building a stronger and stronger case for the Bible during the past hundred years of extensive research in the Near East.

We are discovering piece by piece (1) that the peoples, places and events of Scripture are to be found in the same locale and under the precise geographical circumstances as those described in the Bible; (2) that whenever statements are made in the Bible concerning kinship, origin, or customs of peoples, these statements can be depended upon to be in accordance with the finds of archaeology;

C. Testimony of the apostles

It is evident from their inspired writing that the apostles of Christ considered the Old Testament Scriptures prophetic of and inseparable from the authority, power and ministry of Christ.

Peter

1. From whom did the apostle Peter say the writings of the Old Testament come (2 Peter 1:21; Acts 1:16)? Holy Spirit.

   How did Peter feel about the Old Testament historical account he recorded in 1 Peter 3:20? He accepted it as fact.

   Who did Peter say were inspired by God (Acts 3:20, 21)? Holy prophets.

Paul

2. How much of the Old Testament is inspired by God, according to Paul in 2 Timothy 3:16? _____

   Paul believed the Old Testament to be what (Romans 3:2)? The oracles of God.

James

3. Acceptance of the Old Testament writing is evidenced by references concerning which person in the Book of James?
   (2:21) _Abraham._
   (2:25) _Rahab._
   (5:11) _Job._
   (5:17) _Elijah._

John

4. One of the many evidences that John believed the Old Testament is his acceptance of which story (1 John 3:12)? Cain's slaying of Abel.

N.T.

FULFILLMENT

O.T.

(3) that when we compare events in the Old Testament with the records on the tombs and monuments of Egypt, or the records of Babylonia, Assyria and elsewhere, we find that the different parts of the chronology fit extremely well, in spite of the unscientific chronological systems which the ancients used.

Conclusion and Application

The prophets lay down high standards as characteristic of the Word of God:

1. Above and beyond, outside of the self-centered and sensual interests of sinful men; and powerful, therefore — infallibly effective and invincible — Isaiah 55:6-9, 10-11.

2. Eternal, lasting, universally true — Isaiah 40:6-8.

The writers of the Old Testament were fully convinced that their messages met these standards; and they would be the first to discard them *if* they did not. Such was the quality of their objectivity and devotion to God's truth.

Life Application

H.S. Miller, in his book *General Biblical Introduction*, says,

"The same Old Testament books which had been received by the Jews and by Christ and the New Testament writers as inspired and authoritative were received by the early church. The church, with the exception of a few heretics, held the same high standard of inspiration. However much the fathers may have differed in other doctrines, they all, from various parts of the Empire, differing in character and training, were, with perhaps some slight variations in minor details, unanimous in this one great doctrine. They taught that in the entire Old Testament, God and Christ, the incarnate Word of God, spoke through the Holy Spirit through men, and that all Scripture is permanently fitted for our instruction. The matter was not even discussed, as some doctrines were; it was not considered debatable."

1. The writers of the Old Testament, Jesus Christ the Son of God, the apostles of Christ and the early church fathers all say of the Old Testament, "This is the inspired Word of God."

   What do you say? (See John 8:47 and 1 John 4:6.) _____
   _____

2. Write down *how* the information in this lesson gives you confidence in the authority of the Old Testament. _____

3. Repeat the names of the five books of poetry until you have committed them to memory. Then write them here: _____
   _____
   _____

   Review all those learned earlier.

Suggested Closing Prayer

We praise You, Father, for the trust we can have in Your Word. The testimony of its writers, the testimony of Christ and the testimony of the apostles all back up the claims of the Old Testament to its divine revelation and we praise and thank You for giving it to us.

LESSON FOUR

AUTHORITY OF THE
NEW TESTAMENT

Teacher's Objective: To help the students discover the absolute reliability of the New Testament and increase their confidence in the entire Word of God.

Teacher's Enrichment: (May be shared with class as time permits.)

There are five valid reasons for our belief in the authority of the New Testament as God's Word:

1. Christ's authentication, not only of the Old Testament, but also of the New Testament.
2. Christ's resurrection, proving that His authority was truly divine, and endowing the apostles with unique authority because they were the eyewitnesses of this foundation to salvation.
3. The character, integrity and historical accuracy of the New Testament writers, combined with their claim to be under Christ's authority.
4. The endurance and preservation of God's Word.
5. The witness of the Holy Spirit directly to the Christian, authenticating the New Testament.

CLASS TIME

Suggested Opening Prayer

Our heavenly Father, we pray You will open our understanding to the truth of the authority of the New Testament and what it is based upon. Increase our confidence in the truth of all of Your Word.

(Introduction: Be sure
students understand
    objective
    memory work
    reading assignment.)

> **Introduction**
>
> OBJECTIVE: To gain confidence in the Bible's authority by looking at the reliability of the New Testament.
>
> TO MEMORIZE: Matthew 24:35.
>
> TO READ: Acts 21 and 22.
>
> HEAVEN AND EARTH SHALL PASS AWAY...NOT MY WORD
>
> HOLY BIBLE

Discussion Starter

(Ask the class:) Some people, who have not examined all the evidence, attempt to discredit the authority of the Scripture. If I were one who doubted, could you give me valid reasons for your belief in the authority of the New Testament? What would they be?

Lesson Development

The various New Testament writings have been fairly precisely dated. It is established that they were all written in the first century, so early that the suggestion that myths and legends arose around the figure of Jesus is ruled out. There was not a long enough time lapse between Jesus' life and the writings. Legends require several generations to develop and

> **Bible Study**
>
> A. *Authority given the apostles by Christ*
>
> 1. What four things did Christ say the Holy Spirit would do for the apostles (John 16:12-15)? <u>*"Guide you into*</u> <u>*all the truth...disclose to you what is to*</u> <u>*come...glorify Me...take of Mine, and shall*</u> <u>*disclose it to you."*</u>
>
>   At that time, why do you think the apostles could not know all the truth? _____
>
>   How would they in the future? _____
>
> 2. What authority did Christ give the apostles (John 17:18; 20:21)? <u>*As God sent Him, He sent them.*</u>
>
> 3. On what basis did Christ select the apostles to bear witness of Him (John 15:26, 27; Luke 24:46-48)? <u>*They*</u> <u>*had been with Him and had been witnesses.*</u>

spread, but the New Testament writings came from the first generation, while the actual eye-witnesses still lived.

For the earliest written reports, read 1 Thessalonians 1:10 and Galatians 1:1 (dated 50 A.D., just 20 years after the event); and note especially 1 Corinthians 15:3-9 with its statement that, *25 years after the event,* there were *several hundred* eyewitnesses still alive to tell the story.

For the latest written witness, read John 20:26-31 and 1 John 1:1-3, dated about 90-95 A.D. (And we have a portion of a manuscript of John's Gospel which the experts have dated at 125 A.D., only 30 years after the original writing!)

> How did Paul fit in according to Acts 9:3-6; Acts 26:13-15 and 1 Corinthians 15:7-9? <u>*He saw heavenly light*</u> <u>*and heard voice of Christ.*</u>
>
> How do you think we fit into this witnessing aspect? _____
>
> 4. What authority did Christ give Paul (Acts 26:15-18)? <u>*Christ appointed Paul a minister and witness.*</u>
>
> B. *The apostles wrote under Christ's authority*
>
> 1. *Paul:* What does he call himself at the beginning of the book of Romans and his other letters? _____ <u>*A bond-servant of Christ.*</u>

The strength of Paul's witness lies not only in the fact that he claimed along with the others, to have seen the risen Christ personally; but he also became fully convinced that *all* the aspects of the resurrection story were true. And, as James Martin comments in *Did Jesus Rise from the Dead?*, "Such a man would accept the Christian case only if he were left with no alternative."

From whom did Paul receive what he preached (1 Corinthians 11:23; Galatians 1:11, 12)? *From the Lord/through a revelation of Jesus Christ.*

What was Paul's authority and purpose (2 Corinthians 5:20)? *An ambassador for Christ.*

Read 2 Peter 3:15, 16. What did Peter think about Paul's writings? *He wrote according to wisdom given him.*

2. *Writer of Hebrews:* Where did the writer of Hebrews get his authority (Hebrews 1:1,2)? *Through the Son of God.*

3. *James:* What did this half-brother of Christ (Christ's Father is God) call himself (James 1:1)? *A bond-servant of God and of the Lord Jesus Christ.*

4. *John:* What does John claim as the authority for writing his epistles (1 John 1:1-3)? *He had seen and heard-- and touched--the Word of Life, Christ.*

What about Revelation (Revelation 1:1)? *God gave the revelation to Christ, and He sent it to John*

5. *Jude:* What does this other half-brother of Christ call himself in Jude 1? *A bond-servant of Jesus Christ.*

What do you think Paul, James and Jude meant by saying they were bondservants of Christ? _____

6. *Peter:* He calls himself what (1 Peter 1:1)? *An apostle of Jesus Christ.*

What does Peter make known (2 Peter 1:16)? *The power and coming of the Lord Jesus Christ.*

7. On whose writings is the foundation of the church of Jesus Christ established (Ephesians 2:20)? *Jesus.*

8. What is the gospel of Christ, according to the apostles (Romans 1:16)? *The power of God for salvation*

9. Why were the apostles confident they wrote correctly about Christ (2 Corinthians 4:5, 6)? *God had shone into their hearts to give light of knowledge.*

Life Application

RELIABILITY OF THE NEW TESTAMENT WE HAVE TODAY

"The evidence for our New Testament writings is ever so much greater than the evidence for many writings of classical authors, the authenticity of which no one dreams of questioning. There are in existence about 4,000 Greek manuscripts of the New Testament in whole or in part." — F. F. Bruce, Professor of Biblical History and Literature, University of Sheffield, England: *Are the New Testament Documents Reliable?*

"The interval between the dates of original composition and the earliest extant evidence becomes so small as to be in fact negligible, and the last foundation for any doubt that the Scriptures have come down to use substantially as they were written has now been removed. Both the authenticity and the general integrity of the books of the New Testament may be regarded as finally established." — Sir Frederic Kenyon, British classical scholar, president of the British Academy, president of the British School of Archaeology at Jerusalem: *The Bible and Archaeology.*

True, there are variant readings of some words and phrases in the New Testament. However, Bible scholars tell us that if you would put all the variants of any consequence together, they would take up about one-half of a page. Even if you chose the worst of the variant readings, no doctrine in the New Testament would be changed.

Dr. J. Harold Greenlee, Department of New Testament, Asbury Theological Seminary, says:

Although the known manuscripts of the classical writings number only a few hundred at most, there are literally thousands of known manuscripts of the New Testament. And although the oldest known manuscript of a classical writing may be an umpteenth generation copy written a thousand years or more after the original, there are manuscripts of the New Testament which were written within 300 years after the original, and some parts of manuscripts are dated to within 150 years of the original.

Conclusion and Application

The fact that we, in the twentieth century, still have access to the Word of God, is living proof that God's Word does not pass away. Throughout the centuries attempts to destroy the Bible have been to no avail, for God Himself will not permit it.

1. God has miraculously preserved His Word for us. Although the above study should convince any of us that the New Testament is the Word of God, what is your greatest assurance that it is God's Word (John 16:13; 8:47; 18:37b)? _____

2. How does the information in this lesson help you trust the Bible more than you may have in the past? _____

3. Commit to memory the names of the five books of the Major Prophets. Then write them: _____

Don't forget to review all other books previously learned.

Suggested Closing Prayer

We thank You, our Father, for what we have learned today and for the mountains of evidence for the truth and authority of the New Testament. We recognize that the pivotal point in the faith of each one of us is the resurrection of Christ and we thank You for all the proofs of that, both in the Scriptures and outside it. Thank You for our assurance that the New Testament we have today is reliable.

ADDITIONAL BACKGROUND MATERIAL

Some parallel passages of Scripture which testify to the witness of the resurrection, and of its power, and of the faithfulness of the witnesses in the face of persecution:

John 20:26-31
Acts 2:22-32
Acts 3:13-15
Luke 1:1-4
Acts 4:13-22
Acts 7:54; 8:3
2 Corinthians 11:24-29

LESSON FIVE
THE POWER OF THE BIBLE

Teacher's Objective: To help the students experience the power of God's Word in their daily lives.

Teacher's Enrichment: (May be shared with group members as time permits.)

Campus Crusade for Christ has a short and clear creed. Each year the staff reaffirms their faith as expressed in it. The fourth article is as follows:
"We personally accept the Bible as God's infallible Word, uniquely inspired, the Spirit's supreme and final authority for man in all matters of faith and conduct, His sustenance for every believer."

This states the central issue in a nutshell — it is toward faith and conduct, toward spiritual sustenance, that the Lord's Word is unerringly aimed. We should place our concentration where He places His. Then, and not until then, will our doctrine be characterized by the prophets' and Jesus' and the apostles' *confidence in the power* of the Word itself to do its own work and to carry its own conviction. Read John 7:16-17.

CLASS TIME

Suggested Opening Prayer

Father, we thank You for meeting with us today, and we ask that You will help us understand the power of Your Word and how it may be appropriated in our lives.

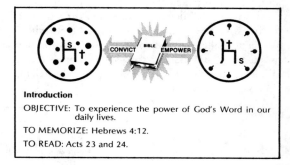

(Introduction: Be sure students understand
    objective
    memory work
    reading assignment)

Introduction

OBJECTIVE: To experience the power of God's Word in our daily lives.

TO MEMORIZE: Hebrews 4:12.

TO READ: Acts 23 and 24.

Discussion Starter

What would be your answer if challenged by another student: "I don't believe the Bible is the Word of God. I can't go along with a lot of the miracles and I don't understand much of it. Do I have to believe the Bible 100% — from cover to cover — to become a Christian?"

Lesson Development

> **Bible Study**
>
> A. The Word of God
>
> Tell what God's Word is or what it does, or both, according to the following Scripture references (use dictionary for definition of key words if needed):
>
> 1. What it is:
>
> Hebrews 5:13 _Milk/word of righteousness._
> Philippians 2:16 _Word of life._
> Ephesians 6:17 _Sword of the Spirit._

Through the written Word, God speaks His living Word to us day by day, hour by hour. And soon we learn what Jesus both practiced and taught (in His wilderness temptations): "Man shall not live on bread alone, but on every word that proceeds out of the mouth of God" (Matthew 4:4).

> 2. What it does:
>
> 1 John 2:5 _Perfects the love of God in us._
> John 12:48 _Will judge the one who rejects Christ_
> Romans 10:17 _Gives faith._
> John 15:3 _(Cleanses.)_
>
> 3. Both:
>
> 1 Peter 1:23 _Is imperishable seed/gives new birth_
> John 8:31, 32 _Is truth/makes free._

"Man's mind becomes free only when its thoughts are brought into captivity to Christ and His Word; till then, it is at the mercy of sinful prejudice and dishonest mental habits within, and of popular opinion, organized propaganda and unquestioned commonplaces without. Tossed about by every wind of intellectual fashion and carried to and fro by cross-currents of reactions, man without God is not free for truth . . . Only as his thoughts are searched, challenged and corrected by God through His Word, may man hope to rise to a way of looking at things which, instead of reflecting merely passing phases of human thought, reflects God's eternal truth. This is the only road to intellectual freedom . . ." (Packer, pp. 143-144).

> John 17:17 _Is truth / sanctifies_
> 1 Peter 2:2 _Is pure milk of the Word / Helps one grow in respect to salvation._
> Hebrews 4:12 (5 things) _Is living, active, sharper than two-edged sword / divides soul and spirit, judges thoughts & intents of heart._

What must occur in one's life in order to

understand and know God and His plan for our lives (John 3:3)?

> B. How to understand the Word of God
> 1. Read 1 Corinthians 2:14.
>
> No one can understand the Word of God by his own ability. Why? <u>Natural man does not accept</u> <u>things of the Spirit of God.</u>

A young woman once picked up a certain book to read but soon laid it down, finding it too dull and difficult. Shortly afterward she met a young man to whom she became quite attached. During the course of their courtship she learned that he was the author of this book. She began to read the book a second time, and this time she read it from cover to cover.

Why the tremendous interest? Now she knew and loved the author. When we come to know and love Jesus Christ, His Book, the Bible becomes alive and vital to us.

Directing the inquiring student to Christ Himself does not deny a rightful place for historical research and hardheaded scientific examination of the Bible; but emphasis in these areas *misses the point.*

To the non-Christian we lay down the challenge: *begin where the Bible applies to you and can therefore be tested by you.* "Come and see" was Andrew's answer to his brother in John 1:39.

> 2. Describe in your own words a natural man's reaction to spiritual things. _____
>
> 3. State again in your own words, how one must come to understand the Word of God. See verses 10-12, John 2:3, Romans 8:9. _____
>
> 4. Why do some individuals deny the authority of Scripture, the deity of Christ, the inspiration of the Bible, and other basic teachings in the printed word of the Holy Spirit? _____
>
> What should be our response to them? _____

Conclusion and Application

You, a new Christian, have the same teacher that great Bible scholars have, the Holy Spirit. Every time you sit down to study the Bible, ask the Holy Spirit to show you the things He wants you to learn from His Word, and to help you understand difficult sections.

> **Life Application**
> "I believe a knowledge of the Bible without a college course is more valuable than a college course without the Bible." — William Lyon Phelps, former professor at Yale University.
> 1. When we approach the Word of God, what is the first thing we should understand (2 Peter 1:20, 21)? _____

2. Name some way the power of the Bible manifests itself according to 2 Timothy 2:15-17. _____

_____

3. How have you experienced that power in your life recently?

_____

_____

4. The 12 books of the Minor Prophets are probably the most difficult of all to learn. Give extra diligence to memorizing this division, then write the names here: _____

_____

_____

Suggested Closing Prayer

Dear God, we praise You for how Your Word can meet every need we have. We confess the need for power in our lives now and ask that You will meet that need. Help us to experience the power of Your Word — what it is and what it can do — and we thank You for the promise of answered prayer.

ADDITIONAL BACKGROUND MATERIAL

Some parallel passages of Scripture illustrating the power of the Word of God.
God's Word shall not return void — Isaiah 55:10-11.
His Word is like a fire and a hammer — Jeremiah 23:29.
The Word to be fulfilled — Matthew 5:17-18.
All of the Word is inspired by God — 2 Timothy 3:16-17.
It is the power of God for salvation — Romans 1:16.

LESSON SIX

THE NEED FOR THE
WORD OF GOD

Teacher's Objective: To help the students discover the value of God's Word as essential for life and to increase their desire for it as daily spiritual food.

CLASS TIME

Suggested Opening Prayer

Our Father, we pray that today as we consider the need for Your Word You will help us understand the value and importance of it and how it affects us and what it will do for us. Thank You for the way You have promised in Your Word to guide us.

(Introduction: Be sure students understand
    objective
    memory work
    reading assignment.)

Introduction

OBJECTIVE: To gain spiritual dependence on God's Word for daily Christian living.

TO MEMORIZE: Psalm 119:105.

TO READ: Acts 25 and 26.

WORD OF GOD
PSALM 119

**PARDON
PURPOSE
PEACE
POWER**

MAN

Discussion Starter

God has promised to guide us by His Word. Why do you think He felt this was necessary?

Lesson Development

There are certain essentials to physical health and growth which find parallels in the spiritual realm. Without food, air, rest and exercise, we cannot live physically. So, too, without spiritual food, air,

---

Bible Study

Read Psalm 119.

A. *Things we need to know about the Bible*

1. What does the psalmist call God's Word in the following verses of Psalm 119?

Verse 1 *The law of the Lord.*

2	*His testimonies.*	7	*Righteous judgments*
3	*His ways.*	43	*Word of truth.*
4	*His precepts.*	72	*Law of His mouth.*
5	*His statutes.*	91	*His ordinance.*
6	*His commandments.*	123	*Righteous word.*

2. What does this tell you of the importance of knowing God's Word? _____

---

rest, and exercise, we shrivel up and die spiritually.

Just what are these spiritual equivalents of food, air, rest and exercise?
1. The Christian's food: the Word — 1 Peter 2:2; Matthew 4:4.
2. The Christian's breathing: prayer — 1 Thessalonians 5:16-18;
   Philippians 4:6-7.
3. The Christian's rest: abiding in Christ — Matthew 11:28-30; John 15:10.
4. The Christian's exercise: witnessing — Acts 1:8.

It is with the first of these absolute necessities that we have been concerned in this Step, and now in this lesson. "Give us this day our daily bread" is a universal prayer of mankind. In answer to that prayer, the Word of God replies, "I am the food of the full-grown man; become a man, and you shall feed on Me."

3. When does God discipline (126)? _When His law is_ _broken._

4. What value does the Word have for us (72)? _More_ _than thousands of gold and silver pieces._

5. What is necessary in order to learn the Word (73)? _Understanding._

B. How God's Word affects our feeling

1. The psalmist found that respecting and learning God's Word resulted in:
   (7) _Uprightness of heart._
   (8) _Will not be forsaken utterly._
   (9) _Young man can keep his way pure._

2. From verses 10-16 list at least three attitudes of the psalmist that show his love for the Word of God: _____ _He sought God with all his heart; treasured_ _His word in his heart; rejoiced in the way of_ _His testimonies; meditated on His precepts,_ _regarded His ways, delighted in His statutes;_ _would not forget His word._

Here is a visual method of demonstrating how we "eat" the Bread of Life. Hold your Bible in your hand with a firm grip, noting that it takes all five fingers for the firmest grip. Then put the book down and count off on your fingers the following *ways of appropriating the Word:* (1) hearing (little finger); (2) reading (next finger); (3) studying (middle finger); (4) memorizing (index finger); (5) meditating (thumb).

(Hearing and Meditating:) We attend church services and we hear the Word preached. Psychologists will tell you that most of what you retain from the worship service will be inspirational; you will actually *remember* only about 5% of what you heard (little finger), though that percentage might run as high as 15% depending on how much meditation (thumb) goes into the hearing. (Pick up your Bible and hold it with the thumb and little finger only.) Hearing is vitally important. Romans 10:17 tells us that "faith comes by hearing" the Word of God. But 5% or even 15% does not give a very strong grip on the Word of God, does it? It would not be difficult for this Bible to be taken away from me when I'm holding it like this.

3. Why is adversity sometimes good for us (67, 71)? _It_
makes us keep His word and learn His statutes.

4. What is the reaction of those who love Christ when His
Word is not kept (136)? _____ _They weep._
(158)? _They loathe the treacherous._

5. How can we have great peace (165)? _____
By loving God's law.

(Reading:) Reading enables us to cover the broad sweep of the Scriptures, and this is absolutely essential. But you will remember ordinarily only about 25% of what you read. (Now hold the Bible with the thumb, little finger and the next finger.) When we add personal reading of the Bible to hearing, we certainly have a firmer hold on God's Word, but it's still a rather weak grip, wouldn't you say?

C. Results of appropriating God's Word
1. What the Word does for us:
Knowing and memorizing the Word makes us (98) _____
Wiser than our enemies.

Meditating on it makes us (99) _____
Have more insight than all our teachers.

Obeying it makes us (100) _____
Understand more than the aged.

Why is this (105)? _(God's Word enlightens--is a_
lamp to our feet and a light to our paths.)

The Word gives us (130) _(Light, and understanding_
to the simple.)

(Studying:) To appropriate God's Word, we must study it. Studying contrasts to merely reading in that we use a pencil. We may make notes, outlines, word studies and file them away for future reference. Or, we may make notations in the margins of our study Bible concerning related passages, chapter outlines, and paragraph titles. Sometimes we may write a synonym above a difficult word. We may retain up to 50% of what we study.

2. What we should do as a result of appropriating the Word:
(74) _Wait for His Word._
(63) _Be a companion of those who fear God._
(11) _Not sin against God._
(32) _Have an enlarged heart._
(157) _Do not turn aside from His testimonies._
(176) _Not forget His commandments._

(Memorizing:) Memorizing may seem like child's play — something that is done in the Junior Department in Sunday school. But think again. Have you ever heard of a doctor, a physicist, a lawyer or a stock broker who has not found it necessary to commit to memory many of the thought-tools of his profession? What good would a football or basketball player be if he refused to memorize the plays? We memorize the things that are absolutely essential, the things we dare not forget. We memorize when we are looking not for 5% retention, or 25%, or 50% but 100%.

(Hold the Bible with all fingers now.) When I add memorization to my methods of learning and understanding God's holy Word, then I have the firmest grip possible.

Conclusion and Application

We need a sure word for the age in which we live; we need clearly spoken directions. This is what God promises to those who study His Word.

> **Life Application**
>
> 1. What impresses you most about Psalm 119? _____
> _____
> _____
>
> 2. Write *three* ways in which you recognize your personal need for God's Word today. _____
> _____
> _____
> _____
>
> 3. Many people can recite the four books of the Gospels. Can you? _____ Add the one book of New Testament history and write all five books here: _____
> _____
>
> Since this division is quite easy, go ahead to the next division, the Pauline epistles and Hebrews. That division is much harder to learn so you should get started on it now.

Suggested Closing Prayer

Dear Father, we appreciate the gift of Your Word. Thank You for the deepened understanding You have given us of how important Your Word is, how extensively it affects us and how far-reaching are the results of appropriating it. Help us continually to recognize it as a vital part of our lives and to study and meditate upon it accordingly.

PRIVATE BIBLE STUDY METHODS

Teacher's Objective: To encourage and motivate students to begin serious personal Bible study.

CLASS TIME

(NOTE TO TEACHER: This is not necessarily a lesson to be used as a full study by groups. The material in brief outline may be incorporated in the discussions which are centered on Lesson Six.)

Suggested Opening Prayer

Dear Lord, in our lesson today we will be looking at the various methods of studying Your Word. We ask that You will motivate all of us to be more serious about our approach to regular systematic Bible study and what we expect to gain from it.

(Introduction: Be sure students understand objective
   memory work
   reading assignment.)

Introduction

OBJECTIVE: To know how to and to establish good habits of regular systematic study of the Bible.

TO MEMORIZE: Colossians 3:16a and 17.

TO READ: Acts 27 and 28.

Discussion Starter

(Rather than using a separate discussion starter, for this lesson, just read and discuss the various points as appropriate for your group.)

"It is a great day for a little child when he learns to feed himself; so it becomes a new era in a believer's life when he forms the habit of going daily to the original sources of spiritual truth for his own personal nourishment.

"Study the Bible as a traveler who seeks to obtain a thorough and experimental knowledge of a new country.

"Go over its vast fields to truth; descend into its valleys; climb its mountains of vision; follow its streams of inspiration; enter its halls of instruction; visit its wondrous portrait galleries.

"Remember that many doctrinal errors have grown out of a lack of spiritual perspective, or a narrow view of scriptural truth. The Savior says, 'Ye do err, not knowing the Scriptures, nor the power of God.'

"Seek to understand the deep things of God. Study 'The Word' as a miner digs for gold, or as a diver plunges into the depths of the sea for pearls.

"Most great truths do not lie upon the surface. They must be brought up into the light by patient toil" — Thompson Chain Reference Bible.

Lesson Development

Bible Study

A. *Proper attitude for Bible study*

When you personally received Christ as your Savior and Lord, you began a great adventure. That great adventure is mapped out in the pages of the Holy Scriptures. As you read and study the Bible in the power of the Holy Spirit you will find strength and direction. You will learn and claim the many great promises God has reserved for His own.

Approach the Bible in prayer, with reverence, awe, expectancy; with a willing mind; with a thirst for truth and righteousness and fullness in the Lord Jesus Christ; with a humble and contrite heart, trusting God the Holy Spirit to engraft therein the cleansing power of His eternal Word. Above all, in the study of God's Word be eager to obey all that He commands and rejoice in the knowledge that you are an ambassador for Christ, beseeching men in His stead to be reconciled to God.

1. How do you feel about Bible study? _____

_____

2. What do you see at this point as your main purpose in studying God's Word? _____

_____

3. Have you established a definite goal regarding Bible study? _____

_____

B. *Tools needed*

First, obtain two translations of the Bible. Study both translations. You would not expect to learn much about the physical laws of our universe without diligent and persistent study. Should you expect to acquire much knowledge of God and the unsearchable riches of His Word without studying with equal diligence and persistence?

Other books you will need, and should plan to add to your study library as soon as possible, are a topical Bible, a concordance and a Bible dictionary. Additional Bible study books are helpful and can be added as convenient. However, always remember, Bible study involves just that — studying the *Bible*. The other things are merely tools to assist you in getting the rich truths God has for you in His Word.

As you consider each study of the Scriptures, may I suggest you record God's Word to you in a journal. This will not only help give a deeper, more serious study, it also will give you a written record of how God speaks to you and of your response to Him.

1. List the tools you now have. _____

_____

2. List the additional tools you desire in the order in which you plan to obtain them. _____

_____

_____

You have been reading a number of Bible books as you have progressed through the study of these Ten Basic Steps To Christian Maturity. This program of study is designed to ground young Christians in the basics of Bible knowledge *and* in good habits of regular, systematic feeding upon the Bread of Life.

C. *Suggested methods*

1. Book Study: The Bible contains many books. Yet the divine plan of God to redeem men in Christ Jesus runs through the whole of it. Be careful to consider each book as a part of the whole. Read it through.

Mark and *underline* as God speaks to you through His Word.

Outline it.

List the principal characters, who they are and their significance.

Select from each chapter key verses to memorize and copy each on a card to carry with you.

List *teachings to obey and promises to claim.*

Consider the characteristics revealed of God the Father, God the Son and God the Holy Spirit.

What book would you particularly like to study using this method? (It is best to start with one of the shorter ones.)

_____

This is the core of any good book study.

2. Chapter Study: To get a grasp of the chapter, answer the following questions:

What is the principal subject of the chapter?

What is the leading lesson?

What is the key verse? Memorize it.

Who are the principal characters?

What does it teach about God the Father? Jesus Christ? the Holy Spirit?

Is there any example for me to follow?

Is there any error for me to avoid?

Is there any duty for me to perform?

Is there any promise for me to claim?

Is there any prayer for me to echo?

To what chapter of which book would you choose to apply these questions? _____

3. Topical Study: Take an important subject, such as grace, truth, prayer, faith, assurance, justification, regeneration, peace, etc., and, using a *topical Bible and concordance,* study the scope of the topic throughout the Bible. You will find it necessary to divide each topic into sub-topics as you accumulate material; e.g., forms of prayer, prayer promises, examples of prayer in Scripture, Christ's teaching on prayer, Christ's ministry as we pray, ministry of the Holy Spirit in prayer, etc.

The first eight Steps are based on this method, so it is familiar already.

What topic do you plan to study first? _____

How much time have you scheduled for it? _____

Step Nine, Lessons 3, 5, 6 and 7 are designed to whet your appetite for the inspiration and education to be found in character studies. Once the taste has been created through the Ten Steps, you will be eager to get going on your own!

4. Biographical Study: There are 2,930 people mentioned in the Bible. The lives of many of these make extremely interesting biographical studies (1 Corinthians 10:11; Romans 15:4). Using a concordance, topical Bible, or the proper name index in your Bible, look up every reference to the person in question. Answer the following questions:

What was the social and political atmosphere in which he lived?

How did that affect his life?

What do we know of his family?

What kind of training did he have in his youth?

What was accomplished by him during his life?

Was there a great crisis in his life? If so, how did he face it?

What were his outstanding character traits?

Who were his friends? What kind of people were they?

What influence did they have on him? What influence did he have on them?

Does his life show any development of character?

What was his experience with God? Notice his prayer life, his faith, his service to God, his knowledge of God's Word, his courage in witnessing, and his attitude toward the worship of God.

Were any particular faults evident in his life?

Was there any outstanding sin in his life? Under what circumstances did he commit this sin? What was its nature and its effect on his future life?

What were his children like?

Was he a type or antitype of Christ?

Was there some lesson in this person's life which is outstanding to you?

Name the person you would like to study. _____

Your reason for choosing that particular person. _____

Conclusion and Application

Most of the material of Lesson 7 is for future reference, rather than immediate usefulness. When the Ten Steps have been completed, you will need to refer to these instructions in order to carry on fruitful personal Bible study without the use of study questions and other aids.

Life Application

By the time you complete the studies outlined in this Handbook for Christian Maturity, you will have been introduced to each of these four methods. You already have taken the first step in the *book* study method by reading the book of Acts. Lessons 2 and 4 of Step 2, The Abundant Life, were chapter studies. You will soon be ready to apply these as well as the other two methods to more advanced work in your own individual Bible study.

1. Which method interests you most now? _____

_____

2. What do you expect serious study of the Bible to do for you?

_____

3. Complete your memorization of the Pauline epistles and the last book of prophecy. Write them all here:

Pauline epistles & Hebrews _____

_____

_____

General epistles & prophecy _____

_____

_____

When you have completed Step Ten, you should be more than ready to launch out into one profitable Bible study after another. However, it is recommended — with emphasis — that *this* foundation of the Ten Steps first be laid before you move to more advanced work.

Always study the Bible with:

a pencil or pen

a paper

a prayer

a purpose.

Suggested Closing Prayer

Thank You, Father, for what you have shown us today. As we continue in our study of the Ten Basic Steps, and of the Bible, we pray You will help us put these things in practice so as to gain the most possible benefit from our study time.

LESSON EIGHT

RECAP

Teacher's Objective: To increase the students' appreciation of the importance of the Bible, its authority and inspiration, its purpose and what daily Bible study can do for the individual Christian.

CLASS TIME

Suggested Opening Prayer

Dear Father, we ask that as we review the last seven lessons You will increase our knowledge, understanding and appreciation of the importance of Your Word. Help us commit these things to our hearts so as to experience spiritual growth.

(Introduction: This review lesson does not have a new student's objective. Previous memory work is to be reviewed, especially 2 Timothy 3:16,17. Reading assignment: reread Psalm 119.)

(NOTE: This Recap lesson could begin with an oral review of the books of the Bible and the divisions into which they fall. After getting them fixed in the minds of the students as well as you can, then you could go on to the Discussion Starter and the development of the rest of the lesson.)

> Write the divisions of the books of the Bible and the names of each book in each division. Go back over any division you do not know well.
>
> _____
> _____
> _____
> _____
> _____
> _____
> _____
> _____

Discussion Starter

(Ask the class:) Do you think a non-Christian should study the Bible? Why or why not?

Lesson Development

(Any Teacher's Enrichment or Additional Background Material that you were not able to use in the previous lessons could be utilized at this time and any point which you might feel was not sufficiently covered before, or which the students do not understand as well as they could, can be dealt with now too.

Then go over the Recap questions and answers. This material will benefit both the students and you by giving you a deeper appreciation of God's Word.)

How would you explain the statement, "Christ is the central person of the Bible"? _____

_____

What do you think is the real source of the authority of the Scriptures? Explain. _____

_____

Name at least three things the Word of God accomplishes that indicate its supernatural power. _____

_____

Why do *you* need the Word of God?   _____

_____

What steps do you still need to take to be fully prepared for serious study of the Bible? _____

_____

_____

Review the names of the books of the Bible and write them one final time here. Be sure the spelling is right.

_____

_____

_____

_____

_____

_____

_____

Conclusion and Application

(Give class members some time to write the books of the Bible one more time, then go on with:) We can readily see the importance of and the need for the Word of God. Someone has said, "Sin will keep me from this Book, but this Book will keep me from sin." That is in accord with Psalm 119:11: "Thy Word I have treasured in my heart, that I may not sin against Thee."

Suggested Closing Prayer

(Give the students a few minutes for silent prayer in which to make any commitments they feel necessary, especially regarding study of God's Word. (Then you pray aloud:)

We thank You, God, that You again have answered prayer and that we have a better understanding of Your Word by looking again at its authority and inspiration as well as its purpose and how it can change our lives. Help us not to forget these things You have taught us today.

SUMMARY LESSON PLAN

THE CHRISTIAN AND THE BIBLE

Teacher's Objective: To impress students with the greatness of the Bible; to show that the unity of the Bible lies in one theme; to give Christians confidence in its authority and inspiration; to discover what the Bible claims for itself; to awaken a desire for the Word of God as daily spiritual food essential for life; and to motivate students toward a regular and systematic study of the Word.

Teacher's Enrichment: (see Teacher's Enrichment sections as they occur in the previous lessons of this Step, and share with the class as time permits.)

CLASS TIME

Suggested Opening Prayer

Dear Father, we ask that as we study this lesson today You will increase our knowledge, understanding and appreciation of the importance of Your Word. Help us to commit these things to our hearts so as to experience spiritual growth.

(Introduction:

STUDENT'S OBJECTIVE: To discover the greatness of the Bible, to see that the unity of the Bible lies in one theme — Christ, to understand the authority and inspiration of the Scriptures and to see what the Bible claims for itself and what it can do in a person's life.

TO MEMORIZE: 2 Peter 3:20,21; 2 Timothy 3:16,17; Psalm 119:11.

READING ASSIGNMENT: Psalm 119; Luke 24:44-48.)

Discussion Starter

Two claims for the Bible are made in 2 Timothy 3:16,17. What are they? If you were a non-Christian and you wanted seriously to investigate Christianity, how would you evaluate these two claims? What would be your criteria for the first claim? The second?

Lesson Development

(Have one of the students read the opening paragraphs — by William W. Orr — of Lesson 1 of this Step. Encourage students to go through the lessons in this Step and learn the books of the Bible and the divisions into which they fall.)

A. Construction of the Bible *(from Lesson 1).*

   1. Old Testament — 5 divisions

      Pentateuch (Law): Genesis, Exodus, Leviticus, Numbers, Deuteronomy

      Historical: Joshua, Judges, Ruth, 1 and 2 Samuel, 1 and 2 Kings, 1 and 2 Chronicles, Ezra, Nehemiah, Esther

      Poetry: Job, Psalms, Proverbs, Ecclesiastes, Song of Solomon

      Major Prophets: Isaiah, Jeremiah, Lamentations, Ezekiel, Daniel

      Minor Prophets: Hosea, Joel, Amos, Obadiah, Jonah, Micah, Nahum, Habakkuk, Zephaniah, Haggai, Zechariah, Malachi

   2. New Testament — 5 divisions

      Gospels: Matthew, Mark, Luke, John

      Historical: Acts

      Epistles — Pauline (and Hebrews): Romans, 1 and 2 Corinthians, Galatians, Ephesians, Philippians, Colossians, 1 and 2 Thessalonians, 1 and 2 Timothy, Titus, Philemon, Hebrews (thought to be written by Paul)

      Epistles — General (named for the author rather than the recipient): James, 1 and 2 Peter, 1, 2 and 3 John, Jude

      Prophecy: Revelation

B. Christ is the central person of the Bible *(from Lesson 2).*

   1. What did Christ say of the Scriptures in John 5:39? (They bear witness of Him.)

   2. What did the apostles think about Christ and the Old Testament?

      Peter (Acts 3:18): (God announced beforehand by the prophets that Christ should suffer, and He has fulfilled it.)

      Paul (1 Corinthians 15:3,4): (Christ fulfilled the Scriptures in His death, burial and resurrection.)

   3. There are more than 300 Old Testament prophecies about the first coming of the Messiah which were fulfilled in the life of Christ and recorded in the New Testament. (Refer students to Lesson 2 of this Step and encourage them to work out section C on their own later.)

   4. Why were the historical facts and teachings of Jesus Christ written (John 20:31)? (That we might believe Jesus is the Christ and might have life in His name.)

C. Authority of the Old Testament *(from Lesson 3).*

   1. What opinion did the writers have of their work in the Old Testament? (Have students look these up and have one person give the answer for each Scripture: 2 Samuel 23:2; Isaiah 8:1; 8:5; 8:11; Jeremiah 1:9; Ezekiel 3:4.) "Thus saith the Lord" occurs 2000 times in the Old Testament.

2. What was Jesus' view of the Old Testament (Matthew 4:4,7,10)? ("It is written" was the basis for his decisions and actions.)

3. What did the apostles consider the Old Testament to be (Acts 1:16 and Romans 3:2)? (The oracles of God, delivered by the Holy Spirit.)

D. Authority of the New Testament, the writings of the first Christians (from Lesson 4).

1. What authority did Christ give the apostles (John 17:18; 20:21)? (As God sent Christ, Christ sent the apostles.)

2. Where did the writer of Hebrews get his authority (Hebrews 1:1,2)? (Through the Son of God.)

3. How about John (1 John 1:1-3)? (He had seen and heard — and touched — the Word of life, Christ.)

E. The power of the Bible (from Lesson 5).

1. Tell what the Bible is or what it does according to: Hebrews 5:13; Ephesians 6:17; Romans 19:17; John 8:31,32.

2. What is the only way a person can understand the Bible, according to 1 Corinthians 2:14? (To become a spiritual man, by being born of the Holy Spirit.)

3. What is the power the Bible has in the life of a person (Hebrews 4:12)? (Can divide the soul from the spirit, and judges the thoughts and intentions of the heart.)

F. The need for the Word of God (from Lesson 6).

1. When does God discipline (Psalm 119:126)? (When His law is broken.)

2. What is God's Word called in Psalm 119:

verse 1? (Law of the Lord)

4? (His precepts)

6? (His commandments)

72? (Law of His mouth)

123? (Righteous Word)

3. How did the psalmist feel about the Word of God (verses 10-16)? Treasured, rejoiced, delighted, etc.)

4. What are some of the results of appropriating God's Word shown in:

verse 98? (Makes us wiser than our enemies)

99? (We have more insight than all our teachers)

100? (We understand more than the aged)

Conclusion and Application

There are certain essentials to physical health and growth which find parallels in the spiritual realm. Without food, air, rest and exercise we cannot live physically. So, too, without spiritual food, air, rest and exercise, we shrivel up and die spiritually.

What are the spiritual equivalents of these essentials?

The Christian's *food:* the Word — 1 Peter 2:2; Matthew 4:4.

The Christian's *breathing:* prayer — 1 Thessalonians 5:16; Philippians 4:6,7.

The Christian's *rest:* abiding in Christ — Matthew 11:28-30; John 15:10.

The Christian's *exercise:* witnessing — Acts 1:8.

(NOTE: Students should be encouraged to read carefully the information in Lesson 7 in order to get a grasp on the various methods of Bible study presented there. You may tell them:) Most of the material of Lesson 7 is for future reference, rather than immediate usefulness. When these Ten Steps have been completed, you will need to refer to those instructions in order to carry on fruitful personal Bible study without the use of study questions or other aids.

Suggested Closing Prayer

(Give the students a few minutes for silent prayer in which to make any commitments they feel necessary regarding study of God's Word. Then you pray aloud:)

We thank You, God, that You have answered prayer and that we have a better understanding of Your Word by looking at its authority and its inspiration as well as its purpose and how it can change our lives. Help us not to forget these things You have taught us today.

STEP SIX

The Christian and Obedience

(Introductory article appearing on page 221 of student's handbook. Discuss with students as appropriate.)

THE OBEDIENT CHRISTIAN

Jesus refers to Himself in John 15 as the vine and to the Christian as a branch. "Abide in Me, and I in you. As the branch cannot bear fruit of itself, unless it abides in the vine, so neither can you, unless you abide in Me" (John 15:4). *To abide is to obey.* The obedient Christian abides in Christ and bears much fruit for His glory.

"The one who says he abides in Him ought himself to walk in the same manner as He walked" (1 John 2:6).

"He who has My commandments, and keeps them, he it is who loves Me . . ." (John 14:21).

"The world has yet to see what God can do *in* and *through* and *for* one individual who is completely yielded to the Lord Jesus Christ." This was the challenge that inspired Dwight L Moody to say, "I want to be that man." God used him, as He used no other man of his time, to reach multitudes.

LESSON ONE

OBEDIENCE AND THE RESULTS
OF DOING GOD'S WILL

Teacher's Objective: To help students desire to know God's will and be completely obedient to Him no matter how the circumstances appear to them.

Teacher's Enrichment: (This material may be shared with class members as time permits.)

Paul's life is an example that one's calling should always precede his preaching.

1. In his earlier ministry Paul prayed, "That I may finish my course, and the ministry, which I received from the Lord Jesus, to testify solemnly of the gospel of the grace of God" (Acts 20:24). At the end of his ministry he stated, "I have fought the good fight, I have finished the course, I have kept the faith" (2 Timothy 4:7-8).

2. Paul obeyed. His faithfulness in the trials of his early Christian life laid the foundation for greater trials and more faith to follow, thus a lifetime testimony to the saving and keeping grace of God was built.

3. Exhortation to believers today: "Brethren, be all the more diligent to make certain about His calling and choosing you; for as long as you practice these things, you will never stumble" (2 Peter 1:10).

CLASS TIME

Suggested Opening Prayer

Our Father, we ask that You will show us the importance of obedience in an effective Christian's life. Help us to understand how our trust in You must be balanced by our obedience to Your commands, and make us willing to discover and do Your will regardless of what the circumstances may seem to be.

(Introduction: Be sure students understand
  objective
  memory work
  reading assignment.)

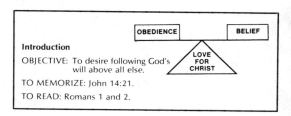

OBEDIENCE   BELIEF

Introduction

OBJECTIVE: To desire following God's
    will above all else.

LOVE
FOR
CHRIST

TO MEMORIZE: John 14:21.

TO READ: Romans 1 and 2.

(Have the class share this material in any of the ways suggested in the Instructions for Teaching on page 21.)

The true test of our love for Christ is *obedience.* Jesus said, "He who has My commandments, and keeps them, he it is who loves Me; and he who loves Me shall be loved by My Father, and I will love him, and will disclose Myself to him" (John 14:21). Just as there are physical laws that govern our physical lives, so are there spiritual laws that govern our spiritual lives. It is only as we are obedient to these laws that we are free. Jesus said that He had come to give us a more abundant life (John 10:10). Satan tempts us to violate the laws of the Spirit, which are confirmed by the Word of God and our hearts. Satan is the enemy of men's souls. Yet, though he wields great power, he cannot defeat us if we are completely yielded and obedient to Christ.

A successful athlete must be obedient to certain regulations. The same applies to doctors, lawyers, teachers, farmers, etc., if they are to be successful in their chosen endeavors. How then can a Christian expect to be an effective and fruitful witness unless he is obedient to the Lord Jesus Christ and to His Word (1 John 2:6, 15-17)?

Some are reluctant to trust God completely with their lives, fearing that He may wish to make a change in their plans. What if He does? Is it not logical that the one who created us knows better than we that purpose for which we were created; and since He loves us enough to die for us, is it not logical to believe that His way is best (Romans 8:32)? Obedience is the true test of our love for Christ.

Discussion Starter

The importance of obedience cannot be overemphasized. We are admonished to discipline our children to save them from spiritual bankruptcy (Proverbs 23:13-14). We are taught also to bring up our spiritual children (2 Timothy 2:2). As a disobedient child grows up to be a problem child, so will the disobedient Christian grow into a problem to himself, to others and especially to the Lord if he does not learn obedience in his early Christian experience. What kinds of problems do you think a disobedient Christian could create?

Lesson Development

God was displeased and dissolved Saul's kingship (verses 11, 23). Saul called

Bible Study

A. *Disobedience of King Saul*
   Read 1 Samuel 15.

   1. What was God's command to Saul through Samuel?
      To utterly destroy Amalek, his company and his possessions.

   2. How did Saul comply? *He spared Agag, the king, and the best of the cattle for sacrifice.*

   3. Summarize the results: _____

   4. The main principle illustrated is stated in verse 22. What is it? *Obedience is better than sacrifice.*

his action 100% obedience. Samuel called it rebellion, stubbornness and rejecting
the Word of the Lord (verses 20,23).

Paul's background is
found in Philippians 3:4-6:

> B. *Obedience of Paul*
> Read Acts 9:1-22.

circumcised (covenant status), stock of Israel (pride of family), Pharisee (pride of
religion) and zealous persecutor of the church (pride of conviction).

We see the transformation of his life in Acts 9: called by God (verse 6), a
chosen vessel to be God's witness (15), restored to sight (8, 17), filled with the
Spirit (17), baptized (18), preached Christ (20).

1. What was God's command to Paul?   *To rise and enter the city where he would be told what to do next.*

2. How did he comply?   *He did exactly what God told him to do.*

3. Summarize the results listed in this passage: _____

4. How do you think Paul's obedience illustrates the truth of the principle listed in A. 4 above? _____

C. *Obedience of Ananias — and its effect*

1. What was God's command to Ananias? *To find Saul and lay his hands on him that Saul might receive his sight.*

2. What human reaction did Ananias exhibit? *Fear.*

3. How did he finally respond? *Complete obedience.*

4. How did his simple obedience indirectly influence us?
   God used Paul to reveal the most abundant life ever possible to mankind.

Conclusion and Application

Henry Drummond once stated, "There is a great instrument for finding God's
will; this instrument can penetrate where others cannot go. It has a name which
every child may understand, even as the stupendous instrument itself with all its

mighty powers is sometimes moved in infant hands when others have tried in vain. The name of the instrument is OBEDIENCE." Perfect obedience can bring perfect happiness when we have perfect confidence in the power we are obeying.

Life Application

1. How would you have felt in Ananias' place? _____

_____

2. What is the most important thing this lesson teaches you about obedience? _____

_____

3. What specific area of weakness in your life do you need to bring into obedience to Christ? _____

_____

_____

Suggested Closing Prayer

We thank You, God, for what You have shown us about the far-reaching results of our obedience or disobedience to Your commands. Help us to remember that You know us and You know what is best for us, and Your commands are all made in love, so we can have confidence in You and in what You ask us to do.

ADDITIONAL BACKGROUND MATERIAL

Some additional passages of Scripture which teach the importance of obedience:
Obedience to God — John 15:10, 14.
Obedience to man — Hebrews 13:17; 1 Peter 5:5-6.
Obedience to higher authority — Romans 13:1-7.
Disobedience leads to slothfulness — Proverbs 18:9; 19:15.

LESSON TWO

OBEDIENCE AND PERSONAL PURITY

Teacher's Objective: To arouse a desire for and motivate students toward purity in their thoughts and actions.

Teacher's Enrichment: (Share this material with group members as time allows.)
- Impurity and its results in the spiritual ministry:
    1. David's sins — 2 Samuel 11:1-4.
    2. Solomon's sin — 1 Kings 11:1-4.
    3. Samson's sin — Judges 14:1-4.
- Purity and its results:
    1. Rebekah — Genesis 24.
    2. Joseph — Genesis 39:7-23; 41:38-44.

Since impure actions are the results of impure thinking, it is especially important that we occupy our minds with Christ.

CLASS TIME

Suggested Opening Prayer

Lord, examine our thoughts and see if there be any wicked ways in us. Show us Your mind regarding purity.

(Introduction: Be sure students understand
  objective
  memory work*
  reading assignment.)

> **Introduction**
> OBJECTIVE: To desire a holy life.
> TO MEMORIZE: 1 Corinthians 6:18.
> TO READ: Romans 3 and 4.

(*Take a few minutes to review the verse together. Ask one person to recite it; then ask another to explain it.)

Discussion Starter

What is sexual temptation and what do you think is the best way to resist it?

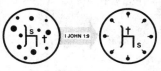

Few areas of life are more important than our relationship to the opposite sex, and few areas are so exposed to temptation. The purpose of this lesson is:

1. To show that immorality originates in the mind, and that God must give us victory there by His Holy Spirit.
2. To show that the Bible gives a healthy outlook on sex. The Bible teaches that the sexual relationship can be a source of enjoyment and blessing when confined to the proper area — marriage. The Bible never pictures sex as sinful, distasteful or dirty. Just as fire may be a great boon to man, but can bring havoc when used improperly, so is sex a great blessing, but it can ruin a life when abusively indulged.
3. To show that our gracious God forgives and cleanses in this area as He does in all others, so that we need carry no unnecessary load of guilt.
4. To show that in all our conduct toward the opposite sex we must set the highest example, and give no occasion for others to doubt our testimony.

Lesson Development

Bible Study

A. *Purity and the mind*

1. What does Christ say of impure thought (Matthew 5:27, 28)? _Shows a wicked heart, which condemns us as quickly as outward sinful actions._

Jesus speaks here of two things, an *outward requirement* and an *inward reality.* Why is meeting the outward requirement without the inward reality unacceptable to God?

The Sermon on the Mount, in which these verses are found, is the classic condemnation of external religion, which is largely obedience to laws and rules. Mark 7:1-23 illustrates this as it was in Jesus' time. In our own time, many believe they are justified before God if they are outwardly moral, cultured, polite, considerate and refined. Many philosophers and social reformers feel that the basic solution to our problems is an external one, merely the improvement of our environment through legislation and welfare programs. Jesus stands against all such thinking. When He says, "There is nothing outside the man, which going into him can defile him; but the things which proceed out of the man are what defile the man" (Mark 7:15), He shows that the real problem is internal. Many Christians are diligent in reading their Bibles, in praying, in church attendance, even in witnessing for Christ, but their works are unacceptable to God because they do not reflect a right heart.

A policeman was shot to death by a gunman in California, and a Michigan business executive shot his best friend in a hunting accident. In the case of the policeman, search was made for the killer and he was prosecuted. In the case of the business executive, there was no prosecution — it obviously was not his fault. He even received sympathy. Both men had done the same thing — they had shot and killed another human being with a gun. But their motives were entirely different.

"For as he thinks within himself, so he is" (Proverbs 23:7). Evil thoughts will eventually result in evil actions. The source of personality is within the thought processes.

As we live each day we are to do it claiming the strength, power and protection Christ provides. The victory over impure thinking does not come from us, but from Christ.

2. List the things on which we are to think (Philippians 4:8). _Whatever is true, honorable, right, pure, lovely, of good repute, excellent and worthy of praise._

Why does the human mind not want to think on these things (Romans 8:7)? _Its nature is to be set on the flesh and hostile toward God--unable to be subject to the Law of God._

3. How, then, do we obtain victory over impure thoughts (Galatians 5:16)? _By walking in the Spirit._

We are to give no occasion, no opportunity to the flesh to fulfill its impure desires. Any choice

4. What else should we do to avoid thinking impure thoughts (Romans 13:14)? _Put on the Lord Jesus Christ--make no provision for lust of flesh._

you face in life will find two voices beckoning, each in opposite directions: the flesh, representing Satan; the Spirit, representing Christ. We often fail because we put ourselves in positions where we will be tempted. To look at or read something which promotes sinful thoughts and then expect God to protect us is equivalent to leaping from a building and asking God to keep us from falling!

Note: _Temptation_ is not the same as _sin_ in the thought life. Evil thoughts may pass through the mind, but sin comes from dwelling on the thought. As an illustration: "You can't stop birds from flying over your head, but you can stop them from building a nest in your hair."

B. _Purity and the opposite sex_

1. What does the Bible say about the sexual relationship in its proper place (Hebrews 13:4)? _Within marriage, it is honorable and undefiled._

2. When tempted by immorality, what is a Christian to do (1 Corinthians 6:18)? _Flee immorality._

Why? _The immoral man sins against his own body which is the temple of the Holy Spirit._

3. List some things you can know when tempted (1 Corinthians 10:13). _It is common to man--you are not the only one, will not be beyond what you can handle, God provides way of escape, you can endure it._

4. Write in your own words the warnings against immorality found in the following Scriptures:

Proverbs 6:26 _____

Proverbs 6:32 _____

1 Thessalonians 4:3 _____

C. *Purity and forgiveness*

1. Write in your own words what the following verses say about God's forgiveness:

Psalm 103:12 _____

Isaiah 43:25 _____

1 John 2:1, 2 _____

Look up "propitiation" and write its meaning: _____

God promises *unconditional* forgiveness which is not based on how guilty we feel or if we promise never to do it again. It is based on the promise of His faithfulness. He alone is faithful and just. He alone can forgive.

When God forgives sin, He also removes and forgets it. Unconditional forgiveness provides complete cleansing.

2. What must we do to obtain God's forgiveness (1 John 1:9)?
Confess our sins--agree with God concerning the sins.

The most difficult aspect of keeping our hearts right before God by confessing our sins is admitting that a particular thing we have done is sin. The human personality is so constructed that it would always prefer to rationalize or justify wrong rather than admit it.

(Ask the class:) To whom does the "we" in 1 John 1:9 refer? (Answer — believers.) The Greek meaning of the word *confess*, "to agree with" God, implies being specific, naming the sin. What is wrong with praying, "Lord, forgive me for all of my sins?" (Answer — It is too general. Unless we identify the sin, we will probably not forsake it.)

When should we confess sin? The *moment* we realize we have failed God, the *moment* we are unkind or unfaithful to a friend we need to ask forgiveness of them and confess the sin to God.

Conclusion and Application

As Christians, we often forget that our relationship to God depends upon our being cleansed, moment by moment, and not on an attitude of "anything goes if I am sincere, or if I am trying."

Life Application

1. What area of impurity in your life do you need to face and deal with? _____

   _____

   _____

2. Choose an appropriate verse or passage from this lesson, apply it to your situation and write the result you expect to attain. _____

   _____

   _____

   _____

Suggested Closing Prayer

We thank You, Father, for what You have shown us in this lesson today about the inward purity of heart and mind which You require, and how we can have that purity by allowing Christ to live within us. Help us to continue to look to You for the leadership and the power for pure lives.

ADDITIONAL BACKGROUND MATERIAL

Christians and Questionable Practices (Romans 14:21)

What is a "questionable practice?" What determines whether I should engage in a questionable practice or not?

The Bible puts the things we do into three general classifications — things that are *wrong* (murder, immorality, drunkenness, etc.), things that are *right* (marriage, eating, worship, etc.), and things that are *dependent on our own personality, the circumstance and the potential effect upon others,* as to whether they are right or wrong. It is like contrasting black, white and gray.

A questionable practice is in the third class.

We may engage in many activities with no personal harm, if we are strong Christians. But those who follow our example may fall. If such happens, God holds us responsible.

Such things are not usually sin in themselves, but our participation in them is to be governed by a "law of love," a consideration for others. If our participation will weaken, or somehow lead another Christian astray or wrongly influence a non-Christian, the law of love says we should refrain.

Fortunately, the Bible is not a book of petty rules and regulations, but of broad principles which span time and culture. The Bible will not tell a girl how long her sleeves should be, or how high the neck on her dress. It will not tell a young man when he should and should not kiss his date. But it gives general principles which by the wisdom of the Holy Spirit we are to apply to our own situations.

We are to avoid two extremes — license and legalism. It is never safe to lay down specific rules in these areas as to what one can and cannot do. Rather each must decide for himself on the basis of the fact that our bodies are temples of God, and that 1 Corinthians 10:31 says, "Do *all* to the glory of God."

LESSON THREE

OBEDIENCE AND THE
PRIVILEGE OF SECURITY

Teacher's Objective: To show the student that physical, material and spiritual security depend on Christ and our obedience to Him.

Teacher's Enrichment: (This material can be shared with students as time permits.)

God's Word says this: "Ask, and it shall be given to you; seek, and you shall find; knock, and it shall be opened to you. For everyone who asks receives, and he who seeks finds, and to him who knocks it shall be opened. Or what man is there among you, when his son shall ask him for a loaf, will give him a stone? Or if he shall ask for a fish, he will not give him a snake, will he? If you then, being evil, know how to give good gifts to your children, how much more shall your Father who is in heaven give what is good to those who ask Him!" (Matthew 7:7-11).

"What then shall we say to these things? If God is for us, who is against us? He who did not spare His own Son, but delivered Him up for us all, how will He not also with Him freely give us all things?" (Romans 8:31-32).

Security is found only in being obedient to God's Word: "Do not love the world, nor the things in the world. If anyone loves the world, the love of the Father is not in him. For all that is in the world, the lust of the flesh and the lust of the eyes and the boastful pride of life, is not from the Father, but is from the world. And the world is passing away, and also its lusts; but the one who does the will of God abides forever" (1 John 2:15-17). False security lies in the world and the things of the world, but true security lies in doing the will of God.

CLASS TIME

Suggested Opening Prayer

Lord, show me that You take care of all my needs, wants and desires, and make me want only You.

(Introduction: Be sure
students understand
    objective
    memory work *
    reading assignment.)

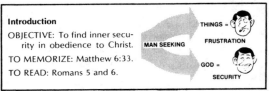

Introduction

OBJECTIVE: To find inner security in obedience to Christ.

TO MEMORIZE: Matthew 6:33.

TO READ: Romans 5 and 6.

MAN SEEKING

THINGS = FRUSTRATION

GOD = SECURITY

(*Review verse individually for a few minutes. Ask someone to quote the verse, and explain what "all these things" means.)

Discussion Starter (Read or relate the following to your group:)

"In 1923 a very important meeting was held at the Edgewater Beach Hotel in Chicago. In attendance were nine of the world's most successful financiers . . . men who had found the secret of making money. Twenty-five years later let's see where these men were:

The president of the largest independent steel company, Charles Schwab, died bankrupt and lived on borrowed money for five years before his death. The president of the largest utility company, Samuel Insull, died a fugitive from justice and penniless in a foreign land. The president of the largest gas company, Howard Hopson, went insane. The greatest wheat speculator, Arthur Cotton, died abroad, insolvent. The president of the New York Stock Exchange, Richard Whitney, was released from Sing Sing Penitentiary. The member of the President's Cabinet, Albert Fall, was pardoned from prison so he could die at home. The greatest "bear" on Wall Street, Jesse Livermore, died a suicide. The head of the greatest monopoly, Ivan Krueger, died a suicide. The president of the Bank of International Settlements, Leon Fraser, died a suicide. All of these men learned well the art of making a living, but not one learned how to live." (From Billy Rose, *Pitching Horse Shoes*, 1948. The meeting at the Edgewater Beach Hotel was a youth congress.) What do you think this tells us?

Lesson Development

(Have the class share this material in any of the ways suggested in the Instructions for Teaching on page 21.)

> Many people search for security and the abundant life through acquiring money and possessions, or through marriage or a career. However, security is found only in a right relationship with almighty God. Why set affections on the gift rather than on the giver? He alone owns the world. The cattle on a thousand hills are His (Psalm 50:10). He alone can supply our every need (Philippians 4:19). There is no security in the plan which denies God as Lord of our lives and of all that we possess.

Books often are written by well-meaning Christians which almost give the impression that if we come to Christ we are guaranteed an improvement in our

> **Bible Study**
>
> A. *The rich fool*
>
> Read Luke 12:13-34.
>
> 1. How did the man in verse 13 feel about spiritual areas of his life? _Was not interested--ignored them._
>
> 2. Why did Jesus deny his request? _Jesus did not come to provide material blessings._
>
> In light of this, why do you think He denies some of our requests? _____

material condition. A recent advertisement told of a book which had discovered the secret of making money and guaranteed this to its readers. The secret, it said, was taken from the teaching of Jesus.

But the blessings of Christianity are not material, though these sometimes incidentally result. They are spiritual and eternal. Don't make Christ just a divine bill-payer!

3. Why was the man in the parable a fool? *He was con-*
   cerned about material problems when the real
   one was spiritual.
4. How do people today make the same mistake this man

This man probably
thought that *after* he had
extended his fortune he

made? _____

could straighten out his life with God. God says "this night" your soul shall be
required. All his efforts in the material direction were useless.

(Ask the class:) In what ways can we be overly concerned about material things,
to the neglect of the spiritual? (See 1 John 2:15-16.) What is the difference
between *using* the things of the world and *loving* them?

A man gave a woman an expensive ring. She came to love the ring more than
the one who gave it. When we love *things* more than God, we are guilty of one of
the worst kinds of sins.

What kind of security can be found in money? in family relationships? in
possession of clothing and goods? in God?

5. Name some illustrations Jesus used in verses 24 - 28 to
   show the uselessness of worrying about material things.
   God feeds ravens; we can't add to our height;
   God arrays lilies and grass and will clothe
   us.

B. A follower of Christ

1. Read Philippians 4:11-19.

   How did Paul react to the lack of money? _____
   He had learned to be content either with
   money or without it.

   Where did Paul obtain the strength to face adverse
   circumstances? _____
   From Christ who strengthened him.

   Study verse 19. Why do you think God promises to
   supply our *needs*, but not necessarily our *desires*? _____

   _____

   _____

2. Read 1 Timothy 6:17-19.

   Against what things did Paul warn the rich? _____
   Being conceited or fixing their hopes
   on the uncertainty of riches.

   What did he exhort them to do? _____
   Fix their hope on God, be rich in good works,
   be generous and ready to share, store up
   treasure of good foundation for future.

   Why? *That they may be able to take hold of*
   that which is life indeed.

C. *Christ Himself*

1. In your own words, write what Jesus Christ did for us according to 2 Corinthians 8:9. *He was rich, but became poor for our sakes, so we through His poverty could become rich.*

The one who spoke of detachment from material things was Himself detached. Jesus, the ruler of the universe, owned no property and often had no place to sleep.

2. Read 2 Corinthians 9:7, 8.

Because of what Jesus Christ has done for us, we should be willing to invest part of our income in His work. When we give toward His work, what should be our attitude (2 Corinthians 9:7)? *It should come from our hearts willingly and cheerfully.*

Note the use of the words "all" and "every" in verse 8. Why can you be cheerful even though you may give sacrificially toward God's work? _____

_____

_____

Conclusion and Application

C. T. Studd was a wealthy young Cambridge student famous for his skill as a cricket player. He studied the Scripture, especially the story of the rich young man to whom Jesus said, "One thing you lack: go and sell all you possess, and give to the poor, and you shall have treasure in heaven; and come, follow me" (Mark 10:21).

C. T. Studd felt impressed to do exactly what the rich young man had failed to do. There was no question of feeling or emotion, nor was there any kind of special supernatural guidance. In simple obedience to the black and white statements of God's Word, he gave away a substantial inheritance. He proved what all prove who put God to the test, that He never fails those who trust Him — neither he nor his wife nor their children ever lacked the necessities of life. He was a great man of God and went as a missionary to China, India and Africa, and through his ministry thousands of people were won to Christ.

Here is what he said: "Seeing that some 40 years ago at God's command I left mother, brethren, friends, fortune and all that is usually thought to make life worth living, and have so continued ever since, I have been called fool and fanatic again and again, yet lived to prove that the worldly counselors were the fools. 'Cursed is he that trusteth in man' does not make a

Life Application

1. Think about the circumstances of your life. What part do they play in your search for security? _____

_____

2. List on this chart your most important possessions and whether or not you have yielded each one to God.

POSSESSION	MINE OR GOD'S

very good pillow for a dying man, but there is much comfort in the other one, 'Blessed is he that trusteth in the Lord.' "

The life of C. T. Studd was a testimony to the world that when a believer is obedient to the commands of Jesus Christ every NEED in life will be supplied.

Suggested Closing Prayer

Our Father, we thank you for what you have shown us today about putting our trust in You and having real security. Reveal to each of us now the areas of our lives in which we are not trusting You. (Teacher, pause a few seconds, then continue:) We commit those particular areas into Your hands right now, and we trust You to take care of us. Thank You for answered prayer.

ADDITIONAL BACKGROUND MATERIAL

For another example of a person who put his trust in material possessions, read Joshua 7.

1. Disobedience of Achan — took of the spoils of battle, verse 1.
2. Reason — coveted them for self, verse 21.
3. Result — Israelites killed in battle, verse 5; Achan and family stoned, verses 24,25.

LESSON FOUR
OBEDIENCE AND THE FEAR OF WHAT MEN WILL THINK

Teacher's Objective: To show the student how and to motivate him to overcome the fear of what men will think and thus be able to obey God more fully.

Teacher's Enrichment: (May be shared with class as time permits.)

We are to please God, not men — Galatians 1:10; Acts 5:29.

Biblical examples of the fear of man:

Abraham — Genesis 12:11-19. He said Sarah was his sister rather than his wife.

Aaron — Exodus 32:22-24. He yielded to the Israelites who were demanding an idol.

The Israelites — 1 Samuel 17:24. They were afraid of men when they faced the Philistines.

Pilate — John 19:12-16. He yielded to the demands of the people.

CLASS TIME

Suggested Opening Prayer

Lord, teach us to be more concerned about what You think of us rather than what others think of us. Help us never to be ashamed of You.

(Introduction: Be sure students understand
  objective
  memory work*
  reading assignment.)

> **Introduction**
>
> OBJECTIVE: To obey God regardless of popular opinion or peer pressure.
> TO MEMORIZE: Luke 9:26.
> TO READ: Romans 7 and 8.

(*Review individually for a few minutes. Ask someone to quote the verse and to tell what it means to be ashamed of Christ and His words — possibly give an example.)

293

Discussion Starter

Jerome Hines, Metropolitan Opera star, before singing at the Presidential Prayer Breakfast, which was attended by the President of the United States, the Cabinet, the House, the Senate, and the Supreme Court, stated clearly his faith in Jesus Christ. He minced no words. His stand was strong and dynamic.

Other Christians, when presented with golden opportunities, become afraid and never say a word for their Lord. What do you think is the reason for the difference?

Lesson Development

(Have the class share this material in any of the ways suggested in the Instructions for Teaching on page 21.)

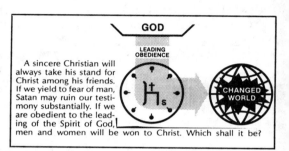

A sincere Christian will always take his stand for Christ among his friends. If we yield to fear of man, Satan may ruin our testimony substantially. If we are obedient to the leading of the Spirit of God, men and women will be won to Christ. Which shall it be?

Bible Study

A. *Peter's renunciation*

Read Matthew 26:57-75 carefully.

1. Peter knew and loved Christ in his heart, but when it came time to openly identify himself as a follower of Christ, what did he do (verse 58)? *He followed Jesus at a distance.*

2. Note the contrasts between Christ and Peter:

Who accused Christ (verse 59)? *The chief priests and the Council.*

Who accused Peter (verses 69, 71)? *Two different servant girls.*

How did Christ answer His accusers (verse 64)? *He told them who He was.*

How did Peter answer his accusers (verses 71-74)? *He said he didn't know Jesus.*

What happened to Christ because He told the truth (verses 67, 68)? *He was spit upon, beaten with fists, and slapped.*

What was the result when Peter told those lies (verse 75)? *He remembered what Jesus had said and wept bitterly.*

3. Some have said Christ's teachings are only for weaklings, cowards, neurotics and those who demand some kind of crutch. As you look at the examples here, of Christ and Peter, how would you evaluate such a statement? _____

_____

_____

_____

Peter's restoration

1. After Christ's resurrection, what did the angel announce to the women in Mark 16:7? *They were to go tell the disciples and Peter that Jesus would meet them.*
Why did the angel single out Peter's name from the rest?

Because of the resurrection he understood the Messiahship of Jesus Christ. Previous to the resurrection he had too much of a human concept of Jesus. After the resurrection he

2. Upon what basis can Christ restore you even though you have sinned against Him and denied Him? _____

_____

understood that Christ is the Messiah who must suffer for our sins and be raised again for our justification, and that was the message he preached!

C. *Peter's transformation*

1. Less than two months later at Pentecost, Peter stood up from among the disciples to give a bold defense of the Christian faith to a ridiculing crowd (Acts 2:14). What do you think made the difference? _____

_____

_____

Because of Pentecost he had living within him the power to tell others the good news of the Gospel. It was a power which rested not in self, but in the Holy Spirit who dwelt within him.

THE EXAMPLE OF PETER

His strong faith (Matthew 16:13-16): He promised Christ that he would never be ashamed of Him (Matthew 26:33).

2. What shocking thing did Peter fearlessly tell the crowd (Acts 2:36)? *That they had crucified Jesus who was both Lord and Christ.*

3. And what resulted (Acts 2:37-42)? *The people were convicted and converted.*

His denial (Matthew 26:69-75): In front of a young girl.

His transformation: He boldly preached Christ before thousands of people (Acts 2:14-44).

Again he preached Christ, before all the leaders in Jerusalem who had been responsible for the death of Christ (Acts 4:8-20). Everyone marveled at his boldness.

Again he prached Christ before the religious leaders, claiming that he must obey God rather than men (Acts 5:29-42).

Christ had predicted
these things:

> 4. What do Acts 1:8 and 4:8 tell us made this dramatic difference in Peter's life? _The power and the filling of the Holy Spirit._

Resurrection — Matthew 16:21; Matthew 26:31-32.
Pentecost — John 14:16-17; John 16:13-14.

Conclusion and Application

This might be the answer to the problem of many professing Christians, who have no power or authority in their lives. They want to be men of God, but they are defeated by the overwhelming sense of the fear of man. The only way to overcome that fear is to yield to God, become obedient to Him and be faithful to the command, "Be filled with the Spirit" (Ephesians 5:18). If you want power and authority and if you want to be a man or woman of God, you must let the Holy Spirit have full and complete control of your life.

Life Application

1. How do you think having natural courage and boldness compares to being filled with the Holy Spirit? _____

2. Write out Proverbs 29:25 in your own words. _____

3. If we know and love Christ in our hearts, why must we also take a bold and open stand for Him? _____

4. How does Matthew 10:32 relate to your present attitudes? _____

5. To whom do you particularly need to confess Christ and take a bold stand for Him? _____

Suggested Closing Prayer

We thank You, Father, for the examples given in Your Word of those who were able to overcome the fear of man. We also thank you for showing us how to overcome that fear in our own lives and we ask that You will enable us to obey You more fully.

ADDITIONAL BACKGROUND MATERIAL

The Example of Esther's Courage:

A. Situation: King Ahasuerus had ordered queen Vashti to appear before a great feast. When she refused his command, he dissolved her queenship and sought a fair young virgin to take her place (Esther 1).

B. Choice of Esther.
1. Preparation:
   a. groomed by God — Esther 2:7.
   b. costly planning — Esther 2:12.
   c. favor gained — Esther 2:15.
   d. loved and crowned — Esther 2:17.
2. Principle: first chosen by God, then the king (Psalm 75:6-7).

C. Esther's great trial — Esther 4:8.
1. Haman, the head of the king's princes, conspired to destroy all Jews (Esther 3:6).
2. Mordecai, who reared Esther, urged her to go to the king in behalf of her people, the Jews. Under the law of the land, however, to go in to the king without his request meant certain death unless the king held out his golden sceptre to indicate his approval of the visitor (Esther 4:8-11).

D. Esther's attitude of ultimate trust — "thus I will go in to the king, which is not according to the law, and if I perish, I perish" (Esther 4:16).
1. We have little conception of what Esther's faithfulness meant in the face of death. With the fate of the whole Jewish race at stake, she fulfilled her duty as Christ commanded in Mark 8:35, ". . . whoever loses his life for My sake and the gospel's, shall save it."
2. God does not require from His children perfect understanding of the circumstances, but perfect obedience. He assumes personal responsibility for the result when we carry out His commandments. Esther feared God more than she feared people and because of this attitude God showed Himself strong in her behalf (2 Chronicles 16:9).

E. Conclusion — a faithful stand and a faithful God — Esther 5:12.
1. Esther approached the king in her royal apparel. Principle of our life — we approach the Father in the perfect imputed righteousness of the Son.
2. The king held out the sceptre to her. Results:
   a. her life was spared.
   b. her people were delivered.
   c. her Lord was glorified.

LESSON FIVE

OBEDIENCE AND THE TONGUE

Teacher's Objective: To lead the students to a realization of the importance of the tongue and how it is used to reflect what is in our hearts and of how it must be controlled if we are to be obedient to God.

CLASS TIME

Suggested Opening Prayer

Our Lord, we pray that You will teach us about the importance of the tongue in relationship to our complete obedience to You. Help us understand the power of such a small thing for great good or for great evil.

(Introduction: Be sure students understand
    objective
    memory work
    reading assignment.)

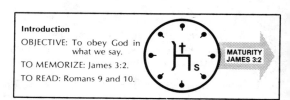

Introduction

OBJECTIVE: To obey God in what we say.
TO MEMORIZE: James 3:2.
TO READ: Romans 9 and 10.

MATURITY
JAMES 3:2

Discussion Starter

Why should we control the tongue? Why do you think the Scriptures devote most of a chapter here, plus numerous passages in other books, and why does Christ Himself have so much to say about the tongue? Why is this so important?

Lesson Development

Bible Study

A. *Effects of the tongue*
  1. Read James 3:1-13.

    Though we may study our Bibles faithfully, attend Christian meetings regularly and even talk to our friends about Christ, one thing marks us as a really perfect (i.e., mature) Christian.

    What is it? _When we do not stumble in what we_ _say._

    What does control of the tongue here indicate? _That_ _we are able to bridle the whole body as well._

An unruly tongue can wreck one's whole Christian life. What is the origin of evil speech? Jesus said, "His mouth speaks from that which fills his heart" (Luke 6:45). The tongue is not something independent; it merely reflects the condition of the heart. Therefore, if we can control it, it indicates a heart which is totally submitted to Christ!

Controlling the tongue keeps us from inconsistency and hypocrisy. Verses 9-12 point out how a person's

> What does the comparison of a wicked tongue to an incorrectly handled steering mechanism on a ship imply to you? _____
>
> What does it take to start a forest fire? *A small fire.*
> _____

tongue may reveal his inconsistent life. Many Christians know all the "language," can pray eloquently, and speak as if they were very holy. But in almost the same breath their gossiping tongues betray their hypocrisy. Remember, your speech is just like a large neon sign telling everyone what you *really* are. (Summarize with James 1:26:) "If anyone thinks himself to be religious, and yet does not bridle his tongue, but deceives his own heart, this man's religion is worthless."

The tongue can do so much damage with so little

> What damage can be caused by just a few words of gossip you pass on? _____
>
> _____

effort. All sin is sin. But some sins do more damage than others. Many times we have sins in our lives for which God will still hold us accountable, but which are not so public. Note the difference between harboring a secret grudge and spreading lies openly.

> B. *Sins of the tongue*
>
> 1. Name the sins of the tongue which are condemned in the following references in Proverbs:
>
>   6:16-19 *A lying tongue, a false witness who utters lies and one who spreads strife.*
>
>   11:13 *A talebearer revealing secrets.*
>
>   15:1 *Harsh words that stir up anger.*
>
>   17:9 *Repeating someone's transgression.)*
>   27:2 *Self-praise.*
>
> 2. Read Ephesians 4:29. How does this apply to profanity, obscene language, off-color jokes, etc.? *They should not proceed from our mouths.*

What other things can you name that could be included here? _____

_____

C. Significance of the tongue

   1. Read Matthew 12:33-37.

     For what shall men give account? _Every careless_ _word that they shall speak._

     What illustration does Christ use? _A good tree and good fruit._

     How does he apply it? _____

_____

     What, then, is the real source of an evil tongue? ____ _An evil heart._

   2. What is the only solution for a believer (Galatians 5:16)? _Walk by the Spirit._

Conclusion and Application

The tongue does not function by itself as an independent member of your body, but is completely controlled by the mind. It responds to thought impulses. "For the mouth speaks out of that which fills the heart" (Matthew 12:34). Since a person's tongue is controlled by his mind, the mind must be renewed (Romans 12:2). Renewal is conformity, not to the world, but to Christ by the Holy Spirit working on the inside.

Life Application

1. How would you obey the instructions indicated in James 1:19 and 26 in your own life? _____

_____

2. Think through the attitudes expressed through your words, and ask yourself,

   Is there an attitude I need to confess and make right with God? _____

_____

   What is it? _____

_____

   Who has been affected by my words to whom I need to go and ask forgiveness? _____

_____

_____

Suggested Closing Prayer

Dear Father, we thank You for what You have taught us today and we pray that You will fill us continually with Your Holy Spirit and that we will appropriate the power You have for us to control our tongues and to be obedient to You in all things. We pray our tongues will be used only to bring glory to You.

ADDITIONAL BACKGROUND MATERIAL

Additional scriptural teachings on the tongue:

Warnings concerning the use of the tongue for evil.
   Psalm 12:3 — against mischief, deceit and lying.
   Psalm 52:2-4 — against flattery and pride.
   Matthew 15:8 — against lip service without life testimony.

The use of the tongue for the glory of God.
   Proverbs 14:25 — soul-winning.
   Proverbs 15:4 — a tree of life.
   Colossians 3:16 — praise.
   Romans 10:9 — confessing Christ.

The tongue and the heart in obedience.
   Luke 6:45 — "His mouth speaks from that which fills his heart."
   Proverbs 23:7 — "For as he thinks within himself, so he is."
   Ephesians 6:5,6 — True servants obey from the heart.

LESSON SIX

INSINCERE OBEDIENCE

Teacher's Objective: To show students that true obedience affects the inward attitude as well as the outward act.

CLASS TIME

Suggested Opening Prayer

(Have two or three students open with short prayers.)

(Introduction: Be sure
students understand
   objective
   memory work*
   reading assignment.)

(*Ask the group to discuss
the relationship between the
memory verse for this
lesson, and the one for the last lesson, James 3:2.)

Introduction

OBJECTIVE: To recognize
   obedience that is
   external only, and
   become obedient
   from the heart.

TO MEMORIZE: Colossians 3:23.
TO READ: Romans 11-13.

GOD
ATTITUDE 2
PLEASING GOD
PLEASING MAN
ATTITUDE 1
MAN

Discussion Starter

Let's think about an apple tree. We do not produce an apple tree by taking a bushel of apples and pinning them on an oak tree. So, mere exhortations to outward obedience neglect the heart of the problem.

On the other hand, if an apple tree is planted and grows properly, the natural result is large red apples. For one to claim he has the right attitude and true faith in God and have nothing to show for it is senseless. "But are you willing to recognize, you foolish fellow, that faith without works is useless?" (James 2:20).

> The epitaph of Amaziah reads, "And he did that which was right in the sight of the Lord, but not with a perfect heart" (2 Chronicles 25:2). Obedience involves attitude, not merely outward actions.

Lesson Development

Bible Study

A. *An example of insincere obedience*

Read Acts 4:32 - 5:11.

1. For a short time Jerusalem Christians held goods as common property. Each Christian put his funds into a common treasury, which then supplied the needs of the Christian community. What made them willing to give up personal possessions as they did (verse 32)? _____

   They were of one heart and soul.

2. One writer has said that many today view the local church as if it were a restaurant where all kinds of people meet for a short time, sit down together in the same room, then part, not knowing or caring anything about each other. Would you say this is true? What is your estimation of the fellowship in our churches today compared with the fellowship of these Jerusalem Christians?

3. When Barnabas sold his land, which was probably valuable, and gave the money to the church, no doubt other Christians praised his devotion. How do you think Barnabas' action influenced Ananias and Sapphira?

4. What do you suppose motivated Ananias and Sapphira to sell their possessions and give the money to the church?

5. How did their motive differ from Barnabas' motive?

Because of insincere hearts, Ananias and Sapphira gave money to God, not to please Him but only to please men. An obedience not backed by the right heart attitude is unacceptable, and will sooner or later reveal itself in sin. Suppose these two had been given the job of handling the funds of the church. No doubt they would have been dishonest in this area also. Note also these things about the sin of Ananias and Sapphira:

This sin of Ananias and Sapphira was within the fellowship of the church. The church is rarely harmed or hindered by opposition from without; it is perpetually harmed or hindered by perils from within. Contrast with the damage wrought by Judas and Saul. Hypocrisy is a sin which can cause irreparable harm.

The sin of Ananias and Sapphira was not in refusing to contribute to the church, nor was it in the amount they gave and the fact they held back part of the price. There was no rule that they should give, or not give, a certain amount. Their sin was that of pretending they had done more than they had — in other words, hypocrisy.

B. *Importance of our Christian testimony*

1. How can it be possible to study the Bible, share Christ with others, attend Christian meetings, etc., for the wrong motives, and thus be committing sin when you think you are pleasing God? _____

2. What did Christ say was the matter with the people of His day (Mark 7:6)? *They honored Him with their lips but their hearts were far away from Him.*

The one thing that made Christ angry, the one thing against which He uttered His severest words, was the sin of hypocrisy. What severe things He said to the men who pretended to be religious; what scorching, blasting words fell from His lips against such! He had no attitude toward the hypocrite but that of denunciation.

3. Why is your heart attitude just as important to God as your outward action? _____

Conclusion and Application

(Have the class give some present-day examples of types of hypocrisy; then add:)

A. **Hypocrisy toward God.** We tell God we are surrendered to Him when we are not, instead of honestly expressing our feelings — no matter how sinful they may be — and obtaining His forgiveness.

We claim to love Him and His will. He who said "I am the truth" never made any peace with a lie! Be *honest* in prayer. If you do not want to do God's will on any issue, it is far better to tell Him so and ask for His help, rather than hide it because we think dedicated Christians are not supposed to have such feelings.

B. **Hypocrisy toward others believers.** We try to put on a show of being dedicated, sincere Christians, experiencing victory in most of our life when in reality we are defeated and in desperate trouble. Do not broadcast your defeats before others, nor wallow in self-pity, but don't be afraid to seek help from mature Christians when help is needed.

C. **Hypocrisy toward non-Christians.** We profess to them that we are Christians; we read our Bibles; we attend church. But we become just as frustrated, worried or exasperated as they are when the pressure comes. Or, even worse, our lives show drastic moral inconsistencies — we sin in the areas of sex or drunkenness, etc. Our lives will never be perfect. But we

Life Application

1. Read 1 Corinthians 13:1-3. The word "charity" in the King James Version means "love." In terms meaningful to you, paraphrase these three verses:

_____
_____
_____
_____

must ask Christ to enable us to live godly lives if we are to impress the non-Christian world for Christ.

2. On the basis of this passage, what would you say is the relationship between love and sincere obedience? _____

_____

_____

_____

3. What action or activity in your life do you see as needing a change in motivation? _____

_____

4. How do you expect that change to affect other people you come in contact with? _____

_____

_____

_____

Suggested Closing Prayer

Thank You, Lord, for opening our hearts and minds to the truth of the importance of the inward attitude regarding obedience to You. We pray that our outward obedience will indicate a heart that is right with You.

LESSON SEVEN

RECAP

Teacher's Objective: To help students better understand the difference between what is true obedience and what is not, and to help each of them make whatever commitment necessary to grow toward a life of obedience from the heart.

CLASS TIME

Suggested Opening Prayer

As we review these lessons on obedience, Father, we ask that You will impress more deeply upon our hearts and minds the importance of a life of true obedience — obedience from the heart rather than for an outward show. Teach us today, dear Father.

(Introduction: The student's objective is to review what has been learned from the preceding seven lessons, especially any particular section that was not clearly understood or well remembered. Memory work from previous lessons should be reviewed, especially John 14:21 and Colossians 3:23. The reading assignment includes a continuation of the book of Romans.)

> Review all memorized verses in this step.
> Read Romans 14-16.
> Reread 1 Samuel 15 and Acts 4:32 - 5:11.

Discussion Starter

(Have students complete these first two statements of the Recap lesson, then ask:) Why do you think God requires inward obedience from the heart rather than outward conformance to rules and regulations? What difference does it make?

> Complete the following statements:
>
> True obedience to God is not _sacrifice or outward conformity to rules and requirements._
>
> True obedience really is _an attitude of the heart which willingly conforms to God's will._

Lesson Development

(Any Teacher's Enrichment or Additional Background Material that you were not able to use in the previous lessons could be utilized at this time and any point which you might feel was not sufficiently covered before, or which the students do not understand as well as they could, can be dealt with now too.

Then go over the remaining Recap questions and answers. This material will benefit both the students and you by giving you a deeper appreciation of God's Word.)

How is your obedience expressed:

In your attitude toward God's will? _____

_____

In the sexual purity of your life? _____

_____

In the degree of satisfaction you find in your possessions?

_____

In your courage in witnessing for Christ? _____

_____

In your speech? _____

_____

In the true motivation for your action? _____

_____

Conclusion and Application

(Give students a few minutes to think about what commitments they need to make, and discuss as appropriate. Then lead in the closing prayer.)

Suggested Closing Prayer

Thank You, Father, for what You have taught us today — for what You have shown us about obedience. There are certain areas in each of our lives which we need to commit to You in order to have that inward attitude of surrender to Your will no matter what the consequences are or what other people think. In this moment of quietness now, Father, we make those commitments. (Pause for a few moments of silent commitment for yourself and for the students. Then proceed:) We ask Your blessings on these commitments and for Your help. We thank You for Your promise of answered prayer.

SUMMARY LESSON PLAN
THE CHRISTIAN AND OBEDIENCE

Teacher's Objective: To help students discover the secret of a fruitful life in Christ: obedience to the Word and being led by the Holy Spirit.

Teacher's Enrichment: (See Teacher's Enrichment sections in each of the preceding lessons of this Step, and share with the class as time permits.)

CLASS TIME

Suggested Opening Prayer

Our Father, we ask that You will show us the importance of obedience in an effective Christian's life. Help us to understand how our trust in You must be balanced by our obedience to Your commands, and make us willing to discover and do Your will regardless of what the circumstances may seem to be.

(Introduction:

STUDENT'S OBJECTIVE: To discover the secret of a fruitful life in Christ, and how to live it.

TO MEMORIZE: John 14:21; Colossians 3:23.

READING ASSIGNMENT: John 15.)

Discussion Starter

(Write the following four key words on a large sheet of paper or blackboard: TRUST, OBEDIENCE, FELLOWSHIP, UNION. Then ask students:) How would you relate the other three words to the word "obedience"? How would you connect them?

(Summarize the students' comments with the following example of our relationship to Christ:)

TRUST: We walk *before* the Lord as children.

OBEDIENCE: We walk *after* the Lord as servants.

FELLOWSHIP: We walk *with* the Lord as friends.

UNION: We walk *in* the Lord as members of the body.

Lesson Development

Since obedience is the supreme test of our love for Christ, we should know what obedience means. First of all, what it is *not:*

Obedience is not telling God what we can or will do for Him. Example: Many Christians spend a lifetime refusing to surrender to the will of God out of fear.

Obedience is not asceticism, or the giving up of all fun and personal possessions in order to *appear* humble and simple.

Obedience is not outward conformity to a list of external rules of do's and don'ts.

What it is:

Obedience is, rather, that attitude of heart which willingly conforms to the instruction of the Spirit of God as set forth in the Word of God. Obedience involves not mere knowledge but the practical application to one's everyday Christian experience of what is learned. True obedience is only initiated and continued by the fullness of the Holy Spirit who alone can live a Christ-honoring life through the believer.

A. Obedience and the result of doing God's will *(from Lesson 1).*

    1. Disobedience of King Saul (1 Samuel 15)

       a. Saul, sent to destroy Amalek and all that they had, spared the king and best of the cattle for sacrifice.

       b. Result: God was displeased and dissolved Saul's kingship.

       c. Principle: To obey is better than sacrifice (verse 22).

    2. Obedience of Paul and Ananias (Acts 9:1-22)

       a. What was God's command to Paul and how did he comply? (To rise and enter the city where he would be told what to do next, and he did exactly as God told him to.)

       b. What was God's command to Ananias; how did he react, and how did he finally respond? (To find Paul and lay his hand on him that he might receive his sight; he reacted in fear, but obeyed completely.)

       c. What resulted from these two men's complete obedience? (God used Paul to reveal the most abundant life ever possible to mankind.)

B. Obedience and personal purity *(from Lesson 2).*

    1. What does Christ say of impure thought (Matthew 5:27,28)? (Shows a wicked heart, which condemns us as quickly as outward sinful actions.)

    2. What does the Bible say about the sexual relationship in its proper place (Hebrews 13:4): (Within marriage, it is honorable and undefiled.)

    3. How are we instructed to deal with impure thoughts? (See 1 Corinthians 6:18, 2 Corinthians 10:5 and Philippians 4:8.) Why is it important? (See 1 Corinthians 6:18-20.)

C. Obedience and the privilege of security *(from Lesson 3).*

    1. Many people search for security and the abundant life through acquiring money and possessions, or through marriage or a career. How do you feel about that?

2. What does Jesus say about security? (Have students give answers based on Luke 12:22-31.)

3. Look at Philippians 4:19. Why do you think God promises to supply our *needs*, but not necessarily our *desires*?

D. Obedience and the fear of what men will think *(from Lesson 4)*.

1. What does Luke 9:26 mean to you?

2. According to Matthew 26:57-75, what was Peter's failing? (He was afraid of people and denied knowing Christ.) What were his feelings afterward? (Remorse — he wept bitterly.) What was the ultimate result? (Peter was restored to fellowship with Christ.)

Because of the resurrection Peter understood the Messiahship of Jesus Christ. Previous to the resurrection he had too much of a human concept of Jesus. After the resurrection he understood that Christ is the Messiah who must suffer for our sins and be raised again for our justification, and that was the message he boldly preached. Upon hearing his first message, thousands of people accepted Christ! (See Acts 2:14-44.)

E. Obedience and the tongue *(from Lesson 5)*.

1. What does the tongue tell us according to Matthew 12:37 and Luke 6:45?

2. How significant is the tongue (James 3:1-12)?

Controlling the tongue keeps us from inconsistency and hypocrisy. Verses 9-12 point out how a person's tongue may reveal his inconsistent life. Many Christians know all the "language," can pray eloquently, and speak as if they were very holy. But in almost the same breath their gossiping tongues betray their hypocrisy. — Remember, your speech is just like a large neon sign telling everyone what you *really* are. (Summarize with James 1:26:) "If anyone thinks himself to be religious, and yet does not bridle his tongue, but deceives his own heart, this man's religion is worthless."

F. Insincere obedience *(from Lesson 6)*.

1. What did Christ say was the matter with the people of His day (Mark 7:6)? (They honored Him with their lips but their hearts were far away from Him.)

The one thing that made Christ angry, the one thing against which He uttered His severest words, was the sin of hypocrisy. What severe things He said to the men who pretended to be religious; what scorching, blasting words fell from His lips against such! He had no attitude toward the hypocrite but that of denunciation.

2. In several places Christ spoke of two things, an *outward requirement* and an *inward reality*. How do Ananias and Sapphira (in Acts 4:32-5:11) illustrate this? (Discuss students' ideas.)

3. How can we apply Colossians 3:23 to our lives in regard to obedience?

Conclusion and Application

There is no substitute for obedience. God calls us individually. He does not call me and expect me to send someone else to take my place. There are no substitutions in the will of God. We are to respond to the highest privilege ever offered to man — to represent the King of Kings and Lord of Lords until He comes again — and in His own Word He has said, "Yes, I am coming quickly!"

Suggested Closing Prayer

We thank You, God, for what You have shown us about the far-reaching results of our obedience or disobedience to Your commands. We pray that You will search us and know our hearts; try us and know our thoughts and lead us into a practical understanding of how to obey You every day. Help us to remember that You know us and You know what is best for us, and Your commands are all made in love, so we can have confidence in You and in what You ask us to do.

STEP SEVEN
The Christian and Witnessing

LESSON ONE

WHY WITNESS?

Teacher's Objective: To demonstrate the reason for a verbal witness and to show students how to remove the barriers which prevent it.

Teacher's Enrichment: (This material may be shared with students as time permits.)

A young man rushed back from a Billy Graham meeting to the apartment he shared with a friend. They had roomed together for several years since they both worked for the same company. "I must tell you something," he said to his friend. "Tonight I invited Christ to be my Savior, and He has changed my life."

His friend smiled and said, "Wonderful, I have been hoping you would do that. I have been living the Christian life before you all these years hoping that you would trust Christ as your Savior."

Much surprised, the new Christian said, "You lived such a perfect life that I kept trying to do it without Christ, the same as you seemed to be doing. Tonight I invited Him to become my Lord and Savior because I failed to live up to your standard. You should have told me why you live the way you do. Why didn't you tell me how I could know Christ too?"

This is a good illustration of the fact that we need to witness with our lips or our life can be misinterpreted, doing harm to the gospel, and perhaps even keeping people from receiving Christ.

Paul preached this message, defining the gospel: "Now I make known to you, brethren, the gospel which I preached to you, which also you received, in which also you stand, by which also you are saved, if you hold fast the word which I preached to you, unless you believed in vain. For I delivered to you as of first importance what I also received, that Christ died for our sins according to the Scriptures, and that He was buried, and that He was raised on the third day according to the Scriptures" (1 Corinthians 15:1-4).

Some people want a god, but they must know the true gospel about the real God if their lives are to be transformed. Paul expressed the exact responsibility of believers in Romans 10:14-15: "How then shall they call upon Him in whom they have not believed? And how shall they believe in Him whom they have not heard?"

CLASS TIME

Suggested Opening Prayer

Lord, remove any false barriers to our verbal witness that Christ may be glorified in us.

(Introduction: Be sure students understand
    objective
    memory work
    reading assignment.)

Introduction

OBJECTIVE: To understand the reasons to witness for Christ.

TO MEMORIZE: 2 Corinthians 5:14, 15.

TO READ: Galatians 1 and 2.

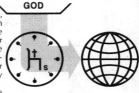

One friend may say to you, "I think a man's religion is such a personal matter that we should not discuss it." Another may say, "I don't like people who are dogmatic and fanatical, who try to force their views of religion on everybody they meet."

Yet, Christ considered the human soul to be of such transcendent value that He gladly exchanged the shining courts of glory for a life of poverty, suffering, shame and death as an expression of His desire to "seek and save the lost." He was "not willing that any should perish, but that all should come to repentance" (2 Peter 3:9).

Christ has a concern for the individual and for the multitude. His concern was so deep that at times the flood of manly tears could no longer be restrained, and rolled down His compassionate face. Jesus, the manliest of men, wept. Paul, the brave, besought men night and day with tears to be reconciled to God. When a young missionary who had been sent home by illness was asked why he was so eager to get back to his people, he said, "Because I cannot sleep for thinking about them."

The aim of this lesson is to discuss why it is important that we share Christ with others.

Discussion Starter

(Ask the group:) What is a witness? (Have students suggest answers and then give this definition:)

A witness is any Christian who bears testimony to the death, burial and resurrection of Jesus Christ by life and by lips.

Lesson Development

Bible Study

A. *What a witness is*

    1. What is the greatest thing that has ever happened to you?

    _____

    _____

2. What is the greatest kindness that you can show to
   another? _____

A witness is one who
first receives the gospel

3. What are you admonished to do in Psalm 107:2? _Let_
   the redeemed of the Lord say so. _____

himself, then proclaims that
truth to others. One can never teach or testify to a truth which he does not first
personally believe and practice.

B. _The motivation for witnessing_

1. What did Jesus command you to do (Mark 16:15;
   Matthew 28:19, 20)? _Go into all the world and_
   preach/make disciples of all nations, teach
                                            them.

The Biblical position
on witnessing:
People are lost and hungry for God — Matthew 9:37-38; John 4:28-39.
Jesus Christ is the Savior people need — John 14:6; Acts 4:12; 1 Timothy 2:5.
Commission and responsibility: "You shall receive power . . . you shall be My
witnesses" — Acts 1:8.
Go with the message and you will bear fruit — Psalm 126:6.
The early church was active in witnessing — Acts 5:42; 8:4; 15:35.
The Lord added the harvest — Acts 2:41, 47; 4:4; 11:18.

2. Read Acts 20:24-27, 31, 32.
   How important would you say Paul's ministry of witnessing was to him? _More than life itself._

3. In 2 Corinthians 5:14, 15:
   What caused Paul to witness? _The love of Christ/_
   His death for all.

   What effect should Christ have on people? _They_
   should no longer live for themselves, but
   for Him.
4. What does Jesus Christ say about the one who is
   ashamed of Him (Luke 9:26)? _Son of Man will be_
   ashamed of that one.
5. If you are faithful to follow Jesus, what does He promise
   to do (Matthew 4:19)? _Make you fishers of men._

C. _The message_

1. What are we called, according to 2 Corinthians 5:20?*
   Ambassadors for Christ. _____

   *An ambassador is one who is appointed to interpret the
   mind of his ruler to those in a foreign land.

As our example, Christ:
   dealt with individuals —
Nicodemus, John 3; the
Samaritan woman, John 4;
   dealt with groups —
5,000, John 6; taught in the
temple, John 8; spoke to
Pharisees, John 8:13 ff.;

2. As a representative of Christ, what would be your
   message to those who do not know Him personally
   (2 Corinthians 5:18-20)? _That of reconciliation_
   to God through Christ.

3. Why did Jesus say He came into this world (Luke 19:10;
   Mark 10:45)? _To seek and save that which was_
   lost.

dealt with the disciples — John 13:1 ff.; John 9:2 ff.

Our responsibility is the same: talk with individuals, talk with groups and talk with family and close friends.

> 4. How does Paul express the message in 1 Corinthians 15:3, 4? *Christ died for our sins, was buried, and raised again according to the Scriptures.*

Conclusion and Application

The desire to witness is not natural to us. Satan uses our old nature, which is still within us, to keep our hearts cold to the spiritual needs of our friends. But if we remember what Christ has done for us and what it would mean to us if those friends came to know Him too, our desire to witness can be awakened. And then when we rely upon the Holy Spirit to do His work in and through us we often see great victories.

> **Life Application**
>
> 1. How would you define the word "witness" as it relates to Christ? _____
> _____
> _____
>
> 2. State one reason you feel it is important that *you*, personally, be a witness for Christ. _____
> _____
> _____

Suggested Closing Prayer

Our Father, we thank You for the desire for witnessing that You give us and for the understanding we have gained today of the reasons for speaking to others about You. We are humbled when we realize the importance of the message we bear, and we are thankful that Your Spirit is the one who does the work through us and is responsible for the results.

ADDITIONAL BACKGROUND MATERIAL

Other reasons for witnessing:
1. Our responsibility — Ezekiel 3:18.
2. To glorify God — John 15:8.
3. That our prayers may be answered — John 15:16.

Acts 20:17-38 is an example of how Paul felt about those to whom he witnessed. Compare Acts 20:20-21 and Ezekiel 33:9.

LESSON TWO

JESUS DEMONSTRATES HOW TO WITNESS

Teacher's Objective: To show the students new approaches and techniques of witnessing as illustrated in Christ's example.

CLASS TIME

Suggested Opening Prayer

(Have one or two students open.)

(Introduction: Be sure students understand
    objective
    memory work
    reading assignment.)

Introduction

OBJECTIVE: To follow Christ's example in witnessing.
TO MEMORIZE: John 4:35.
TO READ: Galatians 3 and 4.

Discussion Starter

(Ask the group:) Suppose you want to share your Christian faith with some person you know. How would you begin? (After one student has answered, make helpful comments, and elicit further suggestions from the group.)

Lesson Development

In the Gospel of John, chapter four, Jesus demonstrated how to witness in the most effective manner as He talked to the woman of Samaria. Study this passage carefully to discover new approaches and techniques of witnessing.

In Lesson 1 we considered the question, "Why witness?" Many reasons were suggested. An additional reason is that we would never have received Christ if someone had not told us. It is because we are debtors to Christ and to the person who told us that we in turn must witness.

One reason that so few Christians never get off the ground, so to speak, in this important area is that they don't know how to go about it. We have not been left to shift for ourselves, but our Lord has given explicit instructions as to the why and how and has given us examples from His own personal life to follow. This methodology has been recorded in the account of His discourse with the Samaritan woman in John's gospel, the fourth chapter.

319

He began His conversation with her on a topic of natural and common interest to both of them. Jesus was

Bible Study

A. *Example of Jesus*

Read John 4:1-42.

1. What everyday experience did Jesus use as a situation for witnessing? _____

_____

sitting by the well at noontime when it was hot, and His being there would suggest to her that He, too, was thirsty. It was obvious she had come for water as she was carrying a water pot.

2. What, in your opinion, is the advantage of beginning a conversation on the level of a person's immediate interest? _____

_____

3. List some of your natural opportunities to witness for Christ: _____

_____

_____

4. Why do you suppose Jesus sent all 12 of His disciples to buy provisions when two of them could have done it?

   He wanted an opportunity to

   talk with the woman alone.

5. Who spoke first — Jesus or the woman of Samaria? _____
   Jesus

   Why is this significant when considering witnessing techniques? *He was willing to talk to anyone who had a need regardless of race, creed or social status.*

It was unheard of for a Jew to go to Samaria, let alone talk to a Samaritan woman.

6. What did Jesus do repeatedly when the woman tried to divert his attention from her sin and her need? *He had a set purpose and would not be sidetracked--He kept bringing the subject back to her need.*

Jesus brought this woman to grips with His own claims about Himself and

her need for what He could do for her. He was tactful, kind and considerate in His dealings with the woman and He answered her questions that were pertinent, but He always returned to her problem.

Jesus was a good listener and did not always try to get over His own points. What a necessary characteristic in witnessing! Often one must listen and hear the other person out before he can give the gospel message. The individual sometimes has misconceptions which he will talk himself out of if we will listen.

B. *Responses of the Samaritan woman*

1. How did the woman first respond to Jesus' approach?
   Surprise and disbelief. ,

   How does verse 15 indicate that her attitude changed?
   She asked for what He could give her.

   What do you think brought it about?   *His gracious-*
   ness had won her respect and admiration.

2. What did Jesus say that demonstrated His divine powers?
   He talked about her husbands.

3. How did Jesus describe God (verse 24)?   *As a Spirit.*

   What do you think is important about this statement?

4. For whom was the woman looking and why?   *For the*
   Messiah--He would tell them everything.

5. What did Jesus claim for Himself?   *"I who speak*
   to you am He."

C. *Effectiveness of Jesus' witness*

1. State briefly your analysis of the approach Jesus used in
   witnessing to this woman of Samaria.

2. What was the result of His witness?   *She believed,*
   and immediately went to tell others.

She knew very little, but she told the whole town what she had seen, heard and felt.

3. How did the people to whom she witnessed respond?
   The whole town came to hear Jesus.

The town turned out to hear Christ because of the woman's report and many believed when they heard Him. Our job is to bring men and women to a hearing of the word of Christ as found in the Scriptures. They will not believe because of what we say but rather what God the Spirit says to them through the written Word. It is as we become skillful in using the Word that we become effective in leading men and women to a saving knowledge of Christ.

There are three "sound barriers" to witnessing. These are much like the sound barrier through which an airplane passes. There is much stress and nervousness.

The first "sound barrier" is just starting to mention to a person the name of Jesus Christ and the value of knowing Him. Once we get the conversation around from girls, guys, the fraternity or sorority, politics, etc., to spiritual things, we have broken the first barrier. It is hard to do, and it never becomes easy. Never!

The second "sound barrier" is to ask the person if he would like to receive Christ. That nervous feeling returns once again. We must blast through this one also. Remember, many people, when they understand who Jesus Christ is and what He has done for them, *will* want Him in their lives.

The last barrier is the most difficult. It is to ask him to receive Christ *right now*. This is the most important step. Often this is the most important step. Often we tell the person how and then just leave him high and dry. We have not really witnessed until we ask the person to trust Christ.

Conclusion and Application

Christ demonstrated clearly that the reason for the woman's conversion was that he drew from her a faith in who He was and all that He said. Obedience to what Christ says is what brings us to fully understand and know Him.

> **Life Application**
>
> 1. State at least one thing you have learned from Christ's example that you can apply in your own witnessing. _____
>   _____
>   _____
>
> 2. What do you think most hinders your witnessing? _____
>   _____
>   _____

The only real way to learn to witness and become effective at it is to *do* it. It is only by trying that one ever succeeds. The Word of God says, "He who is wise wins souls" (Proverbs 11:30). You will be amazed at how many people will appreciate your concern for them and be genuinely pleased that you talked to them.

Suggested Closing Prayer

Father, use us to bring Christ into the lives of our friends that they might find the abundant life He offers.

ADDITIONAL BACKGROUND MATERIAL

Jesus' methods of witnessing to some other individuals as seen in John's gospel:
Nicodemus — John 3:1-15,
The man by the pool — John 5:1-4,
A woman taken in adultery — John 8:1-11,
The man born blind — John 9:1-41.

LESSON THREE

QUALIFICATIONS FOR WITNESSING

Teacher's Objective: To enable the students to take a personal inventory of their spiritual qualifications for witnessing.

CLASS TIME

Suggested Opening Prayer

Our Lord, we thank You for meeting with us today and for the truths which You have for us. As we look at the qualifications necessary for witnessing, we pray You will give us the right understanding of those qualifications and of Your place in our lives.

(Introduction: Be sure
students understand
    objective
    memory work
    reading assignment.)

> **Introduction**
>
> OBJECTIVE: To take "spiritual inventory" in preparation for witnessing.
>
> TO MEMORIZE: Matthew 4:19.
>
> TO READ: Galatians 5 and 6.

Discussion Starter

I am sure that each of you is a sincere Christian and that it is your desire to become an effective witness for Jesus Christ. What qualifications do you think would be necessary in the lives of those who desire to be effective in witnessing for Him?

> Every sincere Christian desires to be an effective witness for Christ. A careful study of the eighth chapter of Acts will call attention to certain qualifications for witnessing. Ask the Holy Spirit to make these qualities real in your own life.

Lesson Development

> **Bible Study**
>
> A. *Philip's opportunity*
>   Read Acts 8:25-40.
>   1. According to verses 25 and 26, why do you think God
>   called Philip for this particular assignment? *He took*
>   *God's message seriously and was actively*
>   *preaching*

You will notice that persecution did not stop Philip. It only opened the door for a vital witness in Samaria.

> 2. To whom did Philip witness (verse 27)? *An Ethiopian*
>   *eunuch, court official and treasurer for queen.*
> 3. Who told Philip to join the chariot (verse 29)? *Spirit*
>   Does the Holy Spirit lead us in this same way today?
>   _____
> 4. Describe Philip's response (verse 30): *He ran up to*
>   *the chariot.*
> 5. How would you describe Philip's approach in verse 30?
>   _____
>   _____
> 6. Was the man ready? *yes.* _____ Why? *He had*
>   *been reading God's Word.*
>   _____
>   What was his response? *He wanted someone to*
>   *help him understand what he was reading.*

The Word of God is the only effective means of opening up the minds and hearts of people to the Gospel. Philosophy, sociology, etc., though good studies in themselves, will not avail in meeting the needs of the heart of man. The reading of the Word had so prepared the Ethiopian for Philip that the man asked him about whom Isaiah was speaking.

> 7. What Old Testament reference was the Ethiopian reading
>   (verses 28, 32, 33)? *Isaiah 53.*
>   To whom did this reference refer? *Christ.*
> 8. What was Philip's message? *The gospel of Jesus.*
>   _____

The Ethiopian was ready because of the Holy Spirit's preparatory work. However, God used a man, a ready, willing man, to win him. Philip had earned the right to be used. God had sent an angel to command Philip to leave a revival and go to the desert and Philip was humble and obedient. Then, after Philip had baptized the eunuch, God's Spirit brought him to Azotus. Philip was God's key man and God depended on him because he was dependable.

B. *Philip's qualifications*

There are at least eight definite qualities stated or referred to in Philip's life that contributed to his effectiveness for Christ. Place appropriate reference verses after the following words:

Knowledge of Word of God	*35*
Boldness	*30*
Compassion	*30*
Humility	*27*
Obedience	*27, 30*
Receptivity, sensitivity to guidance	*26,27,29,30,35,38*
Tact	*30,37*
Enthusiasm	*25,27,30*

The miraculous way the Holy Spirit transported Philip from place to place was a supernatural thing that indicated God's delight in using Philip.

C. *Possible hindrances to our witnessing*

1. Lack of preparation. Personal dedication to Christ and understanding of how to witness and what to say are imperative.
2. Fear of man. We possibly will be persecuted by unbelievers, as well as believers, but "the fear of man bringeth a snare" (Proverbs 29:25). Christ said of those who feared to confess His name, "For they loved the praise of men more than the praise of God."
3. Fear of failure. "They won't believe; they won't accept such simple truth." Certainly some will reject or neglect the gospel, but you should never believe the lie of Satan that people aren't interested. Christ said, "Lift up your eyes, and look on the fields, for they are (present tense . . . 'now') white already to harvest." Matthew 9:37 says, "Then saith He unto His disciples, the harvest truly is plenteous, but the labourers are few; Pray . . . that He will send forth labourers into His harvest."
4. Fear that the new Christian will not go on and grow in the Lord. Review the parable of the sower (Matthew 13:1-23). Every seed of the Word of God will fall on one of these types of soil: wayside, thorny, rocky and good. Some will be disciples. Keep up the faithful search for these disciples!

Conclusion and Application

In the last analysis, it was Christ in Philip who did the work. The flesh is not prayerful, tactful, compassionate or humble. But it is not what you are or were, but what He is through you that wins men. Our responsibility is to deny self and daily take up the cross, an instrument of death, and let Him live through us. We must allow Him, His Spirit, and His Word to be central in our lives.

Life Application

1. What hindrance is the greatest problem to you? _____

_____

2. What steps will you take to overcome it? _____

_____

3. Look back through the list of qualities in Philip's life and list the ones you would like to have God develop in your life.

_____

_____

_____

_____

4. Spend some time in prayer, asking God for those characteristics to be shown through your life and witness. _____

_____

_____

Suggested Closing Prayer

We thank You, Father, that our feelings and attitudes can be under the control of the Holy Spirit, that You can give us the genuine love and compassion that we need for a lost person. To look to You is to possess the answer for that for which we have prayed.

ADDITIONAL BACKGROUND MATERIAL

The apostle Paul was another faithful witness for Christ. He spoke of himself as debtor to everyone because he had Christ (Romans 1:14). Paul's behavior would not usually bring offense. He treated all as creditors. The only offense was the offense of the cross. We see in 1 Corinthians 9:19-27 Paul's concept of himself and how his body should be considered.

Other Scriptures about keeping ourselves within God's will are found in 1 Thessalonians 4:3-5 and 5:18 and 1 Peter 2:15, 16.

LESSON FOUR

WITNESSING AND THE WORD OF GOD

Teacher's Objective: To demonstrate to the students the value of memorizing and using Bible verses when witnessing.

CLASS TIME

Suggested Opening Prayer

Dear God, we ask today that You will show us the value of the use of Your Word in witnessing and that You will help us understand its power.

(Introduction: Be sure students understand objective memory work reading assignment.)

> **Introduction**
> ˙ OBJECTIVE: To learn to appropriate and use the power of the Bible in witnessing.
> TO MEMORIZE: 1 Peter 3:15.
> TO READ: Ephesians 1 and 2.

Discussion Starter

(Ask the group:) What do you think is the most important area of our lives in regard to witnessing? (Then, after a few minutes of discussion, elaborate as appropriate:) One of the most important areas in which many Christians fail in living a life for Christ is the all-important area of memorizing and effectively using the Word of God. The Psalmist states clearly that it is the Word of God which keeps the Christian from sinning against God and it is the means by which the Christian purifies his or her life.

The Word of God is the most effectual weapon in dealing with people about their need of Christ. Their questions are only truly answered in the Word of God. There is convincing power *only* in a presentation of what the Word of God has to say. We are to set aside our hearts for the Lord God according to 1 Peter 3:15. Then we are to be ready to give a scriptural answer to any question which men can ask concerning the hope (which is actually a firm conviction) of our salvation, with reasonableness, humility and respect for them as individuals. For this, we must

study the Scriptures
diligently if we are to
be effective witnesses
for Christ.

When the miracle of Pentecost occurred, the news spread quickly throughout Jerusalem, and a large crowd gathered, seeking the meaning of this phenomenon. Peter, under the control and in the power of the Holy Spirit, addressed the inquisitive crowd. Some of these had during Christ's trial 50 days earlier cried, "Crucify Him," and "His blood be on us, and on our children" (Matthew 27:25).

Possibly some in the front row were those before whom Peter had used profanity when he denied Christ (Matthew 26:73, 74). Under these circumstances of fear and trembling, Peter's resources had to be the Holy Spirit and God's Word. The purpose of this lesson is to demonstrate the use of the Word of God in witnessing, and its results.

Lesson Development

Bible Study

A. *Peter's witness*

Read Acts 2.

1. Of all the disciples, why was Peter the least qualified to witness for Christ, and yet the most qualified, as suggested above and in Acts 2? *He had denied Christ, but he had a thorough knowledge of the Old Testament to base his preaching on.*

Peter had no notes to
which he could refer. His
address was impromptu and
based upon Old Testament
Scripture with which He
had saturated his mind from

2. How much of Peter's sermon involves quotations from the Bible (i.e., Joel, David, etc.)? _____

How much Scripture memorization do you suppose Peter had done in his early life? _____

an early age. No doubt the disciples actively engaged in the study of the Scriptures as they traveled with the Lord Jesus. Often He explained or expounded the Scriptures to the disciples as they journeyed about. The success of what Peter said was due entirely to the Word of God administered to the hearts of the hearers by the Holy Spirit.

Peter's first sermon after
Pentecost contained much

3. What part does the Holy Spirit play:

In those who share Christ's message (John 14:26)? *He will teach and bring to remembrance what Jesus had said.*

In those who hear Christ's message (John 16:8-11)? *He will convict of sin, righteousness and judgment.*

of the Word of God and
was preached in the power
of the Holy Spirit.

> 4. What did Peter say to convict them of sin (Acts 2:23, 36)?
> *They had crucified the one whom God had*
> *sent.*

It was the Word of God
as found in the Old Testament which the Holy Spirit used to bring great conviction about their sins, and particularly the sin of crucifying Christ.

> 5. Name some great things Peter preached about God (verses 24, 34, 35, 38, 39): _____
> _____
> _____
>
> B. The crowd's response
>   1. How many became Christians that day? *3,000*
>   2. List the emotions experienced by the hearers before and after conversion: _____
>   3. What do you think caused anger toward a witnessing Christian? _____
>
> C. The power of the Word
>   1. Summarize Isaiah 55:11. *The Word of God will*
>   *do what God intends it to do.*

The Spirit of God uses
the Word of God to exalt
the Son of God through whom people become the children of God.

> 2. How does the Word of God affect the non-Christian as you witness, according to Hebrews 4:12? *Judges*
>   *the thoughts and intentions of the heart.*
>
> 3. In Ephesians 6:17, what is the Bible called? _____
>   *The sword of the Spirit.*
>   Why? _____ *It is the sharp instrument of*
>   _____ *Hebrews 4:12.* _____ .
>
> As you shall see in more detail in Lesson 6, it is the Holy Spirit who brings men to grips with the issues as we witness.
>
> D. The value of Scripture memorization
>
>   Committing portions of Scripture to memory is the best way to know the Word of God, and as a result, to know Christ. Also by having the promises and commands of the Word memorized, we can apply them to any life situation at a moment's notice, especially when we desire to use them in an unexpected witnessing opportunity.

1. List some things you can know from 2 Peter 1:2-4: _____
   His divine power has granted everything to us;
   precious promises are granted; we are
   partakers of divine nature.

2. List some ways having Scripture memorized will help you according to:

   1 Peter 2:2, 3 and Hebrews 5:12-14 _____
       To grow in respect to salvation,
       and grow to be teachers.

   Joshua 1:8 and Psalm 1:1-3 *We will be careful to*
   do according to all that is written; make our
   way prosperous; have good success; be fruitful.

   Psalm 32:8 *God counsels and instructs with*
                   His eye on us.

3. List some ways in which the Scriptures will nourish your growth.
   Romans 10:17 _____ *In faith.*
   Psalm 119:11 _____ *Will not sin.*
   Psalm 119:165 *Have great peace.*

4. And one thing God's Word was absolutely essential for:
   1 Peter 1:23 *We are born again through it.* _____

Conclusion and Application

The disciples of Christ who have been used most successfully are those who have memorized the Word of God systematically and then obeyed it. In order to win men and women to Christ we must learn the Scriptures, and memorizing is a vital part in the process.

Life Application

1. List specific ways the above Scriptures will help you in your witnessing. _____

2. Which one do you feel you need the most? _____

3. How will you apply it? _____

4. Have you memorized it? _____

Suggested Closing Prayer

Thank You, Father, for showing us the importance of memorizing Your Word and being able to use it properly in witnessing situations. Help us as we grow in our memorization efforts and abilities. Make us effective witnesses for You.

ADDITIONAL BACKGROUND MATERIAL

Some helpful techniques to use in memorizing Bible verses:

Read the verses through several times.

Read the verses that come before and after in order that you might understand the trend of thought.

Read the verses again from comma to comma, colon or semi-colon. Look for the verbs first, as they convey the action of the verse. Note the thought of the words between the commas.

Additional values of a Scripture memory program:

enables us to reap great returns for the time invested;

gives solid doctrinal foundations;

gives guidance in worship — 1 Chronicles 29;11-13; in prayer — John 15:7; 1 John 5:14-15;

builds character — Luke 6:45.

LESSON FIVE

WITNESSING AND PRAYER

Teacher's Objective: To demonstrate to the student the vital part prayer plays in effective witnessing for Christ, and to motivate the student toward believing prayer for boldness.

Teacher's Enrichment: (May be shared with students as time permits.)

A Canadian missionary knelt as his Chinese Communist interrogator commanded him to pray and demonstrate that God answers prayer. The missionary prayed that God would make it apparent that He does answer prayer, even if it meant their brash interrogator would lose his vision. Immediately he was blinded, just as Elymas was (Acts 13:11). Seven clergymen were converted to Christ along with the Communist. The Communist died as a martyr at the hands of his comrades.

Events such as these are little seen today. In the Bible they happen over and over again. God has not changed; we have changed. Our confidence in our own ability and our own self-sufficiency keeps us from asking God to deal with our problems in mighty power. Prayer changes things, even men's lives. One reason we are not seeing more Christians witnessing and more people converted is prayerlessness.

George Mueller of Bristol, England, cared for hundreds of orphans, meeting their needs through daily miracles of answered prayer. He tells the story of one memorable morning when he had them bow their heads to thank God for the provision of breakfast. Unknown to the children, nothing had been prepared — the cupboard was bare. Then it was that a large sack of breakfast meal was delivered by a wealthy man who felt strangely constrained to do so. God met George Mueller's need by answering his prayer.

CLASS TIME

Suggested Opening Prayer

Our Father, show us today the importance of prayer in witnessing. Help us to see how You give us the courage we need, and create in us a burden for those who do not know Christ.

(Introduction: Be sure students understand
   objective
   memory work
   reading assignment)

OBJECTIVE: To make prayer a vital part of witnessing.
TO MEMORIZE: Acts 4:31.
TO READ: Ephesians 3 and 4.

Discussion Starter

Have you ever wondered why some people are successful in their witness for Christ and others are not successful? Why do you think God seems to use some Christians and not others?

(Allow students to answer and then proceed as appropriate:) Prayer is really the place where people are won to Christ; service is just gathering in the fruit. If we really believe this, we should certainly spend more time praying before witnessing.

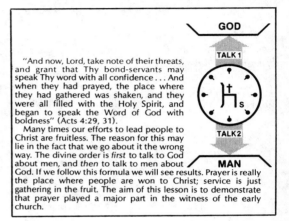

"And now, Lord, take note of their threats, and grant that Thy bond-servants may speak Thy word with all confidence . . . And when they had prayed, the place where they had gathered was shaken, and they were all filled with the Holy Spirit, and began to speak the Word of God with boldness" (Acts 4:29, 31).

Many times our efforts to lead people to Christ are fruitless. The reason for this may lie in the fact that we go about it the wrong way. The divine order is *first* to talk to God about men, and *then* to talk to men about God. If we follow this formula we will see results. Prayer is really the place where people are won to Christ; service is just gathering in the fruit. The aim of this lesson is to demonstrate that prayer played a major part in the witness of the early church.

Lesson Development

Bible Study

A. *What the early Christians prayed for*

   Read Acts 4.

   1. State the problem faced by these Christians. _____
      Persecution and danger.
      _____

   2. What do you think would have happened to Christianity had they stopped witnessing? _____

   3. Of what importance to the cause of Christ today is the soul-winning witness? _____

   4. How did these Christians solve their dilemma:
      Before magistrates? _____ *Glorified God.*
      In private? _____ *Prayed.*
      In public? _____ *Preached Christ.*

   5. What protected them (Acts 4:21)? *The people were glorifying God.*

   6. For what did they pray? *Confidence--boldness.*

They did not pray for themselves that they might be spared nor did they keep silent. They wanted power and boldness that they might not fail to proclaim Christ. One Roman writer said of the early Christians, "These Christians are turning the empire around."

B. *The answer to their prayer*

1. What was the result of their prayer? <u>*The place was*</u> <u>*shaken and they were filled with the Holy Spirit*</u>

The answer to their prayer was immediate and definite. It was in the affirmative. They prayed, and God answered as He had promised. None could stand against them, and they were victorious in Christ.

They spoke the gospel with such boldness that none could stand against them, and they were victorious in Christ.

Boldness is a very scarce commodity today in Christian circles. We are afraid of what men will think of us or do to us. But God has given us not the spirit of fear, but of love and power and of a sound mind (2 Timothy 1:7). We need to pray for boldness!

2. How have you profited from their courage, prayer and effective witness? _____
_____

3. In what ways can other people depend on your courage, prayer and witness? _____
_____

C. *The Christian's opposition*

1. Were the witnessing Christians persecuted by the religious or non-religious people of their day? _____

Although many believe Satan is non-existent, the Word of God verifies his presence and speaks of his

2. Whom do you believe to be the author of resistance to Christian witness, and why? _____
_____

work against God in very concrete terms. But Satan cannot overcome and defeat a praying Christian. Jesus told Peter, "Keep watching and praying, that you may not enter into temptation." (Matthew 26:41). Battles are being waged in the heavens between the hosts of Satan, and Christ and the angels. It is the prayers of the believers that avail to bring victory on earth and in heaven. God has included us in the battles and victories of the ages, and nowhere can we have a more powerful part than in the field of prayer.

We laboriously struggle not against flesh and blood, which appear tangible, but against powers that energize this world system, and against spiritual corruption — high and low and all around us. Seeing this, put on the complete armor of God, that you may be able to bear up under the onslaughts of Satan, and having done all you can do, stand steadfast and immovable. See Ephesians 6:11-13.

Conclusion and Application

Prayer is the God-ordained way to bring Christ into the lives of men that they might live the heavenly life here on earth and afterwards in heaven. We must pray for those without Christ. Praying for them will cause us to reach out and win them to Christ.

(Have the students give some examples of persons who have come to know the Lord as a result of their prayers, or that of someone else. If they cannot give any instances, cite a few of your own experiences.)

Life Application

1. What specific opposition have you encountered recently, and how did you deal with it? _____

_____

_____

2. How could you have handled it better? _____

_____

_____

3. List at least one prospective witnessing situation and spend a few moments praying specifically for God's leading and empowering through your life. _____

_____

_____

Suggested Closing Prayer

Lord Jesus, cause us to see, as You see, the fields white unto harvest. Motivate us to go to them with the message; give us the compassion and the boldness to tell and tell and tell.

ADDITIONAL BACKGROUND MATERIAL

Scripture passages which show some unique answers to prayer:

Jehoshaphat — 2 Chronicles 20:1-30.

Hezekiah — 2 Chronicles 32:1-23.

Peter in prison — Acts 12:1-17.

Paul and Silas in prison — Acts 16:25-40.

LESSON SIX

WITNESSING AND THE HOLY SPIRIT

Teacher's Objective: To demonstrate to the student the vital necessity of the Holy Spirit to our witness, and encourage total dependence upon Him.

Teacher's Enrichment: (This material may be shared with group members as time permits.)

Some parallel passages on witnessing and the Holy Spirit:

2 Corinthians 3:5-18:

How did Paul feel about his capability of winning men, considering he had the finest seminary background in the world at that time?

What happened to Moses when he was in communion with God and what bearing does this have on God's part in Christian service (verse 7)?

Why did Paul have liberty to witness (verse 17)? Does this suggest why you may not have liberty?

1 Corinthians 12:4-11:

How does God's Spirit make Christians differ in function?

What antidote is there for pride at having a more conspicuous gift (1 Corinthians 4:7; 12:12-31)?

Who is a truly superior Christian in God's estimation (1 Corinthians 13:1-3)?

Which Christians are to be witnesses (Matthew 4:19; 2 Timothy 4:5)?

CLASS TIME

Suggested Opening Prayer

Dear Lord, we thank You for meeting with us today. We pray You will, through Your Holy Spirit, reveal the necessity of His power in our lives in order to be effective witnesses.

(Introduction: Be sure
students understand
   objective
   memory work
   reading assignment)

Introduction

OBJECTIVE: To understand and trust in the Holy Spirit's leading as you witness.

TO MEMORIZE: John 15:26, 27.

TO READ: Ephesians 5 and 6.

Discussion Starter

What do you think is the most important attribute we must have to witness and see results?

Self-consciousness and fear of what others will say are great foes to our witness. Stephen as a tablewaiter (Acts 6:2-5), not as an apostle, was brought before the most skilled and wicked opponents of Christianity. Though he might have retreated, conscious of his inadequacy, he yielded to the Holy Spirit's control of his life. By so doing, he became the first Christian martyr, mightily moved the unbelievers and laid the basis for Saul's conversion.

The purpose of this lesson is to demonstrate how the power of the Holy Spirit relates to our witness.

Lesson Development

Bible Study

A. Read Acts 6 and 7

1. Underline every mention of the Holy Spirit.

2. What part did the Holy Spirit play in Stephen's life?
   Controlled him --gave him courage, witness and results

No amount of persuasiveness or imagination or ability on our part will ever avail to move any person toward a saving knowledge of Jesus Christ apart from the work of the Holy Spirit in His convicting and regenerative power. Salvation, as the Psalmist says, is of the Lord, totally and completely. The first Christian martyr, Stephen, was an ordinary man — fearful, inadequate and powerless. As you read Acts 6 and 7, you will note that one cannot locate the techniques which Stephen used to influence people. However, he became fearless, and moved multitudes with the sincerity and power of his life and witness for Christ. By examining his life, we will discover that the reason for his effectual witness was the person and work of the Holy Spirit who produced in him a mighty likeness to the Son of god Himself. The Holy Spirit gave him the courage, the witness and the results.

3. What was the spiritual indictment upon his hearers which cut them to the heart? They were resisting the Holy Spirit, just as their fathers did.

Stephen became absolutely fearless, he did not compromise his message regardless of circumstances, and he told men what was wrong with them. He spoke of the person of Christ, not of pious platitudes.

4. As a Spirit-filled man, Stephen had two purposes which were his greatest concerns, as seen in his desire to witness and in his dying prayer. What were they?
   To present Christ as He is to men as they are and that men's sins might be forgiven.

Another way of stating this is that his fellow Jews might come to know Christ and have His forgiveness of their sins.

A result of being filled
with the Spirit is selflessness.
Stephen did not fear what
man could do to him nor

> 5. How do these concerns show the fullness of the Holy Spirit in Stephen (Galatians 5:22, 23 and 2 Corinthians 5:14, 15)? *He showed fruit of the Spirit and a selfless life, living for the one who died for him.*

was he defeated by self-consciousness. It was not a case of what part should the Holy Spirit play in his life; but rather the Holy Spirit was his life, all of it. Stephen was full of the Holy Spirit.

> B. *Work of the Holy Spirit in witnessing*
> 1. What is the ministry of the Holy Spirit (John 15:26; 16:13, 14)? *Bearing witness of Christ and glorifying Him.*
> 2. How is it accomplished in a person who witnesses of Christ (Acts 1:8, 6:10)? *The Spirit gives that person power that others are unable to cope with.*
> 3. What will the Holy Spirit do for the witnessing person (Acts 8:29, 4:31)? *He will give him guidance and boldness.*
> 4. What will the Holy Spirit do for the person being witnessed to, according to 1 Corinthians 2:10-12? *Open the person's understanding of things of God.*
> 5. How would you compare that to 2 Corinthians 4:3, 4?
>
> It is the Holy Spirit who brings a man face to face with the facts regarding his condition and his need. This action is called "convicting, reproving, exposing, bringing to light." If we were to witness on our own, we would accomplish nothing, but when the Holy Spirit uses our witness, He brings a man face to face with important facts — presenting them so forcefully that these facts must be acknowledged and considered.
> 6. What are these basic facts (John 16:7-11)? *The facts of man's sin, Christ's righteousness, and the judgment of the world and its rulers.*

The presentation of the person of Christ always has a reaction on the part of the hearers. In the case of Stephen, rejection and anger resulted in his death. The other reaction is acceptance of Christ and the man bearing the message about Him.

In any case, the work of the Holy Spirit is the same: to produce conviction of sin in the heart of the sinner.

> 7. What final result is the full responsibility of the Holy Spirit to bring about in the hearer (John 3:5, 6)? *The new, spiritual birth.*

Conclusion and Application

The same power that was evidenced in Stephen's life and ministry and in the life and witness of the early church is also ours if we will but take it. How do we appropriate it? By yielding our lives completely to Christ and appropriating the control or filling of the Holy Spirit.

> **Life Application**
>
> Ask the Holy Spirit of God to prepare individuals to whom you can witness. Ask Him to free the minds of specific individuals so that they can see the issues at stake and be able to make a logical, rational, intelligent choice to receive Christ as Lord and Savior. Record the names of at least three persons you feel God would have you speak to about Christ within the next week.
>
> _____
>
> _____
>
> _____
>
> Ask the Holy Spirit to lead you to these individuals at the proper time, and to speak through you in confronting them with the message of Christ.
>
> As you witness, be conscious of the fact that it is the Holy Spirit who is penetrating the mind of the other person, revealing spiritual truth.
>
> Are you sure you are prepared? If not, review the earlier lessons in this step.

Would you like to pray and ask the Holy Spirit to fill and control your life, and place Christ on the throne of your life? Would you like to do it right now as we conclude in prayer?

Suggested Closing Prayer

Father, we confess the sin of running our lives as we want, and ask the Holy Spirit to take complete control of our lives. We place the Lord Jesus Christ on the throne of our lives right now. Thank you for doing this.

LESSON SEVEN

RECAP

Teacher's Objective: To impress more deeply upon the hearts of the students the importance of witnessing and to review the qualifications, methods and resources available.

CLASS TIME

Suggested opening Prayer

Father, we thank You for what You thus far have taught us about witnessing, the need for it, what the spiritual qualifications are and the place of the Word, of prayer and of the Holy Spirit in regard to witnessing. We pray that as we recap the last six lessons, You will impress these things more deeply upon our hearts and that You may use us more fully in Your service.

(Introduction: The student's objective at this time is to understand more fully why witnessing is important, to become more familiar with methods which may be used and to develop a stronger desire to become fruitful in winning souls.

Memory verses from previous lessons are to be reviewed, and this would be a good time for the students to do any reading in Galatians and Ephesians that they may have missed earlier.)

> Review all verses memorized.
> Reread Galatians and Ephesians.

Discussion Starter

(The first question in the *Handbook,* page 263, may be used to start the discussion of this lesson.

> What is the most important reason you have learned for witnessing for Christ? _____
>
> **GOD**
>
> VISION FOR THE WORLD
>
> TELL THE WORLD

Lesson Development

(Any Teacher's Enrichment or Additional Background Material that you were not able to use in the previous lessons could be utilized at this time and any point which you might feel was not sufficiently covered, or which the students do not understand completely, can be dealt with now too.

Going over the Recap questions will benefit both the students and you by making these truths a more active part of your subconscious, habitual way of life.)

Have you overcome the thing that most hinders your witnessing? _____

What is the next most effective hindrance for you and how do you plan to overcome it? _____
_____
_____

Summarize why you think a knowledge of the Word of God is important in witnessing. _____
_____
_____

How will prayer specifically help you? _____
_____
_____

Why do you think the Holy Spirit does not speak of Himself?
_____
_____

Conclusion and Application

John 15:16 tells us that Christ has especially chosen us to be His witnesses. When He asks us to do something, He always gives us what we need to get it done. A clear understanding of His call, of His own methods of witnessing and of the power available to us through His Holy Spirit will make it easier to be about the Father's business, and it is only for us to decide to allow Him to work through us in this way.

Suggested Closing Prayer

(Give students a time for silent prayer of commitment to being available to the Lord, and an opportunity to appropriate the power of the Holy Spirit for witnessing. Then close with:) We thank You, Father, for the promise of answered prayer, and we thank You for what You will be doing through us.

(Instruct students to write their testimony as suggested here. Help them to understand that by

> Write a personal three-minute testimony of your personal experience with Christ. Briefly share what your life was like before your decision; how you became a Christian; and explain in greater detail what it is like to be a Christian. (Attach testimony to this lesson.)

writing it, they will clarify and organize it in their own minds. By doing whatever rewriting may be needed, they will be able to make it concise and powerful.

Also, point out to the students that pages 264 through 271 in the *Handbook* contain information vital to their ability to witness effectively and encourage them to study the material carefully and learn it well. It will give them the tools they need for witnessing.)

STEP SEVEN

THE CHRISTIAN AND WITNESSING
SUMMARY LESSON PLAN

Teacher's Objective: To help students develop techniques and to motivate them to be effective witnesses for Jesus Christ.

Teacher's Enrichment: (See Teacher's Enrichment sections in each of the preceding lessons of this step, and share with the class as time allows.)

CLASS TIME

Suggested Opening Prayer

Lord, teach us today how we can be effective instruments in bringing others to Christ.

(Introduction:

STUDENT'S OBJECTIVE: To learn how and to begin effectively witnessing for Christ.

TO MEMORIZE: Matthew 28:19,20; 2 Corinthians 5:14,15.

READING ASSIGNMENT: John 3,4; Acts 8:25-40.)

Discussion Starter

Do you think it is important for you personally to bring others to Christ? Why or why not?

Lesson Development

A. Why witness *(from Lesson 1)*?
   1. What is a witness? (Have students suggest answers and then give this definition:) A witness is a person who himself has received the testimony of the death, burial and resurrection of Jesus Christ, and then proclaims that truth to others by his life and by his lips.
   2. Why should we witness?
      a. The Old Testament admonishes us to, Psalm 107:2.
      b. Jesus commanded it, Mark 16:15.
      c. People are lost and hungry for God, Matthew 9:37,38.
      d. They need to know the way to find Him, John 14:6; Acts 4:12.

THE CHRISTIAN AND WITNESSING

3. What is the message we take (1 Corinthians 15:3,4)?
(Christ died for our sins, was buried, and raised again the third day according to the Scriptures.)

B. Jesus demonstrates how to witness *(from Lesson 2)*.
   1. Techniques He used (John 4:1-42):
      a. Jesus spoke first, verse 7.
      b. He talked with the woman alone, verse 8.
      c. He began with an everyday situation, verse 7.
      d. He kept returning to the subject of her need, verses 13-24.
      e. He brought her to a moment of acknowledgment and of decision, verse 26.
   2. Result: She brought the whole town to Him and many received Christ.

C. Qualifications for witnessing *(from Lesson 3)*.
   1. Philip's example — Acts 8:25-40.
      a. He took God's message seriously and was actively preaching, verses 25 and 26. Persecution did not stop Philip.
      b. He was obedient to the Spirit's leading, 27,29,30.
      c. He was enthusiastic and bold, 30.
      d. He was compassionate and tactful, 30,37.
      e. He preached Jesus, 35.
   2. Hindrances we must guard against.
      a. Lack of preparation. We must be prepared spiritually (sin confessed and filled with the Holy Spirit) and mentally (must know how to witness).
      b. Fear of man. (See Matthew 10:32,33 and John 12:42,43.)
      c. Fear of failure. Certainly some will reject, but you must never believe the lie of Satan that people aren't interested. (See Matthew 9:37,38.)

D. Witnessing and the Word of God *(from Lesson 4)*.
   1. Our responsibility. The Word of God is the most effectual weapon we have in dealing with people about their need of Christ. There is convincing power only in a presentation of what the Word of God has to say. We are to be ready to give a scriptural answer to any question which men can ask concerning the hope (which is actually a firm conviction) of our salvation.
   2. Peter's example. His first message, recorded in Acts 2:14-36, showed a remarkable knowledge of the Old Testament, which were the only Scriptures they had at that time. He used it to preach Christ. He had no notes to refer to — his message was impromptu. And three thousand people received Christ that day.
   3. The power of the Word.
      a. What part does the Holy Spirit play (John 14:26; 16:8-11)? (He will teach and bring to remembrance what Jesus has said, and He will convict of sin, righteousness and judgment.)
      b. What promise do we have in Isaiah 55:11 regarding sharing God's Word? (It will do what God intends it to do.)

c. What will the Word do in regard to our witnessing according to:
Hebrews 4:12
Psalm 1:1-3
1 Peter 1:23

E . (Witnessing and prayer *(from Lesson 5).*

1. What did the early Christians pray for (Acts 4:29)? They did not pray for themselves that they might be spared

> "And now, Lord, take note of their threats, and grant that Thy bond-servants may speak Thy word with all confidence . . . And when they had prayed, the place where they had gathered was shaken, and they were all filled with the Holy Spirit, and began to speak the Word of God with boldness" (Acts 4:29, 31).
>
> Many times our efforts to lead people to Christ are fruitless. The reason for this may lie in the fact that we go about it the wrong way. The divine order is *first* to talk to God about men, and *then* to talk to men about God. If we follow this formula we will see results. Prayer is really the place where people are won to Christ; service is just gathering in the fruit. The aim of this lesson is to demonstrate that prayer played a major part in the witness of the early church.

GOD

TALK 1

TALK 2

MAN

nor did they keep silent. They wanted power and boldness that they might not fail to proclaim Christ. One Roman writer said of the early Christians, "These Christians are turning the empire around."

2. How did God answer their prayer (verse 31)? They spoke the gospel with such boldness that none could stand against them, and they were victorious in Christ.

3. What should we be praying for?

F. Witnessing and the Holy Spirit *(from Lesson 6).*

1. The work of the Holy Spirit in Stephen (the first Christian martyr):
   a. Stephen was filled with the Holy Spirit and faith, Acts 5:15.
   b. The Holy Spirit gave him wisdom, 6:10.
   c. He recognized his hearers were resisting the Holy Spirit (not himself), 7:51.
   d. The Holy Spirit comforted him at the time of his death, 7:55

2. The work of the Holy Spirit in us as we witness:
   a. What is the ministry of the Holy Spirit (John 15:26; 16:13,14)? (Bearing witness of Christ and glorifying Him.)
   b. How does He accomplish that in us (Acts 1:8; 6:10)? (He gives us power that others are unable to cope with, and gives us guidance and boldness.)
   c. What will the Holy Spirit do for the person being witnessed to (1 Corinthians 2:10-12)? (Open the person's understanding to the things of God.

3. What final result is the full responsibility of the Holy Spirit to bring about (John 3:5,6)? (The new, spiritual birth.)

Conclusion and Application

John 15:16 tells us that Christ has especially chosen us to be His witnesses. When He asks us to do something, He always gives us what we need to get it done. Understanding His call, His own methods of witnessing and the power available through the Holy Spirit makes it easier for us. Our part is to allow Him to work through us in this way.

Suggested Closing Prayer

(Give students a time for silent prayer of commitment to being available to the Lord, and an opportunity to appropriate the power of the Holy Spirit for witnessing. Then close with:) We thank You Father, for the promise of answered prayer, and we thank You for what You will be doing through us.

(A final note: Instruct students to write their testimony as suggested on page 264 of the *Handbook*. Help them to understand that by writing it, they will clarify and organize it in their own minds. By doing whatever rewriting may be needed they will be able to make it concise and powerful.

Also, point out to the students that pages 264 through 271 of the *Handbook* contain information vital to their ability to witness effectively, and encourage them to study the material carefully and learn it well. It will give them the tools they need for witnessing.)

STEP EIGHT
The Christian and Stewardship

WHAT IS A CHRISTIAN STEWARD?

Of what are we to be stewards? A steward is "a manager or superintendent of another's household." We are stewards of all that God possesses, and His possessions include our money, our talents, our minds, our bodies and the time we live in this world.

God owns everything. He is the creator and sustainer of the universe. "Christ, who is the image of the invisible God, the firstborn of every creature; for by Him were all things created that are in heaven and that are in earth, visible and invisible, whether they be thrones, or dominions, or principalities, or powers: all things were created by Him and for Him; and He is before all things and by Him all things consist" (Colossians 1:15-17).

There is just one thing that God does not, strictly speaking, own — that is, you and me. In creating the human being He allowed us to have the moral choice of whether we would subject ourselves to Him. Initially, all of us made the wrong choice. "All have sinned and come short of the glory of God" (Romans 3:23). By this choice we forfeited our love relationship with God. But, praise be to God, we who have accepted Christ "are not our own, but are bought with a price." The price is God's Son.

A Christian steward is one who realizes that as Christians "we live, and move, and have our being" in Christ. The Christian steward recognizes God as his preeminent master, and lives for Him. The whole of the Christian's life — his personality, time, talent, influence, material substance, everything — is dedicated to Christ. This is true Christian stewardship.

"Each one of us shall give account of himself to God" (Romans 14:12).

"For we must all appear and be revealed as we are before the judgment seat of Christ, so that each one may receive [his pay] according to what he has done in the body, whether good or evil [considering what his purpose and motive have been, and what he has achieved, been busy with and given himself and his attention to accomplishing]" (2 Corinthians 5:10, Amplified New Testament).

So we see that God really does own everything. Therefore we own nothing and are only stewards of what He gives us. God holds the key to every material and spiritual thing, and the only reason that we have had anything, or have it now, or will have it, is that God loves us enough to give it to us.

347

LESSON ONE

THE OWNERSHIP OF GOD OUR FATHER

Teacher's Objective: To show that God owns our lives and to encourage absolute surrender to Him.

Teacher's Enrichment: (This material may be shared with class members as time permits.)

God's Ownership

A. Proofs:

1. He created us through His Son — Genesis 1:1; John 1:1-3; Colossians 1:16.
2. His Son purchased us with His blood — 1 Corinthians 7:23; Mark 10:45.
3. He drew us to Himself and gave us to His Son — John 6:37, 44; Ephesians 1:22-23.
4. He convicted and converted us by His Spirit, giving us life — John 3:17; 16:7-11.

B. Purpose:

1. God loves us and He has shown it — Romans 5:8; John 3:16.
2. Evidences of God's character — Psalm 86:5, 15, and His concern for us — Psalm 32:8.
3. We lost blessings by going our own way and failing to recognize His ownership — Isaiah 48:17-19.

CLASS TIME

Suggested Opening Prayer

Lord, teach us to realize that You are the supreme owner of the universe and that You rightfully own each one of us. Help us to understand what it means for us to be good stewards of what You own.

(Introduction: Be sure
students understand
    objective
    memory work*
    reading assignment.)

Introduction   **GOD**

OBJECTIVE: To surrender every
thing we have to God,
because we can rest in
His ownership of all.

TO MEMORIZE: 1 Chronicles 29:11.

TO READ: Genesis 1-3.

(*Have students review this
verse individually and ask a couple of students to quote it.)

Discussion Starter

The steward is not the owner. He does not possess the estate he manages. It is
derived property, the ownership of which is vested in another. The true owner has
the right to demand an accounting from the one to whom his possessions have been
entrusted. What examples can you give of present-day stewardship?

Lesson Development

Bible Study

A. *Creation and fall of man*

  1. After what pattern did God create man (Genesis 1:26)?
     After Himself--in the image of God.

  Theologians have long debated just what it is in man
that constitutes the image of God. That image seems to
include the basic characteristics of personality — intellect, emotion and will. Adam and Eve had intellect
(Genesis 2:19), emotion and will (Genesis 3:6), just as
God does.

Man is not *physically* in
God's image, for "God is a
Spirit" (John 4:24). Man is
not *morally* in God's image, for man is sinful and God is holy (Romans 3:23). With
intellect, emotions and will — the elements of personality — man, then, is *constitu-
tionally* in God's image. Man was given intellect with which he might know God,
emotions with which he might love God and a will with which he might serve
God. Man was created not only *by* God but *for* God. Of all His earthly creatures,
man alone could have real fellowship with God. The most intelligent animals lack
any God-consciousness, but God and man *conversed.*

---

  2. What did man do to bring about separation between
    himself and God (Genesis 3:1-8)? *Disobeyed God's
    command not to eat of the tree of the
    knowledge of good and evil.*

  Note: This passage gives important insight into the
character of sin. Adam did not get drunk or commit
immoral acts — murder or the like. He and Eve merely
asserted their independence from God, rebelled against
His command and took control of their own lives. Sin is
being independent of God and running your own life.

Man fell from God, not
vice versa. Earth's first
couple decided that they
could no longer depend on

God to give them the best, but that they themselves must strive to gain what God could not give them. They wanted to remove their lives from divine control. "Godlessness" is nothing more than being independent of God.

Man could no longer know God. (1 Corinthians 2:14).

> 3. How did the sin of man affect his:
> intellect (2 Corinthians 4:2, 4)? _Man is blinded to_
> _the light of the gospel of the glory of Christ._

Some non-Christian scholars have suggested in all honesty that Jesus fed the 5,000 with five loaves and two fishes by hiding the bread in a cave and having His disciples secretly pass it out to them. Millions of intelligent people believe in such obvious foolishness. They say Jesus did not exist, or that God does not exist (it is our imagination); even that death does not exist, or that sin does not exist. Others teach that Adam is God, that Jesus got married to Mary and Martha and had children, that only 144,000 will be saved, etc. The modern cults of our day suggest the blindness of the human mind.

Man's emotions became perverted. He could still

> emotions (Jeremiah 17:9)? _Heart is more deceit-_
> _ful than all else and is desperately sick._

love, but he could not love God. Ephesians 2:1 tells us that man became spiritually dead. Total chaos invaded humanity.

The brutalities of Naziism and Communism, the love for sex which drenches our society, the pursuit of wealth above all things and the worship of idols throughout history are testimony to this. In ancient religions of New Testament times, some pagan temples had prostitutes serving as part of the religious worship, and this was considered devotion to God.

The will of man is now enslaved—the non-Christian

> will (Romans 5:12; 6:20)? _____
> _All have sinned; all are slaves to sin._

is the servant (lit., "bondslave") of sin. Man does not serve God because he cannot. Thus Adam in the garden (1) hid from God, (2) became afraid of God, (3) became ashamed before God. The sweet communion was broken.

Adam's act of independence ruined the human race, and yet God in His grace, at the price of Christ's

> 4. How did this act of rebellion affect the world (Romans
> 5:12)? _Death entered into the world and_
> _spread to all men along with all misery,_
> _suffering and sorrow._

blood, has redeemed us and restored us. The Christian who refuses to submit to the Lordship of Christ _repeats Adam's sin all over again._

Who is the Holy Spirit
(Romans 8:9)? (Answer: the
Spirit of God and the Spirit
of Christ.)
Where does the Holy
Spirit live (Galatians 4:6)? (In the hearts of the believers.)

> **B.** *Reconciliation.*
>
> 1. How did God bring us back and reconcile us to Himself (Romans 5:8-10)? *While we were yet sinners, Christ died for us.*
>
> 2. What has God given us to enable us to live for Him (John 14:16, 17)? *A Helper, the Spirit of truth, the Holy Spirit.*

What has he come to do (Acts 1:8; Galatians 5:22-23)? To empower believers for witnessing, and to produce godly fruit in the life of the believer.)
How must I cooperate (Acts 4:31; Ephesians 5:18-20)? (Pray, and be filled with the Holy Spirit.)

> 3. God now has restored us to a position of fellowship similar to what Adam had. What does that declare about our present relationship with God (1 Corinthians 6:19, 20)? *We are not our own; we belong to God because He has bought us.*
>
> **C.** *Our responsibility*
>
> 1. What, then, is to be our response to God (Romans 12:1, 2)? *Present our bodies, be transformed in our minds.*
>
> 2. Many people attempt to compromise and give God less than full allegiance. How did Jesus regard that practice in Matthew 12:30? *"He who is not with Me is against Me"--no middle ground.*
>
> 3. How did Jesus describe His attitude toward those who will stand neither for nor against Him in Revelation 3:15, 16)? *They are lukewarm, repulsive to Him--He would "spit you out of My mouth."*
>
> 4. What logical choice did Elijah present to the people (1 Kings 18:21)? *"If the Lord is God, follow Him; but if Baal, follow him."*
>
> If Elijah's logic is true, we must take one of two positions. If we determine Jesus Christ is Lord and God, we must serve Him loyally. If He is not, Christianity is obviously a hoax, and we should dissuade men from being Christians. But it is one or the other! We must stand either with Christ or against Him, but never try to stand in between.

Conclusion and Application

The Bible speaks of God's ownership of man as being two-fold: (1) God created man in the beginning; and (2) He redeemed man, or brought him back, after man had turned from Him and become enslaved in sin. And what a price God paid — the death of His only Son! In view of this, it

> **Life Application**
>
> 1. Is there something in your life which you have not surrendered to the control of your heavenly Father?

would be foolish for us to turn back to the things of the world, but it shows true wisdom when we surrender fully to God's will and to the control of the Holy Spirit.

_____ What is it and how will you now deal with it? _____

_____

2. How much of your life are you willing for God to control?

_____

How much of it does He control? _____

3. What do you think God will do with your life if you surrender it all to Him? _____

_____

4. Read Isaiah 48:17-19. What blessings would you lose by going your own way and failing to recognize God's ownership? _____

_____

_____

God does own us — every bit of our time, talents and treasure. Scripture tells us that Christ died for us, that we should "not henceforth live unto ourselves, but unto Him who died for us and rose again" (2 Corinthians 5:15). Not to acknowledge and act upon God's total ownership of everything we are, have or will be is to rob ourselves of His blessing and make ourselves unfit for His service and use (2 Timothy 2:19-21).

Suggested Closing Prayer

(Give students a moment for silent prayer of confession and dedication and then you close with:)

We thank You, Father, for redeeming us, for bringing us back into Your ownership, and for the fact that we can now rest in that relationship. Thank You for hearing and answering our prayers.

LESSON TWO

EXAMPLES OF PERFECT STEWARDSHIP

Teacher's Objective: To show how the life of the Lord Jesus Christ is an example of good stewardship and to demonstrate how that life is possible for every believer, and that it is necessary for an effective witness; to motivate students toward that Spirit-controlled life.

CLASS TIME

Suggested Opening Prayer

Dear Lord, impress upon our hearts and minds the perfect stewardship of Your Son and of the Holy Spirit, and teach us how our lives may become better examples of good stewardship.

(Introduction: Be sure students understand
  objective
  memory work*
  reading assignment.)

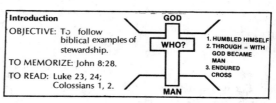

Introduction
OBJECTIVE: To follow biblical examples of stewardship.
TO MEMORIZE: John 8:28.
TO READ: Luke 23, 24; Colossians 1, 2.

GOD
WHO?
MAN

1. HUMBLED HIMSELF
2. THROUGH = WITH GOD BECAME MAN
3. ENDURED CROSS

(*Have students review this verse individually and ask a couple of students to quote it.)

Discussion Starter

Do you think it was necessary for Christ to be an example of perfect stewardship? Why or why not?

Lesson Development

Imagine it! A life without a single moment of sin. Even those who were closest

> **Bible Study**
>
> A. *Stewardship of God the Son*
>
>   1. List acts of Christ that were indicative of perfection in His stewardship (Philippians 2:5-8): *Did not grasp at equality with God, emptied Himself, took form of bondservant, made in likeness of men, humbled Himself, obedient to death on cross.*

to Him, His own disciples who would certainly have seen any flaws which would have been in His character, testify strongly to His sinlessness. "Fifteen million

minutes of life on this earth, in the midst of a wicked and corrupt generation —
every thought, every deed, every purpose, every word, privately and publicly,
from the time He opened His baby eyes until He expired on the cross, were all
approved of God. Never once did our Lord have to confess any sin, for He had no
sin. Here was One who . . . never shed a tear of repentance; never regretted a
single thought, word, or deed; never needed or asked divine pardon; was never
concerned about the salvation of His own soul; and boldly faced all His present and
future enemies in the absolute certainty of His spotless purity before God and
man" (Smith, Wilbur M., *Have You Considered Him?* Chicago: Moody Press,
n.d., p. 10).

What was the most
important aspect of His

> 2. What was Christ's supreme purpose in life (John 6:38;
> Hebrews 10:7)? *To do the will of God.*

Father's will that Jesus came to do (Luke 19:10; 1 Timothy 2:3-4)?
How well did He fulfill His Father's will (John 8:29, 46; 2 Corinthians 5:21;
1 Peter 2:22; 1 John 3:5)?

But was Christ sent
merely to give us an example
— merely to show us a
model of life to which we
could never attain? No!!!
The Scripture says He came

> 3. Read John 12:23-33.
> As part of God's will for Jesus, what was involved (verses
> 32, 33)?
> *A particular kind of death--crucifixion.*
>
> In verse 24 Jesus uses the example of a grain of wheat
> which is planted in the earth. In what sense does a grain
> of wheat have to "die" to bring forth fruit?
>
> How does it apply to us (compare verse 25)?

to save us from (not in) our sins (Matthew 1:21). He promised, "Blessed are they
which do hunger and thirst after righteousness, for they shall (not might) be filled"
(Matthew 5:6).

Jesus told His disciples
that it was profitable for
them for Him to leave
because when He left, He

> If, as a Christian, you are unwilling to make any sacrifice
> to reach others for Christ, to suffer any hardship, to face
> any self-denial, to suffer some persecution; but rather,
> you want everything to be comfortable, easy and effort-
> less, how much fruit will you bear?

would send the Holy Spirit to indwell them (John 16:7). The Holy Spirit is the
Spirit of Christ, and, as Christ lived in absolute dependence on His Father (cf.
John 5:19, 30; 6:57; 8:28), so we are to live in absolute dependence on Christ. "As
ye have therefore received Christ Jesus the Lord, so walk ye in Him" (Colossians
2:6), the Scripture commands. When we came to Christ, we came as sinners, as
those who had no strength and had to depend on Jesus Christ absolutely. We
surrendered ourselves to Him (Romans 5:6-9). He did all the rest.

B. *Stewardship of God the Holy Spirit*

1. What are some duties the Holy Spirit performs as God's steward, as revealed in the following verses?

   John 16:8-11 _Convicts the world concerning sin, righteousness and judgment._

   In what way does this convicting ministry of the Holy Spirit help us in evangelism? _____

   John 16:13 _Guide us into all truth, will disclose what is to come._
   Note: In a general way, the Holy Spirit guides the believer into the realms of spiritual truth. In a specific way, He guided the apostles and early Christians in writing the New Testament Scriptures. This is undoubtedly what Christ had in mind.

   Romans 5:5 _Pours out the love of God within our hearts._

   Romans 8:14 _Leads the sons of God._

   Romans 8:16 _Bears witness with our spirit that we are children of God._

   Romans 8:26 _Helps our weakness; intercedes for us in prayer._

2. When the Holy Spirit controls a person or a group, is the evidence of it a glorifying of the Holy Spirit, or a glorifying of Jesus Christ (John 16:14)? _____
   Of Christ. "He shall glorify Me (Christ)."

Conclusion and Application

Smith also says, "The outstanding characteristic of Jesus in His earthly life was the one in which all of us acknowledge we fall so short, and yet which at the same time all men recognize as the most priceless characteristic any man can have, namely, *absolute goodness,* or to phrase it otherwise, perfect *purity,* genuine *holiness,* and, in the case of Jesus, nothing less than sinlessness" (ibid.)

Life Application

1. How can you best apply to your life the example that Jesus set? Be specific. _____

2. What does the Holy Spirit want to do in your life at this time? _____

3. List ways you can cooperate as suggested in Acts 4:31; Ephesians 5:18-20 and Romans 12:1, 2. _____

Suggested Closing Prayer

(This would be another good time to give students an opportunity to pray the prayer for appropriation of the filling of the Holy Spirit as indicated in Step Three, Lesson 4.)

LESSON THREE

STEWARDSHIP OF OUR TIME

Teacher's Objective: To bring each student to an awareness of the importance of a wise use of the time granted by the Lord and to demonstrate how a right relationship with God will enable the student to be a better steward of that time.

CLASS TIME

Suggested Opening Prayer

Our Father, we ask that You will open our hearts and our minds to the importance of using wisely the hours and days You have given us. Help us learn to be good stewards of our time.

(Introduction: Be sure
students understand
    objective
    memory work
    reading assignment.)

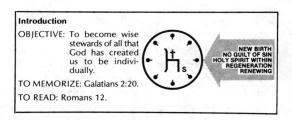

Introduction

OBJECTIVE: To become wise stewards of all that God has created us to be individually.

TO MEMORIZE: Galatians 2:20.

TO READ: Romans 12.

NEW BIRTH
NO GUILT OF SIN
HOLY SPIRIT WITHIN
REGENERATION
RENEWING

(NOTE: The Discussion Starter and Lesson Development material in this lesson is taken from *Managing Yourself* by Stephen B. Douglass, San Bernardino, CA: Here's Life Publishers, 1978. For further help in being a good steward of the time God has given you, you may want to read that book.)

Discussion Starter

Have you ever heard the story about the farmer who told his wife one morning that he was going out to plow the "south forty"? He got off to an early start so he could oil the tractor. He needed more oil, so he went to the shop to get it. On the way to the shop, he noticed the pigs weren't fed. So he proceeded to the corncrib, where he found some sacks of feed. The sacks reminded him that his potatoes were sprouting. When he started for the potato pit, he passed the woodpile and remembered that his wife wanted wood in the house. As he picked up a few sticks, an ailing chicken passed by. He dropped the wood and reached for the chicken. When evening arrived, the frustrated farmer had not even gotten to the tractor, let alone to the field!

When was the last time you found yourself in that kind of situation? How could you have changed it?

Lesson Development

God expects us to fruitfully invest whatever He gives us. Often we think of God's blessings in terms of

Bible Study

Read Psalm 90:12.

What should be our prayer concerning the use of time that God gives us? *That we might use it wisely. "Teach us to number our days, that we may present to Thee a heart of wisdom."*

A. *Right attitude about time*

1. As good stewards, what will we do (Ephesians 5:16)? *Make the most of our time, because the days are are evil.*

money or material goods. But time is also a gift of God, one that He has given all of us equally each day, and we are expected, in fact, commanded, to use it wisely.

The Bible confirms that God intends to help us make the most of our lives.

2. Why is the proper use of our time today so important (James 4:14)? *We don't know about tomorrow.*

3. What does God demand of us in the stewardship of our time (Psalm 62:8)? *That we always trust in Him.*

Consider, for example, the promise of Psalms 32:8 as recorded in the Living Bible: "I will instruct you (says the Lord) and guide you along the best pathway for your life; I will advise you and watch your progress." The Bible further assures us that God is available for consultation on any matter, great or small, on a regular basis: "But if any of you lacks wisdom, let Him ask of God, who gives to all men generously and without reproach, and it will be given to him" (James 1:5).

In Ecclesiastes 3:1, we learn, "There is an appointed time for everything . . . a time to do everything God wants you to do."

4. What does Christ admonish us to do as stewards of time until He comes again (Mark 13:33-37)? *Be on the alert--we don't know when He will come.*

5. If we are wise stewards and heed the commands of our Master, how will we use our time (Ephesians 5:15, 16)? *We will be wise, making the most of our time.*

We have an example of this in the life of Christ. Jesus' ministry on earth lasted only three and one-half years, and yet He fit into this short span of time all the activities necessary to accomplish God's purpose for Him. "I glorified Thee on earth, having accomplished the work which Thou hast given Me to do" (John 17:4). By focusing on what was important, Jesus accomplished in His brief ministry a more significant mission than any other person in history and launched a world-wide movement that has continued for nearly 2,000 years.

When you are walking in the Spirit — that is to say, when God is in control of your life — you will know what He would have

B. **Right relationship with God**

1. As wise stewards concerned over the use of our time, what will we want to understand (Ephesians 5:17)?
   What the will of the Lord is.

2. What is necessary in order to know fully what is the will of God concerning the duties of our stewardship (Ephesians 5:18)? _To be filled with the Holy Spirit._

you do, for He will put His thoughts in your mind, and you will find that you are doing the right thing.

Proverbs 3:5, 6 confirms the fact that, if you "trust in the Lord with all your heart" and "in all your ways acknowledge Him," He will direct your path in life.

The most crucial quality in a disciple is *power* from God. This enables him to be

3. The Holy Spirit will enable the faithful steward to perform the duties of stewardship by giving him (Acts 1:8): _____
   Power to witness.

sensitive to God moment by moment and to be able to fulfill what He asks him to do. Two other key qualities are *direction* and *action*. A disciple should be increasingly willing to follow the commands and principles of God's Word in his daily response to God, others and himself. He should seek to be a person of action, willing to take the initiative not only in sharing the message of Christ with non-Christians, but also in ministering meaningfully and practically to fellow Christians.

"And from everyone who has been given much shall much be required; and to whom they entrusted much, of him they will ask all the more" (Luke 12:48b).

4. He will perform these duties in the name of (Colossians 3:17): _The Lord Jesus Christ._

5. What then will be our attitude as we so utilize the time over which God has made us stewards (Ephesians 5:19, 20)? _Praise and thanksgiving, making melody in our hearts to the Lord._

6. How would you describe such a useful and joyous life (John 10:10b)? _Abundant._

C. **Most important use of time**

1. As wise stewards who know and are obedient to the will of God, we can be sure that we will spend much of our time aggressively doing what (Mark 16:15)? _____
   Preaching the gospel to all creation.

2. What does God say about a soul winner in Proverbs 11:30? _He is wise._

3. Of what value is only one soul according to Christ in Mark 8:36? _More than the whole world._

4. What then is the greatest thing you can do for another?
   Win him to Christ.

> 5. What happens in God's presence when one repents and receives Christ (Luke 15:7, 10)? ___There is joy___ _in heaven in the presence of the angels._
>
> 6. How did Paul feel about those whom he had won to Christ (1 Thessalonians 2:19, 20)? _____ _____ _They were his glory and joy._

Conclusion and Application

"Go therefore and make disciples of all the nations, baptizing them in the name of the Father and the Son and the Holy Spirit, teaching them to observe all that I commanded you; and lo, I am with you always, even to the end of the age" (Matthew 28:19, 20).

Increasingly a disciple: 1) views his life as an opportunity to actively serve his Lord; 2) wins others to Christ; 3) helps to build them in their faith; and, 4) sends them forth as spiritual multipliers to win and build others for the Savior. He seeks to live for Christ in his own sphere of influence, help fulfill the Great Commission in his generation and thus help change the world. He is prepared to serve God in the area of service to which God leads him.

Life Application

1. How many hours are there in a week? ___168___

2. Why is it that some may accomplish more than others in the same amount of time? _They are better organized, have a stronger purpose, more controlled by Spirit._

The following chart can be of great value in the stewardship of your time. Fill in the hours spent on: class, sleep, Christian service, business, recreation, etc. Place the total hours per week used in each activity at the bottom of the chart. By listing the totals you can discover if you have achieved the balanced use of time required of a good steward.

	MON.	TUES.	WED.	THURS.	FRI.	SAT.	SUN.
6:00							
7:00							
8:00							
9:00							
10:00							
11:00							
12:00							
1:00							
2:00							
3:00							
4:00							
5:00							
6:00							
7:00							
8:00							
9:00							
10:00							
11:00							
12:00							

Stewardship of Time
1. Study and class
2. Devotional life
3. Christian service
4. Rest
5. Recreation and social life
6. Activities and athletics
7. Commuting
8. Employment
9. Laundry and clean-up
10. Miscellaneous

Suggested Closing Prayer

Dear Lord, we thank You for showing us that You desire to use us and to work through us in the time You have given us. We ask that we always will be found walking in Your Spirit and that we will have the spiritual fruit You intend for us to have so that we may rejoice together with You.

LESSON FOUR

STEWARDSHIP OF OUR BODIES

Teacher's Objective: To motivate each student toward faithful stewardship of his body and soul. This lesson should not "preach on externals," but should present the biblical view of a dedicated body.

Teacher's Enrichment: (The following material may be shared with the class members as time allows.)

David and Joseph and Temptation

- David was considered a man after God's own heart (Acts 13:22), yet he failed under the attack of Satan. As we study the story of David's fall (2 Samuel 11:1-5), we notice that David was vulnerable to the sin of adultery because he had committed other sins previously.

    First we see the sin of *laziness.* Instead of leading his men into battle, he sent them to fight while he stayed in Jerusalem. He did not spend time with God in prayer and the study of the Scriptures, but went about his own business. These sins broke his vital fellowship with God and he was helpless in the face of the attack of Satan.

    David, walking on the palace roof, saw a woman bathing. Note how the verbs denote David's descent into adultery. He *saw, inquired, sent, took,* and *lay.* Then *adultery* led to *betrayal,* and *murder,* and *open disgrace.* There is more in the Bible about David's sin than there is about any victory he ever had.

- How different is the story of Joseph! (Genesis 39:7-12). When tempted by Potiphar's wife, so vital and real was his fellowship with his Lord that his first thought was that this would be a sin against God (verse 9). This kept him from falling under the weight of constant temptation (verse 10). When faced with a direct assault by Satan, his fear of God had given the needed wisdom (see Proverbs 1:7) to foresee the biblical injunction to flee from immorality (1 Corinthians 6:18) rather than stay there, try to resist it, entertain it, and possibly be overcome by it. His obedience did not result in immediate happiness for him. He was imprisoned. But ultimately Joseph was given a place of honor and power and was used to save his people from death.

CLASS TIME

Suggested Opening Prayer

Our Father, we ask that Your Holy Spirit will teach us and convict each of us of any lack of dedication of our bodies to You.

(Introduction: Be sure
students understand
objective
memory work
reading assignment.)

Introduction

OBJECTIVE: To surrender our
bodies to Christ,
from the heart.

TO MEMORIZE: Psalm 139:23,
24

TO READ: Psalm 51;
Galatians 5;
Ephesians 5.

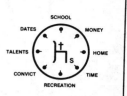

Discussion Starter

How is your standard of morality determined? By your conscience? The crowd?
Circumstances? Christ? How is it possible to keep His standards?

Lesson Development

Conversion means to
change one's mind, and to
be converted to Christ one
must change his mind about
who Christ is and what He

Bible Study

A. *The spirit and the body*

Read Hebrews 10:1-10.

1. Man is to be renewed in the spirit of his mind if he is to
be converted to Christ. How was that conversion made
possible (Hebrews 10:1-10)? *Through the offering
of the body of Jesus Christ.*

---

did on the cross to present us to God perfectly restored to righteousness.
Romans 8:8 says, "those who are in the flesh [old nature in control] cannot please
God." We are to have the mind and spirit of Christ.

God was not satisfied with burnt offerings and sacrifices, but rather prepared a
body for Christ to offer (verse 5). This, too, is to be our offering to the Father. The
only thing which many Christians have offered to the Lord is a set of excuses. As
C. T. Studd said, "We are among the 'I pray Thee have me excused' Apostles."

Our lives will either be
used to further the cause

---

2. What do you learn about the body of the Christian from
Romans 8:8, 9 and Romans 12:1? *It is the only
thing we can present to Christ for service.*

---

of Christ or to hinder His purposes and further the ends of Satan, depending upon
to whom we have yielded our bodies.

God shows His nature to
the world when we glorify
Him in our bodies. 2 Corin-

---

3. Express in your own words the additional reasons given in
1 Corinthians 6:19, 20 for being a good steward of your
body. _____

---

thians 4:7 says, "We have this treasure [meaning the gospel of Christ] in earthen
vessels, that the surpassing greatness of the power may be of God and not from
ourselves." The showcase of the gospel is the body of a Christian. Every vessel
should be clean, empty of self and filled with Christ.

> **B. Individual parts of the body**
>
> **1. The tongue.**
>
> Why is it so important to be a good steward of the tongue (James 3:2-6)? _Though small, it controls entire body and the course of our life._
>
> What should you know concerning its use (Matthew 12:36)? _We shall give an account in the judgment for every careless word we speak._

See Proverbs 6:17, 19 and 1 Peter 3:10 for more on sin in relation to the tongue.

Why should we be stewards of our minds and hearts, our thought life?

> **2. The heart.**
>
> What must we understand about the heart (Jeremiah 17:9)? _It is deceitful and sick._

Because our actions proceed from our thoughts! This is what Jesus said:

Matthew 23:27-28 — "Woe to you, scribes and Pharisees, hypocrites! For you are like whitewashed tombs which on the outside appear beautiful, but inside they are full of dead men's bones and all uncleanness. Even so you too outwardly appear righteous to men, but inwardly you are full of hypocrisy and lawlessness."

Matthew 15:18-19 — "But the things that proceed out of the mouth come from the heart, and those defile the man. For out of the heart come evil thoughts, murders, adulteries, fornications, thefts, false witness, slanders."

How can our thought life be pure?

By thinking on the things of God . . . occupation with Christ! "Destroying speculations and every lofty thing raised up against the knowledge of God, and taking every thought captive to the obedience of Christ" (2 Corinthians 10:5).

See Mark 7:21-23 for more about sin in relation to the heart and mind.

> Therefore, what should a steward of God continually pray (Psalm 139:23, 24)? _For God's searching and leading._
>
> What should be done about sin (1 John 1:9)? _It must be confessed and cleansed._
>
> What condition of heart does God require (Psalm 51:17)? _A broken spirit and a contrite heart._
>
> What kind of heart does God look for and why (2 Chronicles 16:9)? _One that is completely Hi. so He can strongly support it_

> **3. The mind.**
>
> What is your responsibility in being a steward of your mind (1 Peter 1:13)? _We are to gird it for action--to be prepared for vigorous thinking._
>
> Whose mind and which qualities thereof should you have (Philippians 2:5-8; 1 Corinthians 2:12-16)? _The mind of Christ--spiritual thoughts, humble and obedient to God._

We find in 1 Thessalonians 4:3-8: "God's plan is to make you holy, and that entails first of all a clean cut with sexual immorality. Every one of you should learn to control his body, keeping it pure and treating it with respect, and never regarding it as an instrument for self-gratification, as do pagans with no knowledge of God. You cannot break this rule without in

What is the result of keeping your mind stayed on God (Isaiah 26:3)? _We will have perfect peace._

How can you keep your mind on Him (Philippians 4:6, 7 Proverbs 4:20-22)? _Give thanks in prayer for everything; pay attention to what God says._

C. Sexual expression

1. What do the sins spoken against in 1 Corinthians 6:9, 10 13-18 mainly involve? _Sexual immorality._

2. God considered David a man after His own heart, yet David's great sin was what (2 Samuel 11:14, 15, 26, 27)? _Covetousness, adultery, murder--rebellion against God's laws._

3. What is God's stern judgment against misusers and abusers of sex (1 Corinthians 6:9-11)? _They shall not inherit the kingdom of God._

Why is it especially tragic if a Christian becomes involved in the misuse of sex (1 Corinthians 6:15-18)? _He sins against his own body which is the temple of the Holy Spirit._

some way cheating your fellowmen. And you must remember that God will punish all who do offend in this matter, and we have warned you how we have seen this work out in our experience of life. The calling of God is not to impurity but to the most thorough purity, and anyone who makes light of the matter is not making light of a man's ruling but of God's command. It is not for nothing that the Spirit God gives us is called the HOLY Spirit" (Phillips N.T.).

Whatever the standard of the non-Christian, the

How serious is sexual lust, according to Christ (Matthew 5:28)? _It is equal to actual adultery._

standard for the Christian is clear: his body is a sacred trust from God; its functions are meant to be restricted to and preserved for the ends designed by God.

Additional scriptural helps in dealing with sexual temptation:
Negative aspects:
2 Timothy 2:22 — "Flee from youthful lusts."

4. How can the application of the following verses enable you to overcome sexual lust? _Mind is to dwell on honorable, pure._
Philippians 4:8 _Memorized scripture keeps us from sin._
Psalm 119:11
1 Corinthians 10:13 _God will give way of escape._
Romans 6:14 _Sin is not our master--we have ability to resist._

1 Corinthians 6:18a — "Flee immorality."
Romans 13:14b — "Give no chances to the flesh to have its fling" (Phillips).
1 Thessalonians 5:22 — "Abstain from every form of evil."
Postive aspects: The Lordship of Christ.
Romans 14:8 — "For if we live, we live for the Lord, or if we die, we die for the Lord; therefore, whether we live or die, we are the Lord's. For to this end Christ died, and lived again, that He might be Lord both of the dead and of the living."

Colossians 3:23 — "and whatever you do, do your work heartily, as for the Lord, rather than for men."

Conclusion and Application

To keep our bodies and souls for Christ, we must:

1. Dedicate them once and for all to God (Romans 12:1-2).
2. Not yield the body's members to sin, but to God (Romans 6:11-13).
3. Walk by means of the Holy Spirit (Galatians 5:16-17).

As a Christian, a part of the Church, the bride of Christ, each of us must guard against being guilty in any way of *spiritual* immorality. See James 4:4-8; Jeremiah 3:1, 13-14; Matthew 22:37.

1 Timothy 4:12 . . . "Let no one look down on your youthfulness." We are to have a good time, plenty of recreation, some rest and relaxation. But, "show yourself an example of those who believe." We can show the world who Christ is and what He is like; we are to live like regenerate believers, unbelieving members of the world system. How are we examples? "In speech, conduct, love, faith, and purity." Do all to the glory of God!

Life Application

1. How would you say stewardship of each individual part of the body could affect each other part? _____
_____
How could it affect the body as a whole? _____
_____

2. How would you apply 1 Thessalonians 5:22 to:
the use of your tongue? _____
the desires of your heart? _____
the control of your mind? _____
your conduct with members of the opposite sex? _____
_____

Suggested Closing Prayer

(Give group members an opportunity to surrender themselves in silent prayer to the King of Kings, giving Him all that they are and all that they have — both in material things and in their bodies — to be used in His service. Then you close:) We thank You, Father, that You hear and answer prayer, and that we can have a well-balanced life in Christ.

ADDITIONAL BACKGROUND MATERIAL

If we could get a comprehensive grasp of the power and relentlessness of that dread monster, death, our attitude would change toward it. The world's population is now over four billion. Suppose the average life of a man is about 45 years, then one-forty-fifth of the total is 88+ millions who die every year, more than 243,000 every day, over 10,000 every hour, at least 170 every minute and more than two every time the clock ticks a second. Think of it: A city with a population of nearly 250,000 passes into eternity every day!

Some things to consider as we each think about the stewardship of our bodies:

Does my thought life meet the standard of Philippians 4:8? Compare this with Psalm 1:1-3.

Are there things in my life that Christ might not love?

Proverbs 4:23.

Mark 7:20-23.

John 13:34-35 — What is God's standard of love? Are there those whom I know, but do not truly love?

How do my eyes compare with the stewardship Christ demands?

Matthew 5:27-28 — Christ warns of lustful looks.

2 Peter 2:14 — Peter warns of the same.

Hebrews 12:2 — The needed standard.

For what is my mouth used? Compare the following:

Romans 3:14 — Cursing and bitterness.

Proverbs 19:5 — False witnesses which speak lies.

Mark 16:15 — Spreading the gospel.

Psalms 146:1-2 — Praising the Lord.

Testimony of what I hear and listen to is important.

Proverbs 21:13 — Shows a lack of mercy.

2 Timothy 4:3-4 — The refusal to hear sound doctrine and truth.

Romans 10:17 — Hearing the Word to gain faith.

Proverbs 23:12 — Hear the words of knowledge.

My feet should walk the paths of righteousness.

Proverbs 6:18 — Not running into mischief.

Ephesians 6:15 — Feet should be walking about sharing Christ.

●   ●   ●

THE BIBLICAL VIEW OF SEXUAL EXPRESSION

Sex is a gift of God, good and holy, to be expressed only within the marriage bond. Sex needs marriage and marriage needs sex. The two are interdependent in the design of God.

Genesis 2:18-24 — God said it was not good for man to be alone, so he instituted marriage.

Verse 18 — "I will make him a help meet for him" — literally means: "I will make a helper who will in every way complement and supplement him." Verse 21 — "God caused" and He "took," and verse 22 — God "brought." We can see clearly, it was all of God!

The Bible views the body as the vehicle for the expression of spiritual values. Thus, sex cannot be separated from the love which gives it true meaning:

Ephesians 5:22-25 — Marital love compared to Christ's love for the Church.

Colossians 3:18-19 — Christ's instructions for the relationship between husband and wife.

1 Peter 3:8 — The basis for a rewarding sexual relationship.

LESSON FIVE

STEWARDSHIP OF OUR GIFTS

Teacher's Objective: To lead students to recognize their talents and abilities and surrender them to God for His use and glory; also to show them that the most important thing is to recognize God has a plan for each life and He gives direction and power by His Holy Spirit to accomplish that plan — and that it is the responsibility of each Christian to live his life in accordance with God's plan.

CLASS TIME

Suggested Opening Prayer

Dear Lord, we ask that You will help us to understand this exciting subject of spiritual gifts and to discover what each of our own may be. Show us how to be good stewards of these spiritual gifts and how they are to be used in Your service.

(Introduction: Be sure students understand
    objective
    memory work
    reading assignment.)

Introduction

OBJECTIVE: To recognize our talents and abilities and to surrender them to God for His use and glory.

TO MEMORIZE: 1 Peter 4:10.

TO READ: 1 Corinthians 12.

MINISTERING
TEACHING
GIVING
HELPING
EXHORTING
FAITH
SHOWING MERCY
RULING

(Have the class share this material in any of the ways suggested in the Instructions for Teaching on page 21.)

God created man with a great variety of talents. The Christian church is composed of people endowed with different gifts and abilities. All that the Christian possesses should be dedicated fully to God to be used as He directs.

The Scriptures refer to the church as the body of Christ. Christ is its Head (1 Corinthians 12:27; Ephesians 5:23). Just as your body has many specialized parts, each having its own function, so the church is composed of many individuals, each with his own special function to perform — and contribution to make — to the rest of the body.

Every Christian possesses both natural and spiritual gifts. All men have natural gifts (abilities and talents), for they come to us at physical birth. Spiritual gifts are special abilities imparted by the Holy Spirit to Christians. These enable Christians to minister to others in behalf of Christ.

Discussion Starter

Each of us has been given at least one spiritual gift from the Holy Spirit according to 1 Corinthians 12:7, but there is a great variety of gifts given and some seem to be given in a fuller measure than others. They obviously are not the same. Do you think we should aim for spiritual *equality* with each other rather than spiritual *sameness?* Why?

Lesson Development

NOTE: The lesson development material for this lesson has been taken from *The Holy Spirit* by Bill Bright (San Bernardino, CA: Here's Life Publishers, Inc., ©1980 Campus Crusade for Christ, Inc.)

> **Bible Study**
> A. *Natural gifts*
>   1. What talents and natural abilities do you have? _____
>   _____
>   _____
>   2. How did you acquire them? _____
>   _____

Often I have been asked, "What is the difference between a spiritual gift and natural ability?" Well, the difference is not always clear. Keep in mind, though, that spiritual gifts as well as natural abilities come from God.

Whether a certain ability you have is the result of being spiritually gifted or naturally talented really is not that important. What matters is that you develop that gift or ability to its fullest potential through the control and empowering of the Holy Spirit and through much hard work, and that you use it according to God's will and for His glory.

> 3. According to 1 Corinthians 4:6, 7, what should your attitude be about them? *We should not become arrogant; must realize no one considers us superior; we have nothing that was not given to us.*
>
> 4. How would you apply Colossians 3:17 to the stewardship of your natural gifts? *We are to do all and use all in the name of the Lord Jesus, thanking the Father through Him.*

Within the body of Christ, each of us has a unique function. True, two people might have similar functions — just as a body has two hands that function similarly. But those two hands are not identical. Just try to wear a left-hand glove on your right hand! You and I might have similar abilities, but we are not identical. We are unique creations of God.

Therefore, we should not look upon our abilities with pride or be boastful of them. On the other hand, we should not be envious or look with disdain on others because of their different abilities.

We see that each of us has the obligation first of all to *use* our gifts in a scriptural way. We would be poor stewards of what the Holy Spirit has given us if we ignored the special abilities He has given to us.

Next, we must use our gifts to glorify Christ — not to glorify ourselves, or to glorify some other person, or even to glorify the gift itself.

It is important for us always to exercise our gifts in the power and control of the Holy Spirit — never through our own, fleshly efforts. When this happens, then Christ is glorified and the saints are built up in the faith as a body.

B. *Spiritual gifts*

1. Major passages on spiritual gifts in the Bible are:
   Romans 12:3-8
   1 Corinthians 12:1-31
   Ephesians 4:4-16
   1 Peter 4:10, 11

   From these passages make a composite list of the spiritual gifts (combine any two that might be identical). After each one you list, give your brief definition of the gift. (You may wish to consult a concordance or a Bible dictionary.)

Spiritual Gift	Definition
Teaching	
Helps, service, mercy	
Leadership	
Giving	
Wisdom, knowledge	
Faith	
Healing, miracles	
Prophecy	
Discerning of spirits	
Tongues	
Exhortation	
Apostleship	
Evangelism	
Pastoring	

2. List additional spiritual gifts you can think of that might be included: *Interpretation of tongues, 1 Corinthians 14:13; administration, 1 Corinthians 11:2; others--.*

   Why do you think so? _____

3. What are some reasons God has given gifted men to the church (Ephesians 4:11-16)? *Equip saints for work of service, build up body of Christ, unity of faith, knowledge, maturity, growth of body in love.*

4. Why will two people not exercise the same gift in the same manner (1 Corinthians 12:4-6)? *Variety given.*

Some of the gifts of the Spirit are supernatural enhancements of abilities common to all men — like *wisdom.* Other gifts — such as healing — are granted by the Holy Spirit to only a select few.

But the gifts differ in another way, too. Some are *instantaneous,* and others are *developmental* in nature. The gift of tongues at Pentecost was *instantaneous,* while the gifts of preaching and teaching are more *developmental.*

The developmental gifts are developed by the Holy Spirit within us over a period of time, just as the fruit of the Spirit, and usually require some hard work on our part in the process. One is not born into the spiritual kingdom a mature Christian, for the fruit of the Spirit — which is love in its various aspects of joy, peace, patience, kindness, goodness, faithfulness, gentleness and discipline — is developed in time as we walk and work in faith and obedience.

With this in mind, we need to understand and remember that whatever God calls us to do He will enable us to do. Again, however, three elements play a part in the developmental gifts: the empowering of the Holy Spirit, dedicated work on our part and an appreciable amount of time over which the work of the Holy Spirit coupled with our efforts bring about a degree of maturity in our lives and the use of the particular gifts God has given us.

The apostle Paul explains this wonderful truth: "For it is God who works in you, both to will and to work for His good pleasure" (Philippians 2:13, NAS).

God's Holy Spirit is at work in our lives, empowering and controlling us — but we must, as a matter of our own wills, consecrate our lives to God and oftentimes work hard and long, with wisdom, power and the enabling of the Holy Spirit to accomplish what God calls us to do.

---

5. Though some spiritual gifts seem to be of greater value than others (1 Corinthians 12:28-31), what ideas does Paul stress to keep Christians from personal pride because of those they may possess (Romans 12:4, 5; 1 Corinthians 12:12-26; 1 Corinthians 13; Ephesians 4:11-16)? *Many members, not same function but one in Christ; need each other; should be no division; same care for one another; suffer and rejoice with each other; love most important, unity, maturity in love is our aim.*

6. List the principles concerning what your attitude and responsibilities are to be toward your spiritual gifts (Romans 12:3-8). *Don't think more highly of self than ought to, exercise gifts in way proper to each gift.*

Conclusion and Application

My advice to you is this: if you strongly desire to serve the Lord in some particular way — such as teaching, ask the Holy Spirit in faith to empower you to become an effective teacher. Now, it may be that the Holy Spirit will see fit to make you a great teacher overnight, but this is most unlikely. So if it does not happen, do not be discouraged. Have faith!

Continue to ask and believe that the Holy Spirit will make you an effective teacher of the Word of God and *work hard to develop teaching skills and methods.* Be prepared to sacrifice. And be patient — it might take considerable time before anyone will even listen to you.

But, by all means, have faith that the Holy Spirit will bestow spiritual gifts upon you, though they might be developmental in nature and you might have to work hard and long to develop your gift. The Bible reminds us that "faith without works is useless" (James 2:20, NAS).

Life Application

Realize that you have at least one spiritual gift, probably more (1 Corinthians 12:11).

To find our what they are, pray that God will make them known to you. Determine which of your activities the Lord seems to bless and inquire of other mature Christians who know you well what your spiritual gifts might be.

Seek to develop your gifts in the power of the Holy Spirit, according to the scriptural exhortations. Realize that you may have other gifts of which you are not presently aware, so exercise various gifts. Take spiritual responsibility.

Be aware that you are accountable to God for stewardship of your spiritual gifts.

List what you feel might be your spiritual gifts. _____

_____

_____

_____

A Final Word

The tragedy of many Christian lives is that believers are so involved in trying to discover or receive additional spiritual gifts that they are not developing and using their own known gifts and abilities to do God's will.

For this reason, when I counsel in the area of Christian service, I do not suggest going to great lengths to discover spiritual gifts. Rather, I encourage full surrender to Jesus Christ and the importance of being filled with the Holy Spirit. Only then should one seek God's direction in life. Then, by faith and hard work, a person can set out with determination to accomplish that to which God has called him.

Spiritual gifts can be a vibrant part of your supernatural life. But, as I have already cautioned, do not place such emphasis on gifts that your life becomes off-balance. The gifts of the Spirit are given for glorifying Christ *in love,* for equipping the saints *in love,* and for unifying the body of Christ *in love.*

Suggested Closing Prayer

Our Father, we thank You for what You have shown us about Your spiritual gifts to us and for helping us to identify the ones we may have. Help us to remember, though, that the most important spiritual gift is love and that it is more important to surrender what we have to you than it is to be concerned about what our gifts are or are not. Help us to allow You to develop in us whatever You desire to.

LESSON SIX

STEWARDSHIP OF OUR POSSESSIONS

Teacher's Objective: To encourage students to begin giving faithfully to God's work both in their local churches and throughout the world.

Teacher's Enrichment: (This material may be shared with students as time permits.)

THE NECESSITY OF TITHING

Today we are under grace, not law. We are to give "not grudgingly or under compulsion, for God loves a cheerful giver" (2 Corinthians 9:7). "Moreover, it is required of stewards, that one be found trustworthy" (1 Corinthians 4:2).

● Bob Pierce, president of World Vision, tells this story of an outstanding physician — "When he was in his early twenties the Lord called him to be a missionary. He thought about it at length and finally came to this decision, 'Instead of being a missionary, I'll stay here in the homeland and build up the finest practice I can. Then I'll take on the financial support of several missionaries. Instead of going I'll send others.'

"Do you know the result? Well, last year he contributed $4,000 to missions. That's a lot of money — a big donation. Do you know what he kept for himself? $36,000.

"In other words his contribution to sending missionaries in his place was exactly ten percent of his income. I say that this physician has failed miserably in fulfilling God's purpose for his life. It hasn't cost him anything. He had $36,000 for comfort and ease last year" (Savage, Robert, *At Your Orders, Lord!* Grand Rapids: Zondervan, pp. 52, 55.)

● William Borden was a dedicated young Christian. As a student at Yale University he was extremely active in Christian service. It was said of him by a European visitor that what impressed him the most about America was: "The sight of that young millionaire kneeling with his arms around a 'bum' in the Yale Hope Mission."

While a missionary in Egypt at the age of 25, Borden died of cerebral meningitis. Two remarkable wills were probated within a few days after Borden's death. One was his own, and the other was that of J. Pierpont Morgan, who died possessing almost a hundred million dollars. Mr. Morgan at the age of seventy-five left little more than half as much to the work of God as William Borden left at twenty-five! (Taylor, Mrs. Howard, *Borden of Yale,* Moody Press, pp. 202, 205.)

CLASS TIME

Suggested Opening Prayer

Lord, impart to each one of us an understanding of Your instructions for giving. Show us the needs of the world, then give us the desire to help meet those needs.

(Introduction: Be sure
students understand
    objective
    memory work
    reading assignment.)

Introduction

OBJECTIVE: To surrender all our material
wealth to God, and to give
in joy and gratitude.

TO MEMORIZE: Luke 16:13.

TO READ: 2 Corinthians 9;
Matthew 6:19-34; 25:14-30;
Luke 12:15-21.

Discussion Starter

(Ask each individual to think for a moment and estimate how much of his material wealth is given over to God for His use. Show the results of poor stewardship according to Luke 6:38. Ask:) How much do you think this has to do with a person's lack of power and victory and the provision of needs in his life?

Lesson Development

Bible Study

A. *Money — the old standard*

1. What did God command those under the law of Moses to do (Malachi 3:8-10)? *To bring the whole tithe into the storehouse.*

2. What would you say the "storehouse" is (Deuteronomy 16:11 and 12:5, 6)? *"The place where the Lord your God chooses to establish His name."*

3. How much is a tithe (Hebrews 7:2)? *A tenth part.*

In the Old Testament the tenth of all produce, flocks and cattle was declared to be sacred to Jehovah. These tithes were a symbol of the people's recognition and acknowledgment that the whole land belonged to God.

"And he blessed him and said, 'Blessed be Abram of God Most High, possessor of heaven and earth: And blessed by God Most High, who has delivered your enemies into your hand.' And he gave him a tenth of all" (Genesis 14:19-20).

B. Money — the new standard

1. As believers in Christ, we are under grace, rather than law. Whereas the law in itself did not provide eternal life for those who attempted to keep it (Galatians 2:16; 3:21, 22), we have received life by the favor of God — though we do not deserve it and could not possibly earn it. Therefore, do we have a *higher* or *lower* motivation and standard for stewardship of our possessions, than those under the law? _A higher motivation._

2. How did Jesus regard a person's responsibility in that area (Matthew 23:23)? _It should be done._

3. Read 2 Corinthians 8, 9.

In this passage, Paul attempts to encourage the Corinthian church to give financially to help needy Christians. He first points them to the example of the Macedonian church. What did the Macedonians do before they gave their money to God (2 Corinthians 8:5)? _____

Gave themselves to the Lord "and to us."

"With eyes wide open to the mercies of God, I beg you, my brothers, as an act of intelligent worship, to give Him your bodies, as a living sacrifice, consecrated to Him and acceptable by Him. Don't let the world around you squeeze you into its own mold, but let God remold your minds from within, so that you may prove in practice that the plan of God for you is good, meets all His demands, and moves towards the goal of true maturity" (Romans 12:1-2 — Phillips N.T.).

In light of this, what do you think God is interested in? _____

Nevertheless, why is giving of money an important part of our Christian life (2 Corinthians 8:7)? _____

It is a gracious work.

Giving is one of the greatest privileges that we as believers in Christ enjoy. Think of it, God has need of nothing, yet we have the privilege of giving *things* to the God of the universe. How can we resist giving in gladness?

At the most we enjoy the privilege for only 75 years. Compare this with the immeasurable treasure that we will inherit with Christ in heaven. "The Spirit himself bears witness with our spirit that we are the children of God: and if children, heirs of God and fellow heirs with Christ" (Romans 8:16-17). For all of eternity we will enjoy riches that we do not deserve to enjoy, that were given to us, that were paid for by the death of the very Son of the everlasting God. In heaven we will not have this priceless privilege of giving.

Who is the great example of giving (2 Corinthians 8:9)? _The Lord Jesus Christ._

In what sense does the one who "sows" (gives) sparingly reap sparingly (2 Corinthians 9:6)? _____

What kind of giver does God love (2 Corinthians 9:7)? _Cheerful._

C. *Other possessions*
1. To whom do you and your possessions belong (1 Corinthians 6:19, 20)? _The Holy Spirit of God._
2. What should be your motive in the use of whatever you possess (1 Corinthians 10:31)? _To glorify God._

Conclusion and Application

According to Revelation 4:10-11 everything was created for the Lord's pleasure. This includes our material possessions.

Life Application
1. Consider your income and possessions. What should you keep for yourself as God's steward? _____
_____

2. List some Christian groups or churches which are working to fulfill the Great Commission, in which you would like to invest financially. _____
_____

3. Ask yourself, "Is my heart attitude one of joy and gratefulness as I give?" _____
_____

Suggested Closing Prayer

Father, thank You for giving us such clear instructions as to how our material possessions and money are to be used. We pray You will give us a continual desire to be found faithful in the stewardship of our goods and income. Keep before us a vision of the needs of the world and how we can help.

ADDITIONAL BACKGROUND MATERIAL

Some parallel passages regarding stewardship of our possessions:

1 Timothy 6:6-11; Hebrews 13:5 — Be content with what you have. Don't seek to be rich.

Matthew 6:19-21 — Don't lay up treasures on earth (big bank account), but have treasures in heaven. Earthly treasures are temporal; heavenly treasures are eternal.

Mark 10:23-25 — Jesus gives a warning to the rich.

Luke 6:38; 2 Corinthians 9:6, Proverbs 11:24-25; Matthew 7:7-11 — God promises to meet the needs of the giver.

LESSON SEVEN

STEWARDSHIP ACCOUNTING
TO OUR MASTER

Teacher's Objective: To motivate students to be faithful stewards by showing them that Christ will hold them accountable for what He has given them and commanded them to do.

Teacher's Enrichment: (This material may be shared with group members as time permits.)

CHRISTIANS WILL RECEIVE REWARDS

A crown of righteousness, granted for loving the appearing of Christ — 2 Timothy 4:8.

A crown of rejoicing, granted for souls won to Christ — 1 Thessalonians 2:19.

A crown of life, granted for loving Christ and enduring temptation — James 1:12.

A crown of glory, granted for being an example to the flock of God — 1 Peter 5:4.

CLASS TIME

Suggested Opening Prayer

Our Father, thank You for meeting with us today and for being our teacher. Help us understand how important it is to be able to give a good account at the judgment seat of Christ and show us just what that involves.

(Introduction: Be sure students understand
    objective
    memory work
    reading assignment.)

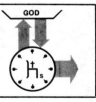

Introduction

OBJECTIVE: To recognize our ultimate accountability to God.

TO MEMORIZE: 2 Corinthians 5:10.

TO READ: Luke 19:12-27;
         Matthew 24 and 25.

Discussion Starter

Imagine that Jesus Christ were to return to earth and walk into this room and ask you: "How have you used the time, treasure and talents I have given you?" How would you feel? How would you answer?

Lesson Development

Romans 14:12 says, "So then each one of us shall give account of himself to God."

Bible Study

A. *The Christian at Christ's coming*

  1. According to 2 Corinthians 5:10, what will Christ do when He comes again? _____
     He will judge each Christian
     and recompense him for the deeds done in
     the body.

---

  2. Notice that Paul says "we all." Who is this primarily for? _____
     Christians.

     Note: A believer's sins have already been judged in Christ (Romans 8:1). The judgment here is of his works since he became a believer.

  3. Read 1 Corinthians 3:11-15.

     God's judgment of our works is compared to the reaction of certain materials to fire. According to this passage, what is God most interested in regarding the works we do for Him (verse 13)? *The quality of the work.*

     How is it then possible for us to spend long hours working for God, but have no reward whatsoever? _____
     _____

We are warned in 1 John 2:28, "And now, little children, abide in Him, so that when He appears, we may have confidence and not shrink away from Him in shame at His coming."

B. *The time of Christ's coming*

  1. The judgment of the Christian will take place when Christ comes again. When will that be (Acts 1:6, 7)? _____
     It is not for us to know--only God knows.

  2. Upon what should we concentrate until He comes (Acts 1:8)? *Being His witnesses.*
     _____

  3. Why has Christ waited so long already before coming (2 Peter 3:9)? *He does not wish for any to*
     perish, but for all to come to repentance.

C. *The earth at Christ's coming*

  Read Mark 13, which foretells the world conditions as Christ's coming approaches. As we see the world today becoming more like this, we know His coming is drawing nearer.

  1. What will we see happening in religion (verses 5, 6)?
     Many people will come claiming to be Christ
     and will mislead many others.

  2. What will the world situation be (verses 7, 8)? *Wars,*
     rumors of wars, nations against nations.

When Christ comes, we, His stewards, should be:

watching — Matthew 24:42;

ready — Matthew 24:44.

Matthew 25:14-29 — the parable of the servants (also 1 Corinthians 4:2):

The first servant is given five talents, the second

3. What will occur in nature (verse 8)? _____
   _____ Earthquakes and famines.

4. What will the attitude be toward true believers (verses 12, 13)? _They will be hated because of Him._

5. Describe in your own words what you think Christ's coming will be like (verses 26, 27). _____
   _____
   _____

servant is given two talents, and the third servant is given one talent. The first two servants double the number of talents they have and when their master returns he praises them and calls them good and faithful servants. The third servant hid his one talent, and his master, upon returning, calls him wicked and slothful.

Conclusion and Application

Christ will come again, but not as a meek child in a manger. He shall come in all His glory (Revelation 19-20). Light dispels darkness and reveals what had been hidden by it. In the same way, the radiance of the risen Christ will reveal the sinfulness of man and will expose to us what kind of life we have been living. He came the first time to die. This time He comes to judge. We do not know when He will come but we are admonished to watch.

James likens life to "a vapor." Life is too short to be wasted; in fact, the most precious possession we have is time. God wants our lives available to Him, that he might use us to do His will. It has been said that in times of peril such as just before an accident, a person sees his life pass before him. The urgency of the hour demands Christian discipleship. We know not when Christ will come; so we must live every day as if it were our last. We want to be able to say with the writer of Revelation, "Amen. Come, Lord Jesus."

Life Application

1. What are you as a believer to do as His coming draws near (verse 33)? _____ _Keep on the alert._
   _____

2. How will obedience to that instruction affect:
   Your employment? _____
   Your social life? _____
   Your worship? _____

Dr. J. Sidlow Baxter gave this illustration of the second coming of Christ: A Scotchman and his two sons were returning from a fishing trip. The younger son said: "I can see her now, my precious wife, waiting at home for me — oh yes, she is indeed a faithful one." The elder son said; "My wife will not only be waiting, but she will be perched on the window sill watching for me to come home. That is what I call faithfulness." The father Scotchman said, "Sons, I can show you where your mother, bless her dear heart, excels them both. She will not only be waiting and watching for me to come home, but she will be fixing my dinner as well!"

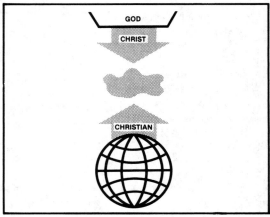

Suggested Closing Prayer

Lord Jesus, help us to invest and spend our lives wisely so we will not be ashamed to give an account to You when You come again to claim us for Your own.

ADDITIONAL BACKGROUND MATERIAL

HIS PLAN FOR ME

"When I stand at the judgment seat of Christ,
    And He shows me His plan for me,
The plan of my life as it might have been
    Had he had His way, and I see how
I blocked Him here and checked Him there,
    And I would not yield my will,
Will there be grief in my Saviour's eyes,
    Grief though He loves me still?
He would have me rich, but I stand there poor
    Stripped of all but His grace,
While memory runs like a hunted thing,
    Down the paths I cannot retrace.
Then my desolate heart will well-nigh
    Break with the tears I cannot shed.
I shall cover my face with my empty hands,
    And bow my uncrowned head.
Lord, of the years that are left to me,
    I give them to Thy hand.
Take me and break me, mold me,
    To the pattern Thou hast planned."

                    — Author Unknown.

Additional Scriptures which encourage Christians to be faithful in God's service:

1 Corinthians 15:58: Therefore, my beloved brethren, be steadfast, immovable, always abounding in the work of the Lord, knowing that your toil is not *in* vain in the Lord.

2 Timothy 4:5: But you, be sober in all things, endure hardship, do the work of an evangelist, fulfill your ministry.

Other verses which also can be used include: 2 Timothy 2:2-4; 2:15; 4:2; 1 Corinthians 4:1,2.

LESSON EIGHT

RECAP

Teacher's Objective: To be sure students have a good understanding of the concept of stewardship and of what good stewardship toward God means personally to them.

Teacher's Enrichment: (May be shared with students as time allows.)

ATTRIBUTES OF OUR MASTER

Omnipotent — All power and authority belong to Him. No individual, nation or combination of forces, terrestrial or celestial, can thwart His sovereign purposes.

Psalm 33:6-10: By the word of the LORD the heavens were made,
And by the breath of His mouth all their host.
He gathers the waters of the sea together as a heap;
He lays up the deeps in storehouses.
Let all the earth fear the LORD;
Let all the inhabitants of the world stand in awe of Him.
For He spoke, and it was done;
He commanded, and it stood fast.
The LORD nullifies the counsel of the nations;
He frustrates the plans of the peoples.

Matthew 28:18: And Jesus came up and spoke to them, saying, "All authority has been given to Me in heaven and on earth."

Omnipresent — He is present everywhere; not just a part of Him, but all of Him.

Jeremiah 23:34: "Can a man hide himself in hiding places,
So I do not see him?" declares the LORD.
"Do I not fill the heavens and the earth?" declares the LORD.

Matthew 28:20: "And lo, I am with you always, even to the end of the age."

Omniscient — He knows the past, present and future. His knowledge comprehends not only all things, but also all possibilities. We suffer when we deny His knowledge and do not lean upon Him for guidance.

Isaiah 46:9, 10: "Remember the former things long past,
For I am God, and there is no other;
I am God, and there is no one like Me,
Declaring the end from the beginning
And from ancient times things which have not been done,
Saying, 'My purpose will be established,
And I will accomplish all My good pleasure.' "

Luke 5:22: "But Jesus, aware of their reasonings . . ."

Immutable — He never changes, develops or grows.

> "Change and decay in all around I see;
> Oh, Thou who changest not, abide with me."

Numbers 23:19: "God is not a man, that He should lie,
> Nor a son of man, that He should repent;
> Has He said, and will He not do it?
> Or has He spoken, and will He not make it good?"

Hebrews 13:8: Jesus Christ is the same yesterday and today, *yes* and forever.

Eternal — There never was a time when He was not; there never will be a time when He will cease to be. He is the everlasting God.

Psalm 90:2,4:   Before the mountains were born,
> Or Thou didst give birth to the earth and the world,
> Even from everlasting to everlasting, Thou art God.
> For a thousand years in Thy sight
> Are like yesterday when it passes by,
> Or as a watch in the night.

Hebrews 13:8: Jesus Christ is the same yesterday and today, *yes* and forever.

Holy — He is separate from that which is morally evil or sinful. At the contemplation of God's holiness one is prone, not to analyze, but to worship!

Psalm 99:9:   Exalt the LORD our God,
> And worship at His holy hill;
> For holy is the LORD our God.

Isaiah 6:3:   "Holy, Holy, Holy, is the LORD of hosts,
> The whole earth is full of His glory."

Just — He is impartial in all His dealings, equitable in all His works.

Deuteronomy 32:4:   "The Rock! His work is perfect,
> For all His ways are just;
> A God of faithfulness and without injustice,
> Righteous and upright is He."

Revelation 15:3:   "Great and marvelous are Thy works,
> O Lord God, the Almighty;
> Righteous and true are Thy ways,
> Thou King of the nations."

Loving — His holiness and justice caused Him to mete out the penalty of death for our sins. But His love caused Him to send His Son to bear the penalty for sin. At the cross God's holiness and love were beautifully merged and revealed.

Psalm 85:10:   Lovingkindness and truth have met together;
> Righteousness and peace have kissed each other.

1 John 4:10:   In this is love, not that we loved God, but that He loved us and sent His Son to be the propitiation for our sins.

CLASS TIME

Suggested Opening Prayer

Our Father, as we review these seven lessons on stewardship, we pray You will clarify anything which we have been unsure of and refresh our minds with the importance of being good stewards.

(Introduction: There is no new student's objective for this lesson, but the objectives for the previous lessons can be looked at again. The previous memory work is to be reviewed and some of the earlier reading assignments are repeated. Any other reading assignments that were missed can be made up now.)

> Review all verses memorized.
> Reread Romans 12; 1 Corinthians 12; James 3:1, 2.

Discussion Starter

(The first question in the students' books may be used to start the discussion of this lesson.)

> Define "Christian steward" in your own words. _____
> _____

Lesson Development

(Any Teacher's Enrichment or Additional Background Material that you were not able to use in the previous lessons of this Step could be utilized at this time and any point which you might feel was not sufficiently covered, or which the students do not understand completely, can be dealt with now too.

Going over the Recap material will benefit both the students and you by making these truths a more active part of your subconscious, habitual way of life.)

> Why are we referred to as Christian stewards? _____
> _____
>
> Summarize your responsibilities as a steward of God as you now understand them. _____
> _____
> _____
> _____
>
> List several things over which you exercise that stewardship.
> _____
> _____
> _____
>
> What is the most important thing for you to realize about your attitude toward stewardship? _____
> _____

In what particular area of your life have you seen a change for the better in your Christian stewardship? _____

_____

_____

Conclusion and Application

We have seen again that God is sovereign owner of everything, and that His standards of stewardship as expressed by Christ and by the Holy Spirit are nothing short of perfection. We have looked at how we can become good stewards of our time, of our bodies, of our gifts and of our possessions, and we have realized that we are and will be accountable to God for the exercise of our stewardship responsibilities. It remains now only for us to decide to allow God to rule in our hearts and through the power of the Holy Spirit to produce the growth toward maturity that he desires in us.

Suggested Closing Prayer

Our heavenly Father, we thank You for your Word which gives us perfect instruction as to how we can grow in our spiritual maturity. We also thank You for the indwelling Holy Spirit and the power available to us, and we pray that You will take over our lives completely. Make us good stewards of that which You have entrusted to us.

(Special note to teacher: Encourage students also to read and become familiar with the Paul V. Brown letter which appears on pages 298 through 306 in the *Handbook*. It is a study on how to know the will of God for your life.)

SUMMARY LESSON PLAN
THE CHRISTIAN AND STEWARDSHIP

Teacher's Objective: To show students that God, by right of creation, owns everything, even our very lives, and that we are responsible to Him — we are accountable — for right and proper use of our time, talents, abilities, gifts, even our bodies; to encourage students' absolute surrender of all they have and all they are to God.

Teacher's Enrichment: (See Teacher's Enrichment sections in each of the preceding lessons of this Step, and share with the class as time allows.)

CLASS TIME

Suggested Opening Prayer

Lord, teach us to realize that You are the supreme owner of the universe and that You rightfully own each one of us. Help us to understand what it means for us to be good stewards of what *You* own. Show us how we may be better examples of good stewardship in every area of our lives.

(Introduction:

STUDENT'S OBJECTIVE: To understand God's ownership of everything; to desire to be wise stewards of all God has made student to be; to recognize personal responsibility to God and to surrender everything he has and everything he is to God.

TO MEMORIZE: 1 Peter 4:10; 2 Corinthians 5:10.

READING ASSIGNMENT: Matthew 24, 25; Romans 12; Ephesians 5.)

Discussion Starter

The steward is not the owner. He does not possess the estate he manages. It is derived property, the ownership of which is vested in another. The true owner has the right to demand an accounting from the one to whom his possession has been entrusted. What examples can you give of present-day stewardship?

Lesson Development

A. The ownership of God our Father *(from Lesson 1)*.

   1. Why does God have the original right of ownership of man? (He created man.)

   2. What did man do to bring about separation between himself and God (Genesis 3:1-8)? (Disobeyed God's command not to eat of the tree of the knowledge of good and evil.)

   3. How did God bring us back and reconcile us to Himself (Romans 5:8-10)? (While we were still sinners, Christ died for us.)

   4. What is His right of ownership now (1 Corinthians 6:19,20)? (We are not our own; we belong to God because He has bought us.)

   5. In the light of that purchase what is our responsibility to God now (Romans 12:1,2)? (Present our bodies, be transformed in our minds.)

B. Examples of perfect stewardship *(from Lesson 2)*.

   1. How did Christ portray perfect stewardship according to:
Philippians 2:5-8? (Did not grasp at equality with God, emptied Himself, took form of bond-servant, made in likeness of men, humbled Himself, was obedient even to death on the cross.)
John 5:38? (Came to do the will of God.)
John 12:27,28? (Came to glorify the Father's name.)

   2. How does the Holy Spirit portray perfect stewardship according to:
John 16:8-11? (Convicts the world of sin, righteousness and judgment.)
John 16:14? (Glorifies Christ.)
Romans 5:15? (Pours out the love of God within our hearts.)
Romans 8:14? (Leads the sons of God.)
Romans 8:16? (Bears witness with our spirits that we are children of God.)
Romans 8:26? (Helps our weakness; intercedes for us in prayer.)

C. Stewardship of our time *(from Lesson 3)*.

   1. What would be the right attitude about time and how can we develop that attitude?
     a. We must use it wisely — Psalm 90:12.
     b. We must make the most of it because the days are evil — Ephesians 5:16.
     c. We don't know about tomorrow — James 4:14.
     d. We don't know when Christ will return — Mark 13:4, 33.

   2. How can a right relationship with God help us be better stewards of our time?
     a. We will understand His will, especially as to being filled with His Holy Spirit — Ephesians 5:17,18.
     b. We will be empowered for witnessing — Acts 1:8.
     c. We will be living a useful and joyous abundant life — John 10:10.

   3. What is the most important use to which we can put our time?
     a. Preaching the gospel to all creation — Mark 16:15.

b. Be involved in the wisdom of soul-winning — Proverbs 11:30.

c. Reflect in our lives Christ's opinion of the value of a soul — Mark 8:36.
"And from everyone who has been given much shall much be required; and to whom they entrusted much, of him they will ask all the more" (Luke 12:48b).

(This chart appears on page 283 of the *Handbook*. Discuss its use and its value with the students.)

The following chart can be of great value in the stewardship of your time. Fill in the hours spent on: class, sleep, Christian service, business, recreation, etc. Place the total hours per week used in each activity at the bottom of the chart. By listing the totals you can discover if you have achieved the balanced use of time required of a good steward.

	MON.	TUES.	WED.	THURS.	FRI.	SAT.	SUN.
6:00							
7:00							
8:00							
9:00							
10:00							
11:00							
12:00							
1:00							
2:00							
3:00							
4:00							
5:00							
6:00							
7:00							
8:00							
9:00							
10:00							
11:00							
12:00							

Stewardship of Time
1. Study and class_____   4. Rest_____   7. Commuting_____
2. Devotional life_____   5. Recreation   8. Employment_____
3. Christian service_____   and social life_____   9. Laundry and clean-up_____
                              6. Activities and athletics_____   10. Miscellaneous_____

D. Stewardship of our bodies *(from Lesson 4)*.

1. What part of Himself did Christ offer to make our conversion possible: (His body.)

2. What do you learn about the body of the Christian from Romans 8:8,9 and Romans 12:1? (It is the only thing we can present to Christ for service.)

3. Why must we be good stewards of these individual parts of our bodies:
The tongue (James 3:2-6)? (Though small, it controls the entire body, and the course of a person's life.)
The heart (Jeremiah 17:9)? (It is deceitful and sick.)
The mind (1 Peter 1:13)? (It is to be girded for action, prepared for vigorous thinking.)

4. How important to God — and to us — is good stewardship of sexual expression according to:
Matthew 5:28? (Sexual lust is equal to actual adultery.)
1 Corinthians 6:9-11? (Misusers and abusers of sex shall not inherit the kingdom of God.)
1 Corinthians 6:15-18? (The person who is involved in the misuse of sex is

sinning against his own body which is the temple of the Holy Spirit.)

Whatever the standard of the non-Christian may be, the standard for the Christian is clear: his body is a sacred trust from God; its functions are meant to be restricted to and preserved for the ends designed by God.

Application of the following verses can enable us to overcome sexual lust: Philippians 4:8; Psalm 119:11; 1 Corinthians 10:13; Romans 6:14; 2 Timothy 2:22; 1 Corinthians 6:18a; Romans 13:14b; 1 Thessalonians 5:22; Romans 14:8; Colossians 3:23.

E. Stewardship of our gifts *(from Lesson 5)*.

  1. Natural gifts.

    a. Where do our natural talents and abilities come from (James 1:17)?

    b. What should be our attitude about them (1 Corinthians 4:6,7)?

    c. How can we be good stewards of our natural gifts (Colossians 3:17)?

  2. Spiritual gifts. (Major Scripture passages on spiritual gifts are: Romans 12:3-8; 1 Corinthians 12:1-31; Ephesians 4:4-16; 1 Peter 4:10,11.)

    a. Each of us has been given at least one spiritual gift from the Holy Spirit according to 1 Corinthians 12:7, but there is a great variety of them and some seem to be given in a fuller measure than others. What spiritual gift do you think you might have?

    b. What are some results God expects from our use of the spiritual gifts He has given us (1 Corinthians 4:12-16)?

    c. Some spiritual gifts are *instantaneous,* such as the gift of tongues at Pentecost, but most are *developmental,* such as teaching or preaching ability. There are three elements necessary for the developmental gifts to come to fruition. They are: (1) the empowering of the Holy Spirit, (2) dedicated work on our part, and (3) time. (See Philippians 2:13.) How can we be good stewards of our spiritual gifts?

  3. What are the most important things to realize about natural or spiritual gifts? (They are both given by God, they are to be developed for His use, and we must not be proud because of them.)

F. Stewardship of our possessions *(from Lesson 6)*.

  1. What was the Old Testament standard regarding money (Malachi 3:8-10)? (The people were to bring the whole tithe, which is a tenth, into the storehouse.)

  2. What was Jesus' attitude about giving the tithe (Matthew 23:23)? (He said it should not be neglected.)

  3. What would you say is the New Testament standard regarding money (2 Corinthians 8:1-5)? Put it in your own words.

  4. What should be our attitude about giving (2 Corinthians 9:6, 7)?

G. Stewardship accounting to our Master

    1. According to 2 Corinthians 5:10, what will Christ do when He comes again? (He will judge each Christian and recompense him for the deeds done in the body. See also 1 John 2:28.)

    2. When will the time of Christ's coming again be (Acts 1:6,7)? (It is not for us to know — only God knows.)

    3. What are we to do until Christ returns (Matthew 24:42,44; 28:19-20)? (Be watching, be ready, and be active in the work of fulfilling the Great Commission.)

Conclusion and Application

Isaiah 64:8: But now, O Lord, Thou art our Father; we are the clay, and Thou our potter; and all of us are the work of Thy hand.

Isaiah 45:9: Woe to the one who quarrels with his maker! . . . Will the clay say to the potter, "What are you doing?"

God is the sovereign owner of everything and everyone. His attributes are wonderful, beyond all comprehension. All He desires of His stewards is that they be yielded and faithful to Him. In consideration of who He is, we should certainly allow Him to reign in our lives.

Suggested Closing Prayer

Lord Jesus, help us to invest and spend our lives wisely so we will not be ashamed to give an account to You when You come again to claim us for Your own.

Old Testament Highlights

INTRODUCTION

The Bible is the record of God's revelation of Himself to man. This record was written by men chosen by God, and inspired by His Spirit so that the record is free from error and free from human reasonings (2 Peter 1:21). The Old Testament is the account of man's creation, his fall because of sin, and the preparation of the world for the coming of Jesus Christ, God's Son, to redeem man from his fallen state.

This preparation of the world was accomplished through the nation Israel. In this study we shall survey the record of these happenings; we shall look at the lives of some of the men God used to live, speak and write this record; and we shall look at the truths revealed in both.

Keep in mind that we are going to cover a period of time that has been estimated to be from 4,000 to 400,000,000 years long. Naturally we shall have to be selective, but in a few incidents we look at, we shall see what God did to prepare the way for Jesus Christ.

HISTORICAL SKETCH

Date	History in the Bible		Contemporaneous History
?	ADAM	The drama begins	
2,000 B.C.	ABRAHAM	The spiritual race begun	The Bronze Age – the Egyptian and Babylonian civilizations had existed for centuries before Abraham
1,400 B.C.	MOSES	Birth of the Hebrew nation	
			The Iron Age begins
1,000 B.C.	DAVID	Height of Hebrew power	
			Rise of Assyrian power
850 B.C.	ELIJAH	The nation in division; two kingdoms	
590 B.C.	JEREMIAH	The nation in demolition: the Babylonian captivity	Beginning of Greek classical culture

450 B.C. EZRA	The Jewish puppet state established	Rise of Persia
		Era of Plato
	— under Persians	
400-year break between the Old and the New Testaments	— under Greeks	
		Alexander's conquests
	— under Romans	
		Pompey's and Caesar's campaigns

LESSON ONE

THE DRAMA BEGINS

Teacher's Objective: To teach students the relevance of Genesis to today's living.

Teacher's Enrichment: (This material can be shared with students as time permits.)

These doctrines are found in Genesis, chapters 1-3:

Creation by God 1:1

Sin....................................... 3:6-7

Salvation by Christ 3:15

Satan .... 3:1; Revelation 12:9; 20:2

Sin nature .... 2:17; Romans 5:12

Death, suffering and toil................. 3:16-19

Satanic persecution of God's people 3:15

Virgin birth............................. 3:15

Subordination of wife to husband 3:16

Marriage and its sanctity are presented in Genesis 2:18, 21-25, wherein man received "a helper fit for him" (Genesis 2:20 RSV). As one scholar noted, "Let us notice that God did not take the woman from man's *feet,* to be trampled upon and enslaved; nor from his *head* that she should dominate him; but from his *side* to be his companion; from beneath his *arm* to receive his protection; and from near his *heart* to have his love and affection" (Johnson, S.L., Jr., "Bibliotheca Sacra," V. 121, #482, Apr.-June, 1964, p. 110).

CLASS TIME

Suggested Opening Prayer

Father, we pray that our lives will be changed as the result of seeing how You do things. Open our hearts to let You begin a new work in them today.

(Introduction: Be sure
students understand
    objective
    memory work*
    reading assignment.)

(*Review verse by having
several in the group
quote it.)

Introduction

OBJECTIVE: To recognize how
        the book of
        Genesis relates
        to us today.

IN THE BEGINNING
GENESIS 1,2,3

TO MEMORIZE: Romans 5:12.

TO READ: Genesis 1, 2, and 3.

The Old Testament is an
account of a Nation.
The New Testament is an account of a Man.
The Nation was founded and nurtured of God to bring the Man
into the world.

Discussion Starter

Of the 39 books of the Old Testament, Genesis is perhaps one of the most important. It answers one of the greatest mysteries of all time, the mystery of how things came into existence. This book deals with the origins of the world, man, woman, sin, marriage (and its sanctity) and the nations. How else is Genesis significant to us today? This book is important because it tells us of God's acts of redemption in our behalf.

Lesson Development

The opening sentence of
Genesis, "In the beginning
God . . ." places God-the-
creator at the center of the

Bible Study

A. *Origin of man*

  1. How did our world come into existence? _____
             It was created by God.

  2. What was the condition of the world and everything that
    was in it at this time (Genesis 1:10b, 12b, 18b, 21b,
    and 25b)? _____ *Good.*

---

stage. One scholar notes that this is a doctrine of the creator, more than a doctrine of creation. As one reads the next three chapters, he then realized that man is at the climax of creation. Throughout the Bible, God and man are great Bible themes.

---

  3. How did man come into existence (Genesis 1:27)? _____
             God created him.

  4. Was man an intelligent being at this time (2:20)? *Yes.*
    How do you know? *He gave all the animals and*
    birds names that they still retain.

  5. How was woman brought into existence (2:21, 22)?
    She was fashioned from a rib taken from
                  the man.

According to Genesis
1:26, God made man in His
own image. What is the
image of God? The image
of God is:

(1) What each man now possesses which makes him different from any other

created being (Genesis 9:6, 1 Corinthians 11:7, James 3:9).

(2) "Original" righteousness, or a true knowledge, righteousness and holiness (Genesis 1:31, Ecclesiastes 7:29). This was *lost* through sin and is restored in Christ by means of progressive sanctification, i.e., true knowledge (Colossians 3:10), righteousness and holiness (Ephesians 4:24).

The qualities which make man different from any created being are the natural capacities of morality, rationality, spirituality, immortality and dominion over lower creation. When we speak of spirituality we mean that life principle breathed into him by God in Genesis 2:7, a "living soul" which exists apart from the body.

For the redeemed, the soul will, in the future, have a perfect spiritual body (Philippians 3:21, 1 John 3:2) which will be governed by the Holy Spirit and will become a perfect instrument for the soul's expression. The reference to immortality applies to the soul. Originally the body was immortal, but this immortality was lost through sin (Romans 5:12, 6:23; 1 Corinthians 15:20-21). The Christian looks forward to receiving an immortal body fashioned in the image of Christ.

> **B. Origin of sin**
>
> 1. What was man's commission from God (1:28-30)? _____
>   *To be fruitful, subdue the earth, rule over living things.*
>   What was man's relationship with God at this time (1:28a)?   *He was blessed of God.*
>
> 2. How would you describe Satan's personality characteristics when he appeared as a serpent and confronted Eve?   *Sly, crafty, deceitful.*

Genesis 3:1 introduces Satan indwelling a serpent for his attack upon creation. The book of Revelation pictures his punishment and, interestingly enough, uses the name serpent:

"And the great dragon was thrown down, the serpent of old, who is called the devil and Satan, who deceives the whole world; he was thrown down to the earth, and his angels were thrown down with him" (Revelation 12:9).

(For more information on the work of Satan, see Additional Background Material at the end of this lesson.)

> How has he used these same personality characteristics in confronting you? _____
>
> 3. Whose word did Satan question (3:1)? *(God's)*
>   Did Eve answer truthfully (3:2, 3 — look particularly at the last phrase of verse 3, then at 2:17)? *(No, she added to.)*
>   To what did Satan appeal in speaking to Eve (3:5)? *(Her intellectual pride--thirst for knowledge.)*
>
> 4. In the light of 1 John 2:16, analyze the temptation and give the three parts of it (3:6). *(Lust of the flesh, lust of the eyes, boastful pride of life.)*

We learn here how sin came into the world and what it is. Sin is the greatest single problem of mankind. In Christ alone the Christian can face it with a realistic solution.

> **5. Why was it wrong for Adam and Eve to eat of this tree (2:17)?** *It would be disobedience to God's command.*

> **C. Sin's result**
>
> **1. What was the result of the sin of the man and the woman (3:7, 8)?** *Eyes were opened; knew nakedness; tried to cover it; hid; fellowship with God broken.*
>
> **2. What was the penalty for sin for (3:14-19):**
>
> **the serpent?** *Crawl on belly; eat dust; enmity with woman and her seed; ultimate defeat.*
>
> **the woman?** *Pain in childbirth; desire to be for husband; subjection to him.*
>
> **the man?** *Ground cursed; he would have to work very hard for food.*
>
> **How was man's relationship to God altered (3:8-10)?** *No longer walking with God; now fearful and ashamed.*
>
> **3. What did God promise regarding Satan's destiny (3:15)? Explain.** *He would be defeated by woman's seed--Christ.*

Man was created to have fellowship with God. We see how the fellowship was broken, and how it can be restored. Christianity has revealed that man is not just a species of protoplasm, but that he is God's special creation.

Conclusion and Application

We have seen from Genesis the great spiritual events which have influenced the world ever since. And we have learned that God is the creator and ruler of all things. This makes us realize our responsibility to Him as creator, and gives us a glimpse of His omnipotent power. Anyone who denies God as creator automatically is faced with an empty, purposeless existence.

> **Life Application**
>
> **1. How does Adam and Eve's sin affect you today (Romans 5:12)?** *All men are under sin.*
>
> Man was created to have fellowship with God, but because of his stubborn self-will, he chose to go his own independent way and fellowship was broken. This is what the Bible calls sin.
>
> The Bible says, "For all have sinned and come short of the glory of God" (Romans 3:23); "for the wages of sin is death, but the gift of God is eternal life through Jesus Christ our Lord" (Romans 6:23).
>
> It is this first act in the drama that sets the stage for all that is to follow. If there had been no sin, there would have been no need for redemption and no need for a Bible to tell us of the need for redemption and the way of redemption.
>
> **2.** Starting with Genesis 3:15, God begins to point to the time when the penalty for sin would be paid on man's behalf by the seed of the woman. In the chart on the next page, notice the prophecies pointing to Christ and their fulfillment in Him.

GOD'S PROMISED MESSIAH

PROMISE	*FULFILLMENT*
1. Born of a Virgin Genesis 3:15, Isaiah 7:14	Matthew 1:18-23
2. From Nation of Israel Genesis 12:3, Numbers 24:17, 19	Matthew 1:1-17
3. Tribe of Judah, Family of David Genesis 49:10, Isaiah 11:1, 10	Luke 1:31-33
4. Born in Bethlehem Micah 5:2	Luke 2:4, 6, 7
5. Time of Coming Daniel 9:24-26	Galatians 4:4
6. Part of Childhood in Egypt Hosea 11:1	Matthew 2:14, 15
7. Suffering and Atonement Isaiah 53:4-6	2 Corinthians 5:21
8. Triumphal Entry Zechariah 9:9	Matthew 21:2, 4, 5
9. Crucifixion Psalm 22	Matthew 27
10. Resurrection Psalm 16:9, 10	Acts 2:31, 32

These are only a few of the more than 300 Old Testament references to the coming of the Messiah that were fulfilled in the life, ministry, death and resurrection of Jesus of Nazareth.

Look up all the references listed above regarding the promises and their fulfillment and read them.

What is the overall picture they present to you? _____

_____

_____

Suggested Closing Prayer

Dear Lord, we thank You today for what You have recorded in Your Word — the account of how our world came to be and the answers to the greatest questions of all time, also for the provision of redemption for man which makes it possible for each one of us to have salvation and a close walk with You. We thank You for that expression of Your love for us.

ADDITIONAL BACKGROUND MATERIAL
THE BOOK OF GENESIS

This world is cursed and at odds with itself (Romans 8:19-25) and we are a considerable portion of its problem.

In Genesis, the "Fall" is followed by the promise of a Redeemer (3:15). Furthermore, we see God choosing a people (12:1-3) and guiding them to a land where He could give them a spiritual education and a Messiah, even the Son of God. Later portions of the Old Testament announce that the Messiah would come from the tribe of Judah and even specify a certain family of that tribe, that of David, their great king (Micah 5:2, 2 Samuel 7:16, Matthew 1:1).

An outline of Genesis is as follows:

A. Primeval history, chapters 1-11.
   1. The Creation-Hymn — 1:1 - 2:3.
   2. "The account of the heavens and earth — 2:4 - 4:26.
   3. "The book of the generations of Adam" — 5:1 - 6:8.
   4. "The generations of Noah" — 6:9 - 9:28.
   5. "The generations of the sons of Noah" — 10:1 - 11:9.

B. The history of God's people, chapters 12-50.
   1. "The generations of Shem" — 11:10-26.
   2. "The generations of Terah" (Abraham) — 11:27 - 25:11.
   3. "The generations of Ishmael" — 25:12-18.
   4. "The generations of Isaac" — 25:19 - 35:29.
   5. "The generations of Esau" — 36:1-43.
   6. "The generations of Jacob" — 37:2 - 50:26.

The Work of Satan

Concerning the work of Satan, a helpful statement is concisely made by H. C. Thiessen, formerly head of the faculty of the Graduate School of Wheaton College:

"There are indications of Satan's work in the various names given to him, for each name expresses a quality of character, or a method of operation, or both; e.g., as Satan he opposes, as devil he slanders and accuses, while as tempter he seeks to lure men to commit sin.

"In addition the Scriptures reveal the nature of his work directly. Generally speaking, Satan's object is expressed in Isaiah 14:14: 'I will make myself like the Most High' . . . In order to achieve his avowed purpose he sought to kill the child Jesus (Matthew 2:16, Revelation 12:4) and when that effort failed, to induce Him to worship him (Luke 4:6-7).

"Satan employs various methods for the realization of his purpose. Since he cannot attack God directly, he attacks God's master-creation, man. The Scriptures mention the following methods used by Satan:

(1) lying (John 8:44; 2 Corinthians 11:3);

(2) tempting (Matthew 4:1);

(3) robbing (Matthew 13:19);

(4) harassing (2 Corinthians 12:7; Job 1 and 2);

(5) hindering (Zechariah 3:1; 1 Thessalonians 2:18; Ephesians 6:12);

(6) sifting (Luke 22:31);

(7) imitating (2 Corinthians 11:14-15; Matthew 13:25);

(8) accusing (Revelation 12:9-10);

(9) smiting with disease (Luke 13:16, cf. 1 Corinthians 5:5);

(10) possessing (John 13:27), and

(11) killing and devouring (John 8:44; 1 Peter 5:8).

The believer must not let Satan gain an advantage over him by remaining ignorant of his devices (2 Corinthians 2:11), but should be sober and vigilant and resist him (1 Peter 5:8; Ephesians 4:27; James 4:7). He should not speak lightly of him (2 Peter 2:10; Jude 8-9), but put on the whole armor of God and take his stand against him (Ephesians 6:11)" (Thiessen, H.C., *Lectures in Systematic Theology*, Grand Rapids: Eerdmans, 1956, pp. 210-211).

LESSON TWO

FROM ADAM THROUGH ABRAHAM

Teacher's Objective: To promote obedience to the Word of God by demonstrating successful living as a result of obedience, and failure as a result of disobedience.

Teacher's Enrichment: (This material may be shared with group members as time allows.)

- Spiritual living profits more than carnal living:
    1. God's discipline — Galatians 6:7-8; 1 Corinthians 11:30-32; Hebrews 12:5-13.
    2. God's bounty for spiritual Christians — Romans 8:32.
- Chastisement for disobedience is unavoidable. Famine in Israel was God's discipline for disobedience and sin.

    One of the judgments for sinfulness — Deuteronomy 28:23-25.

    David given a choice by God — 2 Samuel 24:13.

    Recognized by Solomon as a discipline of God — 2 Chronicles 6:26-31.

CLASS TIME

Suggested Opening Prayer

Lord, help us understand today the importance of obedience to You. Reveal to us more clearly our relationship to You and to the Bible so that we will be neither rebellious to nor ignorant of Your Word.

(Introduction: Be sure
students understand
    objective
    memory work
    reading assignment.)

Introduction

OBJECTIVE: To learn from biblical example the importance of obedience in the Christian life.

ADAM— ABRAHAM
GENESIS 4-22

TO MEMORIZE: Romans 4:20, 21.

TO READ: Genesis 4, 6, 7, 12 and 22.

Discussion Starter

(Ask a person in the group to share how God was faithful in fulfilling a promise. Have him mention the exercise of will involved in committing his problem to the Lord. If no one in the group is able to do this, then the leader should.)

Lesson Development

> **Bible Study**
>
> A. *Cain and Abel*
>
> 1. In Genesis 4, two sacrifices are made. Evaluate each and indicate its acceptability to God. *Cain's, a sacrifice of pride, his choice, disobedient, God rejected; Abel's, as God required, obedient, accepted.*

Cain had no sense of sin or need for atonement. Abel's sacrifice involved confession of sin and expression of faith in God's substitute.

> 2. What do you think verse 7 is all about? *A proper sacrifice was available to Cain if he wanted it.*
> 3. Give at least one present-day counterpart to the two types of sacrifices offered by Cain and Abel. _____

Parallel passages on the sacrifice of Cain and Abel:
Cain — 1 John 3:12;
Isaiah 64:6; Ephesians 2:8-10; Titus 3:5.
Abel — Hebrews 9:22; Leviticus 17:11; Hebrews 11:4.

> B. *Noah*
>
> 1. Why was God sorry He had made man on the earth? (See Matthew 24:37-39.) *Because man was disobedient, wicked, and would not understand about God.*
>
> 2. Why was Noah chosen by God to build an ark? *He had found favor in the eyes of the Lord.*
>
> 3. What do you think God accomplished through Noah? (See also Hebrews 11:7.) *Saved Noah's household, condemned the world; taught the necessity of obedience.*

It takes a choice of will to act on a promise. The "flesh" does not desire to launch out. Noah gave evidence of his trust in God when he persisted in preparing the ark while in adverse surroundings. Repercussions of faithless behavior are great, but the blessings of obedience are unending.

Abraham's lack of faith
in the promise resulted in
the birth of Ishmael and
Moslem persecution of Jews,
which continues today.

> **C.** *Abraham*
>
> 1. Abraham holds a unique place in the history of the world. Three religions point to Abraham as the founder of their faiths: Judaism, Islam and Christianity. On the basis of Genesis 12:2, 3; 16:4, 15; and 17:19, do all three have a right to call him the founder or father of their faiths?
>   ___No.___ Explain. _God's covenant was_
>   _to be established with the son of promise--_
>   ~~_the son of Sarah--only._~~

Abraham is the forbear of the Moslem people through Ishmael.

But Abraham is father of the believing Jews, not the unbelieving; the father of the Judaism which pointed to Christ (Romans 2:17-29; Romans 3:4). At Christ's death the veil of the Holy of Holies was rent. True Judaism no longer exists — no temple, no blood sacrifice, no holy of holies, etc.

Read Genesis 17:15-16
and Genesis 22:8. What
discipline of faith had to
transpire in Abraham?

> 2. Why do you suppose God made the request of Abraham recorded in Genesis 22:1, 2? _To test his faith._
> 3. Study Genesis 22:8 thoroughly and give your explanation of it. _An example showing God will provide the_
>   _necessary sacrifice, and we can trust His_
>   _promise._

Isaac was a sacrifice of his father just as Christ was. Turn to Matthew 1:1 and read it aloud. Note that this is an outline of Matthew. In chapters 1-25 Christ is Son of David, the king. In chapters 26-28 he is Son of Abraham, sacrifice of His Father.

Conclusion and Application

One can trust the promises of God because, "God is not a man, that He should lie; neither a son of man, that He should repent; has He said, and will He not do it? Or has He spoken, and will He not make it good?" (Numbers 23:19).

Spiritual problems usually arise from a problem in our relationship to the Bible. Either we do not trust God's promises, or we are ignorant of them; so we worry. We have not made God's Word a part of our lives. When we get out of fellowship with God we do not confess our sin according to 1 John 1:9 and receive cleansing and restoration.

> **Life Application**
> 1. What important lesson has God's response to Cain taught you? _____
> _____
> _____

> 2. Do you think you would have boarded the ark with Noah? _____ Upon what do you base that opinion? _____
> _____
> _____
>
> 3. How have you and your family been blessed in Abraham as promised in Genesis 12:3? _____
> _____
> _____

Suggested Closing Prayer

Dear Father, thank You for teaching us that we can trust Your promises because You are not a man that You should lie — what You have spoken, You will do. Strengthen our trust in Your Word and help us stand firm on it and guide our lives accordingly.

ADDITIONAL BACKGROUND MATERIAL

Famous expressions of trust in God's promises:

1. Moses — Exodus 14:13, "Stand still and see the salvation of the Lord."
2. David — 1 Samuel 17:47, "The battle is the Lord's."

Illustrations of God and Christ in Abraham and Isaac in Genesis 22:

1. Isaac
   a. Philippians 2:5-8, obedient unto death.
   b. Hebrews 11:17-19; James 2:23, illustration of resurrection.
2. Abraham — John 3:16; Romans 8:32, spared not His own Son *for us!*

Successful living demands obedience to the Bible. Many men have said this in so many words.

"If I am asked to name the one comfort in sorrow, the safe rule of conduct, the true guide of life, I must point to what, in the words of a popular hymn, is called 'the old, old story' told in an old Book, God's best and richest gift to mankind" — Gladstone.

"The promises of the Bible have behind them God's knowledge and power" — John Wanamaker.

"If I were to have my way, I would take the torch out of the hand of the Statue of Liberty and in its stead, place an open Bible" — Marshall, Vice-President of the United States.

LESSON THREE

MOSES, THE PASSOVER AND
THE EXODUS (EXIT)

Teacher's Objective: To illustrate for the students what it means to walk by faith, to arouse their desire for that kind of life and to motivate them to rest in the Lord so that he can use them in whatever way he chooses.

CLASS TIME

Suggested Opening Prayer

Father, help us realize today that the Christian life is a life of faith. Give us the faith to live by the promises which You have made to us.

(Introduction: Be sure students understand
    objective
    memory work*
    reading assignment.)

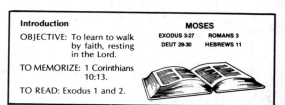

Introduction

MOSES

EXODUS 3-27   ROMANS 3
DEUT 29-30   HEBREWS 11

OBJECTIVE: To learn to walk by faith, resting in the Lord.

TO MEMORIZE: 1 Corinthians 10:13.

TO READ: Exodus 1 and 2.

(*Have several group members explain the verse after others quote it from memory.) (Optional — Use 1 Corinthians 10:11 as additional memory verse. Discuss its meaning and importance in understanding the purpose of the Old Testament.)

Discussion Starter

Susan is ready to start her last year at nursing school. A fine Christian fellow has proposed to her. She loves him and would like to marry him. The problem is that when she was sixteen she felt God called her to foreign missions as a nurse. What should she do?

(Have the class share this material in any of the ways suggested in the Instructions for Teaching on page 21.)

> Jacob, the grandson of Abraham, had taken his family to Egypt to escape a famine. After 400 years, his descendants had multiplied greatly. A new king of Egypt arose, and because he was concerned about their numbers he subjected the Israelites to cruel slavery. Exodus 1 and 2 give an account of this development, of the birth and life of Moses and of the people's cry to God for deliverance. God heard their cry, and sent Moses to lead them out of Egypt.

Lesson Development

> **Bible Study**
>
> A. *Moses, the leader*
>
> 1. Read Hebrews 11:23-29.
>
>   Why do you think God chose Moses to lead His people?
>   _He was a man of faith._

This period of Moses' life illustrates the blessings of trusting God.

The "hall of fame" listed in Hebrews 11 contains men and women made great, not by inherent talent or their own greatness, but by trust in God. No man *ever* counted for God without faith (Hebrews 11:6). Note the change which faith made in Moses' life:

Before faith	*After faith*
Had great opportunities, lost them, Exodus 2:11-15.	Accomplished tremendous feats — performed miracles, led Israel out of Egypt, gave Law, wrote first five books of Bible.
Spent 40 wasted years, Acts 4:23, 30.	Became one of history's greatest men, after he was 80 years old.
Fled as a coward, Exodus 2:15.	Defied the greatest empire of his day.

> 2. Read Exodus 3 and 4.
>
>   When God told Moses what He wanted him to do, how did He say the people would react (Exodus 3:18)? _____
>   _They would pay heed to what Moses said._
>
>   In Exodus 3:17, 20, 21 and 4:12, note the "I will's" of God. Whose work was this going to be? _God's._
>
>   Where did Moses fit in? _He was to gather the elders of Israel together and give them God's message, and Moses was to be the leader._

The simple act of trusting God completely transforms a life. Note what God called Moses to do — defy the greatest ruler of his day, with no backing but the promise of God. God usually calls us to do far greater things than we have ever imagined.

3. **How did Moses respond and how did God handle those responses?** *Afraid people wouldn't believe him,*
Exodus 4:1-9 *God gave him miraculous proofs.*

Verses 10-12 *Pleaded slow speech, tongue. God assured him He would be with his mouth.*

Verses 13-17 *Didn't want to be the one. God gave him Aaron and a special staff.*

Note how well God had things planned — He has all things planned for us, also. He expects us only to fit into His plans.

4. **In 4:1, Moses said of the people, "They will not believe me." When Moses was obedient, how did the people respond (4:31)?** *They believed, and they bowed down and worshipped.*

Moses could have disobeyed God's call, with the result that he would have faded into oblivion. When we accept God's program for our lives, we are the winners.

B. The Passover

Read Exodus 12.

1. **Why was God sending plagues at this time?** _____
To compel Pharaoh to let His people go.

2. **What was the most vital instruction given to the children of Israel?** *To slay a perfect lamb and apply its blood to their doorpost.*

3. **What are the correlations between Christ's death and the Passover as indicated in these Scriptures?**

Exodus 12:3 _____ John 1:29 _____
       A lamb.   *Christ is Lamb of God.*

Exodus 12:5, 6 _____ 1 Peter 2:22 _____
   Without blemish.   *Jesus was sinless.*

Exodus 12:6 _____ 1 Corinthians 5:7 _____
   To be slain.   *Christ sacrificed for us.*

Note how clear this makes the issue of salvation. Salvation is based *solely* on what one does with Christ.

Blood applied to the two doorposts (sides) and to the lintel (top) creates what kind of picture? *A cross.*

4. **What do you suppose happened to those who may have disobeyed the instructions given through Moses?** _____

What spiritual truth do you believe this illustrates? _____

A man is either saved or lost. There is no in-between or second chance for "good" people, any more than there was an in-between for those who, whatever their social

5. **What does Exodus 12:29 teach about God being a respecter of persons?** *He is not. Pharaoh and the captives were equal.*

How does this apply to the condition of any person who has not received Christ? _____

status and personality, refused to apply the blood.

> C. The Exodus ("going out")
>
> 1. One of the most important events in the history of Israel occurred immediately following the Passover. What was it (Exodus 12:40, 41)? *All the hosts of the Lord went out from the land of Egypt.*
>
> 2. Compare Exodus 3:7, 8 and John 3:16. How do you see them relating to each other? *Both show His love, His awareness of need and the provision He made, both contain promises.*
>
> 3. One of the most remarkable and well-known miracles in the world is recorded in Exodus 14. Summarize it here. *Crossing of the Red Sea.*
>
>   What spiritual truth does this experience suggest to you?
>
> 4. While the Israelites were in the wilderness, they had many trials and hardships; several times in the many years of wandering before coming into the land which had been promised to them, they failed God. (See Exodus 17:1-7; 32:1-6, 15-20 and Numbers 21:5-9.) What practical value do these events recorded in the Old Testament have for you today (1 Corinthians 10:5-11)? *They were examples to us, instructions as to desires and actions.*
>
> 5. In summary of the wilderness wanderings mentioned in 1 Corinthians 10:1-15, what is God's promise to you?
>
>   (Write out verse and reference and claim it.) *Verse 13: the promise that no temptation will be too great, and that God's help is always there.*

Conclusion and Application

Israel's mistakes in this instance all were made in spite of the fact that the people recently had witnessed tremendous miracles by God on their behalf and they should have been able to rest in Him. But they committed idolatry (1 Corinthians 10:7) and fornication (8), they tempted Christ (9), and they complained against God (10). For these things God sent judgment upon them. (This is a good place to apply Galatians 5:7,8.)

According to 1 Corinthians 10:12, it is possible for us to fall into the same types of sins despite whatever degree of Christian maturity we may have attained. But when temptations come to us, if we will appropriate God's promise given in verse 13, sin's judgment will be averted, and God will be able to use us. It remains for us only to surrender ourselves and whatever He has put into our hands — whatever abilities and gifts He has placed within us — totally to Him for His use in accomplishing His purpose. When we trust in His pro-

> **Life Application**
>
> 1. God asked Moses a question in Exodus 4:2. What was it? *"What is that in your hand?"*

visions and rest in His
promises He will work
through us.

> 2. God expects us to use what we have. Moses used a rod; David used a sling; Gideon used lanterns, pitchers and trumpets. What is in your hands? _____
>
> _____
>
> 3. How do you think God wants you to use it? _____
>
> _____
>
> _____

Suggested Closing Prayer

We thank You, Father, for the way You provided for Moses and the children of Israel in their flight from captivity in Egypt and for the example that is for us. We appreciate the way our salvation is so graphically portrayed in the Passover and we thank You again for sending Jesus and for giving us eternal life through Him. We surrender our lives and whatever is in our hands — those abilities and gifts You have given us — freely to You and we pray You will use us and work through us.

ADDITIONAL BACKGROUND MATERIAL

Some parallel passages on the passover and the exodus:

Christ our passover — John 1:29; 19:31; 1 Corinthians 5:7; 1 Peter 1:18-20.

Old Testament types (or pictures) of Christ's death:

Brass serpent — Numbers 21:6-9; John 3:14-15.

Abraham offering his son — Genesis 22.

Wilderness wanderings — Deuteronomy 1:2-3; Numbers 14:20-35.

LESSON FOUR

LAW AND GRACE

Teacher's Objective: To help students understand our inability to keep the law and our need for grace, and to motivate them to live under grace instead of trying, even subconsciously, to keep any kind of law.

CLASS TIME

Suggested Opening Prayer

Lord, make clear to us the difference between law and grace that we might know better how to serve You.

(Introduction: Be sure
students understand
    objective
    memory work
    reading assignment.)

> **Introduction**
>
> OBJECTIVE: To understand our inability to keep the law and our need for God's grace.
>
> TO MEMORIZE: Romans 6:23.
>
> TO READ: Galatians 3.

Discussion Starter

(Ask the group:) What is law? What is grace? What is the difference between the two? (Let group members express their answers without giving the answer yourself, and then move into the lesson.)

Lesson Development

> **Bible Study**
>
> A. *The Law*
>
> When "The Law" is mentioned, the thing that most commonly comes to mind is the Decalogue, or the Ten Commandments.
>
> The Ten Commandments are listed in Exodus 20 and are repeated in Deuteronomy 5. They are:
>
>   I.   You shall have no other gods before Me.
>
>   II. You shall not make for yourself an idol, or any likeness . . . You shall not worship them or serve them.
>
>   III. You shall not take the name of the Lord your God in vain.
>
>   IV. Remember the sabbath day, to keep it holy.
>
>   V.   Honor your father and your mother.

VI.   You shall not murder.
VII. You shall not commit adultery.
VIII. You shall not steal.
IX.   You shall not bear false witness against your neighbor.
X.   You shall not covet . . . anything that belongs to your neighbor.

1. Jesus condensed these ten into two in Matthew 22:37-40. What are they? 1. *Love God with heart, soul, mind.* 2. *Love your neighbor as yourself.*

2. What was James' pronouncement concerning the seriousness of breaking even one of these laws (James 2:10)? *If we stumble in one point, we are guilty of all.*

B. What the Law does

Read Deuteronomy 29:29 and 30:11-20.

The law of Moses was a covenant of works. God said, "Thou shalt," and, "Thou shalt not." The laws were definite and the attached penalties were definite if the conditions were not obeyed.

Webster defines law as "a rule of conduct or action prescribed by the supreme governing authority and enforced by a sanction." Law always implies two things, a *standard* and a *penalty*.

These laws were presented as *God's standard of righteousness* for that time. They were literally a yardstick for man. The New Testament reveals that "by the law is the knowledge of sin." Jesus Christ came to "fulfill the law" and now God's standard of righteousness is Christ Himself, a much higher standard.

1. How are God's people to respond to the things of God that He has revealed of Himself (Deuteronomy 29:29; 30:11)? *Observe all the words of the law.*

2. Briefly, what is the summary of all the law (Deuteronomy 30:16, 20)? *Love the Lord your God, walk in His ways, keep His commandments, obey His voice.*

In the New Testament, "law" describes the legal method of approach to God, seeking to be justified before Him by obeying His righteous standards. The law of Moses is the highest and best representative of the legal approach to God. All religions and moral systems which take God into account, approach Him legally *except* true Christianity. Of these legal systems, the law of Moses is the only one ordained of God. All who seek salvation or blessing on the basis of *obedience,* even if it be obedience to the Ten Commandments or Sermon on the Mount, are approaching God by *law.*

3. How did Jesus Christ summarize the will of God for man in Mark 12:29-31? *Love God with heart, soul, mind and strength; love neighbor as self.*

4. On the basis of Matthew 5:17, what do you think was Christ's assessment of the law? *It was to be kept— He came to fulfill it.*

5. Read Romans 3:19-26.
   What does the law reveal (3:19, 20)? *The knowledge of sin.*

6. To what did the law bear witness while failing to reveal it fully (3:21)? *The righteousness of God.*

Grace is an entirely different way of approaching God (Romans 6:14). Law and grace are two different systems ordained for two different purposes, and are never to be mingled. Each is complete in itself. We are under either one system or the other, not both. All Christians, whether they realize it or not, whether they enjoy the privilege or not are under the grace system.

7. How has a full revelation been made to us (3:22-24)?
   (Through faith in Jesus Christ.)

C. *Grace.*

1. You will find a modern translation of this Romans passage (3:19-26) helpful. As you read the following excerpt from Williams' translation, *underline the explanatory paraphrase which replaces the term "the righteousness of God."*

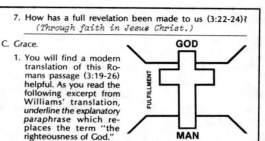

(v. 19) Now we know that everything the law says is spoken to those who are under its authority, that every mouth may be stopped and the whole world be held responsible to God; (v. 20) because no human creature can be brought in right standing with God by observing the law. For all the law can do is to make men conscious of sin.

(v. 21) But now God's way of giving men right standing with Himself has come to light; a way without connection with the law, and yet a way to which the law and the prophets testify.

(v. 22) God's own way of giving men right standing with Himself is through faith in Jesus Christ. It is for everybody who has faith, for no distinction at all is made.

(v. 23) For everybody has sinned and everybody continues to come short of God's glory.

(v. 24) But anybody may have right standing with God as a free gift of His undeserved favor, through the ransom provided in Christ Jesus.

Grace is the kindness and love of God expressed toward us entirely apart from what we deserve (Titus 3:5-6; Romans 4:4-5). Under the law, we earn whatever we get. Under grace, whatever we get is a free gift.

Since grace depends only on our accepting it, and not on what we deserve, it is in no way dependent on how good we are, and can *never* be limited by how bad we are (Romans 5:8). God did the most for us when we deserved the least from Him.

2. Compare Romans 3:20 and Ephesians 2:8, 9 and write your conclusions. _____

Conclusion and Application

There are thousands of Christians today who have all that they have by God's free grace. yet, because of their own weakness, they labor in misery and defeat, plagued with guilt and feelings of condemnation because they live as though still under law. God is to them a very hard, exacting, and scrupulous taskmaster. They spend all their lives trying to make up for sins, trying to earn His love and acceptance, trying to lift themselves toward heaven with their good works. But the one whom Jesus lovingly called Father, forgave freely, gave bountifully and was a

Life Application

1. How would you explain the difference between law and grace to someone who was depending upon his own good works to please the Father? _____

joy to know. He is the God of grace.

2. What is Christ's relationship with:

the law? _____

grace? _____

What is your relationship with:

the law? _____

grace? _____

3. What difference will an understanding of law and grace make in your motivation? _____

Suggested Closing Prayer

Lord, we thank You for all Your grace and power and for being willing to do for us all that these make it possible for You to do.

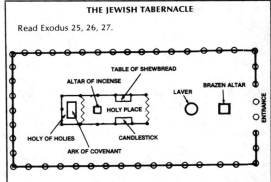

THE JEWISH TABERNACLE

Read Exodus 25, 26, 27.

The Tabernacle and its furnishings have many lessons for us.

The first piece of furniture is the Brazen Altar, which was used for sacrifice and atonement. This teaches us the importance of having a sacrifice for our sins first.

Then came the Laver, which was used for cleansing. This shows our need for a daily cleansing from our sins.

As we proceed into the Holy Place, we observe on our right the Table of Shewbread, which teaches us two truths — Christ is our Bread come down from heaven, and the Bible is the Bread with which man is to feed his soul.

On our left is the Candlestick, which reminds us of Christ — the light of the world.

Straight ahead of us is the Altar of Incense — the reminder of our prayers which are our incense to God.

In front of us now is the veil of the tabernacle that was rent from top to bottom when Christ died. No longer is the believer's way obscured into the Holy of Holies, where God Himself dwells. Here we find the Ark which was the earthly dwelling place of God.

We must remember to keep the proper sequence in our Christian lives if we are to live victoriously for Christ.

ADDITIONAL BACKGROUND MATERIAL

Law and grace — the purpose of each:
The purpose of the law is to condemn and expose sin (1 Timothy 1:8-10). It *never* saves, *never* encourages, *never* comforts, *never* enables. Your bathroom mirror shows you what you look like. If you have dirt on your face, your mirror does not remove it, it only shows you it is there. It reveals your need of cleansing. The law reveals our need of grace.

The purpose of grace is to save, to comfort, to encourage, to enable (Ephesians 2:8-9; Romans 6:1-2). It does not condemn, discourage or judge. The mirror exposes the dirt on my face — the soap and water wash it off. The law shows us our need of cleansing — grace cleanses.

The practical application of being under grace:
Practically the whole New Testament repeats over and over that the Christian is under the grace system, and is delivered from the law system. No truth of the Bible is so clear, yet so misunderstood. These applications follow:

The burden of guilt is now removed from life. All my sins have been forgiven by Christ (1 John 2:2). Although I have not obeyed all of God's laws, I do not labor under a burden of guilt. God has forgiven forever all my sin. Christians who labor under a burden of guilt, who look at God as an awful judge, who feel perplexed because they never seem to please Him, have put themselves under law. But Romans 8:1 tells us there is no condemnation to the Christian.

The burden of a false motive for living the Christian life is now removed. I do not live the Christian life to earn God's approval. He sees only my life in Christ. he looks on Christ instead of me. Nothing I ever have done or ever will do has the slightest effect on whether I will go to heaven. Only the cross justifies me —not witnessing, Bible study, etc. Thus what I do for God I do freely, out of love, because I want to, not because of fear or threat. Many Christians have surrounded their lives with laws of their own which they obey not out of love, but out of a desire to earn God's approval. They witness once a day, they read the Bible early in the morning for a set period of time, they rigorously use a prayer list, and when they fail to obey these laws they have set up, they live under a load of guilt. Some of these habits may be good, but they should never be followed from any motive other than love.

Further, we must be careful that we do not set laws on ourselves and make them moral issues. Murder is a moral issue according to the Bible. Witnessing once a day, or reading the Bible in the morning is *not* a moral issue. Our standards are the New Testament standards alone, without the additions of well-meaning men.

The burden of weakness is now removed. The law set up a standard, but gave no enablement (Romans 8:3). Grace gives the Holy Spirit to enable us to follow its standards. Grace is liberty. But liberty is not license. My life is not worse under grace, but better:

" 'This do and live,' the law commands,
But gives neither feet nor hands,
A better word the Gospel brings,
It bids me fly, and gives me wings."

Author Unknown

Thus, under grace, I have a higher standard, the life of Christ, but also His life within me to aid in fulfillment. And even though I never fulfill the standards completely, I approach them and am forgiven freely and instantly where I fall short.

LESSON FIVE

DELIVERANCE AND FORGIVENESS

Teacher's Objective: To teach the students how to rest by faith in the promises of God, and to encourage them to keep an unhindered fellowship with the Lord by confession of sin.

Teacher's Enrichment: (This material may be shared with group members as time allows.)

RESULTS OF THE LIFE OF FAITH AND OBEDIENCE AS SET FORTH BY JOSHUA

MODERN APPLICATION

Reproach of Egypt was rolled away — Joshua 5:9. Egypt represented a land of misery, hardship and stress. What a great burden was lifted when God took away the guilt of 40 years of wandering in the wilderness and opened up the gates of Canaan.

The blood of Jesus Christ rolls away the reproach of sin and all its defeats; we become perfectly clean (Ephesians 1:7).

New food for a new place — 5:11. The children of Israel began to enjoy the fruit of the land instead of the manna they had eaten for so long. They finally possessed their promise of long ago — a land flowing with milk and honey. No one can ever possess wilderness; one only wanders in the wilderness.

There is a new fruit of love, joy, peace, etc., to thrive upon when we abide in Christ and allow His Spirit to live through us (Galatians 5:22-23).

God conquered as He had promised — 6:20. The walls of Jericho fell flat and Israel took possession.

God fights our battles while we rest in Him (Psalm 108:13).

Each tribe received its own personal inheritance of promised land — Chapters 13-19; 21:43.

Each believer has a particular place in the body of Christ and a special service to perform (1 Corinthians 12:18-31).

Joshua chose obedience and eternal reward — 24:15.

When we choose for God, we lay up eternal rewards, and are said to be building upon gold, silver and precious stones (1 Corinthians 3:12, 13; Matthew 6:20).

Summary of God's goodness — 24:13. "And I gave you a land on which you had not labored, and cities which you had not built, and you have lived in them; you are eating of vineyards and olive groves which you did not plant."

There is nothing which the Lord will not supply if and when we need it (Matthew 6:31-33).

CLASS TIME

Suggested Opening Prayer

Dear Father, help us understand the principles of confession for deliverance from sin and of resting in our faith in You. Teach us as we study these things in the lives of Joshua and David.

(Introduction: Be sure students understand
   objective
   memory work
   reading assignment.)

Introduction

OBJECTIVE: To maintain fellowship with God, unhindered by sin.

TO MEMORIZE: Joshua 1:9.
TO READ: Joshua 1, 7, 8, 23.

JOSHUA
JOSHUA 1-23

Discussion Starter

How do you think sin in our lives would hinder our fellowship with God?

Lesson Development

Bible Study

A. *Joshua and deliverance*

Joshua's name gives us some insight into the book. His name means "Jehovah is Salvation." It is carried over into the New Testament in the name of our Lord — "Jesus."

1. Read Joshua 1:1-9 and list God's promises to Joshua.
   Would give him every place he walked on, strength and victory, God's presence and comfort, success and prosperity.

What was the condition on which these promises would be fulfilled? *Joshua's willingness to arise and go.*

How much of Chapter 1:1-9 depended on Joshua?
How much of our Christian life depends on us?
See 1 Thessalonians 5:24

— "Faithful is He who calls you, and He also will bring it to pass."
2 Timothy 2:13 — "If we are faithless, yet He remains faithful; for He cannot deny Himself!"

See Abraham's example of believing God — Romans 4:20-21.

When God gives a command, He also must open the way of our ability to obey. God was faithful to Joshua as He was previously to Moses — He is no respecter of persons (Joshua 4:23).

> Can you apply any of these promises to your life? _____
> Which, and how? _____
> _____
> _____
>
> 2. In Joshua 7, why did God tell Joshua to stop praying?
>   *Israel had sinned and disobeyed Him.*
>
>   What does God say to you in Psalm 66:18? *"If I regard wickedness in my heart, the Lord will not hear."* Apply Numbers 32:23 to this passage. *"Your sin will find you out."*
>
> 3. What happened after the sin was taken away (Joshua 8:1)? *God's promise of blessings was restored.*

To what lengths did God go in order to complete His will and promise to Joshua? (Joshua 10:13-14).

Has God changed? See Hebrews 13:8 — "Jesus Christ, the same yesterday, and today, and forever."

> 4. What was Joshua's command to the people before he died (Joshua 23:6)? *To be certain and strong in keeping all of God's law and not to turn away from it.*

David's position: God graciously had chosen this young man, brought him out from feeding sheep and anointed him King of Israel.

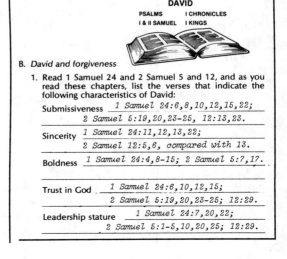

DAVID

PSALMS   I CHRONICLES
I & II SAMUEL   I KINGS

B. *David and forgiveness*

1. Read 1 Samuel 24 and 2 Samuel 5 and 12, and as you read these chapters, list the verses that indicate the following characteristics of David:

   Submissiveness *1 Samuel 24:6,8,10,12,15,22; 2 Samuel 5:19,20,23-25, 12:13,23.*

   Sincerity *1 Samuel 24:11,12,13,22; 2 Samuel 12:5,6, compared with 13.*

   Boldness *1 Samuel 24:4,8-15; 2 Samuel 5:7,17.*

   Trust in God *1 Samuel 24:6,10,12,15; 2 Samuel 5:19,20,23-25; 12:29.*

   Leadership stature *1 Samuel 24:7,20,22; 2 Samuel 5:1-5,10,20,25; 12:29.*

God's dealing with David:

The Jewish new year ended with March, and it was customary for kings to go to battle at this time; however, David sent Joab (verse 1) and disobeyed the Lord. Result of disobedience: loss of fellowship with God.

Psalms 5:3; 63:1, 143:8, all reveal that as a rule David was faithful in meeting God daily and seeking guidance early. But 2 Samuel 11:2 shows a time

Sinful passion _____ *2 Samuel 12:4,9.*

Sorrow for sin   *1 Samuel 24:5; 2 Samuel 12:13.*

2. The nobility of David's character is seen in many of the recorded instances from his career, including some of those which you have just read. He is described as a "man after God's own heart" and as such, he occupies a high position among the heroes of the faith. Jesus' title as the ruler of God's people is "the Son of David."

Many people, however, find the stories of David's terrible sins to be absolutely contradictory to this exalted position of spiritual leadership. How can you hold up such a man as an outstanding example of "a man after God's own heart"? _____

_____

If you can answer this question, you will have grasped the essence of biblical faith. Read 2 Samuel 12 again, and then Psalm 51, which David wrote at that time. (You might find help in Romans 4:1-8 or Luke 7:36-50; 18:9-14.)

when David arose at eventide instead of early morning. While walking on his balcony, he was overwhelmed by the temptation of a beautiful woman.

One who walks away from God always walks into trouble. David's sins included: adultery (verse 4), murder (verse 15) and hypocrisy (verse 25).

The Bible says that man can enjoy sin only for a season, and Psalms 32, 38 and 51 all reveal David's distress and misery during this year's period of being out of fellowship with God.

David paid an awesome price for his sin:

His child of adultery died — 2 Samuel 12:18.

One son, Amnon, committed incest — 13:14.

Another son, Absalom, committed murder — 13:28,29.

The same son rebelled and suffered a dreadful, accidental death — Chapters 15-18.

David confessed and received complete forgiveness and restoration:

Admitted his guilt — 2 Samuel 12:13; Psalm 51:3;

prayed for the joy of his salvation to be returned — Psalm 51:12;

realized he must have a clean heart in order to be used of God — Psalm 51:13.

Conclusion and Application

The blessings of Christian experience depend upon obedience to Christ. Confession of disobedience restores the sense of right standing or joy of our salvation. In this, one must not wait for feelings of restoration, but simply believe it, just as the Bible teaches in Proverbs 28:13, "He who conceals his transgressions

will not prosper, but he
who confesses and forsakes
them will find compassion."

> **Life Application**
>
> 1. What sin, or problem, do you need deliverance from today?
>   _____
>
> 2. Read Proverbs 28:13. How can you appropriate it for your
>   problem? _____
>   _____
>
> 3. Read Joshua 24. Circle all the "I's" in verses 3 through13 and
>   notice all the things God accomplished for the people of
>   Israel. What do you need Him to accomplish for you? _____
>   _____
>
> 4. How does your heart attitude compare with that of Joshua
>   and David? _____
>   _____

Suggested Closing Prayer

We thank You, Father, for what You have shown us about how to maintain an unhindered fellowship with You and we pray that You would apply the principles of confessing sin and of faith-rest to each of our lives.

ADDITIONAL BACKGROUND MATERIAL

Here are some parallel passages for further study on deliverance by resting in faith, and on confession and forgiveness.

Deliverance:

1. Rest in activity: Hebrews 4:1-10; 1 Corinthians 10:13; 1 Peter 5:7.
2. Failure due to self-activity:
   a. Elijah — 1 Kings 19:2-3, 15-16, 18 (Carnal solution to spiritual problem.)
   b. Saul — 1 Samuel 9:1-2, 15-16, 21-22; 13:7-9; 15:13-23 (Carnal capacities substituted for spiritual).
3. Paul — Incapable in own strength: Galatians 2:7-9; Philippians 3:4-6 (Health forced him to depend upon the Spirit).

Forgiveness:

1. Chastening is in the plan of God for man — Hebrews 13:5-11.
2. Suffering for Christ's sake brings glory to God — 1 Peter 2:19.
3. Privilege of confession is based on priesthood of every believer as seen in the Old Testament. Examples:
   a. Priest by birth — Exodus 28:1; John 3:3.
   b. Priest bathed by another upon entering priesthood — Exodus 29:4; Colossians 2:13; Titus 3:5.
   c. Priesthood for life — Hebrews 7:23.
   d. Priestly functions of New Testament believers:
      1) access to God — Hebrews 10:19-22;
      2) sacrifice — Romans 12:1; Philippians 2:17; Hebrews 13:15-16;
      3) intercessory prayer — 1 Timothy 2:1; Colossians 1:9-12.

LESSON SIX

ELIJAH: THE POWER OF THE SPIRIT-LED MAN

Teacher's Objective: To encourage the students, through an examination of the life of Elijah, toward spiritually powerful Christian service.

Teacher's Enrichment: (You may share this material with students as time allows.)

Some parallel passages on the power available when we are Spirit-led:

God's power to work miracles for those who fearlessly stand for Him:
David and Goliath — 1 Samuel 17:32-54.
Jehoshaphat—2 Chronicles 20:1-13, 20-25.
Hezekiah's prayer — 2 Kings 19:10-19, 35.
Elisha — 2 Kings 6:13-23.
Daniel — Daniel 6:16-24.
Esther — Esther 6:1-14; 7:10; 8:1-11.
Spirit-filled ministry — 1 Kings 17:1; Hebrews 11:6; Luke 1:17.
Instant obedience — Acts 8:26-39.
Answers to prayers — John 15:7; 1 John 3:22; 5:14-15.

CLASS TIME

Suggested Opening Prayer

Lord, we pray today that You will open our hearts and minds and spirits to receive Your instructions concerning the power of being Spirit-led. Teach us about how we can maintain a spirit of fearlessness.

(Introduction: Be sure students understand
 objective
 memory work*
 reading assignment.)

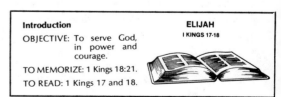

Introduction	ELIJAH
OBJECTIVE: To serve God, in power and courage.	I KINGS 17-18
TO MEMORIZE: 1 Kings 18:21.	
TO READ: 1 Kings 17 and 18.	

(*Have at least two students share what this verse has meant to them.)

Discussion Starter

Two Christians have the same background. However, one is fearless in his witness and the other is not. Instead, he is a spiritual "milquetoast." Why do you think that is?

Lesson Development

> **Bible Study**
> A. *Elijah*
> **Read 1 Kings 17:1-7.**

"To understand the history of Elijah, let us briefly consider the condition of affairs when Elijah made his appearance. Ahab had taken for a wife, Jezebel, a Canaanite woman, daughter of Eth-baal. Of a weak and yielding character, he allowed Jezebel to establish the Phoenician worship on a grand scale — priests and prophets of Baal were appointed in crowds — the prophets of Jehovah were persecuted and slain, or only escaped by hiding in caves. It seemed as if the last remnants of true religion were about to perish. Jezebel had also induced Ahab to issue orders for the violent death of all the prophets of Jehovah who, since the expulsion of the Levites, had been the only firm support of the ancient religion.

"Elijah suddenly appeared before Ahab and proclaimed the vengeance of Jehovah for the apostasy of the king" (*Unger's Bible Dictionary,* Chicago: Moody Press, p. 302).

> Indicate whether the following statements are true or false:
>
> _T_ 1. The cessation of rain is said to rest upon *all* of these factors:
> God lives.
> Elijah lived in His presence.
> Elijah's word controlled the rain.

"This was probably the conclusion of a warning, given to the king, of the consequences of his iniquitous course" *(ibid.).*

> _F_ 2. The Bible says that Elijah searched eagerly for the will of God.
>
> _T_ 3. The prophet obeyed orders for the immediate future, though he did not know how it would turn out.
>
> What step of duty have you not taken because you cannot see its outcome? _____
>
> _F_ 4. Elijah thought the plan was absurd, and hesitated.
>
> _F_ 5. The brook dried up, proving he was right.
>
> B. *The widow*
> Read 1 Kings 17:8-24.
>
> _T_ 1. Strict, implicit obedience characterized Elijah.

"For three years and six months, there had been no rain. At last the full horrors of famine, caused by the failure of the crops, descended on Samaria. Elijah, returning to Israel, found Ahab yet alive and unreformed, Jezebel still occupied with her idols, and the prophets of Baal still deceiving the people. Elijah first presented himself to Obadiah, the principal servant of Ahab and a true

Do you think it was humiliating to take a step of faith that made him dependent upon a very poor widow?

_____ Why do you think God deals with us in such a way? _____

_T_ 2. When her boy died, guilt turned the widow's eyes upon herself.

_T_ 3. God desires to remove from our lives now the guilt that can cripple our faith in time of crisis.

C. Ahab

Read 1 Kings 18:1-18.

_T_ 1. Ahab was at least concerned for his animals.

_T_ 2. He had refused to acknowledge the real reason for the problem (verses 17, 18).

_T_ 3. Nevertheless Elijah recognized the real reason (verses 17, 18).

servant of God. He requested him to announce his return to Ahab; and Obadiah, his fears having been removed by the prophet, consented. The conversation between Ahab and Elijah, when they met soon after, began with the question of the king, 'Art thou he that troubleth Israel?' Elijah answered, unhesitatingly, 'I have not troubled Israel, but thou and thy father's house, in that ye have forsaken the commandments of the Lord, and thou hast followed Baalim.'" *(ibid.)*

Elijah challenged Ahab to "exercise his authority in summoning an assembly to Mount Carmel that the controversy between them might be decided.

D. Prophets of Baal

Read 1 Kings 18:18-40.

1. Write in the verse number(s) in which Elijah spoke as follows:

Rebuked the people for compromise __21__
Challenged the enemies of God to a contest __24__
Blasted them with withering sarcasm __27__
Ordered water poured __33,34__
Prayed to God to make Himself known __36__
Ordered the priests executed __40__

"Whatever were his secret purposes, Ahab accepted this proposal, and the people also consented. Fire was the element over which Baal was supposed to preside. Elijah proposed (wishing to give them every advantage) that two bullocks be slain and laid each upon a separate altar, the one for Baal, the other for Jehovah; whichever should be consumed by fire would be He whom it was their duty to serve . . . The Baalites were allowed to make trial first. All day long these false prophets cried to Baal, leaped upon the altar, and mingled their blood with that of the sacrifice; but all was in vain, for at the time of the evening sacrifice the altar was still cold and the bullock lay stark thereon — 'there was no voice, no one answered, and no one paid attention.' Then Elijah prayed, 'O Lord, the God of Abraham, Isaac and Israel, today let it be known that Thou art God in Israel, and that I am Thy servant, and that I have done all these things at Thy word.' The answer was all that could be desired for 'the fire of the Lord fell, and consumed the burnt offering, and the wood and the stones and the dust, and licked up the water that was in the trench.' The people acknowledged the presence of God, exclaiming with one voice, 'The Lord, He is God; the Lord, He is God.' " *(ibid.)*

> 2. Elijah's prayer in verse 36 provides a superb revelation of the Spirit-led life. Why do you think that's true? _____
> _____

Conclusion and Application

Life Application

1. Describe the relationship you think Elijah had with God.
_____
_____
_____

"Elijah's character is one of moral sublimity. His faith in God seemed to know no limit nor questions. His zeal for Jehovah was an all-absorbing motive of his life, so that he justly said, 'I have been very zealous for the Lord, the God of hosts' (1 Kings 19:9). No danger nor duty was too severe to shake his confidence — no labor too great for his Lord. His courage was undaunted, even in the presence of royalty or famine. His obedience was simple and as unquestioning as a child's. Tender of soul, he could sympathize with the widow when she lost her child, or weep over the sad condition of his deluded countrymen. Stern in principle, he was, in his opposition to sin, as fierce as the fire that more than once answered his command. He was by nature a recluse, only appearing before men to deliver his message from God, and enforce it by a miracle, and then disappearing from sight again". *(ibid.)*

> 2. How does your relationship and power with God compare to Elijah's? _____
>
> 3. How has God's power been exerted through you upon other lives? _____
> _____
>
> 4. What changes in your mental and spiritual thinking do you feel need to take place in order for you to find the power with God which you desire? _____
> _____
>
> "God's promises are given, not to restrain, but to incite to prayer. . . . They are the signed check, made payable to us, which we must endorse and present for payment.
> "We have an irresistible purchase power with God when we can put our finger on His own promise and say, 'Do as You have said.' . . . All prayer, like Elijah's, should be based on promise."
>
> F. B. Meyer

Suggested Closing Prayer

(Have students end in a good season of prayer. Try to inspire them to close the time with a sense of fearlessness, unlimited confidence in God and absolute desire to serve Him.)

ADDITIONAL BACKGROUND MATERIAL

A dynamic Christian is one whose morale is high. He or she is abandoned to God enthusiastically. The fearful Christian has his eyes upon self, situations and people; and he sinks, as Peter did when he took his eyes from Christ to look at the wind and waves. Being Spirit-filled is the difference between the "milquetoast" Christian and the Christian conqueror. Faith in the promises, abandonment to God, knowledge of the Bible and a good devotional life all enter in to produce a Christian leader.

Elijah was later guilty of turning his eyes upon self and the situation. Read 1 Kings 19. It merely demonstrates that failure can come on the heels of victory as we take our eyes from God and put them upon ourselves and situations.

The answer to the question, "How can I maintain my enthusiasm?" may be found in the acrostic, GROWTH:

Go to God in prayer.

Read your Bible every day.

Obey God.

Witness.

Treasury (our stewardship).

Holy Spirit.

Mere zealous feelings are not what we propose, but faithfulness expressed in abandonment to service. The word GROWTH gives us a handle for keeping God and Christ central in our lives, being controlled by the Holy Spirit so that Christ can live the CHRISTian life through us.

LESSON SEVEN

JEREMIAH: A WITNESS WHO STOOD ALONE

Teacher's Objective: To produce in the student faithfulness in the face of discouragements.

Teacher's Enrichment: (This material may be shared with students as time allows.)

CONCERNING JEREMIAH'S POSITION:

In the thirteenth year of Josiah, King of Judah, Jeremiah began his ministry (626 B.C.). A three-way struggle for power between declining Assyria, rising Babylon and aspiring Egypt had begun. Jeremiah knew that God had selected Babylon as His potential instrument to thresh Judah for her sinfulness.

Early in Jeremiah's prophetic career two encouraging situations prevailed. They were:

— In 621 B.C., Josiah began his religious reform, removing impurity and idolatry. Nation-wide revival was beginning, and Jeremiah preached genuine repentance as the only means of averting Babylonian destruction.

— Other prophets were early contemporaries of Jeremiah with their ministries overlapping his: Zephaniah (640-621 B.C.); Habakkuk (625-608 B.C.), who backed up Jeremiah's proclamation that Babylon would demolish Judah unless there was repentance; Nahum, prophesying the fall of the Assyrian capital, Nineveh; Obadiah, who prophesied judgment for Edom because of their attacks (before and during Jeremiah's ministry) on Judah.

In the 40 years that followed, 626-586 B.C., Jeremiah ministered faithfully. Many years before, Isaiah had been God's man in Jerusalem. The Assyrian conqueror, Sennacherib, had been turned from siege by the angel of the Lord, who struck down the whole camp of 185,000 Assyrians in one night (2 Kings 19:35). That was in 701 B.C., but now Jeremiah was God's man in this doomed city. Israel, the northern Kingdom, had fallen to Assyria with most of the people carried away in two major deportations. Now the threat of Babylonian judgment hung over Jerusalem. Judah was following the same idolatrous, sinful path Israel had, and in 597 B.C. Jehoiachin surrendered to Nebuchadnezzar. Many of the Jews were removed to Babylon along with Jehoiachin. In 586 B.C. Nebuchadnezzar laid siege and decimated Jerusalem because Zedekiah, whom he had put in power after Jehoiachin, made league with the Egyptians to revolt. All but the poorest of the people were taken to Babylon as captives (Jeremiah 39:4-10).

The question arises, if Jeremiah began his ministry during national revival and in such auspicious circumstances, how could the country deteriorate so

425

rapidly? In 2 Kings 23:28-30 and 2 Chronicles 35:20-27 we read of what may have been the cause. Josiah, the last spiritual king, nevertheless went to attack Pharaoh Neco contrary to God's will (2 Chronicles 35:22) and lost his life. Without the backing of the throne, the great revival crumbled and the wicked kings who followed resisted Jeremiah's message.

Jeremiah is called the weeping prophet for obvious reasons (Jeremiah 9:1,10; 14:17). He was the model of a weeping evangelist in Jeremiah 2-20. His messages were constantly unheeded, even after Jerusalem had fallen as he had warned. He called for repentance before the siege, for surrender to Babylon during the siege and for the remnant to remain in Judah after the siege — but they chose flight to Egypt. He followed.

In faithfulness he suffered with them until, according to one tradition, five years later they stoned him to death in Tahpenes, Egypt. How much this parallels Christ who did not cling to equality with God, but humbled Himself, became a servant and was obedient unto death (Philippians 2:5-11). It also parallels the experience Paul relates in 2 Timothy 4:16-18.

Jeremiah forms a bridge between the prophets of Judah and those of the exile (Daniel and Ezekiel). He inspired Daniel with his prophecy of the restoration after 70 years of Babylonian captivity (Jeremiah 25:11; 29:10). Daniel, as he read that prophecy, began to pray (Daniel 9:2), and he received the vision of the 70 weeks (Daniel 9:20-27). This is one of the most famous prophecies of the whole Old Testament and describes Christ and the millenial restoration of Israel. Jeremiah speaks of that restoration in Jeremiah 30:3-10 and 23:6, but at that time there was no other prophet and no encouragement or fellowship for Jeremiah, so God used his work later to inspire Daniel as well as others, including ourselves.

CLASS TIME

Suggested Opening Prayer

Lord, we pray that You will teach us the joyous privilege of sharing Your sufferings in order that we might be conformed to the image of Christ.

(Introduction: Be sure students understand
   objective
   memory work*
   reading assignment.)

Introduction
OBJECTIVE: To serve God faithfully in the face of discouragement.
TO MEMORIZE: Jeremiah 23:29.
TO READ: Jeremiah 1, 20, 21.

JEREMIAH
JEREMIAH 1-21

(*Discuss the words *fire, hammer* and *rock* as they apply to the Word of God. Have one student give the verse from memory.)

Discussion Starter

(Ask the group:) In your experiences in dealing with people who need Christ, have you ever felt incapable? Would you tell us about it?

Lesson Development

> If you think it is difficult to stand for Christ in your house, and on your campus, or in your community, take a few lessons from Jeremiah.
>
> **Bible Study**
>
> A. *Jeremiah's call*
>
>   Read Jeremiah 1
>
>   1. When facing Scripture verses that command you to speak for Christ, have you ever said: "Why, I could never do that; I have no training for it"? What did Jeremiah say (1:6)? *"I do not know how to speak, because I am a youth."*
>
>   2. To be effective in speaking, one must have something to say. Where do you get this (see 1:7-17)? *God will give us what He wants us to say.*

If we have hidden God's Word in our hearts and are controlled by the Holy Spirit, then the Spirit will call to mind the words needed to answer every man in every situation (John 14:26; Colossians 4:5-6).

> 3. Opposition of the intensity that faced Jeremiah is unknown in America, though it is common in some parts of the world. How can a man face such overwhelming odds (see 1:8, 18, 19)? *God has promised to be with that person and deliver him.*

Paul had a testimony regarding persecution in 2 Timothy 3:10-12. What was it?

What is the promise of God for a life of service to the Lord (Luke 18:29-30)?

> B. *Jeremiah's arrest and prayer.*
>
>   Read Jeremiah 19:14, 15 for setting. In verse 14 we see that not only *what* Jeremiah said but *where* he spoke (and to *whom*) were under the Lord's direct guidance. This was also observed in Elijah's life as one of the secrets of effectiveness. We must not distribute tracts promiscuously, nor witness to every man in sight. Let God lead.
>
>   Verse 15 was Jeremiah's unpopular message in a nutshell: condemnation upon the capital city, Jerusalem; the Babylonian armies would destroy the city. He advised the people to sue for surrender terms and avoid the horrors of a siege that could not be resisted for long, since God was on the enemy's side.
>
>   Read Jeremiah 20.
>
>   1. How did punishment affect Jeremiah's testimony (20:1-6)? *Just made it more sure and more specific.*

What are some practical lessons we can gain from standing alone with the Lord? (Have several members suggest applications to life. Leader may point out the following:)

God's faithfulness — Lamentations 3:22-23.

His mercy overcoming our distress — Psalm 103:17-18.
Grace during human weakness — 2 Corinthians 12:9-10.
Confidence in God rather than men — Hebrews 10:35-36.
Communion of knowing and loving the Lord — Jeremiah 24:7.

Jeremiah's prayer indicates that though he was a strong witness, inner doubts and fears had to be dealt

> 2. Verses 7-18 are an example of the abrupt interruptions interspersed throughout the book of Jeremiah. What do these prayers reveal about the apparent fearlessness of the prophet? _Inwardly he was afraid and miserable--he wished he'd never been born._

with in prayer. Note his understanding of the total inadequacy of the flesh and the capability of God to meet the situation. Note how fully he unloads his burdens and hardships on his Lord. He is completely open in the presence of God, hiding nothing. He is abiding in Christ, letting Him bear every weight, just as the branch allows the trunk of the tree to support it in a storm (John 15:4-5). The reason he was fearless in public was that he dealt with and removed these fears through his prayer life (see Philippians 4:6-7; 1 Peter 5:7).

Have you had similar feelings? Would you rather have remained silent when

> 3. Since his message brought him so much unpopularity, what did Jeremiah consider (20:8, 9)? _Not speaking, holding it all in._

the Bible instructed you to reprove unfruitful works in yourself and others (Ephesians 5:8-11)? (Have the members of your group share these experiences with one another in order to understand better what the text means.)

> 4. How did his enemies think they could get the best of him (20:10)? _By denouncing and deceiving him._
> _____
>
> 5. What thoughts restored his confidence (20:11)? _____
>   _The Lord was with him, like a dread champion._
>
> 6. How would you describe Jeremiah's prayer? _____
>   _____
>
> C. Jeremiah's prophecy
>   Read Jeremiah 21.
>   1. How do you think feelings of despair and frustration influenced the prophet's obedience to God? _____
>   _____
>
>   2. When asked by the government for a word of comfort and security, what response did Jeremiah make (21:1-7)? _God was going to fight against them and they would be taken into captivity._

Being true to God and conscience is the source of peace and happiness. What

mental and even physical state could Jeremiah have suffered if he had given in to pressures?

God has given us the
"ministry of reconciliation"

> 3. What decision did the prophet declare his hearers must make (21:8-14)? _To surrender and live, or to fight and die._

(2 Corinthians 5:18). It is our privilege to share the gospel frankly, as did Jeremiah.
Ours, however, is a message of life and freedom, not one of condemnation
and captivity.

Conclusion and Application

We are faithful, like Jeremiah, not because we always shall see a favorable
resolution of the difficulties, but because "The love of Christ controls us"
(2 Corinthians 5:14). What we receive is far more than success. Jeremiah had a
personal relationship with God and, though he could become despondent, he
conducted his life not by feelings but by the principle of obedience to the One
whom he loved. Suffering adds a deep quality to our lives:

"Millions of human beings but for suffering would never develop an atom of
affection. The man who would spare due suffering is not wise. It is folly to
conclude a thing ought not to be because it hurts. There are powers to be born,
creations to be perfected, sinners to be redeemed through the ministry of pain,
that could be born, perfected, redeemed, in no other way" — George ,
Macdonald (Robertson, J.D., *Handbook of Preaching Resources from English
Literature,* Macmillan, 1962, p. 222).

Life Application

With this chart, list discouragements you may be facing, and
what you have learned from Jeremiah's life that will help you
cope with them.

DISCOURAGEMENT	LEARNING FROM JEREMIAH

Suggested Closing Prayer

(Use the following poem as the opening part of your prayer:
"I thank God for the bitter things; they've been a 'friend to grace';
They've driven me from the paths of ease to storm the secret place.
I thank Him for the friends who failed to fill my heart's deep need;
They've driven me to the Saviour's feet upon His love to feed.
I'm grateful too, through all life's way no one could satisfy,
And so I've found in God alone my rich, my full supply!"
                                                                    — Author unknown

(Conclude with:) Thank You, Father for Your faithfulness in meeting our needs with your rich, full supply. Keep us ever true to You alone.

ADDITIONAL BACKGROUND MATERIAL

Outline of Jeremiah:

A. Prophet's call — Chapter 1.

B. Prophecies concerning Judah — 2-45.

    1. Six sermons during the reigns of Josiah to Jehoiakim (repent or perish) — 2-20.

Parallel passages on serving God in the face of discouragement.

A. Dealing with an inferiority complex.
    1. Great men have dealt with this through prayer.
        a. Moses — Exodus 4:10-16.
        b. Isaiah — Isaiah 6:4-7.
        c. Solomon — 1 Kings 3:7-13.
        d. Jeremiah — Jeremiah 1:5-10.
    2. We are formed by God and we must not claim imperfect construction for the task for which we were created, Jeremiah 1:5-7.

B. Dealing with discouragement and fearfulness.
    1. Results of failure in dealing with discouragement.
        a. Elijah lost his power — 1 Kings 19:9-18.
        b. Peter denied Christ because he had his eyes on circumstances — John 21:3; Matthew 14:22-23; 27:69-75.
    2. How to deal with discouragement and fearfulness.
        a. Abound in the work of the Lord, do not stop — 1 Corinthians 15:58.
        b. Disregard suffering — 1 Peter 4:1-2, 19.
        c. Know experiences are conforming us to Christ — Romans 8:28-29.
        d. Realize God does not give us fear — 2 Timothy 1:7.

LESSON EIGHT

RECAP

Teacher's Objective: To make sure the students understand the difference between law and grace and to bring them to a clear awareness of how the law teaches our need for grace.

CLASS TIME

Suggested Opening Prayer

Help us, Father, to understand that Your revelation of Yourself in the Old Testament was for the purpose of showing us Your plan for redeeming man from his fallen state. Help us to realize that the Old Testament *is* Your Word and is relevant to today's living.

(Introduction: The student's objective in this lesson is to see again how the examples of the Old Testament relate to us, and how we can walk in faith resting in the Lord and to understand the difference between law and grace and how they show the need for Christ in our lives. Memory verses should be reviewed and Genesis 3 and 4 should be read again along with Galatians 3.)

Discussion Starter

Someone has said you can open the Old Testament, turn to any passage and see the red line of Jesus' blood drawn through it. What do you think that means?

Lesson Development

(Any Teacher's Enrichment or Additional Background Material on the Old Testament that you were not able to use before could be utilized at this time and any point which you might feel was not sufficiently covered in the previous seven lessons can be dealt with now too.

Going over the Recap material will benefit both the students and you by making these truths a more vital part of your subconscious, habitual way of life.)

Review verses memorized.

Now that we have been through the Old Testament at a rapid pace, you have some idea of what it contains and what it teaches. Imagine yourself a Jew, possessing only the Old Testament Scriptures. Can you find God's plan for man in it?

Write it in your own words. _____

_____

_____

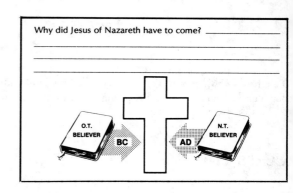

Conclusion and Application

(Ask these questions but do not require students to answer aloud:) Have you understood why Jesus came? And have you invited Him into your life? Have you confessed sin and appropriated the filling of the Holy Spirit to empower your life for service? If you have not taken these steps before, perhaps this is the time for you to do so.

Suggested Closing Prayer

(Close with an appropriate prayer, giving students an opportunity to make whatever commitments they are led to at this time.)

SUMMARY LESSON PLAN

OLD TESTAMENT HIGHLIGHTS

Teacher's Objective: To illustrate to the students the main message of the Old Testament: the sin and failure of man, and the grace and mercy of God.

Teacher's Enrichment: (See Teacher's Enrichment sections as they occur in the previous lessons of this Step, and share with the class as time permits.)

CLASS TIME

Suggested Opening Prayer

Lord, we thank You for allowing us to know about the fears and failures of Your people. We thank You also for the examples of their faith and courage recorded in the Old Testament. We ask that we might learn from their experiences.

(Introduction:

STUDENT'S OBJECTIVE: To recognize how the Old Testament relates to us today, to see that it is a history of man's fall from innocence and from God's standards, to understand what God's requirements are and that they are impossible for us to reach on our own, to learn about God's promise to provide a way for us to come back to Him through His Son, and to appreciate the importance of serving Him faithfully no matter what the circumstances.

TO MEMORIZE: Romans 5:19 and 6:23; Genesis 3:15 and Galatians 4:4,5.

READING ASSIGNMENT: Genesis 3; Exodus 20; Galatians 3,4)

Discussion Starter

You probably have heard this statement: "Every day in every way man is getting better and better." Do you think it is true? Why or why not?

The Old Testament is a perfect illustration of whether man is improving or not.

Lesson Development

(Note to teacher: You should encourage your students to read carefully the section "Old Testament," on pages 18—22 of the student's Handbook, in order for them to get an understanding of the divisions of the Old Testament and a brief overview of what each of these books contains.)

A. The drama begins *(from Lesson 1).*

    1. What do you think "in the image of God" in Genesis 1:27 means as it refers to the creation of man? (He is different from other creatures — Genesis 9:6; he had original righteousness and holiness — Genesis 1:31; his life was breathed into him by God Himself — 2:7, giving him a living soul which exists apart from the body.)

    2. What happened to that original goodness (Genesis 2:17; 3:6; Romans 5:12)? (Because of stubborn self-will, Eve added to God's Word and gave in to deceit and temptation, and Adam disobeyed God's command. Their fellowship with God was broken and their guilt made them fearful and ashamed. Then they brought forth children after their own kind — with that sinful nature.

    3. What was God's response to Adam and Eve's disobedience (3:14-21)? (He pronounced judgment, illustrating the truth of Galatians 6:7,8. But at the same time, in His grace, God provided a covering for their sin and then began to point to the time when the penalty for sin would be paid on man's behalf by the seed of the woman — Christ.)

B. From Adam through Abraham *(from Lesson 2).*

    1. We see in Genesis 3:21 that man had been taught the proper kind of sacrifice. Compare Cain's and Abel's attitudes toward God's instructions, indicated by their sacrifices (Genesis 4:1-7).

        What was the disastrous result of these differences?

    2. Noah gave evidence of his trust in God when he persisted in preparing the ark while in adverse surroundings. What do you think God accomplished through him? (See Hebrews 11:7.) (God saved Noah's household, condemned the world, taught necessity of obedience.)

    3. Abraham and his two sons, Ishmael and Isaac, are a picture of a person's relationship to God — either as a bondslave to sin through the son of the flesh, or as free in the son of promise. Chapters 15 through 18, plus chapter 21 of Genesis give the historical account of this, and Galatians 4:21-31 gives the spiritual explanation. Then in Genesis 22:1,2 Abraham was asked to sacrifice his beloved son, born of his free wife, Sarah.

        Why do you suppose God made this request? (To test his faith.)

        How would you explain Genesis 22:8 and 13? (It is an example of the fact that God will provide the necessary sacrifice and that we can trust His promises.)

        Isaac was a sacrifice of his father just as Christ was. In chapters 26 through 28 of Matthew we see Christ presented as the Son of Abraham, sacrifice of His Father.

C. Moses, the Passover and the Exodus *(from Lesson 3).*

    Jacob, Abraham's grandson, had taken his family to Egypt to escape a famine. After 400 years, his descendants had multiplied so much that the new king of

Egypt was concerned and subjected them to cruel slavery. In Exodus 1 and 2 we see the birth and life of Moses and the cry of the people to God for deliverance.

1. Moses is referred to in Hebrews 11:23-29. Why do you think God chose Moses to lead His people? (He was a man of faith.)

2. Why did God instruct the children of Israel as He did in Exodus 12:3-7, 12,13? (To picture the sacrifice of Christ, the perfect, sinless Lamb of God, and our safety through that sacrifice.)

3. The exodus ("going out") from Egypt, one of the most important events in the history of Israel, occurred immediately after the Passover (Exodus 12:41). In connection with this, one of the most remarkable and well-known miracles in the world took place, recorded in Exodus 14 (see verses 21,22). What spiritual truth does all this suggest to you? (Teacher, after several students have expressed their thoughts, you may add if appropriate: God will deliver us from our bondage of sin and He will keep us safe from the destroyer, Satan.)

D. Law and grace *(from Lesson 4)*.

1. When "the law" is mentioned, what usually comes to mind? (The Decalogue, or the Ten Commandments. See Exodus 20:3-17.)

2. Jesus condensed these ten into two in Matthew 22:37-40. What are they? (1) Love God with all your heart, soul and mind, and 2) love your neighbor as yourself.)

3. According to Romans 3:19,20, what does the law reveal? (The knowledge of sin.)

4. Law and grace are two different system ordained for two different purposes. We are under either one system or the other; they cannot be mixed. Grace is the kindness and love of God expressed toward us entirely apart from what we deserve. Compare Ephesians 2:8,9 with Romans 3:20.

    How do we obtain grace? (We simply accept it. It is a free gift. See Romans 6:23.)

E. Deliverance and forgiveness *(from Lesson 5)*.

1. Joshua's name means "Jehovah is Salvation." How as that expressed in Joshua 1:2-3? (God would be responsible for delivering the Israelites from defeat at the hands of the people already in that new land, and He would empower the Israelites to possess the land.)

2. In Joshua 7:10-12, why did God tell Joshua to stop praying? (The people had sinned.)

    What does God say to us in Psalms 66:18? ("If I regard wickedness in my heart, the Lord will not hear.")

    What happened after the sin of Israel was taken care of (Joshua 8:1)? (God's promise of blessing was restored.)

3. David, the exalted king and spiritual leader of God's people, nevertheless was capable of grievous sin — 2 Samuel 11. This one occurrence included

adultery (verse 4), murder (15) and hypocrisy (25). Considering this, how could David also be called a "man after God's own heart" as in Acts 13:22? (See 2 Samuel 12:13 and Psalm 51:3.) (Though David paid an awesome price for his sin, he also confessed it and received complete forgiveness and restoration.)

F. Elijah, the power of the Spirit-led man *(from Lesson 6)*.

Weak, evil king Ahab and his wicked Canaanite wife, Jezebel, did not worship God and in fact were killing His prophets when Elijah boldly appeared before the king.

1. Where did Elijah's courage come from (1 Kings 17;1)? And why did he proclaim to Ahab that there would be no rain except at his word? (He stood firm in the Lord, and God was bringing judgment on the land because of Ahab's wickedness.)

2. After those three and a half years of drought, Elijah appeared again before king Ahab in 1 Kings 18 and demanded a show-down with the prophets of Baal. After all the efforts of those heathen prophets, Elijah prayed a simple prayer in verse 36.

    What did he ask for, and how do you think that prayer reveals his Spirit-led life? (He merely asked that God let it be known that He was God and that Elijah was His servant. (Teacher, allow students to answer second part of the question in their own words.)

G. Jeremiah, a witness who stood alone *(from Lesson 7)*.

1. Jeremiah ministered to Judah during the times of the last spiritual king, several wicked kings, the Babylonian siege, and the flight of some of the people to Egypt. He was faithful to God and to the people, but they constantly ignored his warnings.

    How could he consistently remain steadfast in the face of such frustration (Jeremiah 1:4-9)? (He knew God had called and prepared him for a special purpose and would give him what he was to say.)

2. Jeremiah was even persecuted by the religious leaders of his day. How did punishment affect his testimony (20:1-6)? (Just made it more sure and more specific.)

3. Because of the unpopularity of his message, what did Jeremiah consider (20:8,9)? (Not speaking, holding it all in.)
    But how was he encouraged (verse 11)? (He knew the Lord was with him like a dread champion.)

4. How does that help you?

Conclusion and Application

Many people feel that the Old Testament is a book of fables and myths with very little value. How would you describe its value to the world? What impact has it had on history? In the pages of the Old Testament are some of the greatest dramas, poems, speeches and truths ever recorded. it is superseded, perhaps, only by the new Testament. We should be diligent students of it as Christ was. Note that one of its main themes is the total depravity of all men and the infinite grace of God.

(Ask these questions, but do not require students to answer aloud:) Have you now understood why Jesus came? And have you invited Him into your life? Have you confessed sin and appropriated the filling of the Holy Spirit to empower your life for service? If you have not taken these steps before, perhaps this is the time for you to do so.

Suggested Closing Prayer

(Close with an appropriate prayer, giving students an opportunity to make whatever commitments they are led to at this time.)

ADDITIONAL BACKGROUND MATERIAL

Parallel Passages illustrating man's failure and God's grace:

	God's promise	Man's failure	God's grace
A. Pentateuch	Genesis 12:1-3	Genesis 3:6-7	Genesis 3:15,21
	Exodus 6:6-8	Genesis 16:1-3	Genesis 21:1-3
		Exodus 6:9	Numbers 14:30-34
B. Historical books	2 Samuel 7:8-13	Judges 2:11-13	1 Kings 11:9-13
		Judges 21:25	1 Kings 15:3-4
		2 Samuel 2	

New Testament Highlights

WHY THE "NEW" TESTAMENT?

The name for the last 27 books of the Bible is taken from the words of Jesus uttered on the eve of His crucifixion: "This cup which is poured out for you is the new covenant [or testament] in My blood" (Luke 22:20). This covenant, instituted at this time, was new in contrast with the Mosaic Law, or old covenant, which was instituted with the people of Israel at Mt. Sinai (Exodus 19:5; 20:1-17; Jeremiah 31:31-34). In the old covenant, God wrote His requirements for living a righteous life on tablets of stone. But because of his sinful heart, man finds it impossible to keep the commands of the law by his unaided efforts. Hence the law of the old covenant made the fact of man's sin obvious by showing him to be a transgressor of explicit commands that God had given (Galatians 3:19; Romans 7:7-25). In thus revealing man's sin, the law readies men to receive Christ, for it shows them their inability to save themselves — they must look instead to that which God does for them.

God in His mercy "did not send the Son into the world to judge the world; but that the world should be saved through Him" (John 3:17). Jesus kept the Mosaic Law perfectly. Then when He shed His blood on the cross, He made it possible for the Holy Spirit to be poured out on men who believed so they might receive not only the forgiveness of sins, but also the ability to make progress in living the holy life whose standards are set forth in the Ten Commandments (Exodus 20:1-7). In this new covenant the law is written on the heart of the believer (Jeremiah 31:33), which simply means that God graciously provides the ability to do what the law demands (Ezekiel 26:27).

Though this new covenant was officially instituted at the time of Christ's death and resurrection, it was on the basis of Christ's death (Romans 3:25) and through the Holy Spirit that God had been saving men in the ages before the cross. Hence the new covenant had really been in effect all along. However, since it was officially instituted at Christ's first advent and since the last 27 books of the Bible concern the events leading up to and following the death and resurrection of Christ, these books have been aptly titled, "The New Testament."

LESSON ONE

MATTHEW AND MARK

Teacher's Objective: To let the student see how the life and teachings of Christ relate to the prophecy and the moral teachings of the Old Testament and to show the basic distinction between Matthew's and Mark's presentation of the life of Christ. Example: Matthew contains what Jesus said and particularly emphasizes prophecy; Mark contains what Jesus did and emphasizes miracles.

Teacher's Enrichment: (This material may be shared with class members as time permits.)

OLD TESTAMENT PROPHECY FULFILLED IN MATTHEW

Prophecy is the oral or written message of a prophet. Its purpose is to demonstrate God's power and wisdom, and to disclose His plans and purposes for the future. The fulfilled prophecy throughout the book of Matthew strengthens our faith in Christ, the Messiah:

1. Of David's family — Matthew 22:44; Isaiah 9:6-7.
2. Born of a virgin — Matthew 1:23; Isaiah 7:14.
3. Born in Bethlehem — Matthew 2:6; Micah 5:2.
4. Sojourn in Egypt — Matthew 2:15; Hosea 11:1.
5. Live in Galilee — Matthew 4:15; Isaiah 9:1-2.
6. Coming announced by an Elijah-like herald — Matthew 3:1-11; Isaiah 40:3-5.
7. Coming to be the occasion of weeping for Bethlehem's children — Matthew 2:18; Jeremiah 31:15.
8. Mission to Gentiles — Matthew 12:18-21; Isaiah 41:1-4.
9. Ministry to be one of healing — Matthew 8:17; Isaiah 53:4.
10. Teach by parables — Matthew 13:14; Isaiah 6:9-10.
11. Be disbelieved, hated and rejected by the rulers — Matthew 15:8-9; Isaiah 53:1.
12. Make a triumphal entry into Jerusalem — Matthew 21:5; Zechariah 9:9.
13. Like a smitten shepherd — Matthew 26:31; Zechariah 13:7.
14. Betrayed by a friend for 30 pieces of silver — Matthew 27:9-10; Psalm 41:9.
15. Buried by a rich man — Matthew 27:57-60; Isaiah 53:9.
16. Dying words foretold — Matthew 27:46; Psalm 22:1.
17. Rise the third day — Matthew 12:40; Psalm 16:10-11.

CLASS TIME

Suggested Opening Prayer

Lord Jesus, thank You for Yourself. May we love You more as we see You revealed in these two gospels.

(Introduction: Be sure
students understand
    objective
    memory work
    reading assignment.)

> **Introduction**
>
> OBJECTIVE: To see the relationship of Christ to the Old Testament, and to recognize different facets of Christ presented by Matthew and Mark.
>
> **MATTHEW**   **MARK**
> CHRIST AS KING   CHRIST AS SERVANT
>
> TO MEMORIZE: Matthew 28:18, 19.
>
> TO READ: Matthew 5-7.

Discussion Starter

Why do you think we have four gospels?

(Have the class share this
material in any of the ways
suggested in the Instructions
for Teaching on page 21.)

> Matthew was written to the Jews presenting Christ as King. Mark was written to the Romans presenting Christ as Servant. Luke was written to the Greeks presenting Him as Perfect Man, and John was written to the world presenting Christ as Son of God, the Savior.

Lesson Development

In the report of an accident, four witnesses give a clearer and more complete picture than one because of their different positions. So in the gospels we have four accounts, each from a different point of view, but all in perfect harmony. They present a perfect portrait of Christ.

1. *Matthew* presents Jesus as King, the Jewish Messiah. It was written with the Jew in mind. Illustration: Matthew 5:17-19.

2. *Mark* presents Jesus as the great conqueror — of storm, demons, disease and death. Also, He is presented as servant, conquering, suffering and finally triumphant. Illustration: Mark 10:45. Mark was probably written at Rome, and primarily for the Romans.

3. *Luke* presents Jesus as the perfect man, as well as the divine Savior. It was written with the Greek in mind. Illustration: Luke 2:11 and 19:10.

4. *John* presents Jesus as God. It was written with everyone in mind. Illustration: John 1:1-14.

Bible Study

A. *Matthew*

In presenting his record of the life of Jesus, Matthew is careful to record the major sermons that Jesus preached. The longest sermon on record is the "Sermon on the Mount," which is found in chapters 5 through 7.

1. As you read and re-read this sermon, see if you can answer the following questions which bring out some of its more important points:

Give one reason that Jesus considers it important for His disciples to live according to the moral standards of the Old Testament law and prophets. *To be called greatest in kingdom of heaven, to enter it, to be spiritually mature and wise.*

In one passage of Scripture Jesus summarized all the moral teachings of the Old Testament (Matthew 5:21-48). List several of them: *Love your neighbor, do not commit murder or adultery, make no false vows, do not take revenge, etc.*

What promise does Jesus give that helps the Christian overcome his desire for man's praise as he does good deeds (Matthew 6:1-18)? *Your Father who sees in secret will repay you.*

What assurance does Jesus give that helps the Christian overcome his anxiety regarding his physical needs such as food and clothing (Matthew 6:25-34)? *(Your Father knows your needs and will take care of you.*

The Sermon on the Mount is probably the most well-known oration in history. Its influence has been immense. There are several views as to its purpose in the ministry of Jesus:

1. Some feel it was addressed to the church, giving it a standard for righteousness. This could not be, however, because the church, as we know it, did not come into existence until Pentecost, and great church truths are not here presented. There is nothing about the Holy Spirit, our position in Christ or redemption through the blood of Christ in this sermon.
2. Some feel it was addressed to mankind in general.
3. Some feel it was meant for the kingdom which Jesus would establish. But verses 11 and 12 show that there is persecution and evil, which are not present in His kingdom. Besides, Jesus would have been giving a message which did not apply to his audience.

The best view is that Jesus was addressing the Jews of His time, showing them what would be required for entrance into His kingdom, contrasting God's righteousness with that of the scribes and Pharisees.

Does the Sermon on the Mount have a definite value for us today? As a way of salvation it is useless. No one has yet lived up to its standards. It is legal, not gracious in character, and is full of judgment and threats (Matthew 5:22-29). It offers no salvation to any man. The non-Christian world, which so admires this sermon, is condemned to hell by it.

As a way of sanctification it is also useless. It represents the law at its best, which condemns all and comforts none. The way of grace is not here.

But as a revelation of the moral requirements of God, it is a mountain peak in Scripture. Here we see how shallow and external human morality is; here we see God at His purest. *If we then take these requirements as a guide for personal living, put them in the context of grace, where all judgment, penalty and fear is removed, and supply the enablement of the Holy Spirit, we have made it of real value.*

2. This Sermon on the Mount is a revelation of the moral requirements of God. In it we see what a holy God expects of man and we come to understand that by it the world is condemned to hell. The sermon gives a standard, but no enablement. The motive is fear, not love. Its value to us is that it reveals our utter inability and need. What is the only way that a human being can escape this judgment and approach the standards set forth here? *By using this as a guide for personal living through the enablement of the Holy Spirit.*

The sermon condemns the world, that the world might seek salvation in the cross. The sermon guides the Christian who, under the power of the Spirit alone, can approach its standards.

The background of the Sermon on the Mount is instructive. Jesus is addressing an audience living in the atmosphere of Pharisaism. The ruling religious party of Jesus' day had twisted the Old Testament law from its true meaning with their perverted interpretations, as men also pervert the Bible today. They had made it an external, hypocritical, superficial thing. Jesus now comes to the fore to show what real godliness is.

3. Read the rest of Jesus' sermons recorded by Matthew in the chapters listed below and give in your own words a phrase that would summarize each.

Chapter 10 _____

Chapter 13 _____

Chapter 18 _____

Chapters 24, 25 _____

B. *Mark*

One of the most striking ways in which the Gospel of Mark differs from Matthew is that it emphasizes more *what Jesus did* than *what He said.*

1. What were some of the things that Jesus did which caused the religious leaders of Jesus' day to be so angry with Him (Mark 2:1-3:5)? *Forgave sins, ate with tax-gatherers and sinners, disciples did not fast, picked grain on Sabbath, healed a man on Sabbath.*

Mark manifests the servant character of the incarnate Son. He emptied Himself of the "form of God" and being found in fashion as a man, gave Himself on the cross. The ministry of Jesus the Servant-Son is now exalted to all authority at the right hand of the Father, where He makes constant intercession for the saints.

The overcoming life of every Christian is always found in what *we are* because of what Christ *is,* rather than our own sinful natures manifesting what we were without Him. "We are more than conquerors through Him that loved us!"

Miracles are supernatural
manifestations of divine
power in the external world,
in themselves special revelations of the presence and

2. Note the four miracles Jesus performed in Mark 4:35-5:43. List the various forces which, according to these records, Jesus had complete control:

4:35-41: _Nature--weather._

5:1-20: _Demon possesion._

5:21-23, 35-43: _Death_

5:25-34: _Disease_

3. What is the one thing that hinders Jesus from exercising His power in the lives of men (Mark 6:1-6)? _____
Lack of faith--unbelief.

power of God. The purpose of miracles is to arrest the attention of men, and aid in winning their acceptance of revealed truth.

Other miracles recorded in Mark include:
Bodily cures:
    Peter's mother-in-law — Mark 1:29-31;
    a leper — Mark 1:30-45;
    a paralytic — Mark 2:3-12;
    a man with a withered hand — Mark 3:1-16;
    a deaf and dumb man — Mark 7:31-37;
    a blind man — Mark 8:22-26.
Nature:
    5,000 fed — Mark 6:34-44;
    Jesus walked on the water — Mark 6:45-52;
    4,000 fed — Mark 8:1-9;
    fig tree withered — Mark 11:12-14.
Cures of demoniacs:
    a demoniac in the synagogue — Mark 1:21-28;
    the Syro-phoenician's daughter — Mark 7:24-30;
    the epileptic boy — Mark 9:14-29.

Conclusion and Application

The complete story of Jesus' life, its main features, events and accompanying incidents, even to many of the minutest details, are plainly foretold in the Old Testament Scriptures. The miracles were a part of God's way of authenticating Jesus' mission. Jesus said that if he had not done works that no other ever did, they would not have had sin (John 15:24), thus indicating that he regarded His miracles as proofs that He was from God. Christ's miracles were always profound, helpful, illustrative of an important truth and majestic.

Life Application

1. Which instruction from Jesus' sermons in Matthew do you need to pay particular heed to? _____

2. How will you apply that teaching to the appropriate area of your life? _____

3. To what degree does unbelief hinder Christ from exercising His power in your life? _____

4. What other attitude of yours could be a hindrance to your Christian growth? _____

Suggested Closing Prayer

We thank You, Father, for Jesus' ministry as the Servant-Son though He was born King of the Jews. We praise You for sending Him to give Himself on the cross for us that we might have eternal life in Him.

ADDITIONAL BACKGROUND MATERIAL

The following outline presents the Sermon on the Mount as a series of contrasts — Jesus contasts his view of the Old Testament with that of the Pharisees:

1. Spiritual Reality Transcends Material Society — Matthew 5:1-16. Jesus gives the Beatitudes in these verses. The word "blessed" is the same as the word "happy." The truly satisfied person is described. Blessedness is not here associated with material possessions or external righteousness, but with holy character, with real spirituality.

2. Internal Purity Transcends External Piety — Matthew 5:17-6:18. Jesus now takes the Pharisees to task for their externalism. He shows that true belief is of the heart, and that God's laws reach inside a man.

3. Godly Faith Transcends Worldly Anxiety — Matthew 6:19-34. The Pharisees were "lovers of money," and Jesus rebukes materialism.

4. Brotherly Love Transcends Critical Judging — Matthew 7:1-12. Jesus sees through another sin of hypocrites — that of judging unjustly.

5. True Devotion Transcends False Doctrine — Matthew 7:14-28. Jesus concludes by making a believer's responsibility clear and by warning of false prophets, whom we are to avoid.

LESSON TWO

LUKE AND JOHN

Teacher's Objective: To compare with the students these two accounts of the life of Jesus so that they will understand His ministry and person better.

Teacher's Enrichment: (This material may be shared with students as time allows.)

Some comparisons between the Gospel of Luke and the Gospel of John:
Different details concerning the Incarnation:
1. Luke 1:26-38; 2:1-20.
2. John 1:1-14.
Different treatments of the same miracle. (One was a self-evident event, the other was used as a background for a discourse):
1. Luke 9:10-17.
2. John 6:1-14; 22-59.

CLASS TIME

Suggested Opening Prayer

Dear Lord, we ask Your Holy Spirit to teach us today and to guide us as we compare the two gospels of Luke and John in their presentation of the life of Christ. Help us better understand His ministry and how it applies to our lives.

(Introduction: Be sure students understand objective memory work.)

> **Introduction**
>
> OBJECTIVE: To understand more deeply the ministry and person of Christ.
>
> TO MEMORIZE: John 7:37, 38.
>
> The writers of the last two Gospels — Luke and John — record and arrange incidents from Christ's life according to the specific objectives they wish to achieve.
>
> **LUKE**
> CHRIST AS MAN
>
> **JOHN**
> CHRIST AS DEITY
>
>

Discussion Starter

(Have someone read aloud Luke 1:1-4; have another student read John 20:30,31. Then ask:) From these two passages what would you say is the specific objective of each of these gospels? What similarities or contrasts are there?

Lesson Development

> **Bible Study**
>
> A. *Luke*
>
>   1. Read Luke 1:1-4.
>
>   To whom was this Gospel originally written? _____
>   *Theophilus.*

Theophilus was probably a Greek. Luke therefore appeals to the thoughtful, cultured, philosophic Greek mind in an orderly and classical story which has been called, "the most beautiful book ever written." He depicts the beauty and perfection of the life of Jesus: the ideal, universal man.

> What evidence is there that the recipient of this Gospel had been given some prior instruction in Christianity?
> *Verse 4: "you have been taught."*
>
> What was Luke's objective in writing to Theophilus?
> *That he might know the truth.*

Although a physician, Luke was primarily a missionary and in this case an eyewitness with a good understanding of the gospel of Christ (Luke 1:1-4).

What way of effective witnessing do you see in Luke's example? God's best ways to carry out His work often take time and organization. How does this apply to the gospel that Luke wrote?

Luke is also the author of the Book of Acts. Paul calls him "the beloved physician" (Colossians 4:14) and "my fellow-laborer" (Philemon 24 — "Lucas"). In Acts, Luke is seen as a frequent companion of Paul. Timothy tells us Luke was with Paul just before Paul's death (2 Timothy 4:11).

> 2. One of the great emphases of Luke is that Jesus, though He is the Christ, must nevertheless suffer and die at the hands of sinful men (2:33-35; 9:22-31, 43, 44; 13:31-35; 18:31-34; 24:7, 25-27, 44-47). Read Luke 20-24, the account of the last week leading up to Jesus' death and resurrection.
>
> What are some qualities of Jesus' character that stand out prominently in these chapters? *Straight-forward truthful, bold, determined, compassionate, perceptive, appreciative, authoratative, earnest, humble, encouraging, submissive, forgiving, understanding.*

The first thirty years of Jesus' life are often termed "the silent years." Scripture gives few details of these years, but the growth and development of the character of Christ are extremely important. Let's read Luke 2:39-52 and name some qualities of Christ's early life as recorded in this passage.

(Leader may present the following suggestions:)

a. Strong in spirit, filled with wisdom — 2:40.

b. Independent and desirous of learning — 2:43.

   c. Able to talk and learn from doctors at only twelve years of age — 2:46.

   d. Astounded men by His understanding — 2:47.

   e. Primarily concerned with the business of the Father, even more so than that of home and family — 2:49.

   f. Obedient to parents, however — 2:51.

   g. Pleased other men while honoring God — 2:52.

> **What qualities of character in Jesus' enemies stand out prominently in these chapters?** *Accusative, evasive, crafty, deceitful, cowardly, murderous, cruel, blasphemous, liars, violent, rebellious, unreasonable, stubborn, gamblers, abusive.*
>
> **Why, then, did men seek to have Jesus crucified?** *Because of who He said He was: the Son of God. Accused Him of blasphemy; fearful of His power and His popularity.*
>
> **How were the disciples — and thus Theophilus and all the readers of Luke — assured that Jesus' suffering and death occurred according to God's plan instead of accidently, simply because of men's evil hearts?** *Jesus foretold it in so many places.*
>
> **What difference does that make to you?** _____

The special emphasis of Luke is the humanity of Jesus. Like the other Gospel writers, he represents Jesus as the Son of God, but he features Jesus' sympathy for the weak, the suffering and the outcast.

Another area of importance in the Gospel of Luke is the genealogy of Christ traced through the line of Mary:

   a. Many Bible readers tend to skip over the passages listing the various generations recorded in Scripture, failing to realize that these passages prove the identity of Jesus Christ as the Messiah, and the fulfillment of the promises of God's Word to the nation Israel.

   b. In the past God chose one particular family, that of Abraham (and later the family of David within Abraham's line), to be the vehicle through which His Son would come into the world. The Hebrew nation was founded and protected by God through the ages in order to preserve the line of descent of His Son to come.

   c. Matthew goes back to Abraham in its record of the genealogy; Luke goes back to Adam. Neither contradicts the other, but each traces the ancestry of Christ through a different line — one is Joseph's, the other Mary's.

> **B. John**
>
> 1. Why did John take the trouble to relate the various signs, or miracles, found in his Gospel (John 20:30, 31)?
>   *That we may believe that Jesus is the Christ, the Son of God, and might have life in His name.*

This is the overall key verse.

The first three gospels are called the Synoptic Gospels. The word "synoptic" implies that the three writers look at the life of Christ from a similar point of view. About one-half of Matthew's material is found in Mark also. About one-third of Luke is found in a similar form in Mark. All but 55 verses of Mark can be found in Matthew or Luke. About one-fourth of Matthew's and Luke's gospels is similar material that is not found in Mark.

Each gives a sort of running account of the life and teaching of Christ but with a different slant. Matthew was an eyewitness of many things in his gospel. Mark, it is believed, wrote with the help of his eyewitness companion, Peter. Luke, a historian of first caliber, admittedly used various first-hand source material (Luke 1:1-4).

The fourth gospel written by John is radically different from the other three. It, too, is the testimony of an eyewitness (John 21:24). But it is not a rapidly moving account of Christ's life and teachings. This had already been provided in the other three which were written a number of years before. John's account is more reflective, more philosophical, more subjective, more interpretative.

He largely brings out new material omitted by the other three writers. He takes a few events and enlarges and amplifies their treatment. The miracles he incorporates are chosen with special purpose of fostering belief in Him.

> 2. Skim through this Gospel and see if you can list below the seven miracles of Jesus that are recorded in John.
>   *1)Turned water to wine--John 2:1-11 2)Healed nobleman's son--4:46-54 3)Healed sick man at pool--5:1-9 4)Fed five thousand--6:1-14 5)Walked on water--6:15-20 6)Healed blind man--9:1-7,25 7)Raised Lazarus from dead--11:38-44.*

The significance of these miracles of Jesus:

(1) John 2:1-11 — *turning the water into wine.* Jesus commanded the servants to fill the waterpots (picture the thirsty human heart, empty without Christ, needing his fullness) and the servants obeyed His word. Salvation is always by the agency of the Word of God. John 3:5 — the water of the Word of God is the means to salvation (1 Peter 1:23). What Christ provided was better than a rich man's best (John 2:10).

(2) John 4:46-54 — *healing the nobleman's son.* The nobleman heard of Jesus; hearing is not enough for salvation. The nobleman besought him; that wasn't adequate. The man believed the word that Jesus had spoken and his son was healed. This is also a picture of our salvation — believing the Word of God.

(3) John 5:1-9 — *healing the sick man at the pool.* This man, sick for thirty-eight years, was completely unable to help himself. He was unable to climb into the pool — a picture of man's inability to help himself or do anything to deserve salvation. The Lord chose this man and healed him. Salvation is obtained by grace!

(4) John 6:1-14 — *feeding the five thousand.* Whatever one may have of his own, whether five loaves and two fishes, or position, popularity or wealth, no one but Jesus Christ can ever supply his present need. Jesus took what the boy had and multiplied it into more than necessary to meet the need of the crowd. Christ broke the loaves to provide physical sustenance; he broke His own body on the cross to provide an eternal redemption for the whole human race. Spiritual feeding at the cross is the only food which eternally satisfies and presently blesses.

(5) John 6:15-20 — *walking on the water.* The disciples, trying to reach the other shore, became frightened at their helpless position in the storm. When they saw Jesus unnaturally walking on the sea, they grew even more anxious. But He spoke to them, and they instantly recognized Him — His power and authority — and gladly received Him into their ship. This pictures an unbeliever who, becoming alarmed at his own need, recognizes Christ's supernatural ability to meet that need. As the disciples immediately reached their destination and were out of danger, so the unbeliever, when he receives Christ into His heart, immediately arrives at an eternally safe haven for his soul.

(6) John 9:1-7, 25 — *healing the blind man.* To be blind from birth indicates total darkness. This is evident in the unbeliever so far as spiritual things are concerned; he is in spiritual darkness, unable to perceive spiritual truth. After receiving Christ, one of the first miracles is that one begins to see spiritual truth, understand the Bible and take note of the guidance of the Lord in one's life. Spiritual light follows new birth, just as seeing physical light follows normal birth into this life.

(7) John 11:38-44 — *raising Lazarus from the dead.* Before one is born into the family of God and has experienced regeneration, he is said to be spiritually dead and without hope in this world or in the next. Christ's raising of Lazarus is a complete likeness of His miraculous work in the human heart when He brings a person out of spiritual death into spiritual life.

The special emphasis in John is the deity of Christ. The emphasis is on belief and faith. However, there is a strong counter theme of willful rejection and unbelief on the part of some.

---

3. What climactic event did most to confirm the disciples' — and thus the reader's — faith in Jesus as the Christ? *His resurrection.*

4. Read John 13 and 14.

   What attitude of heart must you demonstrate if other people are to realize that you are Christ's representative in the world (13:34, 35)? *Love for one another.*

> What is God's provision for enabling Christians to be true representatives of Christ in the world (14:16-18)? _A helper--the Holy Spirit--who abides within._
>
> What conditions must you fulfill in order to experience fully this provision (14:15, 21, 23, 24)? _Must keep His commandments._

Conclusion and Application

Luke presents Christ as a perfect man. As a man He always reacted to every situation as a man should. Luke 20:19-26 is an illustration of His conduct under stress. The Lord Jesus was continually dependent on the Father and absolutely obedient (John 14:10). He was a perfect man walking in the power of the Holy Spirit throughout His life on earth. We, in turn, are dependent on the Son.

> **Life Application**
>
> 1. Luke presented Christ as the Son of Man. What does that say to you? _____
> _____
> _____
>
> 2. According to John 15:16, 27, what was to be the disciples' function after Jesus left the earth? _To be witnesses of Him and to go and bear fruit._
>
> How does that refer to you? _____
> _____
> _____
>
> What promises can you claim from these verses? _____
> _____
> _____

Suggested Closing Prayer

We thank You, Father, for the record You have given us through Luke of Jesus, the Son of Man, and the one You have given us through John of Jesus, the Son of God. Help us apply the teachings of these to our own lives and move us to share them with others.

ADDITIONAL BACKGROUND MATERIAL

John was one of the inner circle of the disciples — Peter, James and John. He often speaks of himself as the "disciple whom Jesus loved" (John 13:23; 19:26; 20:2; 21:7, 20).

Many of the expressions used by Jesus about Himself (recorded by John), can be predicated only by His deity:

"I am the truth" — John 14:6.

"I am the way" — 14:6.

"I am the door; if anyone enters through Me, he shall be saved, and shall go in and out, and find pasture" — 10:9.

"No man comes to the Father but through Me" — 14:6.

"I am the bread of life" — 6:35, 48.

"I am the life" — 14:6; 11:25.

"I am the resurrection" — 11:25.

"And everyone who lives and believes in Me shall never die" — 11:26a.

"I am [the Messiah]" — 4:26.

"Before Abraham was born, I am" — 8:58.

" . . . glorify Thou Me . . . with the glory which I had with Thee before the world was" — 17:5.

"He who has seen Me has seen the Father" — 14:9.

"I and the Father are one" — 10:30.

LESSON THREE

THE ACTS OF THE APOSTLES

Teacher's Objective: To help students trace the lives of Peter and Paul and their respective ministries as seen in the early New Testament Church, and to motivate students to emulate their obedience and faithfulness.

Teacher's Enrichment: (This material may be shared with students as time allows.)

Who is the author of the book of Acts? (Luke 1:1-4; Acts 1:1,2.) Dr. F. F. Bruce says — "The Book of Acts is the sequel to the Third Gospel and is written by the same author, Luke, the beloved physician, and companion of the Apostle Paul. The external evidence of various writers from the second century onward is unanimous and adequate on this point, and the internal evidence of the style, outlook and subject matter of the two books is equally satisfactory."

In much of the latter part of the book, Luke uses the personal pronoun *we*, indicating that he traveled with Paul and was an eyewitness of much that is recorded in Acts. He quite possibly kept a log or diary from which he could draw in writing this book.

CLASS TIME

Suggested Opening Prayer

Lord, we thank You for Your chosen men in ages past, and we pray that You will teach us obedience and faithfulness to Your kingdom just as they learned it from You.

(Introduction: Be sure
students understand
    objective
    memory work*.)

Introduction
OBJECTIVE: To view the dynamic establishment of the first-century church.
ACTS
WORKS OF THE HOLY SPIRIT
TO MEMORIZE: Acts 1:8.

(*Have a student quote the memory verse and state its importance to his personal life and to the life of every believer. Ask for volunteers to share any other verses which they have memorized.)

Discussion Starter

Action is important in our daily life. Can you think of several examples of activities which would fit under the following three categories? Can you give Scripture verses to back any of them up?

Acts for Christ:
(Suggestions:)
    be His ambassadors — 2 Corinthians 5:20;
    be obedient — Genesis 12:1,4.

Acts for others:
    be an example to believers — 2 Timothy 4:12;
    maintain a loving, long-suffering attitude toward other believers — Colossians 3:12-14.

Acts for self:
    profitable study — 1 Timothy 2:15;
    proper attitude toward self — Romans 12:3.

Lesson Development

The book of Acts is a record of the early church in action, getting the gospel to the Roman world. Acts 1:8 is a prophetic outline of what happens later in the

> The Book of Acts begins by referring to the material presented in the Gospels as "all that Jesus began to do and teach" (Acts 1:1). Acts tells of the works that the resurrected and ascended Christ continued to do through the Holy Spirit, poured out on His disciples at Pentecost. Acts 1:8 has often been considered as the key verse of this book. Survey the book and answer these questions: What chapters tell of the witness of the disciples at Jerusalem? _2-7_ At Samaria? _8-9_
> To the uttermost parts of the earth? _10-28_.

book in the spreading of the gospel. The gospel was first preached to the Jews in Jerusalem (Acts 2:6). Next, the gospel spread throughout the regions of Judea and Samaria (Acts 8:14). The Samaritans were a kind of half-breed Jew and Gentile. Their reception of the gospel was one step toward Gentile evangelism (Acts 8:14). God gave a vision to Peter, and then arranged circumstances so that the gospel was taken to the Gentiles (Acts 10; especially verse 45). As the book continues, Gentile acceptance of the truth grows, and Jewish rejection becomes more and more pronounced (Acts 13:46; 18;6; 28:25-29).

In the first part of the book, Peter is the prominent personage. Jerusalem is the center of his activities

> **Bible Study**
>
> A. *Peter*
>
> The following are some of the major messages that Peter gave as he witnessed for Christ: Acts 2:14-36; 3:11-26; 10:34-43.
>
> What was the most important point about the life of Christ that Peter was trying to get across? _His death for sin, and His resurrection._

and his ministry is primarily to Jews. His characteristics include boldness and preparedness.

> **B. Paul**
>
> Of all the apostles, Paul stands out most prominently in Acts and the New Testament.
>
> 1. What kind of a man was Paul before he was converted (8:1-3; 9:1; 22:1-6; 26:4-12)? *Strict and zealous for God, persecuting Christians, murderous, hostile.*
> When Jesus appeared to Paul on the road to Damascus, what did He tell him he was to do? *Continue to Damascus where he would be given further instructions.*

The key to Paul's effective ministry was:
1. instantaneous obedience — Acts 9:6; 26:19;
2. filling of the Spirit — Acts 13:4. (See parallel passages in Additional

Background Material and compare our lives to Paul's at various points if time allows.)

> 2. The first missionary journey of Paul is recorded in Acts 13 and 14. How did Paul and his friend Barnabas know they were to go forth to preach the gospel (13:1-4)? *The Holy Spirit instructed the church to send them out.*

Where did Paul preach (Acts 13:5)? What significance does this have for us?
(We should share Christ in key centers of learning as well as other places.)

> To whom did Paul seek to minister first at Cypress (13:4-12), at Antioch of Pisidia (13:13-52) and at Iconium (14:1-7)? *To the Jews in the synagogues.*
>
> To whom did Paul preach after this first group rejected the gospel? *The Gentiles.*
>
> In preaching to the Jews, Paul was able to make a point of contact with them by referring to the Old Testament Scriptures. What was the point of contact Paul used in speaking to the pagan Gentiles at Lystra (14:8-18)? *Their attempt to sacrifice to Paul and Barnabus as to gods.*
> What did Paul do to establish his converts in the faith (14:21-23)? *Strengthened the souls, encouraged them, appointed elders, commended them to God.*
>
> Romans 15:20 tells us one more thing about Paul's evangelism strategy. What is it? *He went to areas which had not heard the Gospel before.*

Paul's strategy of evangelism also included the following:
1. He concentrated on centers of culture, commerce and influence. Examples: Antioch, Athens, Corinth, Ephesus, Jerusalem, Rome.
2. When he came to a city, he first went

to the Jews, if possible. He built on their religious foundation of the Old Testament, showing that Jesus of Nazareth was the Messiah. He then presented the message to the Gentiles.

3. When he went to Gentiles, he appealed to their innate knowledge of God, the creator and sustainer of the world. He explained Christ's relationship to making this true God known to man (Acts 17:22-34).

4. He built up the converts and established local organized groups of believers (Acts 14:21-23; 16:5).

5. He trained the believers to be witnesses for Christ (Acts 19:8-10; 1 Thessalonians 1:6-8).

What might be a good strategy for evangelism today?

(Have group refer to 1 Peter 3:15; 2 Timothy 2:2, 15; and 1 Thessalonians 5:19 and ask the members to use their imagination.) What of Paul's strategy should we employ? Should we wait for people to come to church meetings in order to tell them about Christ?

Who in the early church proclaimed the gospel to the lost?

Everyone — Acts 8:1, 4. It is not the duty of the pastors alone to win the lost. They are to build up the Christians so that they can evangelize as well (Ephesians 4:11-13).

---

3. Several of Paul's messages are recorded in Acts. The two major ones are found in 13:16-41 and in 17:22-31. What was the most important truth he presented in each of these? _The death of Christ and His_ _resurrection._

NOTE: The places mentioned in this and the other missionary journeys of Paul may be found on maps found in the back of many Bibles.

C. *The Holy Spirit*

1. What are some of the ways in which the Holy Spirit empowered the early church?

Acts 1:8 _Gave power in witnessing._

4:31 _Gave boldness in witnessing._

2:4-8; 10:46; 19:6 _Gave power to speak in other languages._

7:54-60 _Gave peace and confidence in the face of danger and death._

10:19-20; 13:2-4 _Gave guidance to the early church._

11:28; 21:10-13 _Gave power to prophesy._

2. How did the Holy Spirit work through Paul as he ministered at Cypress (13:4-12)? _He gave Paul insight into the motive of the magician._

At Iconium (13:52-14:3)? _He granted Paul and the others the ability to perform signs and wonders._

Why does the church today lack power?

The early church was enabled for tasks by the filling of the Holy Spirit — Acts 2:4; 4:8, 31; 6:3, 5, 8; 7:55; 9:17; 11:24; 13:9, 52. Today the church needs that message of the filling of the Holy Spirit. We cannot expect to do God's work by our own power, but only by that of the Holy Spirit. We also need to know how to share with others the means of being Spirit-filled — John 14:16-17; 16:7-15.

Conclusion and Application

The early church was commissioned of Christ and empowered by the Spirit to take the message of Christ to every creature. In its generation the known world heard the claims of Christ. The commission has not changed. But only as the church of today avails itself of the power of the Holy Spirit can we reach our entire generation with the message of life.

Life Application

1. What is the most important thing you now try to tell others about Christ? _____

_____

_____

How does that compare with what Peter and Paul preached?

_____

_____

2. What can you learn from Paul in your discipling of others?

_____

Suggested Closing Prayer

(Have several group members pray briefly, expressing thanksgiving for the privilege of sharing in bringing others to the Lord.)

ADDITIONAL BACKGROUND MATERIAL

Some parallel passages of Scripture on:

A. The work of the Holy Spirit:

1. Before conversion: conviction — John 16:7-11.
2. At conversion:
   a. seals — Ephesians 1:13;
   b. baptizes — 1 Corinthians 12:13;
   c. regenerates — Titus 3:5;
   d. indwells — 1 Corinthians 3:16-17;
   e. fills — Ephesians 5:18.
3. Following conversion:
   a. filling should occur — Ephesians 5:18;
   b. guides into all truth — John 16:13;
   c. shows us things to come — John 16:13;
   d. glorifies Christ — John 16:14.

B. Paul's ministry:
   1. Paul's motivation — Philippians 3:7-14.
   2. Paul's obligation — Romans 1:14-17.
   3. Paul's message — 1 Corinthians 1:18-25.
   4. Paul's attitude — 1 Thessalonians 2:3-12; Acts 20:24.
   5. God's results — 1 Thessalonians 1:5-10.
       a. Paul's prayer in his early ministry — Acts 22:10.
       b. Assurance at end of life — 2 Timothy 4:7,8.

LESSON FOUR

ROMANS, 1 AND 2 CORINTHIANS AND GALATIANS

Teacher's Objective: To understand what the gospel is and how it is personally appropriated, and to show the need of sharing the good news with others.

Teacher's Enrichment: (The following material may be shared with class members as time permits.)

Parallel Scripture passages on the gospel:

A. The source of the gospel — Galatians 1:11,12.

B. The basic content of the gospel — 1 Corinthians 15:1-8.

C. Paul's attitude toward those who would proclaim a perverted gospel — Galatians 1:6-9.

D. Various reactions to the gospel — 1 Corinthians 1:17-25.

E. The reason why people are blind to the gospel — 2 Corinthians 4:3,4.

F. Paul's attitude toward proclaiming the gospel to others — Romans 1:14-17.

CLASS TIME

Suggested Opening Prayer

Father, we will be studying today what the gospel is and how it can be personally appropriated. Please show us the importance of sharing it with others with whom we come into contact.

(Introduction: Be sure
students understand
   objective
   memory work
   reading assignment.)

Introduction

OBJECTIVE: To understand
         the essence of
         the gospel.

TO MEMORIZE: Romans 1:16.

TO READ: Galatians.

Discussion Starter

(Explain that the word "gospel" means good news. Have students write on a sheet of paper four reasons why they feel that the Christian message is good news. Have each person read his answers.)

459

Lesson Development

(Have the class share this material in any of the ways suggested in the Instructions for Teaching on page 21.)

ROMANS	I & 2 COR	GAL
LAW	CHURCH	GRACE

Out of the 27 books of the New Testament, 21 are letters and 13 of these were definitely written by Paul. They were written to meet the needs and circumstances of actual persons and communities. Paul, the man God used to write so much of the New Testament, was a Roman citizen, a Jew of Tarsus, a Hebrew of the Hebrews, brought up at the feet of a great teacher, Gamaliel, but became a bond slave and missionary to Jesus Christ. His Lord calls him "a chosen instrument of Mine, to bear My name before the Gentiles and kings and the children of Israel" (Acts 9:15). From the day of his conversion, Paul's very life was Christ (Philippians 1:21).

Bible Study

A. *Romans*

This epistle was written from the city of Corinth shortly after Paul had finished his work in Ephesus. Rome was the center of the civilized world, the great metropolis of a vast empire. The city was already the home of many Christians. The immediate reason for this letter was Paul's anticipated visit to Rome. He is telling the Romans the good news concerning the way in which God, in His infinite love, has provided free and full salvation for sinners. Paul's main insistence is that man's justification before God rests not on the Law of Moses, but on the mercy of Christ.

1. Read Romans 1:1-3, 16, 17.

What is the main theme of Romans? _____
    _____ The Gospel of Christ.

What is the gospel of Christ? _____ His death for our sins, His burial and His resurrection for our justification.

What does it reveal? God's grace and His love for mankind.

An outline of the book of Romans shows what all the gospel of Jesus Christ includes.

1. Provisions for forgiveness of sin — Chapters 1-5.
2. Power to live a victorious life — Chapters 6-8.
3. Program for the ages — Chapters 9-11.
4. Precepts for Christian living — Chapters 12-16.

Many think the gospel refers only to the fact that a Christian is saved from hell. But as this outline shows us, it is much more inclusive. The gospel guarantees that we shall go to heaven; but, because of our position in Christ (Chapter 6) and the Holy Spirit in our hearts (Chapter 8), it also guarantees we can live the life God wants us to live here on earth. Furthermore, the gospel includes the future salvation of the Jewish nation (Chapters 9:11); and finally, it gives us practical instructions on how to live (Chapters 12-16). As Paul contemplated all the gospel, he broke into an exclamation of praise: "O the depth of the riches both of the wisdom and knowledge of God! How unsearchable are His judgments, and unfathomable His ways!" (11:33). The gospel of Jesus Christ is God's answer to every human dilemma. There is no problem it will not solve, no need it cannot satisfy, no question it cannot answer. Paul was not ashamed of it, and he felt a debtor to preach it to every creature (1:14-16).

What is sin?

The condition of man before a holy God is sinful.

> 2. **Read Romans 3:9-18.** Man is sinful and lives a life separated from God. Man is self-centered rather than God-centered. God's Word describes how He looks at man in his sinful state.

Sin originated with Satan (Isaiah 14:12-14), entered the world through Adam (Romans 5:12), was and is universal (Christ alone excepted — Romans 3:23), incurs the penalties of spiritual and physical death (Genesis 2:17; 3:19, Romans 6:23) and has no remedy but the sacrificial death of Christ (Hebrews 9:26; Acts 4:12) which must be accepted by faith (Acts 13:38-39).

Sin may be summarized as: the violation of or lack of obedience to the revealed will of God, the absence of righteousness, a natural attitude of opposition or indifference toward God.

What has God done for us to bring us into a right relationship with Himself?

He has redeemed us — Romans 3:24; 5:6-8; Galatians 3:13.

Redemption means "to deliver by paying a price." The underlying thought is to be purchased out of a slave market, in this case,

> **List five characteristics of a sinful man:**
> verse 9 _All under sin._
> verse 10 _None righteous._
> verse 11 _None understand or seek for God._
> verse 17 _Do not know the path of peace._
> verse 18 _Have no fear of God._
>
> **According to Romans 2:11 and 3:9, 10, 23, who is included in this sinful condition?** _Everyone._
>
> **What righteousness does a man have that he can offer God (Romans 3:10)?** _None._
>
> 3. Read Romans 3:21-28; 5:1-5.
>
> **What is it that God declared unto you (verses 25, 26)?** _His righteousness._
>
> **Why has He declared this (two reasons)?** _That He might be just and that He might also be the justifier of those who have faith in Jesus._
>
> **Therefore, how are you justified (1:17; 3:28; 5:1)?** _By faith, apart from the works of the law._

the slavery of sin. Only a free man can purchase the slave's freedom.

He has justified us — Romans 3:26; 4:25-5:2; Galatians 2:16.

To be justified is the judicial act of God whereby He justly declares righteous one who believes on Jesus Christ. Literally, God imputes or credits to our account His righteousness, which is in reality the only righteousness.

Herein lies the gospel! God redeems us, justifies us and gives us his righteousness. He does it all because of His grace. This is certainly good news!

> What are some results of justification (5:17)? _____
> *Abundance of grace, gift of righteousness,*
> *life through Jesus Christ.*
>
> **4.** Being justified by faith, what is your spiritual resource
> (5:5)? *The Holy Spirit has been given to us.*

God has given us the
power to live for Him —
Romans 8:11, 15; 6:11-13; Galatians 5:16, 22-23.

> **5.** Being justified by faith, what is your reasonable service
> (12:1)? *To present our bodies a living and*
> *holy sacrifice, acceptable to God.*
>
> **6.** List five ways in which this service will affect your daily
> walk (12:6-13:10)
> *Love will be without hypocrisy; will abhor*
> *evil and cling to good; etc.*
> _____
> _____

The main theme of
1 Corinthians is Christian
conduct — 1 Corinthians
10:13, 31-33.

    Morality — 6:18-20.

    Marriage — 7:1-40.

    Questionable practices
— 8:1-13.

> **B.** *1 Corinthians*
>
> This epistle was written three years after Paul left Corinth.
> A delegation of the leaders of the Corinthian church was
> sent to Ephesus to consult Paul about some very serious
> problems that had arisen in the church. There were
> thousands of Christians in Corinth and yet they had no one
> central meeting place. Paul dealt with individual problems
> and endeavored to unite the groups into units that would
> cooperate in the general cause of Christ.

Divisions among the Christians — 1:10-17.

Conduct had to be stressed because these Christians were carnal (walking "after
the flesh"), thus remaining babes in Christ (1 Corinthians 3:1-4).

Outline of 1 Corinthians:

1. Problem of divisions — 1:10-4:21.
2. Problem of immorality — Chapters 5-7.
3. Problem of food offered to idols — 8:1-11:1.
4. Problem of public worship — 11:2-14:40.
5. Doctrine of the resurrection — Chapter 15.
6. Practical concern of Paul — Chapter 16.

> **1.** Read 1 Corinthians 1:17-29. Paul makes it clear that God
> is wiser than men and chooses the foolish things of the
> world to confound the mighty.
>
> How has God ordained that men should hear and
> believe? *Through the preaching of His Word.*
> _____
>
> Whom has He chosen for this task? _____
> *The foolish, the weak and the base.*
>
> Why? *That no man should boast before God.*

2. Read 1 Corinthians 9:22-24.

   Give in your own words definite proof that Paul had

   forsaken all that he had to follow Christ (verse 22). _____
   "I have become all things to all men."

   To what does he liken his task?   *A race.*

   Why is this so appropriate? *Because of the need*
   for learning and exercising self-control.

3. Read 1 Corinthians 13. In verses 4-8, insert your own
   name in the place of "love" or "charity." As you read it,

   does it paint a true picture of your life? _____

   Which verse does not fit you and what do you think God

   would have you do about it? _____

C. 2 Corinthians

Soon after Paul had written 1 Corinthians, he met Titus on his way to Corinth. Titus brought word that Paul's letter had accomplished much good but that there were still some who were disloyal and that there were problems with legalizers. Paul's condition was one of physical weakness, weariness and pain. His spiritual burdens were great: first, the maintenance of the churches; second, his concern about the legalists; and third, his anguish over the distrust felt toward him by some of the members of the churches.

The main theme of 2 Corinthians is the vindication of Paul's apostleship (2 Corinthians 4:1-7).

Outline of 2 Corinthians:
1. Ministry: Paul's defense 1:1-7:16.
2. Money: for the Christians at Jerusalem — 8:1–9:15.
3. Ministry: Paul's defense — 10:1–13:14.

1. Read 2 Corinthians 4:1-6. Paul is careful in his handling of
   the Word of God.

   What is the tragic result of handling the Word of God
   deceitfully (verse 3)?   *Some will perish.*

   Why did God shine into our hearts (verse 6)? *To give*
   us light so we could know the glory of God
   in Christ.

2. What is it that Paul fears and of which we all must be
   well aware (2 Corinthians 11:3)? *Being led astray.*

3. Paul prayed to be relieved of his "thorn in the flesh."

   What was the Lord's answer to his prayer (2 Corinthians
   12:9)? *"My grace is sufficient for you."*

   What was Paul's attitude toward the final outcome?
   He would boast about his weakness because he
   knew the power of Christ would dwell in him.

   What lesson can you learn from his experience (12:10)?
   Be content; we have Christ's strength when
   we are weak.

D. Galatians

Some time after Paul had left Galatia, certain Jewish teachers began to insist that Gentiles could not be Christian without keeping the Law of Moses. The objective of this epistle is the defense of the gospel of grace that Paul had received by the revelation of Jesus.

The main theme of Galatians is that the gospel of God comes by grace and is sustained by grace. Law has nothing to do with it. We can do nothing to receive grace or to keep it. All is of God and of His grace. Example: Galatians 3:1-3, 10,11; 4:9,10; 5:1-6.

What is grace?

Grace is the unmerited love of God shown toward sinful men. Grace means that God has *given* us the gospel as a gift, without any strings attached; we can do nothing to *earn* it. We must simply receive it by faith, just as any gift is received. Faith is the only channel through which grace can operate. (See Ephesians 2:8-10.)

The Galatians were making the mistake of trying to impose the law of Moses on the gospel. They said it was necessary to do some work, such as submit to circumcision, to be saved.

Many Christians today, though they realize they cannot do anything to be saved but receive God's gift, make the mistake of trying to earn their way thereafter in the Christian life. In Galatians 3:1-5, Paul speaks against these heresies.

Outline of Galatians:

1. The gospel of grace: Paul's apostolic authority — Chapters 1-2.
2. The gospel of grace: contrasted with the law — Chapters 3-4.
3. The gospel of grace: results in practical living — Chapters 5-6.

---

1. Paul shows that the gospel was not of man, neither did he receive it of man nor was he taught it of man. What was its true origin (Galatians 1;12)? _____
   A revelation of Jesus Christ.

2. According to Galatians 2:20, who indwells Paul? *Christ.* What effect does this have on his daily life? *It is no longer he who lives, but Christ lives in him.*

3. Read Galatians 5:16-21. In this passage Paul lists the works of the flesh. How can we as Christians avoid doing the works of the flesh? *Walk by the Spirit.*

Conclusion and Application

Grace transforms Christian living from moralistic striving in our own effort, to an attitude of rest and faith, where we let Christ live in us and through us. Galatians 2:20 and 5:16 are two of the key passages of the book, teaching us that our only responsibility is to trust Jesus Christ to live through us by the Holy Spirit. Here is the secret to victory. We give up our own struggling and striving — our own efforts to please God — and by faith we trust Him to live through us.

Life Application

1. According to Galatians 5:22, 23, what will be the result in your life of this type of walk? List the definite characteristics. *Love, joy, peace, patience, kindness, goodness, faithfulness, gentleness, self-control.*

> Which work of your flesh do you most need to surrender to the Holy Spirit's control today? _____
>
> _____
>
> Why not take time right now to do that?

Suggested Closing Prayer

(Give students a few minutes of silent prayer time in which to surrender to the Lord's control any part of their lives they may feel necessary. Then close with:) Father, we thank You for hearing and answering our prayers, and for forgiving us of sin and cleansing our lives. Give us the boldness needed to become effective witnesses for You.

ADDITIONAL BACKGROUND MATERIAL

A. Receiving the gospel:

It is not man's wisdom, religion, or good works that bring him salvation; it is the simple gospel of Christ received by faith (Romans 1:16).

B. Sharing the gospel with others:

Notice the three "I am's" of Paul:

1. "I am under obligation" (Romans 1:14). We need to realize the debt that we have toward all men to tell them the good news. We gain a sense of obligation as we study the Bible and see man's desperate need and God's provision for this need through Jesus Christ.

2. "I am eager [ready]" (Romans 1:15). We need to be prepared to share the gospel with others. We need to know how to explain the gospel in terms that people can understand and respond to.

3. "I am not ashamed" (Romans 1:16). If we are ashamed of the gospel of Christ, this means that we need the filling of the Holy Spirit to give us boldness (Acts 4:31).

LESSON FIVE

THE PRISON, THESSALONIAN AND PASTORAL EPISTLES

Teacher's Objective: To help students get a brief survey of the Prison, Thessalonian and Pastoral Epistles; particularly to note how they reflect the character of Paul.

Teacher's Enrichment: (This material can be shared with students as time permits.)

These are some of Christ's teachings which parallel Paul's examples.

A. Christ's teaching on prayer — Luke 11:11-13; John 15:7; 16:23,24.

B. Christ's teaching on suffering for the gospel's sake — Matthew 5:11,12.

C. Christ's teaching on personal example — Matthew 5:13-48.

D. Christ's teaching on money — Matthew 6:19-34.

E. Christ's teaching on good works — Matthew 5:16.

CLASS TIME

Suggested Opening Prayer

Lord, teach us to be like Thy servant Paul.

(Introduction: Be sure students understand
objective
memory work
reading assignment.)

Introduction		
OBJECTIVE: To examine the character of the apostle Paul as presented in his epistles.	EPH PHIL COL PHILEMON	◊ PRISON
	I & 2 THESS	◊ LETTERS
TO MEMORIZE: Colossians 2:6, 7.	I & 2 TIMOTHY TITUS	◊ CO-WORKERS
TO READ: Ephesians.		

Discussion Starter

(Read the following to the group:)

A particular church was in need of a pastor. One of the elders was interested in knowing just what kind of a minister they desired. He therefore wrote the following letter, as if he had received it from the applicant and read the letter before the pulpit committee.

"Gentlemen: Understanding that your pulpit is vacant, I should like to apply for the position. I have many qualifications which I think you would appreciate. I have been able to preach with power and have had success as a writer. I have been told that I am a good organizer. I have been a leader in most places I've gone.

"Some folk, however, have things against me. I am over fifty years of age. I have never preached in one place for over three years at a time. In some places I have left town, after my work caused riots and disturbances. I have to admit that I have been in jail three times, but not because of any wrong doing. My health is not good, though I still get a good deal done. I have had to work at my trade to help pay my way. The churches I have preached in have been small though several were located in large cities.

"I have not gotten along too well with the religious leaders in different towns where I have preached. In fact, some of them have threatened me, taken me to court, and even attacked me physically. I am not too good at keeping records. I have been known to forget whom I have baptized. If you can use me, however, I shall do my best for you, even if I have to work to help with my support."

(Stop here and ask:) How do you suppose the committee responded? (After hearing some replies, continue reading.)

The elder read this letter to the committee, asking for a reply. The committee said he would never do for that church. They were not interested in an unhealthy, contentious, troublemaking, absent-minded jail-bird. After inquiring about the name of the presumptuous applicant, the elder answered, "The Apostle Paul."

This illustrates how modern Christians are often more concerned with surface issues in a man's life, and know little of true spirituality. In Paul we have a man who is truly spiritual. This lesson gives us many interesting insights into his life.

> Ephesians, Philippians, Colossians and Philemon are called the "prison" epistles because they were written by Paul during his first imprisonment, mentioned in Acts 28.

Lesson Development

> **Bible Study**
>
> A. *Prison Epistles*
>
> 1. Ephesians.
>   Through his own labors, Paul had founded the church at Ephesus (Acts 19), but since, in this letter, he includes as his readers those who had never known him, most scholars agree that Paul wrote this letter not just to Ephesus, but for all Gentile Christians wherever they might be. The purpose of this letter was to show the Gentiles that they were on an equal footing with the Jews in receiving the blessings of salvation (see Ephesians 2:19-22; 3:6).

Paul gives us interesting pictures of his spiritual life in the epistles. His two recorded prayers in Ephesians are monumental. He prays not for material blessings, nor that the saints would receive spiritual blessings, but that they should know of the spiritual blessings they already possess. Ephesians 1:18 — "The eyes of your

heart may be enlightened"; 3:18,19 — that they may "comprehend" and "know."
This is in accord with Ephesians 1:3. We already have all we need in Christ; we
only need to realize it and make use of it. It is not wrong to pray for things which
are material, especially
when they affect our spiritual well-being. But our
real concern should always
be a spiritual one.

> **What had been the prospects of Gentiles receiving the blessings of salvation in previous times (2:11, 12)?** _None— they were separate from Christ, excluded from Israel, strangers to the promise, with no hope and without God_
>
> **Through what event were the blessings of salvation made available to all (2:13-18)?** _He abolished in His flesh the enmity. His death destroyed the barriers, reconciling the two through the cross._
>
> **From the prayer that Paul prays in Ephesians 3:14-19, list the blessings of salvation that all Christians now enjoy.** _A heavenly name, power through the Spirit, Christ dwells in hearts, knowledge of love of Christ, fulness of God._

2. Philippians.

> Paul wrote this letter to the church he had founded (Acts 16) to thank them for the money they had sent him for his support while in prison. In writing it, he also sought to overcome the disunity in the church between two women, Euodia and Syntyche (4:2). With this disunity overcome, the church could stand firmly together in preaching the gospel without fear to those round about them (1:27, 28).
>
> **Read Philippians 1:12-30. What had Paul been doing in Rome that would encourage the Philippians to be bold in proclaiming the gospel (1:13, 14)?** _Witnessing to everyone._

Paul was a prisoner in
Rome. Not many prisoners
are happy about it, even
when justly punished. Paul
was unjustly punished, yet
rejoiced. Why? Because his
great concern was Christ
and His work. For him,
"life" was Christ and his
misfortunes did not overcome him. Note reasons which would otherwise have
discouraged Paul:

(1) He was unjustly in prison.
(2) He had been there for some time (first jailed in Jerusalem).
(3) He was opposed by others who claimed to be Christians.
(4) He was rejected by his own race.
(5) He was probably alone and inactive much of the time.
(6) He was in a large, strange city.
(7) He was uncertain about his future.
(8) He had to take charity from others (Chapter 4).

These reasons would tend to throw a lesser Christian into self-pity and keep
him from witnessing at all. But Paul considered them an open door for spreading
the gospel in a new place.

How did Paul's attitude regarding the future help to encourage the Philippians to stand fearlessly for Christ (verses 18-25)? *He was not afraid of death, rather, he desired it as much as life.*

What was Paul's chief reason for being happy about the gift the Philippians had sent him (4:10-19)? *Because of the profit which would increase to their accounts.*

3. Colossians.

Paul had never visited the church at Colossae, but reports regarding the increase of false teaching there had reached him in Rome. Since he was an apostle to all the Gentiles, he felt it was necessary to write and warn that church.

This false teaching stated that in addition to Christ being the only mediator between God and man, there were certain angelic beings through whom man must also go in order to know God. Consequently Paul's main stress in this epistle is the deity and all-sufficiency of Jesus Christ.

List at least three things Paul says about Jesus Christ which show that it is unnecessary to seek any additional way to reach God (Colossians 1:12-22). *In Him all things were created; He is before all things; in Him all things hold together; etc.*

Since Christ is all-sufficient, what is the Christian to be content to do (2:6, 7)? *Walk in Him.*

What practical effect will submission to the lordship and uniqueness of Christ have upon the Christian's life (3:1-11)? *He will not be so concerned with his position or his circumstances on earth.*

4. Philemon.

For some reason this fourth prison epistle was not joined with the other three, but rather stands by itself at the end of the Pastoral Epistles. Though the shortest of Paul's epistles, this is, nevertheless, one of the most profound and beautiful of all.

While in prison at Rome, Paul had led Onesimus, a runaway slave, to the Lord. He discovered that this slave's master was Philemon, a personal friend of Paul's, living at Colossae. In those days the penalty for a slave who had run away was either death or brutal punishment, but Paul writes Philemon to ask him to forgive Onesimus for what he had done and to receive him as a Christian brother.

This epistle stands as a great example of the profound change for good that Christ makes in all human relations. State in your own words at least three arguments Paul used to persuade Philemon to receive Onesimus in love.

Onesimus' conversion; in Paul's stead; Philemon is indebted to Paul; etc.

There is a phrase, "like father, like son." We are often exhorted to win others to Christ but some carry the importance of evangelism so far that they put no emphasis on Christian character. A person who witnesses all the time and has many so-called "results," yet whose life is un-Christlike, dishonors God and harms his converts. He gives them the wrong example to copy, and his spiritual children are unhealthy and spiritually malformed, just like he is.

B. The Thessalonian Epistles

The first epistles Paul ever wrote were those to the church he had founded at Thessalonica in Macedonia. These were written from Corinth (Acts 18:1-18) soon after Paul had been at Thessalonica.

1. 1 Thessalonians.

Paul had had to leave Thessalonica very hastily because of persecution (Acts 17:10), and the enemies of the gospel there had tried to disillusion the newly won Christians by charging that Paul was only a fair-weather friend who had left them alone because of difficult circumstances. To answer this charge Paul wrote 1 Thessalonians.

What effect had the Thessalonians' conversion had on the Christians of the surrounding area (1 Thessalonians 1:7-10)? _They became an example of faith._

The lives of those to whom Paul wrote had been changed. How did this prove that those who had preached the gospel to them were godly men (1 Thessalonians 1:5,6)? _We tend to copy those we follow, and these new Christians were Spirit-filled._

Give two ways in which Paul's ministry at Thessalonica made it impossible for him to be an insincere person (1 Thessalonians 2:1-10). _Did not try to please men, and worked to support self--endured hardship._

There is *no* substitute for Christian character. This is why Paul was successful. Note some of his characteristics in 1 Thessalonians 2:1-10: (1) boldness; (2) sincerity; (3) ability to please God; (4) not seeking to please men; (5) gentleness (not harsh, argumentative or unkind); (6) love for converts; (7) hardworking; (8) holiness, righteousness, blamelessness.

2. 2 Thessalonians.

Some questions regarding the circumstances of Christ's second coming had arisen after the Thessalonians had received Paul's first epistle. They were troubled because they had to endure unjustly great sufferings and persecutions for Christ (2 Thessalonians 1:3-12). Some also had become slack in doing their work because they thought that Christ's second coming would occur at any moment. What do you think the Christian's attitude toward persecution should be (2 Thessalonians 1:3-12)? _____

What is to be his attitude toward work (3:6-15)? _____

C. The Pastoral Epistles

From the time of his first missionary journey, Paul had always had co-workers. The Pastoral Epistles are three letters that Paul wrote to his co-workers who were helping him to strengthen the churches already founded.

These letters were written in the period between Paul's first Roman imprisonment in A.D. 60-62 (Acts 28) and his final martyrdom under the emperor Nero in A.D. 66. 1 and 2 Timothy were written to help Timothy in his work with the church at Ephesus. Titus was written to the co-worker who was laboring on the island of Crete.

1. 1 Timothy.

Read 1 Timothy 6. What are the two things that are necessary for contentment in life (1 Timothy 6:6-8)?
  Food and clothing--and godliness.

Paul here speaks much of material possessions. Why? Because in his day, as now, this was the consuming drive in the lives of many. Perhaps there were many wealthy people in Timothy's church.

Money is like luggage on a trip. It is a necessity for the trip — we have to take luggage along — but it is not the main thing. We are concerned about where we are going, what we will see on the way, etc., not our luggage.

What great danger confronts those who seek after riches (verses 9-12)? *Falling into temptation and wandering away from the faith.*

What attitude should Christians who are wealthy have toward money (verses 17-19)? *No conceit, fix hope on God, do good, share, take hold of true life.*

2. 2 Timothy.

Paul wrote 2 Timothy just before he was martyred. He writes as though it may be his last word to his co-worker, Timothy. What are the last commands that Paul gave Timothy (2 Timothy 4:1-5)? *Preach the Word; be ready always; fulfill your ministry; etc.*

What two means will help Timothy remain true to his calling after Paul has gone (2 Timothy 3:10,11 and 14-17)? *Emulate Paul, and continue in what he had learned.*

3. Titus.

What are some of the things that a Christian should be careful to do in light of the unbelieving world in which he lives (Titus 3:1,2)? *Be subject to rulers; be ready for good deeds; malign no one; be considerate of all.*

What reason does Paul give for a Christian's living this way (3:3-7)? *We were once foolish, etc., ourselves, but God saved us and we are renewed.*

Note the concern about "good works." It is important to understand Titus 3:5 and 8. Christians do good works, but *never* to earn God's approval or our salvation. Salvation is a free gift, received by faith alone (Ephesians 2:8-9). This is contrary to the notion that many of us are good enough to "get by" with God. Good works are the result, not the cause, of becoming a Christian. If a man is sick, I do not tell him to play a game of tennis to get well. But if he is well, he can play without trouble.

Conclusion and Application

Christ is our supreme example (1 John 2:6), but lest we become weary in well-doing, the Scriptures have given us the example of Paul, a man of the same passions as ours. He is proof that Christianity works. All we need is one case that works to refute the claims of those who would reject Christianity because of hypocrites in the church. Furthermore, the man with whom it worked was a murderer of Christians and "chief of sinners" (1 Timothy 1:15).

> **Life Application**
>
> 1. Name two things you have learned from Paul's character, as you have studied him in this lesson. _____
> _____
> _____
>
> 2. What do you sense from Philippians 3:1 and 4:4 about an approach to life Paul would advise you to have? _____
> _____
>
> How is that always possible? _____
> _____
> _____

Suggested Closing Prayer

Father, we thank You for Paul and for his testimony and the example of his life. We pray that, like him, we will be found putting You first in all things, understanding and appreciating our spiritual blessings and privileges, and honoring You.

LESSON SIX

THE GENERAL EPISTLES

Teacher's Objective: To help students to understand and apply the gospel that Jesus Christ taught, as it is amplified and defined in the General Epistles.

Teacher's Enrichment: (This material may be shared with students as time allows.)

Some parallel passages of Scripture regarding the strength of our faith:

A. Our position in Christ — Ephesians 1:1-14. We are:
> chosen in Him — verse 4;
> predestined to adoption — 5;
> accepted in the beloved — 6;
> redeemed — 7;
> informed of His will — 9;
> given an inheritance — 11;
> sealed by the Spirit — 13.

B. The reward of faith and obedience (story of Naaman) — 2 Kings 5.

C. Outward testimony of willing death when inward faith faces supreme test (Stephen):
> his death — Acts 7:54-60; 8;
> characteristics of this man of God — 6:8;
> result of his witness and involvement of Paul — 7:58.

D. Building a good foundation of faith — Matthew 7:24-27; 1 Corinthians 3:11-15.

E. Evidences of present-day apostasy — 2 Timothy 3:1-5, 7; Revelation 3:14-18.

CLASS TIME

Suggested Opening Prayer

Our Father, we ask that You will help us to understand the implications of the strength of the gospel in our lives as it is defined in these general epistles we will be studying today.

(Introduction: Be sure students understand
> objective
> memory work
> reading assignment.)

> **Introduction**
>
> OBJECTIVE: To see the gospel amplified and defined.
>
> TO MEMORIZE: Hebrews 1:1, 2.
>
> TO READ: James; 1 and 2 Peter; 1, 2 and 3 John; Jude.

Discussion Starter

In Hebrews, James, 1 and 2 Peter, 1, 2, 3 John and Jude we have a group of inspired writings differing in important respects from

> GENERAL
>
> **HEBREWS   1, 2, 3 JOHN**
> **JAMES   JUDE**
> **I & 2 PETER**
>
> The term "general" is at best only an imperfect way to characterize the last eight epistles of the New Testament. It has been selected because, unlike most of Paul's epistles which are written to specific churches, most of the recipients of these eight epistles are either the churches of some large area or are all Christians (the exceptions: Hebrews, 2 and 3 John). Again, with the exception of Hebrews, these epistles are named for their authors.

Paul's Epistles. But this difference is in no sense one of conflict. All present the same Christ, the same salvation, the same morality. The difference is one of extension, of development. These Jewish-Christian writings deal with the elementary and foundational things of the gospel, while to Paul were given the revelations concerning the church, her place in the counsels of God and the calling and hope of the believer, as vitally united to Christ in the one body.

Paul writes in view of the body of true believers who are assuredly saved, a called-out priesthood, members of Christ's church on earth.

In contrast to these truths, the Judeo-Christian writers view the church as a professing body in which, during this age, the wheat and tares are mingled (Matthew 13:24-30). These writings abound in warning to arouse mere professors of religious beliefs, who are sincere in their practices as far as they go, but do not completely embrace the true gospel of Jesus Christ and commit themselves to Him as Lord.

Which teaching do you think is most important for today's Christian and why?

Lesson Development

Bible Study

A. *Hebrews*

The early church called this book "Hebrews" because it was originally addressed to Jewish Christians. In the early days following their conversion through the preaching of some of Jesus' original disciples (2:3), they had become exemplary Christians, they had helped supply the needs of other Christians (6:10) and they had taken cheerfully the loss of their own possessions as they were persecuted for Christ's name (10:32-34).

However, at the writing of this letter their original teachers and leaders had died (Hebrews 13:7). Now they were on the verge of slipping back from a confession of Christ into the Judaism out of which they had been converted (13:13,14). One reason they might have wanted to do this was that the Roman government in the first century allowed Jewish worship but deemed Christianity an illicit religion. The writer of Hebrews exhorts the readers to remain true to Christ even at the price of having to shed their own blood (12:3,4).

That writer had to have been an outstanding leader in the early Christian church, but his identity is unknown. Origen, the first Christian theologian, writing in the third century, said, "Who wrote the Epistle to the Hebrews, God alone knows." Many believe it was written by the apostle Paul, though this cannot be confirmed.

The first chapter of Hebrews fulfills the declarations of Jesus Christ in Genesis 1:1 and John 1:1. His deity and everlasting glory are plainly evident and he is displayed fully as

> The key passage of Hebrews is 10:19-25. In verses 19,20 the writer speaks of the finality of Jesus Christ in that He is the "new and living way." This summarizes the argument from 4:14-10:18. Then in verse 21 he declares that Jesus is final because He is the great High Priest, and this was the argument of 1:1-4:13. Since Jesus Christ is final, ultimate and all sufficient, all Christians should obey the commands in Hebrews 10:22-25.

the only true Son of God. By an eternal act of God, Jesus once for all, paid the penalty for the sin of the world and provided everlasting salvation for the whole human race.

Major points of doctrine include: Christ's unity with man (Chapter 2), the Christian's rest of faith (Chapter 4), the New Covenant as superior to the old law (Chapters 8, 10), and great heroes of the Old Testament (Chapter 11).

This epistle brings to great reality many various Old Testament doctrines which in the past were mere "shadows" of truths to come in the person of Jesus Christ.

1. What are four things a Christian must do, according to Hebrews 10:22-25? _____
   1--Draw near to God with a sincere heart.
   2--Hold fast the confession of our hope.
   3--Stimulate one another to love and good deeds.
   4--Not forsake assembling together.
2. Summarize in your own words the two lines of argument that the writer uses to support these commands.
   (10:26-31) _____

   (10:32-34) _____

3. What attitude of heart did the original readers of this epistle need to have in order to remain true to Christ in the midst of persecution (Hebrews 10:35-39)? Endurance and hope, faith to the persevering of the the soul.
4. By what means did the Old Testament believers acquire this necessary quality of heart (Hebrews 11:1-39)? _____
   By faith.

1. The position of faith — Hebrews 10:19-21.
   a. We are placed in Christ, a position of perfection, acceptable to the Father.
   b. This position gives boldness rather than fear when approaching God.
   c. The blood cleanses and makes forgiveness of sin possible.
2. The assurance of faith — Hebrews 10:22-25.
   a. Obedience gives one assurance before God.
   b. Is church attendance anywhere implied? (See verse 25.)

5. In view of the way these Old Testament believers lived, what should you do (Hebrews 12:1-4)? _Put aside sin and "run with endurance" in holy living._

B. James

The writer of this epistle is thought to have been the half brother of Jesus. During the days of Jesus' earthly ministry, His brothers were unbelievers (John 7:5). However, after His resurrection, Jesus appeared to James (1 Corinthians 15:7). It would seem that this appearance affected James' conversion and perhaps that of all His brothers, for in the days prior to Pentecost we find them in the upper room praying with the apostles (Acts 1:14).

Though not counted as one of the 12 apostles, James became a prominent leader in the early Jerusalem church (Acts 15:13; Galatians 1:19; 2:9). Because the name "James" was so common in those days, it is felt that only this James who figured so prominently in the early church would have announced himself to the readers of this epistle without going into any detail as to who he was (James 1:1). The original readers of this epistle were Christians scattered abroad. Because they had suffered greatly at the hands of unbelievers (1:2-4; 2:6-7), they had tended to become cold in their devotion to Christ.

James was surnamed "the just" by his country-men and chosen a "bishop of Jerusalem" where he was very influential in the church. He endorsed Paul's Gentile work, but was a Jew himself and primarily concerned with Jews. His life's work was to win Jews and aid them in a smooth change-over to Christianity.

James writes this epistle to remind them about those qualities of heart and life that should characterize true Christian devotion in contrast to dead orthodoxy. In so doing, he made it clear how a Christian can find joy in Christ even when suffering for Him.

Major doctrines and sub-jects include: the value of testing; discrimination; faith and works contrasted; the tongue; worldly-mindedness; difficulties with wealth; a religion of deeds backed up by a faith in Christ.

1. Why should the Christian consider adversity a reason for the greatest happiness (James 1:2-4, 12)? _Because God is perfecting him, and will give him the crown of life._

2. In what way does the Christian receive the necessary resources to stand for Christ while suffering greatly (James 1:5-8)? _Ask God in faith for his needs._

3. What two things should the Christian always remember when he feels tempted to do wrong?
(1:13-16) _Temptation does not come from God._
(1:17,18) _Every good thing does come from God._

The theme of James is the necessity of outward willing service as true evi-dence of an inward faith. Emphasis on certain aspects of Christian conduct is brought out in the follow-

ng passages in James:
  2:1-4 (partiality).
  3:10-12 (conversation
nd the tongue).
  4:6, 17 (humility and
bedience).

4. Note the qualities of heart that should characterize true Christian devotion as opposed to dead orthodoxy:

Instead of simply hearing what God has to say in His Word, the Christian should do what (1:21-25)? _Be a doer of the Word--live what he has learned._

What should we do instead of simply talk about being Christians (1:26,27)? _Control our tongue, and act._

Peter

1 Peter. Peter addresses the various churches scattered throughout Asia Minor (present-day Turkey). But like James, Peter's purpose in writing was to strengthen Christians in standing firmly against the terrible persecutions that the Roman empire was about to unleash against the church. Thus Peter begins by pointing out the wonders of the salvation that his readers possess (1:3-12). Then he gives certain commands which when obeyed will help a person to realize the wonders of this salvation.

Other differences Christ
an make in our lives:
  dead to sin and alive
nto righteousness — 2:24;
  sanctified because of
Christ within — 3:15;
  alive in the will of God
— 4:2;
  relationships in the
ome — 3:1-7.

1. List the five commands Peter gives in 1:13-2:3:

  (1:13) _Keep minds, spirit and hope on Christ._
  (1:14-16) _Be holy as God is holy._
  (1:17-21) _Conduct selves in the fear of God._
  (1:22-25) _Love one another from the heart._
  (2:1-3) _Long for the pure milk of the Word._

2. When one fulfills these commands, how does his attitude toward Christ differ from that of those who do not believe and obey Him (1 Peter 2:4-10)? _The Christian will not be disappointed or offended by Christ._

3. Chapter 2, verses 9 and 10, are in the key verses of 1 Peter. The purpose of the Christian life is not simply to enjoy the glories of salvation, but rather to enjoy these glories in order to testify of their wonders to those who do not know Christ.

How, in general, does the Christian, by his life, witness to those around him (1 Peter 2:11,12)? _They live in such a way that observers will glorify God._

The persecution of
Peter's day was the first
world trial for the church
and, every night, many
Christians were burned in
Nero's gardens. The ex-
mple of the emperor en-
ouraged the enemies of

How, in relationship to the government, does the Christian demonstrate the praises of Christ (1 Peter 2:13-17)? _He obeys the laws as a matter of personal choice, not because of force._

How, in his relationship to an employer, can a Christian demonstrate the praises of Christ (1 Peter 2:18-25)? _Through respectful obedience, even to the unreasonable for the sake of conscience._

How can a Christian wife best testify of Christ to an unbelieving husband (1 Peter 3:1-7)? _Be submissive to him--chaste and respectful._

Christians to take advantage of his permission to persecute, and from Jesus' words in John 21:28, we judge that Peter himself died a martyr's death.

> How may the Christian be an effective witness for Christ in the midst of sufferings (1 Peter 3:8-17)? *Be harmonious, humble, return blessing for evil, suffer for right rather than for wrong.*

Doctrine included in this epistle: the Christian's incorruptible inheritance, the earthly pilgrimage of believers (attitudes toward the elect, government, family, etc.), and the fiery trial and reward of patience and endurance.

> *2 Peter.* As 2 Timothy records Paul's last words before martyrdom, so 2 Peter was Peter's last message before his martyrdom (1:14; cf. John 21:19). (Tradition says he was killed by being crucified head downwards.) This epistle is a continuation of the theme of 1 Peter. The sufferings that his readers had just begun to endure when that epistle was written have continued unabated, and Peter's purpose in writing this second epistle is to encourage his readers to endure steadfastly to the end. He begins by citing the greatness of God's grace to the Christian (1:2-4). Then he follows up the first epistle by declaring certain things the Christian must do to enjoy God's blessings fully (1:5-11). In 1:14-21, Peter relates the basis for feeling so confident regarding God's grace.

This epistle was Peter's second message to the same people as 1 Peter and his objective was to warn them of coming apostasy.

Methods of defending of the faith:

claiming the promises of God — 2 Peter 1:4;

> 1. From what two sources have the readers heard of this grace?
> (1:14-18) *Peter had told of his witness of Christ's majesty.*
> (1:19-21) *They had read the Old Testament Scriptures.*

allowing the world to be an eyewitness of the love and truth of God as seen through lives lived for Him;

recognizing those who are not true to the faith.

> 2. However, there have always been those whose teaching would keep God's people from the truth. Name three ways to recognize those who are false prophets (2 Peter 2:1-22). *1--Have eyes full of adultery and sensuality; 2--have a heart trained in greed; 3--forsake the right way and follow after unrighteousness.*
>
> 3. What great event should determine the present conduct of Christians (2 Peter 3:10-14)? *The coming day of the Lord.*

The principal doctrines of 2 Peter include: the great and precious promises, false teachers, the destruction of the ungodly and the time of the Lord's coming.

D. John

1 John. During his later years the apostle John settled at Ephesus among the Christians, who had found Christ through Paul's ministry.

While he was there a certain false teaching became popular which declared that God did not become truly incarnate in Jesus Christ and that a life of actual holiness was not essential to the Christian life. The first epistle of John was written to counteract this heresy. However, it is more than a mere refutation; it is one of the most beautiful and inspiring documents of the New Testament.

To refute this heresy John showed Christians certain tests by which they could distinguish the true from the false. The key verse is 1 John 5:13: "These things I have written to you. . . that you may know that you have eternal life." When certain things are true in a person's life he may have the assurance that he has eternal life.

See if you can find at least five tests of this assurance in the material leading up to 5:13.

(1:7) *If we walk in the light.*

(2:3) *If we keep His commandments.*

(2:15) *If we do not love the world.*

(3:6) *If we do not habitually sin.*

(4:7) *If we love one another.*

John's first epistle is intensely personal and recognized as a circular letter from John the Apostle to the churches around Ephesus. It emphasized the main essentials of the gospels in addition to warning against heresies.

2 John. It is not clear whether the recipient of this brief epistle is an individual, or whether the term "elect lady" figuratively denotes a church whose members are her "children" (verse 1). Summarize in your own words the burden of the message John gives to this church. _____

_____

_____

What was John's joy in 2 John 4? In 3 John 4?

If a person claims he believes in God, but not in Christ, what does the Word say about him (2 John 9)?

3 John

1. What example is Gaius to continue to follow in the future (3 John 2-8)? *That of truthful brethren.*

_____

2. What is there about Diotrephes that Gaius is to avoid imitating (3 John 9-11)? _____
The evil in Diotrephes' life.

Christianity had been in the world some 60 or 70 years, and in many parts of the Roman Empire it had become an important influence. Feeling the impact of the Church, false teachers arose seeking to neutralize its power. These epistles were written to correct false doctrine and to expound God's love and the Christian's righteousness.

Major doctrines include: how to walk in the light of God, true righteousness, love, false prophets and teachers, and the need for recognizing the authority of the apostles and their chosen servants.

Major doctrines and subjects of Jude include: warnings connected with the imminent apostasy, descriptions of false teachers, fallen angels and their fate, Michael's contention with the devil and the prophecy of Enoch.

The entire tone of this book is that every Christian should contend for the faith once delivered to the saints (verse 3).

E. Jude

Many Biblical scholars believe that Jude was another one of Jesus' brothers who was converted after His earthly ministry. He calls himself "the brother of James" (verse 1), and in verse 17 he indicates that he was not himself an official apostle.

1. What was Jude's reason for writing as he does in this epistle (Jude 3,4)? _To counteract heresy._

2. What are two things that Jude wants his readers to remember?
   (5-16) _How God deals with unbelievers._
   (17-19) _The words of warning spoken by apostles._

3. What is the Christian's responsibility in view of the many false teachers that exist (Jude 20-23)? _To stand firm for their faith._

Conclusion and Application

We can praise God today that in His matchless grace He has given us everything which pertains to life and godliness. Nothing depends upon what we have been in the past, what we are at present, or what we shall become in the flesh in the future. On the cross Christ said, "It is finished," and this was an eternal sign to man that he had completely accomplished everything it will ever take to make man acceptable before God. The only barrier remaining today, which can keep man from God, is the barrier of unbelief.

Life Application

Have you read all these general epistles? _____

Determine one main truth from each which is particularly helpful to you and list it here:

Hebrews: _____

James: _____

1 Peter: _____

2 Peter: _____

1 John: _____

2 John: _____

3 John: _____

Jude: _____

Suggested Closing Prayer

Lord Jesus, in the light of these great scriptural truths which we have reviewed today, we accept by faith Your work for us and we thank You that You alone are worthy to be called the Son of God.

LESSON SEVEN

THE REVELATION OF JESUS CHRIST

Teacher's Objective: To teach the student some fundamentals of God's prophetic program and to help them know how to prepare for the coming of Christ.

Teacher's Enrichment: (As time allows, this material may be shared with class members.)

- These parallel passages can be used in the Bible study to throw more light on the book of Revelation.

  A. Concerning the rapture of the church — the bride of Christ: 1 Thessalonians 4:13-18, 1 Corinthians 15:51-58; John 14:1-3; Titus 2:12-13.

  B. Concerning the great tribulation: Daniel 9:20-27; 12:1-3; Matthew 24-25; 2 Thessalonians 2:1-12.

  C. Concerning the second coming of Christ: Isaiah 63:1-6; Zechariah 14:1-7; Matthew 24:27-31; 2 Thessalonians 2:8; 2 Peter 3:1-11.

  D. Concerning the millennium: Isaiah 61-66; Jeremiah 31:33-40; Ezekiel 36-37; Zechariah 14:8-21; Romans 8:19-21.

  E. Concerning the eternal state: Isaiah 65:17; 2 Peter 3:13.

- Some practical applications as to how a knowledge of God's prophetic program can affect our:

  manner of living — 2 Peter 3:10-14;

  attitude toward the world and material possessions — 1 John 2:15-17;

  attitude toward the difficulties in life — John 14:1-3;

  our attitude toward Christian work and soul winning — 1 Corinthians 15:54-58.

CLASS TIME

Suggested Opening Prayer

Father, as we study the unfolding of the events of the future as recorded in the book of Revelation, we pray You will quicken our minds and hearts to an understanding of the work of our Savior and of the Holy Spirit in preparation for these things.

(Introduction: Be sure
students understand
    objective
    memory work
    reading assignment.)

Discussion Starter

Can you name three major events in God's prophetic program? Why is it
important to be familiar with prophecy?

Lesson Development

(Have the class share this
material in any of the ways
suggested in the Instructions
for Teaching on page 21.)

REVELATION

1-3 7 CHURCHES   4-18 FUTURE   19-22 FINAL
                  PROPHECY   REDEMPTION

The last book of the New
Testament is the record of
the revelation which the
apostle John received during
his imprisonment on the
island of Patmos for being a
Christian (1:9 and following).
Many of the chapters of this
book are very difficult to
interpret. Some of the greatest
theologians in the history of
the church have felt unequal to the task of expounding these
Scriptures. For example, John Calvin, one of the great reformers,
wrote a commentary on every book of the Bible except
Revelation.

However, despite the fact that the meaning of every part of
this book may not be immediately apparent, there is the
promise that those who read (not necessarily understand) it
will be blessed (1:3).

And though some parts may be obscure, certain ideas do
stand out with unquestioned clarity. Chapters 1 through 3 are a
description of Jesus as He appeared to John and a record of the
messages to be sent to the seven churches of Asia Minor, and
they are quite clear in their meaning. Chapters 4 through 18 are
more difficult, but chapters 19 through 22, which concern
those events by which God brings final redemption to the
world, are clear for the most part. These four chapters are of the
utmost importance for completing the history of redemption
outlined since Genesis.

The book is often in-
correctly called the "Revelation of Saint John." It is
precisely, "The Revelation
of Jesus Christ" (Revelation
1:1). That is, it is an un-
veiling of His future plan for the earth and for His redeemed saints, both for time
and eternity.

It is necessary to view the book as in no sense sealed (Revelation 22:10). The
figures and symbols of the book, which furnish the basis of its interpretation, are
found elsewhere in divine revelation and can be understood only in the light of a
coherent and connected study of all other lines of prophecy as they converge upon
the book of Revelation.

It is a book of optimism for God's people, assuring us again and again that we
are under God's protection, with a life of everlasting blessedness ahead.

Alternating scenes between earth and heaven, it is also a book of the "wrath of
God," ever contrasting the joys of the redeemed with the agonies of the lost.

The Background:

There visions were given and the book was written in the lurid light of burning
martyrs. The Church had made enormous strides in growth, although suffering
terrific persecutions.

The Author:

God Himself dictated it, through Christ, by an angel, to John, (Revelation 1
around A.D. 96. John wrote it down and sent the completed book to seven
representative churches. John, called "the beloved disciple," was the most
intimate earthly friend of Jesus (John 21:20, 24).

Bible Study

A. *Jesus Christ*

Write in your own words your impression of Jesus Christ as

John describes Him in Revelation 1:9-20. _____
Students should be encouraged to express in

their own words.

There are several differ-
ent ways of interpreting
Revelation, but the best seems to be to follow the outline suggested in
Revelation 1:19:

A.   "The things which thou hast seen" — including the vision of a glorified
     Christ — are in the first chapter.

B.   "The things which are" — the letters to the seven churches — are in the
     second and third chapters. These seven churches represent all facets of
     Christendom, good and bad, during the Church age.

C.   "The things which shall be" — the unfolding of the prophetic events — are i
the fourth through the
twenty-second chapters.
These chapters contain
descriptions of the great
tribulation, the second
coming of Christ, and the
millennium.

B. *The churches*

Name the seven churches to whom John was to write, and
tell the one main message he was to give to each.
Ephesus: Left your first love, remember and re-
pent. Smyrna: Encouragement in face of suffer-
ing. Pergamum: Warning against their evil
teachers. Thyatira: Warning of judgment upon
their sin. Sardis: Exhorting dead Church to
awaken. Philadelphia: Encouragement and promise.
Laodicea: Warnings against compromise & pride.

C. *Final events*

1. What great events are described in Revelation 19:1-21?
Marriage Supper of Lamb; coming of Christ, doom
of beast and false prophet.
2. What will be the fate of the devil at the beginning of

Christ's thousand-year reign (Revelation 20:1-3)? _____
Chained for 1000 years in abyss(bottomless pit).

3. What will be the devil's final fate at the end of Christ's

thousand-year reign (Revelations 20:7-10)? *Thrown*
into lake of fire and brimstone to be tormented
forever.

> 4. What will be the final fate of all unbelievers (Revelation 20:11-15)? *Thrown into lake of fire.*
>
> 5. Show three ways in which the Christian's ultimate destiny will differ from this present existence (Revelation 21:1-9)? *Christ will dwell among His people; no mourning, crying or pain; separated from wicked and unbelieving.*

Conclusion and Application

WHAT THEN?

When the great plants of our cities
    Have turned out their last finished work;
When our merchants have sold their last yard of silk
    And dismissed the last tired clerk,
When our banks have raked in their last dollar
    And paid the last dividend;
When the Judge of the earth says, "Close for the night,"
    And asks for a balance — WHAT THEN?

When the choir has sung its last anthem,
    And the preacher has made his last prayer;
When the people have heard their last sermon
    And the sound has died out on the air;
When the Bible lies closed on the altar
    And the pews are all empty of men
And each one stands facing his record
    And the great Book is opened — WHAT THEN?

When the actors have played their last drama
    And the mimic has made his last fun,
When the film has flashed it last picture
    And the billboard displayed its last run;
When the crowds seeking pleasure have vanished
    And gone out in the darkness again —
When the trumpet of ages is sounded,
    And we stand before Him — WHAT THEN?
                    — Author Unknown

Jesus Christ will actually return to earth! All the material accomplishments of mankind will be destroyed. Christians will be judged on the basis of what they

have done with Jesus Christ
and what they have allowed
Him to do with and through
their lives.

Life Application

How can you prepare spiritually for Christ's coming and the
events which will be taking place? _____

_____

_____

_____

_____

Suggested Closing Prayer

Thank You, Father, for what You have shown us of the glories to come and of
our part in them. Prepare us for the coming of our Lord and work through us to
reach others with the message of His coming. As we look expectantly toward that
event, we ask also that You will use us to help fulfill Your Great Commission
during whatever time we have left.

ADDITIONAL BACKGROUND MATERIAL

These are some questions that may be used as a guide for further study of
Revelation.
1. What is the tribulation? What are some of the events that happen during
   this time?
2. What events accompany the second advent of Christ?
3. What is the condition of the world during the millennium?
4. What events happen after the millennium?
5. What is the "eternal state?"

LESSON EIGHT
RECAP

Teacher's Objective: To lead students in review of the New Testament highlights covered in the last seven lessons and make sure they understand how Jesus fulfills Old Testament prophecy, how His life and teachings apply to a Christian's life today, and to lead students to make any commitments still necessary to prepare for Jesus' second coming.

CLASS TIME

Suggested Opening Prayer

Help us, dear Father, as we review the last seven lessons on New Testament Highlights to understand better how the Old and New Testaments relate to each other, how Jesus' life and teachings are to be reflected in our own lives, and make even clearer to us how we should be preparing for His second coming.

(Introduction:

STUDENT'S OBJECTIVE is to review what has been learned so as to get a clearer understanding of the content of the New Testament and how it relates to his life today.

MEMORY WORK: Students should review all verses previously memorized in this Step, with special attention given to Matthew 28:18-19, Acts 1:8 and Revelation 21.4.

READING ASSIGNMENT: The Gospel of John.)

Discussion Starter

What benefit do you think a non-Christian would gain from reading the New Testament?

Lesson Development

(Any Teacher's Enrichment or Additional Background Material that you were not able to use in the previous lessons could be utilized at this time and any point which you might feel was not sufficiently covered, or which the students do not understand completely, can be dealt with now too.

Going over the Recap material will benefit both the students and you by giving you a clearer picture of the content and purpose of the New Testament.)

Review all verses memorized.

1. What is the focus in Matthew regarding the person of Christ?
_____
_____

2. How does Mark differ from Matthew? _____
_____
_____

3. How did Luke and John each present Christ? _____
_____
_____

4. What changes took place in Paul's life after he became a Christian? _____
_____
_____

5. What are the three results of justification by faith (Romans 5:1,2)? _____
_____
_____

(Students should all be able by now to write the names of the books of the Old Testament and the New Testament from memory.)

---

6. Write again the names of the books of the Old Testament, listing them by division.
_____
_____
_____
_____
_____
_____
_____

Conclusion and Application

Jesus' fulfilling of prophecy, the miracles He performed as proof of His ministry, the examples of His life and the fact of His death and resurrection all attest to His authority to forgive sin. The gift of the Holy Spirit for power, the establishing of the church, the admonition to live godly in this present world and to carry His message to those who have not yet heard it are evidences of God's continuing love for man. In light of the things foretold in the book of Revelation, we realize how vitally important that message is.

When we invite Christ into our lives, we have just begun our journey with Him and as we walk in the Spirit there are many things in store for us — including the abundant life He has promised us and the ongoing process of being conformed to the image of Christ. As you know, being filled with the Holy Spirit is the only way we can appropriate the fullness of all these blessings.

We want to take a few minutes for silent prayer to allow God's Holy Spirit to speak to each of us individually and show us what we most need to pray about, what we need to surrender to Him, in what area we need to trust Him more, or whatever He wants us to be aware of. So now, during this quiet time, we will all have a chance to make whatever commitment is necessary. Let's pray.

Suggested Closing Prayer

(After an appropriate amount of quiet time you may close simply with:) Thank You, Father, for the promise of answered prayer. We trust and praise You for always guiding us, loving us, and filling us with Yourself.

SUMMARY LESSON
NEW TESTAMENT HIGHLIGHTS

Teacher's Objective: To help students gain insight into the basic teaching of the New Testament, with emphasis upon each individual book; to show students how the New Testament reveals Jesus as the fulfillment of Old Testament prophecy; to show how the life and teachings of Christ as presented in each book of the New Testament apply to the Christian's life in this world today; and to assist students in preparing for the world to come.

Teacher's Enrichment: (See Teacher's Enrichment sections as they occur in the previous lessons of this Step, and share both those and this with the class as time permits.)

FORMATION OF THE NEW TESTAMENT CANON

In the days of Christ there was in the literature of the Jewish nation a group of writings called "The Scriptures" (now known to us as the Old Testament), which the people commonly regarded as having come from God. These writings were called *The Word of God* and were read publicly and taught in the synagogues. Jesus so recognized them, and in Luke 4:16-19 we see Him authoritatively reading from these Scriptures.

Later, certain of the writings of the New Testament apostles began to be collected and placed alongside the Old Testament as the inspired Word of God, some of them while the apostles were still living.

1. Paul claimed inspiration — Galatians 1:11,12; 1 Thessalonians 2:13.

2. John also claimed inspiration — Revelation 1:2.

3. Both Peter and Paul stated that their letters should be kept in the churches and read repeatedly after they themselves were gone — Colossians 4:16; 1 Thessalonians 5:27; 2 Peter 1:15; 3:1,2.

4. Peter classed Paul's epistles with "other Scriptures" — 2 Peter 3:15,16.

The word "canon" literally means "cane," or "rod of measurement." In early Christian use it came to mean the "written rule of faith," and referred to these original apostolic writings.

Some have taught that certain writings of men of God were selected and voted on as authentic Scripture and the books so chosen became the Word of God.

But the "canonical" writings which *had already proved* to be the inspired Word of God and *had been accepted* by the churches actually are what were bound together and became the 27 books of the New Testament as we know them.

The Council of Carthage, A.D. 397, gave its formal ratification to these 27 books. It did not formulate the New Testament canon, but merely expressed the unanimous judgment of the churches and accepted for itself the Book that was destined by God to become man's most precious heritage.

CLASS TIME

Suggested Opening Prayer

(Have one of the group open in prayer.)

(Introduction:

STUDENT'S OBJECTIVE: To become familiar with the content and purpose of the New Testament and how it relates to the life of a Christian today.

TO MEMORIZE: John 20:21; Matthew 28:18-20; Acts 1:8.

READING ASSIGNMENT: 1 John; Galatians; Revelation 1:1-3.)

Discussion Starter

Why do you think God has given us the New Testament?
What is the basic difference between the New and Old Testaments?
How do we know it is the Word of God?

Lesson Development

A. Why the four gospels were written *(from Lessons 1 and 2).*

In the report of an accident, four witnesses give a clearer and more complete picture than one because of their different positions. So in the gospels we have four accounts, each from a different point of view, but all in perfect harmony. They present a perfect portrait of Christ.

1. *The Gospel of Matthew* presents Jesus as King, the Jewish Messiah, and is written particularly to Jews. It contains Jesus' major sermons, The longest of these is the Sermon on the Mount, in which you will find the beatitudes.

   a. Purpose of the Sermon on the Mount: It showed the Jews of Jesus' time what would be required for entrance into His kingdom, contrasting God's righteousness with that of the religious rulers of the day.

   b. Value for today: It is a revelation of the moral requirements of God; it condemns the world that the world might seek salvation; it is a guide for the Christian's personal living. How is it possible, however, with the standard nothing short of absolute purity, for us to approach it? (Only through the enablement of the Holy Spirit.)

2. *The Gospel of Mark,* written probably at Rome and primarily to Romans, presents Jesus as the suffering servant, but with power over all earthly forces. Four miracles are recorded in Mark 4:35 to 5:43. The purpose of miracles is to arrest people's attention, and to aid in winning their acceptance of revealed truth. Over what forces did these four miracles prove Jesus had supernatural power?

4:35-41 (nature); 5:1-20 (demons); 21-23, 35-43 (death); 25-34 (disease).

3. *The Gospel of Luke* presents Jesus the man, perfect in His humanity. What human characteristics does He display in Luke 2:51? (Obedience.) 7:13? (Compassion.) 19:41? (Grief.) 19:45? (Anger, indignation.) 22:42-44? (Anguish, agony.) 23:46? (Physical mortality — as a human, He could die.)

The line of geneology presented in Luke traces the ancestry of Christ through Mary's line all the way back to Adam, the first man, authenticating Jesus' human origins. Luke was written with the Greeks in mind.

4. *The Gospel of John* was written to everyone and presents Jesus as the Son of God and God the Son.

Different from the other three gospels, John's record is not a rapidly moving account of Christ's life and teachings, but is more reflective, philosophical, subjective, interpretative. John takes a few events and enlarges on them to foster belief in Jesus. John's special emphasis on the deity of Christ is shown by the particular miracles he chose to record. In those seven miracles, Jesus:

turned water into wine — 2:1-11;
healed a nobleman's son — 4:46-54;
healed a sick man at the pool of Bethesda — 5:1-9;
fed 5,000 people with five barley loaves and two fish — 6:1-14;
walked on water — 6:15-20;
healed a blind man — 9:1-7;
raised a dead man — 11:38-44.

What climactic event did the most to confirm the disciples' faith, and ours, in Jesus as the Christ, the Son of God? (His resurrection.)

And what is His provision for us to be able to represent Christ in the world (John 14:16-18)? (The indwelling Holy Spirit.)

B. *Acts (from Lesson 3).*

The book of Acts records the early church in action. Acts 1:8 is a prophetic outline of the spreading of the gospel to the Roman world. First preached to the Jews in Jerusalem (2:5,6), the gospel was next taken to Judea and Samaria (8:1,4) and then to the Gentiles (10:45). As Gentile acceptance of the truth grows, Jewish rejection becomes more and more pronounced (13:46; 18:6; 28:25-29).

The two people most prominent in the book of Acts are Peter, in the first several chapters, then Paul.

What was the subject of Peter's preaching? See Acts 2:23,32,36; 3:15, 26; 10:38-40, 43. (The death and resurrection of Christ for our sins.)

What was the subject of Paul's preaching? See Acts 13:28-30,38; 17:31. (The same as Peter's — the death and resurrection of Christ for our sins.)

What was the key element in each of their ministries (2:4,14; 13:4)? (They were filled with the Holy Spirit.)

Notice some of the things the Holy Spirit empowered the early church to do:
1:8 (witness);
2:4-8; 10:46; 19:6 (speak in other languages);
7:55-60 (have peace and confidence in the face of danger and death);

10:19-20; 13:2-4 (understand God's leading);

11:28; 21:10-13 (prophesy);

13:52-14:3 (perform signs and wonders).

C. Epistles of Paul (*from Lessons 4 and 5*).

What was the main theme of:

1. *Romans* (1:16)? (The gospel of Christ.)

2. *1 Corinthians* (10:13, 31-33)? (Christian conduct.)

3. *2 Corinthians* (4:1,7)? (Vindication of Paul's apostleship.)

4. *Galatians* (3:1-3 and 23-26)? (The gospel is by grace, not law.)

5. *Ephesians* (1:3; 2:15,16; 3:6)? (Encouragement to Gentile Christians because of their equality with the Jews in their position in Christ and in His body, the church.)

6. *Philippians* (4:2,13,19)? (Encouragement to be harmoniously united and to live fearlessly in Christ.)

7. *Colossians* (1:15-20)? (The deity and all-sufficiency of Christ as defense against false teachings, 2:4,8.)

8. *1 and 2 Thessalonians* (1 Thessalonians 2:19; 5:11)? (Confirmation of the faith of New Christians and exhortation to holiness in the light of the second coming of Christ.)

9. *1 and 2 Timothy* (2 Timothy 1:13-14)? (To help Timothy in his work with the church at Ephesus and other pastors with their work in churches everywhere.)

10. *Titus* (3:5-8)? (Reasons for Christians to do good works. Also to help Titus with his work in the church at Crete, 1:5.)

11. *Philemon* (verse 6)? (Forgiveness expected because of the change for good that Christ makes in believers.)

D. Other epistles (*from Lesson 6*).

What are the key thoughts in:

1. *Hebrews* (8:6)? (A new and better way for a right relationship with God.)

2. *James* (2:17,18)? (The necessity of outward service as evidence of inward faith.)

3. *1 and 2 Peter* (1 Peter 1:3,7)? (Strength for Christians in standing firmly against persecution.)

4. *1,2,3 John* (1 John 4:1,10; 1:9; 5:13)? (Correction of false doctrine which had arisen, and God's love and the Christian's righteousness.)

5. *Jude* (verses 3,4,20-23)? (Warnings about apostasy and false teachers, and exhortation for Christians to contend for the faith once delivered to the saints.)

E. *Revelation (from Lesson 7).*

   1. Overall them: an unveiling of God's future plan for the earth and for His redeemed saints, both for time and for eternity.

   2. Internal outline (1:19):

      a. "the things which you have seen," chapter 1;

      b. "the things which are," chapters 2 and 3 — letters to the seven churche which represent the history of the church age;

      c. "the things which shall take place after these things," chapters 4 through 22 — the great tribulation, the second coming of Christ and the millenium.

   3. What value do you see in the promise of Revelation 1:3? (The person who reads and responds to the things written in the book of Revelation will be blessed because the time is near.)

   4. What would you say is the significance of Jesus' final invitation in 22:17? (Teacher, allow students to express their own ideas.)

Conclusion and Application

We might compare the New Testament to a bank building that has a tower on top to forecast the weather. The building is complete with foundation, super-structure, internal furnishings, and weather forecaster.

The four gospels present the person and work of Jesus Christ, the central figure of history, and comprise the foundation upon which the rest of the New Testament rests. Without this foundation, the book of Acts, the epistles and the Revelation would have no basis.

Acts represents the superstructure of the building. It presents the historical framework of the New Testament Church, relating the story of the spread of the gospel and growth of the church.

The epistles picture the internal furnishings of the building, the heart of the church. We see the life, the motivation and the spirit of early Christians. We understand what they believed and how this belief affected their lives. We recognize Christ alive in them.

Revelation stands like the weather tower, forecasting what is to come — both good and bad. It points to the climactic return and reign of the "KING OF KINGS, AND LORD OF LORDS" (19:16).

In light of all these things, we realize the vital importance of the message of the gospel, the continuing love of the Father and the power of the indwelling Holy Spirit. When we invite Christ into our lives, we have just begun our journey with Him, and as we walk in the Spirit there are many things in store for us — including the abundant life He has promised us and the ongoing process of being conformed to the image of Christ. As you know, being filled with the Holy Spirit is the only way we can appropriate the fullness of all these blessings.

We want to take a few minutes for silent prayer to allow God's Holy Spirit to speak to each of us individually. We need to ask Him to show us what we most need to pray about, what we need to surrender to Him, in what area we need to trust Him more, or whatever He wants us to be aware of. So now, during this quiet time, we will all have a chance to make whatever commitment is necessary.

Suggested Closing Prayer

(After an appropriate amount of quiet time you may close simply with:) Thank You, Father, for the promise of answered prayer and for a better understanding of the authority and inspiration of Your Word. We trust and praise You for guiding us always, for loving us and for filling us with Yourself.

ADDITIONAL BACKGROUND MATERIAL

● CONCERNING THE WRITTEN WORD

For no prophecy was ever made by an act of human will, but men moved [carried along] by the Holy Spirit spoke from God.
                                                                    2 Peter 1:21

1. Amazing composition — 66 books, 40 authors, written over a 2000-year period in three languages on three continents, yet it is one book with one theme: Jesus Christ.
2. Miraculous preservation — most books are forgotten in 50 years, but the Bible has survived the tests of more than 19 centuries.
   a. The Bible has survived time and attack: Diocletion (303 A.D.) tried to burn all Bibles; 100 years later Constantine made Christianity the state religion.
   b. Today, Bibles are printed in over 1,000 languages.
   c. Voltair predicted the end of Christianity; the house he lived in was used later to publish Bibles.
3. Internal evidence reveals the authority of the Scriptures.
   a. Matthew 5:18 — all the law will be accomplished.
   b. Luke 24:25-27 — Christ taught about Himself, beginning with Moses and including all the prophets.
   c. John 16:13 — the Holy Spirit will show us things to come.
   d. 2 Peter 1:16-21 — the disciples were eyewitnesses of the majesty of Christ, yet they considered and proclaimed the written Word a more sure source of truth.

THE ANVIL OF GOD'S WORD

Last eve I paused beside a blacksmith's door,
    And heard the anvil ring the vesper chime;
Then looking in, I saw upon the floor,
    Old hammers worn with beating years of time.
"How many anvils have you had," said I,
    "To wear and batter all these hammers so?"
"Just one," said he, and then with twinkling eye,
    "The anvil wears the hammers out, you know."
"And so," I thought, "The Anvil of God's Word
    For ages skeptic blows have beat upon,
Yet, though the noise of falling blows was heard,
    The Anvil is unharmed, the hammers gone."

Author Unknown

THE BIBLE

We search the world for truth. We cull
The good, the true, the beautiful,
From graven stone and written scroll,
And all old flower-fields of the soul;
And, weary seekers of the best,
We come back laden from our quest,
To find that all the sages said
Is in the Book our mothers read.

John Greenleaf Whittier

HOW TO STUDY THE BIBLE

Someone has said that four things are necessary in studying the Bible: admit, submit, commit and transmit. First, admit its truth; second, submit to its teachings; third, commit it to memory; and fourth, transmit it to others. If the Christian life is a good thing for you, share it with someone else.

Use a notebook as you study the Bible. Write out the answers to the following questions as you study a portion of the Bible:

1. What persons have I read about, and what have I learned about them?
2. What places have I read about, and what have I learned about them? If the place is not mentioned, can I find out where it is? Do I know its position on the map?
3. Can I relate from memory what I have just been reading?
4. Are there any parallel passages or texts that throw light on this passage?
5. Have I read anything about God the Father? or about Jesus Christ? or about the Holy Ghost?
6. What have I read about myself? about man's sinful nature? about the spiritual new nature?
7. Is there any duty for me to observe? any example to follow? any promise to claim? any exhortation to guide me? any prayer that I may echo?
8. What is the key verse of the chapter or passage? Can I repeat it from memory?

Dwight L. Moody

More Books from Here's Life Publishers

A Handbook for Christian Maturity, compilation of Bill Bright's *Ten Basic Steps to Christian Maturity,* a practical guide to joyful Christian living. May be used by Christians or non-Christians individually or in a group.

Handbook of Concepts for Living by Bill Bright. A practical book conveying the basics of the Christian life. Spiritual truths which can be communicated from one person to another and then on to others, greatly multiplying each person's ministry. For use by individuals or in group settings. Paperback. Same content is also available in nine individual books called the *Transferable Concepts* series. The following topics are included:

> How to Be Sure You Are a Christian
> How to Experience God's Love and Forgiveness
> How to Be Filled With the Spirit
> How to Walk in the Spirit
> How to Witness in the Spirit
> How to Introduce Others to Christ
> How to Help Fulfill the Great Commission
> How to Love by Faith
> How to Pray

The Discipleship Series. Carefully balances the study of Scripture with practical application. Builds around three levels of Christian development. For use in a group discipleship setting. Paperback. Four books are available.

> Book 1:   The Discovery Group
> Book 2:   The Discipleship Group
> Book 3:   The Leadership Group
> The Discipleship Series Leaders Guide

The Holy Spirit: Key to Supernatural Living by Bill Bright. A clear explanation of what the Holy Spirit can do in your life now. Available in both quality paperback and hardback.

Vonette Bright's Prayer and Praise Diary by Vonette Bright. Excellent tool for developing an effective prayer life. Paperback.

Available at Christian bookstores or from Here's Life Publishers.

NOTES

NOTES

NOTES

NOTES

NOTES

NOTES

NOTES

NOTES

NOTES

NOTES

NOTES

NOTES